Other books in O'Reilly's Head First series

Head First Android Development

Head First C#

Head First Design Patterns

Head First Go

Head First iPhone and iPad Development

Head First Java

Head First JavaScript Programming

Head First Learn to Code

Head First Object-Oriented Analysis and Design

Head First Programming

Head First Python

Head First Software Development

Head First Swift

Head First Web Design

Praise for *Head First Git*

"*Head First Git* is a gem. The book is a clear, fun, and engaging introduction to a very powerful and complex tool. The pace, scope, and structure make it approachable while providing readers a solid foundation from which to continue their journey learning Git."

—Matt Cordial, staff software engineer, Experian Decision Analytics

"Software developers depend on their tools to get the job done, but that often means we work with just enough knowledge to be dangerous. And while the basics of Git can be understood in a few hours, the nuance, the power, the depth can take years to master. Seemingly every page of *Head First Git* contains a nugget or explanation of something you only thought you understood. Regardless of your experience level with Git, Raju will make you better at using this invaluable tool."

—Nate Schutta, architect and developer advocate at VMware and author of
Thinking Architecturally and Responsible Microservices

"Version control is hard. Explaining version control is harder. *Head First Git* reforms dry, difficult, highly technical information into an enjoyable and playful story that not only makes learning fun but also very effective. Author Raju Gandhi is sure to delight your neurons with amazing analogies, characters, and adventures in glamping. If you are a first-time Git user, this book will be one you'll want to `git checkout`."

—Daniel Hinojosa, self-employed programmer, speaker, and instructor
at EvolutionNext.com

"I wish this book existed a decade ago when I first started using Git extensively. The book's conversational style, along with real-world analogies for common Git concepts, will make this a fun read. Regardless of your level of experience, you'll enjoy reading this book and will learn something new about Git."

—Nihar Shah, software consultant

Head First **Git**

Wouldn't it be dreamy if there was a book about learning Git that was more fun than getting a root canal and more revealing than reams of documentation? It's probably just a fantasy...

Raju Gandhi

Beijing • Boston • Farnham • Sebastopol • Tokyo   O'REILLY®

Head First Git

by Raju Gandhi

Published by O'Reilly Media, Inc., 1005 Gravenstein Highway North, Sebastopol, CA 95472.

O'Reilly Media books may be purchased for educational, business, or sales promotional use. Online editions are also available for most titles (*http://oreilly.com*). For more information, contact our corporate/institutional sales department: (800) 998-9938 or *corporate@oreilly.com*.

Series Creators:	Kathy Sierra, Bert Bates
Series Advisors:	Eric Freeman, Elisabeth Robson
Acquisitions Editor:	Melissa Duffield
Development Editor:	Sarah Grey
Cover Designer:	Susan Thompson, based on a series design by Ellie Volckhausen
Cover/Interior Illustrations:	José Marzan Jr.
Production Editor:	Kristen Brown
Proofreader:	nSight, Inc.
Indexer:	nSight, Inc.
Page Viewers:	Buddy and Skye (dogs) and Zara (the cat)

Printing History:

January 2022: First Edition.

ISBN: 978-1-492-09251-3
[LSI]

[2022-01-13]

IN MEMORIAM

Mummy

(1945–2020)

Your memory lives on.

Author of Head First Git

Raju Gandhi

Raju Gandhi is the founder of DefMacro Software, LLC. He lives in Columbus, Ohio, along with his wonderful wife, Michelle; their sons, Mason and Micah; and their three furry family members—their two dogs, Buddy and Skye, and Princess Zara, their cat.

Raju is a consultant, author, teacher, and regularly invited speaker at conferences around the world. In his career as both a software developer and a teacher, he believes in keeping things simple. His approach is always to understand and explain the "why," as opposed to the "how."

Raju blogs at *https://www.looselytyped.com*, and can be found on Twitter as @looselytyped. He's always looking to make new friends. You can find his contact information at *https://www.rajugandhi.com*.

Table of Contents (the summary)

Table of Contents (the real thing)

Intro

Your brain on Git. Here you are trying to learn something, while your brain is doing you a favor by making sure the learning doesn't stick. Your brain's thinking, "Better leave room for more important things, like which wild animals to avoid and whether naked snowboarding is a bad idea." So how do you trick your brain into thinking that your life depends on knowing Git?

beginning Git

Get Going with Git

You need version control. Every software project begins with an idea, implemented in source code. These files are the magic that powers our applications, so we must treat them with care. We want to be sure that we keep them safe, retain a history of changes, and attribute credit (or blame!) to the rightful authors. We also want to allow for seamless collaboration between multiple team members.

And we want all this in a tool that stays out of our way, springing into action only at the moment of our choosing.

Does such a ***magical tool*** even exist? If you're reading this, you might have guessed the answer. Its name is Git! Developers and organizations around the world love Git. So what is it that makes Git so popular?

branching out

Multiple Trains of Thought

2

You can walk and chew gum at the same time. Git old-timers will tell you, as they recline in their lawn chairs (sipping their handcrafted green tea), that one of Git's biggest selling points is the ease with which you can create branches. Perhaps you have been assigned a new feature, and while you are working on it, your manager asks you to fix a bug in production. Or maybe you just got around to putting the finishing touches on your latest change, but inspiration has struck and you've just thought of a better way of implementing it. Branches allow you to work on multiple, completely disconnected pieces of work on the same codebase at the same time, independently of one another. Let's see how!

looking around

3

Investigating Your Git Repository

You ready to do some digging, Sherlock? As you continue to work in Git, you'll create branches, make commits, and merge your work back into the integration branches. Each commit represents a step forward, and the commit history represents how you got there. Every so often, you might want to look back to see how you got to where you are, or perhaps if two branches have diverged from one another. We'll start this chapter by showing you how Git can help you visualize your commit history.

Seeing your commit history is one thing—but Git can also help you see how your repository changed. Recall that commits represent changes, and branches represent a series of changes. How do you know what's changed—between commits, between branches, or even between your working directory, the index, and the object database? That's the other topic of this chapter.

Together, we will get to do some seriously interesting Git detective work. Come on, let's level up those investigative skills!

undoing

Fixing Your Mistakes

We all make mistakes, right? Humans have been making mistakes since time immemorial, and for a long time, making mistakes was pretty expensive (with punch cards and typewriters, we had to redo the whole thing). The reason was simple—we didn't have a version control system. But now we do! Git gives you ample opportunities to undo your mistakes, easily and painlessly. Whether you've accidentally added a file to the index, made a typo in a commit message, or made a badly formed commit, Git gives you plenty of levers to pull and buttons to push so that no one will ever know about that little, ahem, "slip-up."

After this chapter, *if* you trip up, it won't matter what kind of mistake you've made, you'll know exactly what to do. So let's go make some mistakes—and learn how to fix 'em.

5

collaborating with Git–part 1
Remote Work

Working by yourself can get dull quickly. So far in this book, we have learned a lot about how Git works, *and* how to work with Git repositories. The repositories we used are ones that we initialized locally using the git init command. Despite that, we've managed to get a lot done—we created branches, merged them, and used Git utilities like the `git log` and `git diff` commands to see how our repository evolved over time. But most projects aren't like that. We often work in teams or with friends or colleagues. Git offers a very powerful collaboration model—one in which we can all share our work using a single repository. It all starts by making our repository "publicly available," which makes the commit history of the project a "shared" history. In a public repository we can do everything we've learned so far, just as we've always done (with a few exceptions). We can create branches and commits and add to the commit history, and so can others; everyone can see and add to that history. That's how we collaborate with Git.

But before we start collaborating, let's spend some time together to understand how public repositories work and how to get started with them. Go team!

collaborating with Git—part II
Go, Team, Go!

6

Ready to bring in the team? Git is a fantastic tool for collaboration, and we've come up with a brilliant idea to teach you all about it—you are going to pair up with someone else in this chapter! You'll be building on what you learned in the last chapter. You know that working with a distributed system like Git involves a lot of moving parts. So what does Git offer us to make this easier, and what do you need to keep in mind as you go about collaborating with others? Are there any workflows that can make it easier to work together? Prepare to find out.

Ready. Set. Clone!

searching Git repositories
Git a Grep

The truth is, your project and its commit history are going to grow over time. Every so often, you will need to search your files for a particular piece of text. Or perhaps you'll want to see who changed a file, when it was changed, and the commit that changed it. Git can help you with all of that.

And then there is your commit history. Each commit represents a change. Git allows you to search not only for every instance of a piece of text in your project, but also for when it was added (or removed). It can help you search your commit messages. To top it off, sometimes you want to find the commit that introduced a bug or a typo. Git offers a special facility that allows you to quickly zero in on that commit.

What are we waiting for? Let's go search some Git repositories, shall we?

making your life easier with Git
#ProTips

8

So far in this book, you've learned how to use Git. But you can also bend Git to your will. That's where the ability to configure Git plays a vital role. You've already seen how to configure Git in previous chapters—in this chapter we'll be exploring a lot more of what you can configure to make your life easier. The configuration can also help you define shortcuts: long-winded Git commands begone!

There's a lot more you can do to make your interaction with Git easier. We'll show how you can tell Git to ignore certain types of files so that you don't accidentally commit them. We'll give you our recommended ways of writing commit messages and tell you how we like to name our branches. And to top it off, we'll even explore how a graphical user interface to Git can play an important role in your workflow. #letsgo #cantwait

appendix: leftovers
The Top Five Topics We Didn't Cover

We've covered a lot of ground, and you're almost finished with this book. We'll miss you, but before we let you go, we wouldn't feel right about sending you out into the world without a *little* more preparation. Git offers a lot of functionality, and we couldn't possibly fit all of it in one book. We saved some really juicy bits for this appendix.

how to use this book

Intro

In this section, we answer the burning question:
"So why DID they put that in a Git book?"

Who is this book for?

If you can answer "yes" to both of these:

1 Do you want to learn about the **world's most popular version control system**?

2 Do you prefer **stimulating dinner-party conversation** to **dry, dull, academic lectures**?

This book is for you.

Who should probably back away from this book?

If you can answer "yes" to any of these:

1 **Are you <u>completely</u> new to computers?**

(You don't need to be advanced, but you should understand folders and files, how to open applications, and how to use a simple text editor.)

2 Are you a version control system maestro looking for a *reference* book?

3 Are you **afraid to try something new**? Would you rather have a root canal than mix stripes with plaid? Do you believe that a technical book can't be serious if it uses mouth-watering menu items to explain branching?

This book is **not** for you.

[Note from marketing: This book is for anyone with a credit card.]

We know what you're thinking

"How can *this* be a serious book on Git?"

"What's with all the graphics?"

"Can I actually *learn* it this way?"

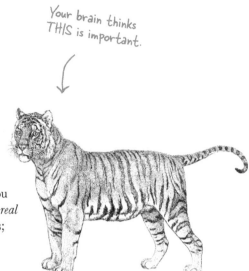

Your brain thinks THIS is important.

We know what your *brain* is thinking

Your brain craves novelty. It's always searching, scanning, *waiting* for something unusual. It was built that way, and it helps you stay alive.

So what does your brain do with all the routine, ordinary, normal things you encounter? Everything it *can* to stop them from interfering with the brain's *real* job—recording things that *matter*. It doesn't bother saving the boring things; they never make it past the "this is obviously not important" filter.

How does your brain *know* what's important? Suppose you're out for a day hike and a tiger jumps in front of you. What happens inside your head and body?

Neurons fire. Emotions crank up. *Chemicals surge.*

And that's how your brain knows...

This must be important! Don't forget it!

But imagine you're at home or in a library. It's a safe, warm, tiger-free zone. You're studying. Getting ready for an exam. Or trying to learn some tough technical topic your boss thinks will take a week, 10 days at the most.

Just one problem. Your brain's trying to do you a big favor. It's trying to make sure that this *obviously* unimportant content doesn't clutter up scarce resources. Resources that are better spent storing the really *big* things. Like tigers. Like the danger of fire. Like how you should never have posted those "party" photos on your Facebook page. And there's no simple way to tell your brain, "Hey brain, thank you very much, but no matter how dull this book is, and how little I'm registering on the emotional Richter scale right now, I really *do* want you to keep this stuff around."

Your brain thinks THIS isn't worth saving.

Great. Only 490 more dull, dry, boring pages.

We think of a "Head First" reader as a learner.

So what does it take to *learn* something? First you have to *get* it, then make sure you don't *forget* it. It's not about pushing facts into your head. Based on the latest research in cognitive science, neurobiology, and educational psychology, *learning* takes a lot more than text on a page. We know what turns your brain on.

Some of the Head First learning principles:

Make it visual. Images are far more memorable than words alone, and make learning much more effective (up to 89% improvement in recall and transfer studies). They also make things more understandable. **Put the words within or near the graphics** they relate to, rather than on the bottom or on another page, and learners will be up to *twice* as likely to be able to solve problems related to the content.

Use a conversational and personalized style. In recent studies, students performed up to 40% better on post-learning tests if the content spoke directly to the reader, using a first-person, conversational style rather than taking a formal tone. Tell stories instead of lecturing. Use casual language. Don't take yourself too seriously. Which would *you* pay more attention to: a stimulating dinner party companion, or a lecture?

Get the learner to think more deeply. Unless you actively flex your neurons, nothing much happens in your head. A reader has to be motivated, engaged, curious, and inspired to solve problems, draw conclusions, and generate new knowledge. And for that, you need challenges, exercises, and thought-provoking questions, and activities that involve both sides of the brain and multiple senses.

Get—and keep—the reader's attention. We've all had the "I really want to learn this but I can't stay awake past page one" experience. Your brain pays attention to things that are out of the ordinary, interesting, strange, eye-catching, unexpected. Learning a new, tough, technical topic doesn't have to be boring. Your brain will learn much more quickly if it's not.

Touch their emotions. We now know that your ability to remember something is largely dependent on its emotional content. You remember what you care about. You remember when you *feel* something. No, we're not talking heart-wrenching stories about a kid and a dog. We're talking emotions like surprise, curiosity, fun, "what the...?" and the feeling of "I rule!" that comes when you solve a puzzle, learn something everybody else thinks is hard, or realize you know something that "I'm more technical than thou" Bob from engineering *doesn't*.

Metacognition: thinking about thinking

If you really want to learn, and you want to learn more quickly and more deeply, pay attention to how you pay attention. Think about how you think. Learn how you learn.

Most of us did not take courses on metacognition or learning theory when we were growing up. We were *expected* to learn, but rarely *taught* to learn.

But we assume that if you're holding this book, you really want to learn how to use Git. And you probably don't want to spend a lot of time on it. If you want to use what you read in this book, you need to *remember* what you read. And for that, you've got to *understand* it. To get the most from this book, or *any* book or learning experience, take responsibility for your brain. Your brain on *this* content.

The trick is to get your brain to see the new material you're learning as Really Important. Crucial to your well-being. As important as a tiger. Otherwise, you're in for a constant battle, with your brain doing its best to keep the new content from sticking.

So just how *DO* you get your brain to treat Git like it's a hungry tiger?

There's the slow, tedious way, or the faster, more effective way. The slow way is about sheer repetition. You obviously know that you *are* able to learn and remember even the dullest of topics if you keep pounding the same thing into your brain. With enough repetition, your brain says, "This doesn't *feel* important, but they keep looking at the same thing *over* and *over* and *over*, so I suppose it must be."

The faster way is to do **anything that increases brain activity**, especially different *types* of brain activity. The things on the previous page are a big part of the solution, and they're all things that have been proven to help your brain work in your favor. For example, studies show that putting words *within* the pictures they describe (as opposed to somewhere else on the page, like a caption or in the body text) causes your brain to try to make sense of how the words and picture relate, and this causes more neurons to fire. More neurons firing = more chances for your brain to *get* that this is something worth paying attention to, and possibly recording.

A conversational style helps because people tend to pay more attention when they perceive that they're in a conversation, since they're expected to follow along and hold up their end. The amazing thing is, your brain doesn't necessarily *care* that the "conversation" is between you and a book! On the other hand, if the writing style is formal and dry, your brain perceives it the same way you experience being lectured to while sitting in a roomful of passive attendees. No need to stay awake.

But pictures and conversational style are just the beginning…

Here's what WE did

We used **visuals**, because your brain is tuned for visuals, not text. As far as your brain's concerned, a visual really *is* worth a thousand words. And when text and visuals work together, we embedded the text *in* the visuals because your brain works more effectively when the text is *within* the thing the text refers to, as opposed to in a caption or buried in a paragraph somewhere.

We used **redundancy**, saying the same thing in *different* ways and with different media types, and *multiple senses*, to increase the chance that the content gets coded into more than one area of your brain.

We used concepts and visuals in **unexpected** ways because your brain is tuned for novelty, and we used visuals and ideas with at least *some* **emotional** *content*, because your brain is tuned to pay attention to the biochemistry of emotions. That which causes you to *feel* something is more likely to be remembered, even if that feeling is nothing more than a little **humor**, **surprise**, or **interest**.

We used a personalized, **conversational style**, because your brain is tuned to pay more attention when it believes you're in a conversation than if it thinks you're passively listening to a presentation. Your brain does this even when you're *reading*.

We included dozens of **activities**, because your brain is tuned to learn and remember more when you **do** things than when you *read* about things. And we made the exercises challenging yet doable, because that's what most people prefer.

We used **multiple learning styles**, because *you* might prefer step-by-step procedures, while someone else wants to understand the big picture first, and someone else just wants to see an example. But regardless of your own learning preference, *everyone* benefits from seeing the same content represented in multiple ways.

We include content for **both sides of your brain**, because the more of your brain you engage, the more likely you are to learn and remember, and the longer you can stay focused. Since working one side of the brain often means giving the other side a chance to rest, you can be more productive at learning for a longer period of time.

And we included **stories** and exercises that present **more than one point of view**, because your brain is tuned to learn more deeply when it's forced to make evaluations and judgments.

We included **challenges**, with exercises, and we asked **questions** that don't always have a straight answer, because your brain is tuned to learn and remember when it has to *work* at something. Think about it—you can't get your *body* in shape just by *watching* people at the gym. But we did our best to make sure that when you're working hard, it's on the *right* things. That **you're not spending one extra dendrite** processing a hard-to-understand example, or parsing difficult, jargon-laden, or overly terse text.

We used **people**. In stories, examples, visuals, etc., because, well, because *you're* a person. And your brain pays more attention to *people* than it does to *things*.

Here's what YOU can do to bend your brain into submission

So, we did our part. The rest is up to you. These tips are a starting point; listen to your brain and figure out what works for you and what doesn't. Try new things.

Cut this out and stick it on your refrigerator.

- -

① Slow down. The more you understand, the less you have to memorize.

Don't just *read*. Stop and think. When the book asks you a question, don't just skip to the answer. Imagine that someone really *is* asking the question. The more deeply you force your brain to think, the better chance you have of learning and remembering.

② Do the exercises. Write your own notes.

We put them in, but if we did them for you, that would be like having someone else do your workouts for you. And don't just *look* at the exercises. **Use a pencil.** There's plenty of evidence that physical activity *while* learning can increase the learning.

③ Read the "There Are No Dumb Questions."

That means all of them. They're not optional sidebars, ***they're part of the core content!*** Don't skip them.

④ Make this the last thing you read before bed. Or at least the last challenging thing.

Part of the learning (especially the transfer to long-term memory) happens *after* you put the book down. Your brain needs time on its own, to do more processing. If you put in something new during that processing time, some of what you just learned will be lost.

⑤ Talk about it. Out loud.

Speaking activates a different part of the brain. If you're trying to understand something, or increase your chance of remembering it later, say it out loud. Better still, try to explain it out loud to someone else. You'll learn more quickly, and you might uncover ideas you hadn't known were there when you were reading about it.

⑥ Drink water. Lots of it.

Your brain works best in a nice bath of fluid. Dehydration (which can happen before you ever feel thirsty) decreases cognitive function.

⑦ Listen to your brain.

Pay attention to whether your brain is getting overloaded. If you find yourself starting to skim the surface or forget what you just read, it's time for a break. Once you go past a certain point, you won't learn faster by trying to shove more in, and you might even hurt the process.

⑧ Feel something.

Your brain needs to know that this *matters*. Get involved with the stories. Make up your own captions for the photos. Groaning over a bad joke is *still* better than feeling nothing at all.

⑨ Use it everyday!

There's only one way to learn how to *really* use Git: **use it everyday**. You are going to be using Git a lot in this book, and like any other skill, and the only way to get good at it is to practice. We're going to give you a lot of practice: every chapter has exercises that pose a problem for you to solve. Don't just skip over them—a lot of the learning happens when you solve the exercises. We included a solution to each exercise—don't be afraid to **peek at the solution** if you get stuck! (It's easy to get snagged on something small.) But try to solve the problem before you look at the solution. And definitely get it working before you move on to the next part of the book.

Read me

This is a learning experience, not a reference book. We deliberately stripped out everything that might get in the way of learning whatever it is we're working on at that point in the book. And the first time through, you need to begin at the beginning, because the book makes assumptions about what you've already seen and learned.

We break things down, then build them back again.

We are fans of teasing things apart. This gives us the chance to focus on one aspect of Git at a time. We use a lot of visuals to explain what Git is doing when you perform any operation. We make sure you have a deep understanding of each aspect and the confidence to know when and how to use them. Only *then* do we start to bring things together, to explain the more complex ideas in Git.

We don't exhaustively cover everything.

We use the 80/20 approach. We assume that if you are going for a PhD in Git, this isn't going to be your only book. So we don't talk about everything. Just the stuff that you'll actually use, and that you'll need to hit the ground running.

The activities are NOT optional.

The exercises and activities are not add-ons; they're part of the core content of the book. Some of them are to help with memory, some are for understanding, and some will help you apply what you've learned. ***Don't skip the exercises.*** The crossword puzzles are the only thing you don't *have* to do, but they're good for giving your brain a chance to think about the words and terms you've been learning in a different context.

The redundancy is intentional and important.

One distinct difference in a Head First book is that we want you to *really* get it. And we want you to finish the book remembering what you've learned. Most reference books don't have retention and recall as a goal, but this book is about *learning*, so you'll see some of the same concepts come up more than once.

The examples are as generic as possible.

Most tutorials for Git specifically target developers, and the examples usually involve code. We make no such assumptions about you. We've deliberately made the examples in this book generic yet interesting, fascinating—and downright fun. We're certain you will be able to relate to them and learn how to use Git, no matter what kind of work you do.

Finally, we want you to learn about Git; we're not looking to teach you how to type. To make things easier, we've placed all the example files on the web so you can simply download them. You'll find instructions at *https://i-love-git.com*.

The Brain Power exercises don't have answers.

For some of them, there is no right answer, and for others, part of the learning experience is for you to decide if and when your answers are right. In some of the Brain Power exercises, you will find hints to point you in the right direction.

Not all Test Drive exercises have answers.

For some exercises, we simply ask that you follow a set of instructions. We'll give you ways to verify if what you did actually worked, but unlike other exercises, there are no right answers.

You're going to have to install Git (macOS)

More than likely your computer doesn't have Git installed, or if it does, it might not have
the right version of Git installed. At the time of writing, Git was at version 2.34. While
you don't need to have the latest and greatest version of Git installed, we'll need you to
install verion 2.23 or later. Here's how:

For macOS, open your browser and enter:

> https://git-scm.com

On this page you should see the macOS download links. If not, look under
the Downloads section on the page.

1. Click the Download button for Git.

2. This page lists several ways to install Git. You can use a package
   manager like Homebrew, or you can get an installer.

3. If you choose to use the installer, download it. Then open the
   installation package in your downloads folder and follow the
   installation instructions.

Note that you'll need administrator privileges to install Git—if you commonly install apps, you should be fine; otherwise, ask your administrator for help.

Using the terminal to verify the installation

The Mac operating system ships with a built-in terminal. You can use the terminal to
verify if your Git installation went well, and given that you are going to be using the
terminal *a lot* in this book, you might as well get a practice session in. You'll find the
`Terminal.app` in the `Applications > Utilities` folder.

You can also use Spotlight to search for the terminal.

When you open the `Terminal.app`, you'll be greeted with a terminal window and a
prompt. Type `git version` and you should see something like this:

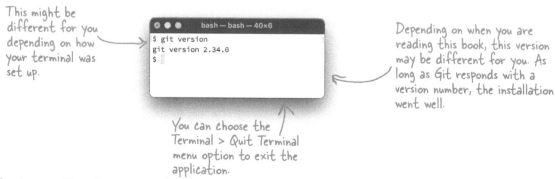

This might be different for you depending on how your terminal was set up.

Depending on when you are reading this book, this version may be different for you. As long as Git responds with a version number, the installation went well.

You can choose the Terminal > Quit Terminal menu option to exit the application.

Don't worry if you've never worked with the terminal before. We have a whole section in
Chapter 1 to get you up to speed with the commands you'll need in this book.

You're going to have to install Git (Windows)

For Windows, open your browser and enter:

> *https://git-scm.com*

1. Click the Download button for Git.

2. Choose to either save or run the executable. If the former, click to run the installer after you've downloaded it.

3. The installer window will appear on your screen. We ask that you stick to the defaults.

   When the installer asks you to "Select Components," make sure that "Windows Explorer integration," "Git Bash Here," and "Git GUI Here" **are all checked**.

   Note that you'll need administrator privileges to install Git—if you commonly install apps, you should be fine; otherwise, ask your administrator for help.

Using Git Bash to verify the installation

As part of your Git installation on Windows, you also installed an application called Git Bash. You are going to be using Git Bash throughout this book as your command-line interface to Git, so let's get a practice session in. Navigate using the Start button, and you should see Git Bash listed under the Git menu option. Click on that and you'll be greeted with a terminal window and a prompt. Type `git version` and you should see something like this:

Going forward, when we say "terminal" or "command line," that's your cue to start the Git Bash application. And worry not! If you are new to using the terminal, we've included a whole section in Chapter 1 to get you up to speed.

Note to Linux users: We're not worried about you; let's be real, you know what you're doing. Just grab the approriate distribution from https://git-scm.com.

You're going to need a text editor (macOS)

Most of the exercises in this book involve using a text editor. If you have one that you prefer to use, feel free to skip this section. On the other hand, if you don't have a text editor, or you trust us enough to want a suggestion, then we recommend using **Visual Studio Code**. This is a free, open source text editor from Microsoft. We love it because it ships with very nice defaults. This means you can start using it immediately, and it integrates well with Git.

Yes, we know we just met, but we can dream, can't we?

For macOS, using your browser, navigate to:

> *https://code.visualstudio.com*

You should see a button to download the installer.

1. Click the Download button for Visual Studio Code for Mac. This will download a zip file to your Downloads folder.

2. Double-click the downloaded zip file to extract the application file. Drag the application file into the Applications folder.

3. Launch Visual Studio Code by double-clicking the application file in the Applications folder.

4. Type `Cmd-Shift-P` to see Visual Studio Code's "Command Palette." Type "shell command" and pick the "Shell Command: Install 'code' command in PATH" option:

This is Visual Studio Code's Command Palette.

That's all there is to it! From now on, forward, anytime we ask that you fire up your text editor or edit a file, you are going to reach for Visual Studio Code. We recommend dropping a shortcut onto your Dock for easy access.

You're going to need a text editor (Windows)

Windows ships with Notepad as its default text editor. We **strongly** advise against using Notepad—it has some idiosyncrasies that are best avoided. If you haven't found a replacement yet, then we highly recommend Visual Studio Code from Microsoft. Visual Studio Code is a batteries-included text editor that can serve as an excellent replacement for Notepad and other text-editing needs.

For Windows, fire up your browser and go to:

> *https://code.visualstudio.com*

You should see a button to download the Windows installer.

1. Click the Download button for Visual Studio Code for Windows.

2. Double-click the executable in your downloads directory. We recommend you accept all the defaults.

   When the installer asks you to "Select Additional Tasks," make sure to check "Register Code as an editor for supported file types" and "Add to PATH (requires shell restart)."

Be sure to read the other options offered on this screen. They can make opening files with Visual Studio Code easier.

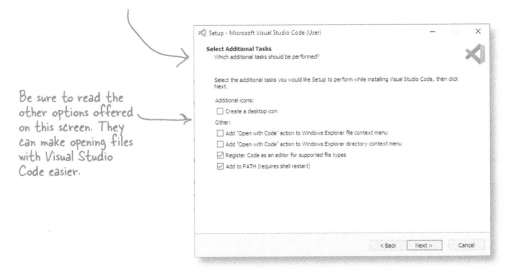

There you go! Anytime we ask you to "edit a file using your text editor," that's when you are going to reach for Visual Studio Code. Notepad begone!

You're (definitely) going to need a GitHub account

If you don't already have a GitHub account, then let's get you set up. If you already have an account with GitHub for work, then we recommend you create a personal account just for this book. (This isn't absolutely necessary, so use your discretion.)

To set up an account on GitHub, fire up your browser and type in the following:

https://github.com

1. You'll see a "Sign up for GitHub" field that requires you to supply an email address.

2. Walk through the wizard, supplying an username and a strong password.

3. You can select the "Free" option. (Don't worry—you can change this later if you like.)

You are all set! Just a few more steps, we promise!

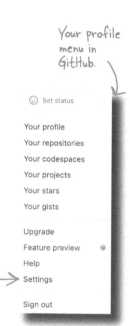

Your profile menu in GitHub.

☺ Set status

Your profile
Your repositories
Your codespaces
Your projects
Your stars
Your gists

Upgrade
Feature preview ●
Help
Settings
Sign out

Setting up a personal access token

GitHub requires you to set up a special token if you ever want to authenticate yourself using the command line. This is something you'll need to do starting in Chapter 5, so we might as well get that knocked out.

1. Sign in to *github.com* using your username and password. Click on your profile icon in the top-right corner to reveal a drop-down menu. Select "Settings."

2. On the next screen, look for "Developer settings" in the left-hand menu. Click that.

3. On the next screen, click on "Personal access tokens." This will lead you to a screen that lets you create a token that you can authenticate with GitHub using the terminal.

4. You should see a "Generate new token" button in the top right-hand corner. Click that.

continued...

5. Next, you are required to supply a "Note" that serves as a reminder of why you created this token. We called ours `headfirst-git`. For the expiration period we picked 90 days. Finally, be sure to check the "repo" box to give this token "Full control of private repositories."

If this book takes you longer than 90 days to finish (and we are sure it won't), you'll have to repeat this exercise. So giddyup! Time's a-wasting!

Give it a note. ———→

Give it an expiration period. ———→

Be sure to check this box! ———→

6. GitHub will show you a final screen that reveals the token. Copy that access token and keep it somewhere secure—this gives you (or anyone else) access to your GitHub account. Treat it with care. If you lose the token you'll have to do this whole exercise all over again.

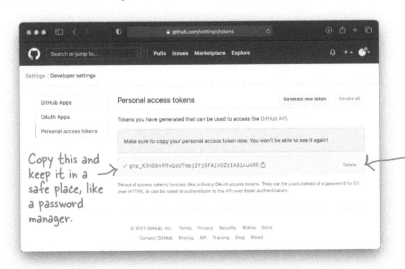

Copy this and keep it in a safe place, like a password manager. ———→

Treat this access token like you'd treat any other password. And if you lose it, just come back here, click the "Delete" button, and repeat the exercise.

A word on organizing your files and projects

Throughout this book, you are going to be working on a series of different projects. We recommend keeping your code organized by chapter. We also assume that you'll be creating one folder per chapter, like this:

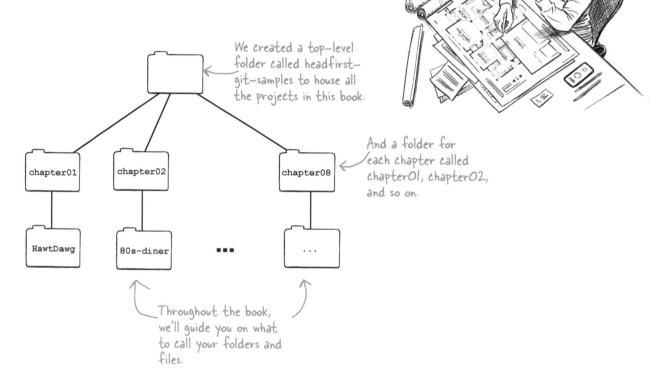

We created a top-level folder called headfirst-git-samples to house all the projects in this book.

And a folder for each chapter called chapter01, chapter02, and so on.

chapter01

chapter02

chapter08

HawtDawg

80s-diner

...

Throughout the book, we'll guide you on what to call your folders and files.

You should also visit:

https://i-love-git.com

There you'll find instructions for downloading all the files (organized by chapter) that you'll need. We suggest you download them and keep them within reach. Feel free to copy them when you need to—they only exist to save you a bunch of typing. We do ask that you follow all the instructions in the exercises and take the time to type out all the commands we ask you to. This will help you develop your muscle memory for working with Git and help things sink into your brain.

Note that, for several exercises, we provide multiple versions for the same file. In these cases, we append a number at the end—for example, FAQ-1.md, FAQ-2.md, and so on. We'll provide detailed instructions in every exercise on how to use these files, but we figured we'd point it out right now.

The technical review team

Meet our review team!

We were lucky enough to round up a powerhouse team of people to review this book, including **senior developers**, **software architects**, **renowned public speakers**, and **prolific book authors**.

These experts read every page, did the exercises, corrected our mistakes, and provided detailed commentary on every single page of this book. They also acted as our sounding board, letting us work through ideas, analogies, and narratives—even helping us think through how this book should be organized.

Every single reviewer here made huge contributions to this book and vastly improved its quality. We deeply appreciate the countless hours they spent poring over the manuscript. We remain indebted to them.

Thank you!

Daniel Hinojosa   Matt Cordial   Matt Forsythe

Nate Schutta   Nihar Shah   Venkat Subramaniam

While we aspire for this book to be error— and omission—free, we'll be the first to admit that's a lofty goal. Just know that any and all omissions are ours and ours alone.

O'Reilly Online Learning

O'REILLY®

For more than 40 years, O'Reilly Media has provided technology and business training, knowledge, and insight to help companies succeed.

Our unique network of experts and innovators share their knowledge and expertise through books, articles, and our online learning platform. O'Reilly's online learning platform gives you on-demand access to live training courses, in-depth learning paths, interactive coding environments, and a vast collection of text and video from O'Reilly and 200+ other publishers. For more information, visit *http://oreilly.com*.

Acknowledgments

Writing a book is often viewed as a solitary activity. But no one is an island. I can only aspire to personify the values imparted upon me by my family, teachers, and mentors. My work is built on the shoulders of giants—technologists from the past and present who worked, and continue to work, tirelessly to make the world a better place. You may see my name on the cover, but a lot of the credit for this book goes to these individuals.

↖ The brilliant Sarah Grey

My editor:

My biggest thanks to my editor **Sarah Grey**. She read every chapter multiple times, did all the exercises, course-corrected when I ventured too deep into the weeds, and kept me on track to deliver this book to you in time. If you find yourself salivating at the delicious menu listings in this book, or getting teary-eyed when reading the poetry, well, the credit for all that goes to Sarah. She has been instrumental in bringing this book from early development all the way to production. I am truly blessed to have an editor like Sarah.

The O'Reilly team:

A big thanks to the entire O'Reilly Media team, including **Kristen Brown** for making sure that our book was production worthy, and to **Sharon Tripp** for the keen and astute eye when copyediting. And like me, if you are someone who routinely uses the index, you have **Tom Dinse** to thank.

I'd like to thank **Melissa Duffield** for being so supportive (and patient) throughout this process and **Ryan Shaw** for considering me for this project.

Much appreciation toward the O'Reilly online training team, specifically **John Devins** and **Yasmina Greco** for giving me a platform to teach Git (among other things) to thousands of developers around the world.

A shoutout to the **Early Release team**, who put out raw and unedited chapters for the audience on the O'Reilly platform to review as they were written. This gave a chance for many of our readers to submit errata and feedback that made this book just that much better.

Finally, I'd be remiss if I did not mention **Elisabeth Robson** and **Eric Freeman**. They took the time to review my work and ensure that it aligned with the vision that is the Head First series—not to mention gave some really useful InDesign tips—thank you!

Just when you thought there wouldn't be any more acknowledgments*

Thanks to:

Jay Zimmerman, director of the No Fluff Just Stuff (NFJS) conference circuit. Thank you for giving me a shot a decade ago. This opened the door for me to speak at conferences throughout the United States and around the world and meet distinguished and accomplished individuals who, to this day, continue to inspire me. Public speaking also gave me the chance to teach and speak about Git, and my regular interactions with smart and talented audiences helped hone a lot of the material you'll find in this book.

Venkat Subramaniam, world-famous speaker, teacher, consultant, prolific author with an uncanny ability to make the hard stuff fun, friend and mentor—you are an inspiration to me. I realize that I can only shoot for the moon and hope that I land among the stars.

Mark Richards, fellow author at O'Reilly, highly regarded architect and speaker around the world, and wonderful human being—you unwittingly set the wheels in motion for this book to happen.

Matthew McCullough and **Tim Berglund**, who a long time ago produced *Mastering Git (https://www.oreilly.com/library/view/mccullough-and-berglund/9781449304737)* and opened my eyes to the elegance of Git. I've been enamored since. You'll always be my canaries.

The countless individuals who contribute to Git, and those who enrich the ecosystem around Git by writing detailed technical blog posts, creating informative videos, and answering questions on Stack Overflow—I am humbled by your work, and I hope that this book will be a valuable addition to your valiant efforts. Thank you.

My eternally patient, much better half, **Michelle**, who shouldered everything that needed to be done so I could focus on this book. Several of the narratives in this book come from her creative mind. I love you.

My family and my sisters, who (despite their fervent denials) forged me into the individual I am.

And finally, you, the readers. Your attention is a scarce resource, and I deeply appreciate the time you'll spend with this book. Happy learning.

Now go on, Git!

We noticed that they started to play the get-off-the-stage music, so we're going to have to stop here.

* The large number of acknowledgments is because we're testing the theory that everyone mentioned in a book acknowledgment will buy at least one copy, probably more, what with relatives and everything. If you'd like to be in the acknowledgments of our next book and you have a large family, write to us.

1 beginning Git

Get Going
with Git

Are you ready to commit?

You need version control. Every software project begins with an idea, implemented in source code. These files are the magic that powers our applications, so we must treat them with care. We want to be sure that we keep them safe, retain a history of changes, and attribute credit (or blame!) to the rightful authors. We also want to allow for seamless collaboration between multiple team members.

And we want all this in a tool that stays out of our way, springing into action only at the moment of our choosing.

Does such a *magical tool* even exist? If you're reading this, you might have guessed the answer. Its name is Git! Developers and organizations around the world love Git. So what is it that makes Git so popular?

Why we need version control

You might have played video games that take more than one sitting to complete. As you progress through the game, you win and lose some battles, and you might acquire some weaponry or an army. Every so often you might try more than once to finish a particular challenge. Many games allow you to save your progress. So now, say you've just slain the fire dragon, and next on the agenda is fighting your way to the massive treasure trove.

You decide, just to be safe, to save your progress and then continue the adventure. This creates a "snapshot" of the game as it stands right now. The good news is that now, even if you meet an untimely demise when you run into the wretched acid-spitting lizards, you won't have to go back to square one. Instead, you simply reload the snapshot you took earlier and try again. Fiery dragons begone!

Version control allows you to do the same with your work—it gives you a way to save your progress. You can do a little bit of work, save your progress, and continue working. This "snapshot" is a way to record a set of changes—so even if you've made changes to a bunch of files in your project, it's all in one snapshot.

Which means if you make a mistake or perhaps are not happy with the current tack, you can just revert back to your previous snapshot. On the other hand, if you are happy, you just create another snapshot and keep chugging along.

Before I started using Git, I was really disorganized. But look at me now!

And there's more. A version control system like Git allows you to confidently collaborate with your fellow developers over the same set of files, without stepping on each others' toes. We will get into details about this in later chapters, but for now it should be enough to know this.

You can think of Git as your memory bank, safety net, and collaboration platform all built into one!

Understanding version control, and Git in particular—understanding what it is capable of and the effect it has on how we work—can help make us really, and we mean *really*, productive.

Congratulations!

Your company has just been awarded the contract to build HawtDawg—the first-ever dating app for humans' furriest best friend. However, it's a dog-eat-dog world out there, and with the competition sniffing around, we don't have much time to waste!

It's hard to swipe right. I wish there was an app that would accommodate my paws. Sigh...

Pug Doctor, Inc.
100 Dover Street
Kennel Hill, OH 45021

Statement of Work

Congratulations on being selected to build a one-of-a-kind mobile application, codenamed HawtDawg.

This app will allow your furriest best friend expand their social network, find friends, maybe even a companion for life! Leveraging the very latest in machine learning, and an intuitive interface specifically designed with your dog's needs in mind, we aim to be the industry leader in a short time.

We believe we have timed this just right, but we are also keenly aware of the competition. Furthermore, this is the first time something like this has been attempted. This requires us to move quickly but also to be prepared to test out ideas. We anticipate we will be working closely with you and your developers as we iterate toward our first release.

We look forward to seeing your initial design and alpha application very soon.

Sincerely,

Johnny Grunt

Johnny Grunt, CEO

Cubicle Conversation

This kind of app has never been developed before. It's going to require a lot of experimentation, a lot of code, and a bunch of developers. How should I be doing this?

Sangita

Marge: We should consider using a version control system.

Sangita: I have heard of version control systems, though I have never had a chance to use one. But we don't exactly have a lot of time here.

Marge: Getting started with Git is super easy. You just create a Git repository and you are off to the races.

Sangita: I create a what now?

Marge: A Git repository is a folder that is managed by Git. Let me take a step back. You are going to need to house all the files for this project somewhere on your computer, right?

Sangita: I prefer to keep all relevant files pertaining to my project, including source, build, and documentation, in one folder. That way, they are easy to find.

Marge: Great! Once you create that folder, you use Git to initialize a repository inside the folder. It's that simple.

Sangita: And what does that do?

Marge: Well, whenever you start a new project that you want to manage with Git, you run a Git command that readies the folder so that you can start to use other Git commands inside that folder. Think of it as turning the key in your car to start the engine. It's the first step so you can now start to use your car.

Sangita: Hmm. OK...

Marge: It's just one command, and now your folder is "Git enabled." Just like kick-starting your engine—you can now put your project in gear.

Sangita: Ah! That makes sense.

Marge: Hit me up if you need something. I will be right here if you need me.

Got Git?

We're not going to get much further if you haven't installed Git yet. If you haven't taken the time to install Git, now is the time. Head back to the section titled "You're going to have to install Git" in the introduction to get started.

Even if you have Git installed, it will help to catch up with a new version of Git just to be sure that everything we discuss in this book works as expected.

Start your engines...

Consider any project you have worked on; it typically involves one or more files—these may be source code files, documentation files, build scripts, what have you. If we want to manage these files with Git, then the first step is to create a Git repository.

So what exactly is a Git repository? Recall that one reason to use a version control system is so we can save the snapshots of our work periodically. Of course, Git needs a place to store these snapshots. That place would be in the Git repository.

The next question is—where does this repository live? Typically we tend to keep all the files for a project in one folder. If we are going to use Git as our version control system for that project, we first create a repository *within* that folder so that Git has a place to store our snapshots. Creating a Git repository involves running the **git init** command inside the top folder of your project.

We will go deeper into the details soon, but for now, all you need to know is, without creating a Git repository, you really can't do much with Git.

No matter how big your project is (in other words, no matter how many files or subdirectories your project has), the **top** (or root) folder of that project needs to have **git init** run to get things started with Git.

They said it couldn't be done. But using Git repositories has really upped my game!

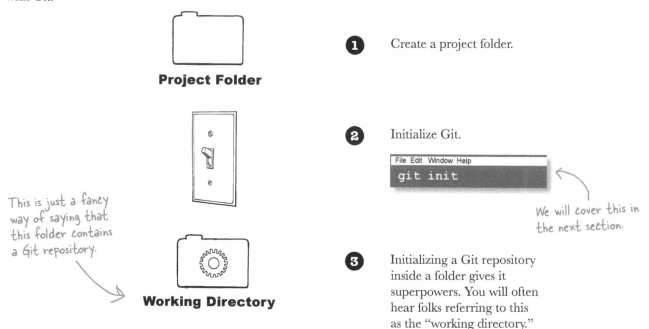

Project Folder

1 Create a project folder.

This is just a fancy way of saying that this folder contains a Git repository.

Working Directory

2 Initialize Git.

```
File Edit Window Help
git init
```

We will cover this in the next section.

3 Initializing a Git repository inside a folder gives it superpowers. You will often hear folks referring to this as the "working directory."

A quick tour of the command line: knowing where you are with pwd

One thing you are going to be using a lot while working the exercises in this book is the command line, so let's spend a little time getting comfortable with it. Start by opening a terminal window like we did in the introduction, and navigate to a location on your hard drive. As a reminder, on the Mac you'll find the **Terminal.app** under **Applications > Utilities** folder. On Windows navigate using the Start button, and you should see Git Bash under the Git menu option. You will be greeted with a prompt, and that is your cue that the terminal is ready to accept commands.

If this sounds unfamiliar, be sure to go back to the introduction. We've listed some instructions for you under the "You're going to have to install Git" section.

This might be different for you depending on how your terminal was set up.

```
File Edit Window Help
~ $
```
Typically you will see a blinking cursor; this is the shell prompt waiting for you to type something.

Windows users—this represents the Git Bash window.

Let's start with something easy. Type **pwd** and hit return; pwd stands for "print working directory" and it displays the path of the directory the terminal is currently running in. In other words, if you were to create a new file or a new directory then they would show up in this directory.

pwd means "I am here".

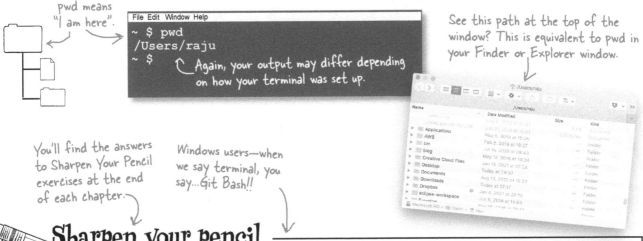

```
File Edit Window Help
~ $ pwd
/Users/raju
~ $
```
Again, your output may differ depending on how your terminal was set up.

See this path at the top of the window? This is equivalent to pwd in your Finder or Explorer window.

You'll find the answers to Sharpen Your Pencil exercises at the end of each chapter.

Windows users—when we say terminal, you say...Git Bash!!

Sharpen your pencil

Time to get busy! Fire up the terminal, and use the pwd command. Jot down the output you see here:

Great! If this is your first time using the terminal, or you are not very familiar with it, then it can be a little daunting. But know this—we will guide you every step of the way, not just for this exercise but all exercises in this book.

Answers on page 44.

More on the command line: creating new directories with mkdir

Knowing the location of the current directory in the terminal using `pwd` is super useful because almost everything you do is relative to the current directory, which includes creating new folders. Speaking of new folders, the command for creating new folders is `mkdir`, which stands for "make directory."

Unlike `pwd`, which simply tells you the path of the current directory, `mkdir` takes an *argument*, which is the name of the directory you wish to create:

This is a Finder or Explorer equivalent of mkdir.

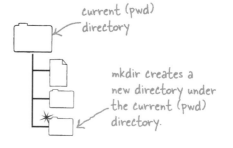

Don't do this just yet. We will have exercises for you to practice in a moment.

```
File  Edit  Window  Help
~ $ mkdir created-using-the-command-line
~ $
```

If all goes well, you'll simply get another prompt.

This is the argument, that is, the name of the new directory.

current (pwd) directory

mkdir creates a new directory under the current (pwd) directory.

Make sure you check your answer with our solution at the end of the chapter.

Watch it!

`mkdir` **will error out if you attempt to create a directory with a name that already exists.**

If you attempt to create a new directory with the same name as one that already exists in the current directory, `mkdir` *will simply report* `File exists` *and not do anything. Also, don't let the "file" in "File exists" confuse you—in this case it simply means folder.*

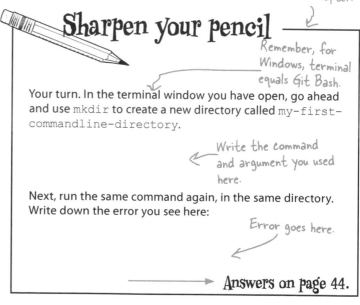

Sharpen your pencil

Remember, for Windows, terminal equals Git Bash.

Your turn. In the terminal window you have open, go ahead and use `mkdir` to create a new directory called `my-first-commandline-directory`.

Write the command and argument you used here.

Next, run the same command again, in the same directory. Write down the error you see here:

Error goes here.

→ **Answers on page 44.**

(Even) More on the command line: listing files with ls

The output of `mkdir` isn't very encouraging, to say the least. But as long as you did not get any errors, it did its job. To confirm if something did happen, you can list all the files in the current directory. The listing command is named `ls` (short for list).

You can use the Finder (Mac) or Explorer (Windows) to navigate to the current directory and see it that way as well.

Running ls here means list all the files and folders in the current (pwd) directory.

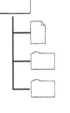

```
File Edit Window Help
~ $ ls
Applications   Movies
Desktop        Music
Documents      Pictures
Downloads      bin
Library        created-using-the-command-line
```

We truncated the output here for brevity.

`ls` by default only lists regular files and folders. Every so often (and we are going to need this soon enough) you want to see hidden files and folders as well. To do that, you can supply ls with a *flag*. Flags, unlike arguments, are prefixed with a hyphen (to differentiate them from arguments). To see "all" files and folders (including hidden ones) we can use the "A" (Yep! Uppercase "A") flag, like so:

Careful with the casing. This is the hyphen followed by an uppercase "A".

The "all" flag. Notice the hyphen.

The ls command.

ls   -A

Here is the output. Yours will probably look very different.

```
File Edit Window Help
~ $ ls -A
.bash_history
.bash_profile
.bashrc
Applications
Desktop
Documents
Downloads
Library
```

These files and folders prefixed with a "." are hidden.

Once again, we truncated the output here for brevity.

Sharpen your pencil

Use the terminal to list all the files in the current directory. See if you can find your recently created `my-first-commandline-directory`.

Then use the `-A` flag and see if there are any hidden folders in the current directory.

Answers on page 45.

More on the command line (almost there): changing directories with cd

Next, moving around! We created a new directory, but how do we navigate to it? For that, we have the cd command, which stands for "change directory." Once we change directories, we can use pwd to make sure that we indeed did move locations.

1 Start here.

2 Change to here.

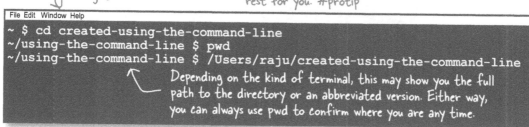

> We must make sure we get the name exactly right.

> Most terminals offer an auto-completion facility. So you can type the first few characters of the directory name, hit the "Tab" key, and the terminal will fill out the rest for you. #protip

```
File Edit Window Help
~ $ cd created-using-the-command-line
~/using-the-command-line $ pwd
~/using-the-command-line $ /Users/raju/created-using-the-command-line
```

> Depending on the kind of terminal, this may show you the full path to the directory or an abbreviated version. Either way, you can always use pwd to confirm where you are any time.

cd navigates to a subdirectory under the current directory. To hop back up to the parent directory, we can also use cd, like so:

> There's a space between cd and the double-dots (..).

cd ..

```
File Edit Window Help
~/using-the-command-line $ cd ..
~ $
```

> Two dots represent the "parent directory."

> That's two dots.

Always keep track of your working directory (using pwd)—most operations on the command line are relative to this directory.

Exercise

Go ahead, give changing directories a spin. Use cd to hop into your newly created my-first-commandline-directory folder, then use pwd to make sure you did change directories, and then use cd .. to go back to the parent folder. Use this space as a scratchpad to practice out the commands as you use them.

Answers on page 45.

No argument there

Command-line functions like pwd and mkdir are the "commands" we are invoking. Some commands, like mkdir and cd, expect you to tell them what you want to create or where to go. The way we supply those is by using "arguments."

We refer to the values we provide to a command as its arguments.

This is the command.

mkdir   created-using-the-command-line

The space is a "delimiter."

You might be wondering why we chose to use hyphens instead of spaces. Turns out, using spaces in arguments can get rather tricky. You see, the command line uses this to separate the command from its arguments. So, it can be super confusing to the command line if your arguments also have spaces in them.

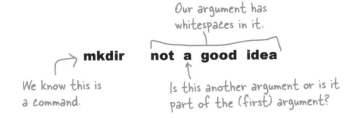

Our argument has whitespaces in it.

mkdir   not a good idea

We know this is a command.

Is this another argument or is it part of the (first) argument?

For the command line, whitespace acts as a separator. But if we put spaces in the arguments, it's hard for the command line to discern whether you are passing in multiple arguments or one argument with multiple words.

So, anytime you have whitespace in an argument and you wish to treat it as one argument, you need to use quotes.

mkdir   "this is how it is done"

Now it is clear that this is the argument.

As you can see, it's easy to trip up when you use whitespaces in arguments. Our advice? Try to avoid whitespace in filenames and paths.

For example, it's better to have C:\my-projects\ than C:\my projects\ as your path.

Does it need to be double quotes? Can I use single quotes? Can I mix and match?

Great question. The command line does not really care if you use double quotes or single quotes. The thing to remember is that you need to be consistent. If you start the argument name with single quotes, end it with a single quote. Likewise for double quotes.

Typically, most folks using the command line tend to prefer double quotes and so do we; however, there is one situation where you will be forced to use double quotes, and that is if your argument has a single quote in it.

Notice that in this case we are using a single quote in the word `sangita's`:

```
mkdir "sangita's_home-folder"
```

To use a single quote here you need to surround the argument with double quotes.

The opposite is also true if you need to use a double quote in your argument, in which case you'll need to surround your argument with single quotes.

However, we alluded to this; it's best if we avoid whitespace in our arguments, particularly in the names of directories and files. **Anytime you need a space, simply use a hyphen or an underscore**. This helps you avoid using quotes (of any kind) when supplying arguments.

Who Does What?

With the command line, there are a lot of commands and flags flying around. In this game of who does what, match each command to its description.

cd   Displays the path of the current directory.

pwd   Creates a new directory.

ls   Navigates to the parent directory.

mkdir   Changes directories.

ls -A   Lists regular files in the current directory.

cd ..   Lists **all** files in the current directory.

⟶ **Answers on page 46.**

Cleaning up

Now that you are done with this section, we suggest you clean up the folders you created like `my-first-commandline-directory` and any others. For this, just use the Explorer or the Finder window and delete them. While the command line offers you ways to do this, deleting files using the command line usually bypasses the trash can. In other words, it's hard to recover if you accidentally delete the wrong folder.

In the future, when you get more familiar with the command line, perhaps you might use the appropriate command to delete files, but for now, let's play it safe.

Creating your first repository

Let's spend a little time to get acquainted with Git. You already have Git installed, so this will give us a chance to make sure everything is set up and get a sense of what it takes to create a Git repository. To do that, you will need a terminal window. That's it!

Start by opening a terminal window like we did in the previous exercise. Just to keep things easier to manage, we suggest you create a **headfirst-git-samples** folder to house **all** the examples in this book. Within that, go ahead and create a new folder for our first exercise for Chapter 1, called **ch01_01**.

If you aren't too familiar with the command line, you can use the Finder (Mac) or Explorer (Windows) to create a new folder. However, we are going to be using the command line a lot, so you should get familiar with the command line.

```
File  Edit  Window  Help
headfirst-git-samples $ mkdir ch01_01
headfirst-git-samples $ cd ch01_01
ch01_01 $
```

Start by making our ch01_01 directory.

Then change to it.

cd stands for "change directory."

Recall that mkdir stands for "make directory."

Now that we are in a brand-new directory, let's create our first Git repository. To do this, we simply run `git init` inside our newly created folder.

Invoke the init command.

Be sure to match the case. Git commands are always lowercase.

Ignore the hints for now. We'll talk about them in the next chapter.

```
File  Edit  Window  Help
ch01_01 $ git init
hint: Using 'master' as the name for the initial branch. This default branch name
hint: is subject to change. To configure the initial branch name to use in all
hint: of your new repositories, which will suppress this warning, call:
hint:
hint:   git config --global init.defaultBranch <name>
hint:
hint: Names commonly chosen instead of 'master' are 'main', 'trunk' and
hint: 'development'. The just-created branch can be renamed via this command:
hint:
hint:   git branch -m <name>
Initialized empty Git repository in ~/headfirst-git-samples/ch01_01/.git/
ch01_01 $
```

Git tells us that all went well.

That was pretty painless, wasn't it? And there you have it—your first Git repository.

Inside the init command

So what exactly did we just accomplish? The `git init` command might not look like much, but it sure packs a punch. Let's peel back the covers to see what it really did.

To begin with, we started with a new, empty directory.

Our project folder →

Using the terminal, we navigated to the folder location and invoked the magic words, `git init`, where `init` is short for **initialize**. Git realizes we are asking it to create a repository at this location, and it responds by creating a hidden folder called `.git` and stuffs it with some configuration files and a subfolder where it will store our snapshots when we ask it to.

All right, fine. I'll show you how I pulled this off. Just this time, though!

Now our project folder contains → the .git folder.

And we have superpowers!

One way to confirm this happened is by listing all the files using our terminal, like so.

Be sure to be in the right directory!

There it is! →

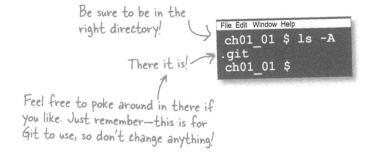

Feel free to poke around in there if you like. Just remember—this is for Git to use, so don't change anything!

This hidden folder represents the Git repository. Its job is to store everything related to your project, including all commits, the project history, configuration files, what have you. It also stores any specific Git configuration and settings that you might have enabled for this particular project.

there are no
Dumb Questions

Q: I prefer to use my filesystem explorer when navigating my computer. Can I use that to see the `.git` folder?

A: Of course! By default most operating systems do not reveal hidden files and folders in the explorer. Be sure to look at your preferences and ensure that you can see hidden files and folders.

Q: What happens if someone accidentally deletes this directory?

A: First of all, let's not do that. Second, this directory is the "vault" in which Git stores all its information—including your entire project history and a bunch of other files that Git needs for housekeeping, and some configuration files that we can use to customize our experience with Git. This means that if you delete this folder, you will lose all project history. However, all the other files in your project folder will remain unaffected.

Q: What happens if I accidentally run `git init` more than once in the same folder?

A: Good question. This is completely safe. Git will simply tell you that it is reinitializing the Git repository, but you will not lose any data nor will you hurt anything. In fact, you should try it in `ch01_01`. We are early in our journey, and the best way to learn is to experiment. Whatcha got to lose?

Q: Other version control systems that I have used have a server component. Don't we need that here?

A: Getting started with Git is *really* easy. `git init` creates a Git repository, and you can get to work. Eventually you will need a mechanism to share your work with your teammates, and we promise we will get to that soon enough. But for now, you are all set.

Code Magnets

We have all the steps listed to create a new folder, change to it, and initialize to create a new Git repository. Being diligent developers, we often check to make sure we are in the correct directory. To help our colleagues we had the code nicely laid out on our fridge using fridge magnets, but they fell on the floor. Your job is to put them back together. Note that some magnets may get used more than once.

Rearrange the magnets here.
↓

`pwd`

`mkdir new-repository`

`git init`

`cd new-repository`

Answers on page 46.

Introduce yourself to Git

There is one more step before we get to work with Git and Git repositories. Git expects you to give it a few details about yourself. This way, when you do create a "snapshot," Git knows who created it. And we are about to start talking about creating snapshots, so let's knock this out right now. You only have to do this once, and this will apply to any and all projects that you work with on your machine.

We will start with our trusty old friend, the terminal, and follow along. **Be sure to use your name and email instead of ours!** (We know you love us, but we wouldn't want to take credit for your work!) Start by opening a new terminal window. Don't worry about changing directories—for this part of our setup it does not matter where you run this.

1   We will start with telling Git our full name.

Fire up your terminal and follow along with us.

```
File Edit Window Help
~ $ git config --global user.name "Raju Gandhi"
```

You can run this in <u>any</u> directory.

Invoke the config command.

2   Next, we tell Git our email address. You can use your personal email here for now; you can always change it later.

```
File Edit Window Help
~ $ git config --global user.email "me@i-love-git.com"
```

Supply your email here.

Note: You can always change these later by running the same command again with different values. So if you choose to use your work email address once you are done with this book, feel free to do just that. You might wanna bookmark this page just in case.

How you will use Git

Let's get a sense of what a typical interaction with Git looks like. Remember how we spoke about video games allowing you to save your progress? Well, asking Git to "save your progress" involves "committing" your work to Git. Essentially, this means that Git stores a revision of your work. Once you do that, you can continue working away merrily till you feel it's time to store another revision, and the cycle continues. Let's see how this works.

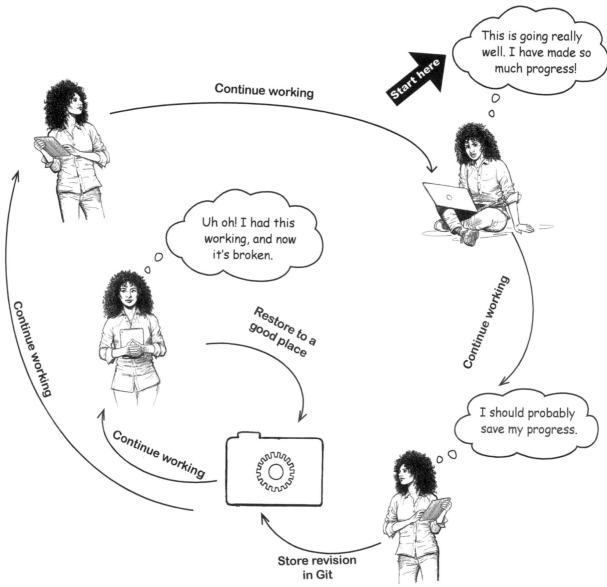

Putting Git to work

We are sure you raring to get started (we know we are!). So far, we have initialized a Git repository, told Git our name and email, and kinda sorta have a sense of how we usually work with Git. So how about we actually put Git to work. We will start small and just put Git through its paces—we will see how to "take a snapshot" in Git by creating a "commit."

For the sake of this exercise, let's pretend to start working on a new project. We usually start with a checklist so we can keep track of everything we have to do. As we progress with the project, we keep checking things off (gotta keep that dopamine flowing!), and as we learn more about the project, we keep adding to it. Naturally, this file is version controlled with the rest of the files in the project, for which we will use Git.

Let's break down what we are going to do, step-by-step.

Step One:

Create a new project folder.

These two steps should be pretty familiar to you.

Step Two:

Initialize a Git repository within that folder.

Step Three:

Create our checklist with a few items to get us started.

Step Four:

Store a snapshot of our checklist in Git by committing the file.

Now that's what we have been waiting for!

Meanwhile, back at the HawtDog Dating Service...

Hey, glad you all are here. We really need to get working on HawtDawg. Lots of pups looking for real love out there. I suggest we start with creating a checklist of all the things we know we need to do so we don't miss anything.

HawtDawg project manager

Since we are just starting off with Git, why don't you fire up a terminal window, and work alongside with us?

Your first step involves creating a new folder under the umbrella **headfirst-git-samples** folder. Be sure you are in the right directory using **pwd**. You may have to use **cd ..** (remember the two dots there) to go up one level if your terminal is still in the ch01_01 directory.

Make our HawtDawg directory.

```
File Edit Window Help
headfirst-git-samples $ mkdir HawtDawg
headfirst-git-samples $ cd HawtDawg
HawtDawg $
```

Yes, we realize that this is repetitive. However, this gives us an opportunity to use these commands again to further cement our knowledge. This is "Head First Git" after all.

Don't forget to switch to it!

Next, we simply initialize a new repository inside **HawtDawg** using the altogether familiar **git init**.

Initialize the Git repository.

```
File Edit Window Help
HawtDawg $ git init
Initialized empty Git repository in ~/headfirst-git-samples/HawtDawg/.git/
HawtDawg $
```

Git kindly tells us it did what we asked of it.

We are not showing the hints that git init displays. You will see these; we'll get to them in the next chapter.

Working with the HawtDawg Git repository

Next, create a new document in your favorite text editor, and type in the following lines of text. If you followed the instructions in the introduction to install Visual Studio Code, then just like the terminal, you will find **Visual Studio Code.app** under the **Applications** folder. In Windows, just click on the Start menu and you should see Visual Studio Code listed under all the applications installed on your machine.

To create a new file, simply click on the File menu item at the top and pick "New File."

We've provided this file to you in the source code for this book, under the chapter01 folder, called Checklist-1.md. You can just copy that over, but be sure to rename it to Checklist.md.

You're still playing along, right?

```
# Getting ready to commit
- [ ] Gather initial set of requirements
- [ ] Adopt a litter of puppies for "user testing"
- [ ] Demo first version
```

Checklist.md

The md extension stands for Markdown. You can find more information about it here— www.markdownguide.org

Save the file as **Checklist.md** in the **HawtDawg** directory.

To save the file, select File from the top menu, select Save, and then navigate to where you created the HawtDawg directory.

Now we are ready to commit our work. This involves two Git commands, namely **git add** and **git commit**.

Again, pay careful attention to every detail of spelling, capitalization, and spacing, as the terminal does not tolerate mistakes very well.

First we add the file to Git.

```
File Edit Window Help
HawtDawg $ git add Checklist.md
HawtDawg $ git commit -m "My first commit"
[master (root-commit) 513141d] My first commit
 1 file changed, 5 insertions(+)
 create mode 100644 Checklist.md
```

Then we commit, which requires we give it a message to explain what we just accomplished.

See that funny sequence of characters and numbers (513141d)? You will get something different. That's fine! As long as you see the "create mode" line, you are good.

You can also use the longhand version of -m, like so—git commit --message followed by the message. We like the shorter version though.

Notice that the git add command takes as its argument the name of the file you wish to add to Git. And the git commit command has a flag, -m, followed by the commit message. The -m stands for "message" and is a mechanism for you to provide a meaningful reminder as to why you made this change.

Speaking of...

Congratulations on your first commit!

You have completed a whirlwind tour of Git. You installed Git, initialized a Git repository, and committed a file to Git's memory. This gives us a great starting point, and we should be ready to dive deeper into Git.

there are no Dumb Questions

Q: Do I need to use Markdown files? I thought Git was a general-purpose version control tool.

A: Oh, no! We are only using Markdown files to make things easy. Teams use Git to version all kinds of different files, including source code, journals, to-do lists, blog posts, what have you. You see, Git is exceptionally good at working with plain-text files—like Markdown, HTML, source code for programming languages like Python—as opposed to rich text (like you would get out of Microsoft Word or Apple Pages). Just know Git is extremely flexible and can accommodate lots of different kinds of files.

Watch it!

Did you get some other output than the one we showed you in the previous exercise?

The command line can be rather unforgiving when it comes to typos, whitespace, and casing. If you did not get the same output as ours, then here are a few things to try:

- *If you see an error like* `fatal: not a git repository`, *be sure that you are in the* `HawtDawg` *directory.*

- *If you got an error like* `command not found`, *then be sure to check to make sure you got the case and the spelling right. Usually the command line tells you which command it did not recognize.*

- *If you see an error along the lines of* `fatal: pathspec checklist.md did not match any files` *when you tried a* `git add`, *know that the filename you supply needs to match the filename exactly, which in our case would be Checklist.md (uppercase "c").*

- *If you get* `error: pathspec '-' did not match any file(s) known to git` *when trying to* `git commit`, *make sure that there is no space between the* - *and* m.

- *If the command line reports an error like* `error: pathspec 'first' did not match any file(s) known to git`, *make sure to wrap the commit message "My first commit" in double quotes.*

- *If you get an error like* `nothing added to commit but untracked files present`, *then try running* `git add Checklist.md` *again, this time making sure you get the filename correct, including the casing.*

What exactly does it mean to commit?

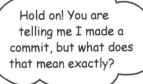

Hold on! You are telling me I made a commit, but what does that mean exactly?

Usually when Git reports commit IDs it tends to display only the first few characters.

We learned that committing to Git is a two-step process. You first `add` the files and then `commit`.

The first thing to know is that only the files that you add are committed. Let's say you had two files, `Checklist.md` and `README.md`, but you only added `Checklist.md`. When you create a commit, Git will **only** store the changes made to `Checklist.md`.

Now, when we commit, Git uses a specialized algorithm to safely tuck away everything that we added to its memory. When we say we "committed" our changes to Git, what that translates into is that Git creates a **commit object** that it stores inside the `.git` folder. This commit object is "stamped" by a unique identifier. You might recall that we got `513141d` when we made our commit in our last exercise (you certainly saw something different)—this is actually a much longer string containing numbers and letters that looks something like this:

`513141d98ccd1bd886b4445c3189cdd14275d04b`

This identifier is computed using a bunch of metadata, including your full name, the time as it was when you made the commit, the commit message you provided, and information derived from the changes you committed.

Let's explore what goes in a commit some more.

Serious Coding

Amazingly enough, the chances that two commits will **ever** have the same ID (and yes, that is across **all** the Git repositories in the world, those that exist and those that haven't even been created yet) is less than 1 in 10^{48}. Yes, that is 10 followed by 48 zeros!

That's 10 followed by 48 zeros!

When we say unique, we mean it!

100000000000000000000000000000000000000000000000

What exactly does it mean to commit? (continued)

The commit object does **not** actually store your changes—well, not directly, anyway. Instead, Git stores your changes in a different location in the Git repository and simply records (in the commit) where your changes have been stored. Along with recording where it stored your changes, the commit records a bunch of other details:

A pointer to the location inside the .git folder where Git has stored your changes, called a tree.

This is another set of alphanumeric characters, the details of which are a topic for another book.

The "author" info—that is, your name and email address.

In an earlier exercise we provided Git with our full name and our email. This is also recorded in the Git so that you can claim full credit for the marvelous work you put in.

tree: 6a36e37
author: Raju Gandhi
email: me@i-love-git.com
timestamp: 1609725692
message: My first commit

commit object 513141

This is why it's important to introduce yourself to Git.

The time the commit was made, represented in seconds elapsed since January 1, 1970.

Git also records the time when you made the commit, along with the time zone your machine is located in.

The commit message you supplied when you invoked git commit -m.

There is a little bit more than what we listed here, but we can leave that aside for now.

Commit objects are stored by Git in binary format, making them very hard for humans to read but super safe and efficient for Git.

Look before you leap

You just made your first commit. Making a commit involves two separate commands—`git add` followed by **`git commit`**. You are probably wondering why it takes two commands to make a commit in Git—why does Git make us jump through all these hoops so we can store a revision of our work in Git?

The answer lies in the design of the Git repository. Remember that the Git repository is housed in the `.git` folder that gets created when you run `git init`.

The Git repository itself is divided into two parts—the first part is called the "index," and the second part is what we will refer to as the "object database."

When we run `git add <filename>`, Git makes a copy of the file and puts it in the index. We can think of the index as the "staging area," wherein we can put things till we are sure we want to commit to them.

Now when we run the `git commit` command, it takes the **contents of the staging area** and stores those in the object database, also known as Git's memory bank. To put it another way, the index is a place to temporarily house changes. Typically, you make some changes, add them to the index, and then decide if you are ready to commit—if yes, then you make a commit. Otherwise, you can continue making changes, add more changes to the staging area, and then when you feel you are in a good place, commit.

Remember, the secret to a great history is to first add, then commit. And don't forget to throw in a meaningful commit message.

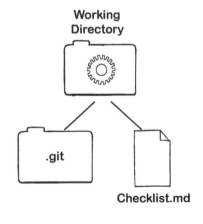

Working Directory

.git

Checklist.md

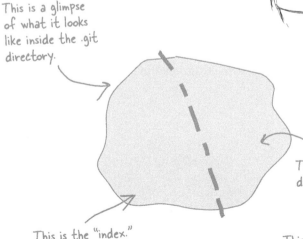

This is a glimpse of what it looks like inside the .git directory.

This is the "object database."

This is the "index."

This is Git's memory.

The three stages of Git

1 Let's start at the top. We have a working directory with just one file.

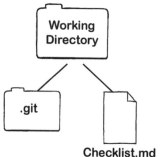

Given that we haven't committed yet, the object database is empty as well.

Initially, the index is empty.

2 When we `git add Checklist.md`, Git stores a **copy** of that file in the index.

Hold on to this thought— we will come back to it in the following pages.

This is a copy of Checklist.md.

adding a file to Git

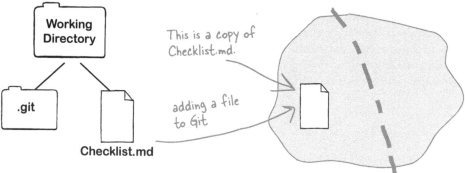

3 Finally, when we commit, Git creates a commit object that records the state of the index in its memory.

FYI, this is the third copy of the file.

This is the commit object. Note that it only records the changes you added to the index.

When we commit, Git copies our changes to its database.

Along with everything else, the commit object has a reference to the changes you committed.

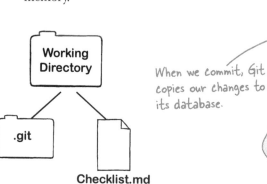

You are telling me that I have to git add and then git commit because of the way Git is designed. I get that. But what does that buy me?

Great question!

We mentioned earlier that the index can be thought of as a staging area. It gives you a way to collect everything you need for the next commit, because Git only creates a snapshot of the changes you've added to the index.

Consider a scenario where you are working on a new feature or fixing a bug. As you navigate the project you notice a typo in a documentation file and, being the good teammate that you are, you fix it. However, this fix is completely unrelated to your original task. So how do you separate the documentation fix from your original task?

Simple.

You finish the task you were working on, and you **only** add the files that were affected by that change to the index. And then you commit, giving it an appropriate message. Remember, Git only commits the files that were added to the index.

Next you `git add` the file in which you fixed the typo and make another commit, this time providing a message that describes your fix.

You see how this allows you to make a bunch of changes, some related and some unrelated, and yet choose which changes make up the next commit!

An analogy that might help would be one of cooking. You are having friends over, and you are feverishly preparing a bunch of delicious dishes. You may start by chopping up everything you know you will need. However, once you start putting things on the stove, you may choose to collect everything you need for that particular dish so they are right there when you need them. You leave everything else by the cutting board. Chefs refer to this as *mise en place*.

The index is your mise en place.

Slice, dice, chop, blend—make all your changes as and when you see fit.

Collect only related changes in the index.

Make a commit to record your changes.

One yummy commit coming up!

mise en place

Git in the command line

We covered some of the idiosyncrasies of the command line previously. This time around let's make sure we understand how we use Git at the command line. As you have seen, Git uses the `git` command, usually followed by a "subcommand," like `add` or `commit`, and finally followed by arguments to the *subcommand*.

The Git command The Git subcommand

`git add Checklist.md` Finally, the argument to the subcommand

> ## Command-line cheat sheet
>
> Git commands and subcommands are always lowercase.
>
> If you want to treat something that has whitespace as a "singular" thing, you **need** to quote it.
>
> If you need to use quotes, prefer using double quotes (though single quotes are allowed).

Since we are using the command line, the same rules that we discussed previously apply. Anytime you have whitespace in an argument, and you wish to treat it as *one* argument, you need to use quotes. Consider a very different scenario where we named our file "This is our Checklist.md". In this case, we will have to use quotes when invoking `git add`, like so:

Wrap the filename in quotes.

The quotes make the whole filename *one* argument.

`git add "This is our Checklist.md"`

You can use single or double quotes, but we like double quotes.

Finally, `git commit` takes both a flag, -m, and a message. -m is a flag, and here, we should **not** put a space between the hyphen and m.

Like many flags, —m is short for ——message. You can use either, but we are lazy so we prefer the shorter version.

`git commit -m "My first commit"`

No whitespace between the hyphen and the letter m

The message flag

Usually our commit messages tend to comprised of several words. So we almost always use double quotes.

there are no Dumb Questions

Q: What if I edited several files? Is there a way to add multiple files to the index?

A: You can supply multiple filenames separated by whitespace to the `git add` command, like so: `git add file1 file2`

Q: What happens if I forget to add before I commit?

A: Git will commit everything that already has been put in the index. However, if you've not added anything to the index, Git will report a `nothing added to commit but untracked files present (use "git add" to track)` error. So now you know you need to add.

A peek behind the curtain

We are going to let you in on Git's little secret. When you add (one or more files) to Git's index, Git doesn't touch any of the files in your working directory. Instead, it copies the contents of those files to the index. This is an important point because it is crucial to how Git tracks the content of our files.

We alluded to this in the previous pages.

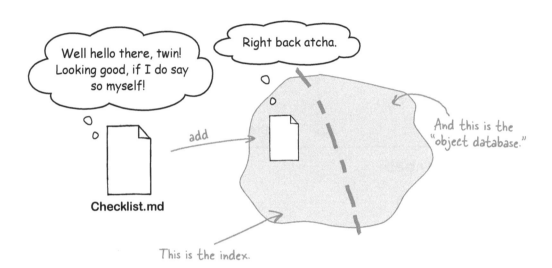

Well hello there, twin! Looking good, if I do say so myself!

Right back atcha.

add

And this is the "object database."

Checklist.md

This is the index.

So what happens when we commit? Well, as we know, Git takes the contents of the index, tucks those safely into its memory bank, and represents that version with a commit object. This means that now Git has a third copy of your files contents in its object database!

Wait a second! A triplet?

Sorry I'm a little late to the party.

Checklist.md

There can be up to three copies of any file in your working directory.

The multiple states of files in a Git repository

Here is what a typical interaction with Git looks like: you make some edits to one or more files, then add them to the index, and when you are ready, you commit them. Now, as you are going through this workflow, Git is attempting to track the state of your files so it knows which files are part of your working directory, which files have been added to the index, and which files have already been committed to its object store.

Throughout, keep in mind that Git is moving *copies* of your file from the working directory, to the index, to its object database.

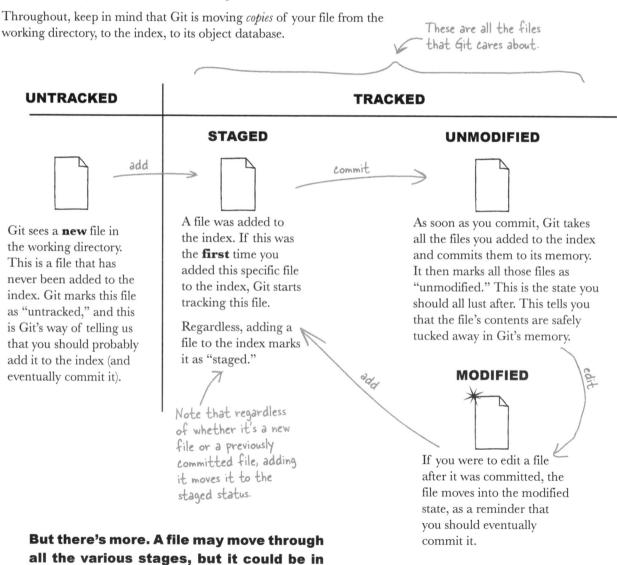

These are all the files that Git cares about.

UNTRACKED   **TRACKED**

STAGED   **UNMODIFIED**

add   commit

Git sees a **new** file in the working directory. This is a file that has never been added to the index. Git marks this file as "untracked," and this is Git's way of telling us that you should probably add it to the index (and eventually commit it).

A file was added to the index. If this was the **first** time you added this specific file to the index, Git starts tracking this file.

Regardless, adding a file to the index marks it as "staged."

As soon as you commit, Git takes all the files you added to the index and commits them to its memory. It then marks all those files as "unmodified." This is the state you should all lust after. This tells you that the file's contents are safely tucked away in Git's memory.

MODIFIED

add   edit

Note that regardless of whether it's a new file or a previously committed file, adding it moves it to the staged status.

If you were to edit a file after it was committed, the file moves into the modified state, as a reminder that you should eventually commit it.

But there's more. A file may move through all the various stages, but it could be in more than one state simultaneously!

A typical day in the life of a <u>new</u> file

When we add a new file to a Git repository, Git sees the file but also chooses **not** to do anything till we explicitly tell it to. A file that Git has never seen before (that is, a file that has never been added to the index) is marked as "untracked." Adding the file to the index is our way of telling Git, "Hey! We'd really like you to keep an eye on this file for us." Any file that Git is watching for us is referred to as a "tracked" file.

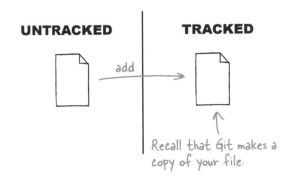

Recall that Git makes a copy of your file.

The object database is the "source of truth"

This time, consider adding a file to the index and then immediately making a commit. Git stores the contents of the index in its object database and then marks the file as "unmodified."

Why unmodified, you ask? Well, Git compares the copy it has in its object database with the one in the index and sees they are the same. It also compares the copy in the index with the one in the working directory and sees that they are the same. So the file has not been modified (or is unmodified) since the last commit.

It does not matter if this is a new or previously committed file.

If these three look identical, then the file is marked as unmodified.

Of course, it follows that if we were to make a change to a file that we had previously committed, Git sees a difference between the file in the working directory and the index but **no difference** between the index and the object database. So Git marks the file as "modified," but it also marks it as "not staged" because we haven't added it to the index yet.

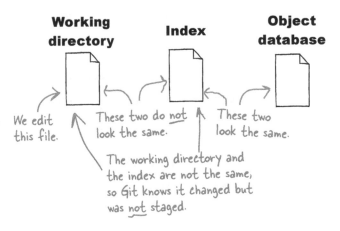

We edit this file.

These two do not look the same.

These two look the same.

The working directory and the index are not the same, so Git knows it changed but was <u>not</u> staged.

Next, if we were to add the *modified* file again to the index, Git sees that the index and the working directory are the same, so the file is marked "staged," or in other words, it is **both** modified and staged.

And we complete the circle—if we commit, the contents of the index will be committed, and the file will be marked as "unmodified."

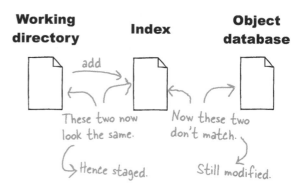

BE Git

Recall that any file in your working directory is either untracked or tracked. Also, a tracked file can be either staged, unmodified, or modified.

In this exercise, assume you just created a new repository. Can you identify the state of the files for each of the following steps?

Answers on page 47.

You create a new file in the repository called `Hello.txt`.

Untracked	Tracked	Staged	Unmodified	Modified

You add `Hello.txt` **to the index (using** `git add`**).**

Untracked	Tracked	Staged	Unmodified	Modified

You commit all the changes that you staged (using `git commit`**).**

Untracked	Tracked	Staged	Unmodified	Modified

You edit `Hello.txt` **with some new content.**

Untracked	Tracked	Staged	Unmodified	Modified

The index is a "scratch pad"

Let's revisit the role of the index. We know that as we edit files in our working directory, we can add them to the index, which marks the file as "staged."

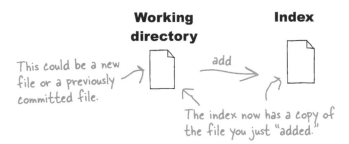

Working directory

Index

This could be a new file or a previously committed file.

add

The index now has a copy of the file you just "added."

Of course, we can continue editing the file even after adding it to the index. Now, we have two versions of the file—one in the working directory and one in the index.

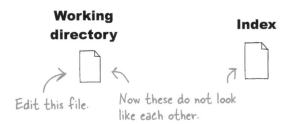

Working directory

Index

Edit this file.

Now these do not look like each other.

Now if you add the file again, Git ***overwrites*** the index with the latest changes reflected in that file. In other words, the index is a temporary scratch pad—one you can use to stuff edits into till you are sure you want to commit.

These are important points. Take a moment for them to sink in before moving on.

There's another subtle aspect to the index—there is no command to "empty" the index. Every time you add a file, Git copies the file to the index, and when you commit, Git copies your changes again. Which means, as you continue to add files to the index, you are either overriding a previous copy of a file (if it was already there), or you are adding new files to the index. So the index keeps growing! Now, this isn't something you need to worry about, but once we talk about the diff command in Chapter 3, this is something to keep in mind.

To give you a sense of how we tend to work, we usually add the files we wish to commit to the index when we feel we are ready. We then make sure that everything looks good, and if so, make a commit. On the other hand, if we spot something (like a typo, or if we missed a minor detail), we make our edits, add those files again to the index, and then commit the files. Wash, rinse, repeat.

Sharpen your pencil

Time to experiment. Navigate to the `headfirst-git-samples` directory, and create a new directory called `play-with-index`, and then `cd` into this directory. Go ahead and initialize a new repository using `git init`. Using your text editor, create a new file in the `play-with-index` called `multiple-add.txt`. **After each step, draw what the working directory and the index look like:**

1. The initial contents of `multiple-add.txt` should be "`This is my first edit`". Be sure to save the file!

We did the first one for you.

Working directory

Index

Index is initially empty.

Untracked file in working directory.

multiple-add.txt

2. Switch back to the terminal, and use `git add multiple-add.txt` to the index.

3. Back in the editor, change the text in the file to "`This is my second edit`". Again, be sure to save.

Use this space for your drawings.

4. Back at the terminal, add the file to the index again.

If you get stuck, remember, our solutions are at the end of the chapter.

———→ Answers on page 48.

Computer, status report!

As you continue to work with Git, it's often useful to check the status of the files in your working directory. One of the most useful commands in your Git arsenal is the `git status` command. This command is particularly useful as your project grows in size, with multiple files.

Remember that the working directory is the directory containing the hidden .git folder.

So let's explore how to use the status command: you'll create Yet Another Git Repository™, except this time you will create multiple files in your repository. This will give you a chance to see what `git status` reports and get an intuitive sense of how Git works.

As you have done before, you will create a brand-new folder inside the umbrella `headfirst-git-samples` folder called **ch01_03**, and initialize a Git repository inside that folder.

Since our last exercise was the second exercise, this is number 3.

Be sure you are back in the headfirst-git-samples folder!

This part should be pretty familiar.

```
File Edit Window Help
headfirst-git-samples $ mkdir ch01_03
headfirst-git-samples $ cd ch01_03
ch01_03 $ git init
Initialized empty Git repository in ~/headfirst-git-samples/ch01_03/.git/
```

Despite not having done anything, you can still check the status of our repository. The command, like others that we have used, is a Git command, called **status**. Let's use that.

Be sure to be in the right directory.

```
File Edit Window Help
ch01_03 $ git status
On branch master
No commits yet

nothing to commit (create/copy files and use "git add" to track)
```

Ignore the branch details for now.

This should be no surprise given this is a new repository.

Your first ever usage of `git status` may seem like a little bit of a letdown, but it does give you a chance to get used to reading its output. Git nicely tells you that you have made no commits yet, and it gives us a useful hint on what you should do next.

Next, you will create the first of **two** files. Open a new document in your text editor, and type in the following lines of text.

> We've provided all the files you need in the chapter01 folder in the source code you downloaded for this book. Be sure to check there if you don't feel like typing all this out.

```
# README
This repository will allow us to play with the git status command.
```

README.md

> Look for a file called README.md under chapter01. You can just copy that here if you like.

Be sure to save the file as **README.md** in the **ch01_03** directory.

Do the same thing to create **another** file called **Checklist.md** with the following text.

> There is a file called Checklist-2.md in the chapter01 folder. Be sure to rename it to Checklist.md!

```
# Checklist
- [ ] Create two files, README.md and Checklist.md
- [ ] Add README.md and make a commit
- [ ] Update Checklist.md, then add it and make a commit
```

Checklist.md

Whoa, easy tiger!

We have done quite a bit very quickly. Let's recap what you have done so far. You created a new folder, and you initialized a brand new Git repository inside that folder. You then created two new files.

Now we will walk Git through its paces, and at every step, ask Git what it thinks is the status of the files. Ready?

You have set up everything to get started. Let's see what `git status` has to report.

```
File Edit Window Help
ch01_03 $ git status
On branch master

No commits yet

Untracked files:
    (use "git add <file>..." to include in what will be committed)
          Checklist.md
          README.md

nothing added to commit but untracked files present (use "git add" to track)
```

No surprise here since we haven't committed yet.

These lines tell us how Git views our newly added files.

What we have:

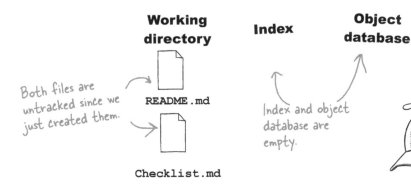

Working directory **Index** **Object database**

README.md

Checklist.md

Both files are untracked since we just created them.

Index and object database are empty.

Recall that when you ask Git for the status of the repository, it tells you the state of all the files in your working directory. In this case, Git sees two **new** files that it has never seen before. So it marks them as "untracked"—in other words, Git has not been introduced to these files, so it is not watching these files just yet. The index is empty since we haven't added either of the files to the index, and the object database has no commits—well, since we haven't committed yet. Let's change that!

Serious Coding

The `git status` command is often referred to as a "safe" command—in that it simply asks the repository for information to display and in no way affects the repository (like, say, creating a commit would). This means that you can and should run `git status` often. We recommend running it before running any other Git command.

We'll start by introducing Git to **one** of our files. **Go ahead and add README.md to Git**, and then check the status again.

Let Checklist.md be for now. We will come to it in a few.

```
File Edit Window Help
ch01_03 $ git add README.md
ch01_03 $ git status
On branch master

No commits yet

Changes to be committed:
  (use "git rm --cached <file>..." to unstage)
        new file:   README.md

Untracked files:
  (use "git add <file>..." to include in what will be committed)
        Checklist.md
```

Add README.md to the index.

README.md is now staged.

Checklist.md is still untracked.

Adding the README.md file to Git's index means now Git knows about this file. Two things changed—the README.md file is now being tracked by Git, and it is in the index, which means it's also staged.

What we have:

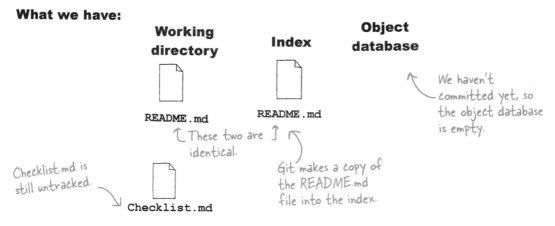

Working directory

Index

Object database

README.md

README.md

We haven't committed yet, so the object database is empty.

These two are identical.

Git makes a copy of the README.md file into the index.

Checklist.md is still untracked.

Checklist.md

Git status is telling us that if make a commit right now, only the README.md will be committed. Which makes sense because only the changes that are staged get to participate in the next commit.

So let's commit!

Brain Power

Before you proceed, can you visualize what would change if we were to make a commit right now? Remember, there are two files, and only one is in the index.

Git commits require that we pass in a message. Let's keep it simple and use "my first commit". Back to the terminal, you!

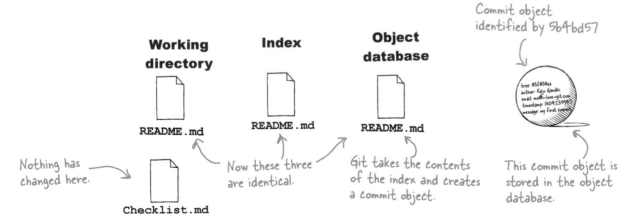

```
File Edit Window Help
ch01_03 $ git commit -m "my first commit"          ←——  Make our first commit in
[master (root-commit) 5b4bd57] my first commit           this repository, supplying it a
 1 file changed, 1 insertion(+)                          commit message.
 create mode 100644 README.md

                                          Git reports a        In our case the commit ID
                                          successful commit.   is 5b4bd57. Yours will be
ch01_03 $ git status                                           different.
On branch master
Untracked files:
    (use "git add <file>..." to include in what will be committed)
        Checklist.md

nothing added to commit but untracked files present (use "git add" to track)
```

What we have:

Working directory **Index** **Object database**

Commit object identified by 5b4bd57

README.md   README.md   README.md

```
tree: 03f039ea
author: Raju Gandhi
email: me@i-love-git.com
timestamp: 1604239467
message: my first commit
```

Nothing has changed here. → Checklist.md

Now these three are identical.

Git takes the contents of the index and creates a commit object.

This commit object is stored in the object database.

 Test Drive

The `ch01_03` repository still has one untracked file, namely `Checklist.md`. Edit it to look like this.

"x" marks to-dos
as done.

```
# Checklist
- [x] Create two files, README.md and Checklist.md
- [x] Add README.md and make a commit
- [ ] Update Checklist.md, then add it and make a commit
```

There is a file called Checklist-3.
md under the chapter01 folder if
you'd rather use that.

Checklist.md

Perform each of the steps below, each time noting the output of `git status`.

1   Add `Checklist.md` to the index (using `git add`).

```
File Edit Window Help
$ git status
```

2   Make a commit with the commit message "`my second commit`".

```
File Edit Window Help
$ git status
```

Answers on page 49.

You've made history!

In the last exercise you made two separate commits as you took both the `README.md` and `Checklist.md` files from being untracked, to being staged, and then finally committed to Git's object database. At the end of it all, you repository now has two commits.

We know that Git commits record the changes you made and added to the index, along with some metadata—like information about the author (you) as well as the commit message. There is one final detail about commits that you ought to know about. For every commit that you make (other than the very first one in a repository), the commit also records the commit ID of the commit that came just before it.

Every commit other than the first one records the ID of the commit that came just before it.

Notice the "parent" attribute.

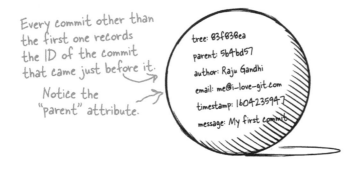

tree: 83f838ea
parent: 5b4bd57
author: Raju Gandhi
email: me@i-love-git.com
timestamp: 1604235947
message: My first commit

In case you are wondering if this is foreshadowing what is to come, well, yes! How very astute of you!

That is to say, the commits form a chain, much like the branch of a tree, or a string of Christmas lights. This means, given a commit ID, Git can trace its lineage by simply following the "parent" pointer. This is referred to as the **commit history** and is an integral piece to how Git works.

Every commit after the first one points to the one that came just before it.

The first commit in the repository. It has no parent.

Note that the arrows are unidirectional—from child to parent.

If we ever made a third commit, it would point to the second one.

Serious Coding

The Git commit history is often referred to as a *directed acyclic graph*, or DAG for short, wherein the commits form the "nodes" and the pointers to the parent form the "edges." They are *directed* because children point to parent, and *acyclic* because parents do **not** point back to their children.

Just know that child commits refer back to their parents, but parents do **not** refer to their children. In other words, the pointers are unidirectional. However, there's nothing to stop a commit from having multiple children or a commit from having multiple parents, as we'll see in the next chapter.

Bullet Points

- A version control system like Git allows you to store snapshots of your work.

- Git is much more than a tool that allows you to record snapshots. Git allows us to confidently collaborate with other team members.

- Using Git effectively requires you to be comfortable with the command line.

- The command line offers a slew of other capabilities, including creating and navigating directories and listing files.

- Git is available as an executable, which you install, and it makes Git available to use in the command line with the name `git`.

- Once you install Git, you need to tell Git your full name and your email address. Git will use this whenever you use Git to take a snapshot of your work.

- If you want Git to manage the files for any project, we have to initialize a Git repository at the root level of the project.

- To initialize Git you use the init command, like so:
  `git init`

- The result of initializing a new Git repository is that Git will create a hidden folder called `.git` in the directory where you ran the `git init` command. This hidden folder is used by Git to store your snapshots, as well as some configuration for Git itself.

- Any directory that is managed by Git is referred to as the working directory.

- Git, by design, has an index, which acts as a "staging area." To add files to the index, you use the `git add <filename>` command.

- Committing in Git translates to taking a snapshop of the changes that were stored in the index. The command to create a commit is `git commit`, which requires that you supply it with a commit message to describe the changes you are commiting, using the `-m` (or `--message`) flag:
  `git commit -m "some message"`

- Every file in the working directory is assigned one or more states.

- A brand new file added to the working directory is marked as "untracked," which suggests that Git does not know about this file.

- Adding a *new* file to Git's index does two things—it marks the file as being "tracked" and creates a copy of that file into the index.

- When you make a commit, Git creates a copy of the files in the index and stores them in the object database. It also creates a commit object that records metadata about the commit, including a pointer to the files that were just stored, the author name and email, and the time the commit was made, as well as the commit message.

- Every commit in Git is identified by a unique identifier, refererred to as the commit ID.

- At any time you can ask Git for the status of the files in the working directory and the Git repository, using the `git status` command.

- Every commit **except** the initial commit in Git stores the commit ID of the commit that appeared just before it, thus creating a string of commits, like leaves on a branch.

- This string of commits is referred to as the commit history.

Crossword Init

You've done a lot in one chapter! Congratulations on getting started with Git. Time to relax with a crossword puzzle—you'll find all of the answers somewhere in this chapter.

Across

1   What this book is all about

5   Git stores your commit message and other data in a commit _____

7   Command to list files

8   Marge is teaching her how to use Git

10   Where Git stores your files

11   Use a hyphen (or two) when you add it to a command

16   Command that tells Git to start tracking your file (2 words)

17   This is where your changes show up when you add them to Git

18   If Git isn't watching it, your file is _____

Down

2   To get started, initialize a repository with the git _____ command

3   Take a "snapshot" of your work using the git ____ command

4   Git is a ___ control system

6   Every dog's favorite dating app

9   Some commands need you to supply these

12   You can work with Git from the ____ line

13   Use the git ____ command to find out what's going on

14   Terminal command to make a directory

15   Use this to find out where you are in the terminal

Answers on page 50.

Sharpen your pencil Solution

From page 7.

Time to get busy! Fire up the terminal, and use the pwd command. Jot down the output you see here:

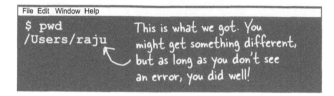

```
File Edit  Window Help
$ pwd
/Users/raju
```

This is what we got. You might get something different, but as long as you don't see an error, you did well!

Sharpen your pencil Solution

From page 8.

Your turn. In the terminal window you have open, go ahead and use mkdir to create a new directory called my-first-commandline-directory.

We invoke the mkdir command, supplying it the name of the new directory as an argument.

```
mkdir my-first-commandline-directory
```

Next, run the same command again, in the same directory. Write down the error you see here:

```
mkdir: my-first-commandline-directory: File exists
```

mkdir errors out if the directory already exists.

Sharpen your pencil
Solution

From page 9.

Use the terminal to list all the files in the current directory. See if you can find your recently created `my-first-commandline-directory`.

Your listing will most certainly be different!

Note that we trimmed our output for brevity.

```
File Edit Window Help
$ ls
Applications          hack
Desktop               headfirst-git-samples
Documents             my-first-commandline-directory
Downloads
Library
```

There it is!

Then use the `-A` flag and see if there are any hidden folders in the current directory.

```
File Edit Window Help
$ ls -A
.DS_Store
.Trash
.bash_history
.bash_profile
.bash_sessions
Applications
Desktop
Documents
Downloads
Library
hack
headfirst-git-samples
my-first-commandline-directory
```

These are some hidden files that we see. Notice the "." prefix.

Again, your listing will be different!

Exercise
Solution

From page 10.

Go ahead, give changing directories a spin. Play around with `cd` to hop into your newly created `my-first-commandline-directory` folder, then use `pwd` to make sure you did change directories, and then use `cd ..` to go back to the parent folder. Use this space as a scratch pad to practice out the commands as you use them.

Show current directory. →
Change directories. →
Where am I? →
Navigate up to parent. →
Display path again. →

```
File Edit Window Help
$ pwd
/Users/raju
$ cd my-first-commandline-directory
~/my-first-commandline-directory
$ pwd
/Users/raju/my-first-commandline-directory
$ cd ..
$ pwd
/Users/raju
```

Who Does What? Solution

From page 13.

With the command line, there are a lot of commands and flags flying around. In this game of who does what, match each command to its description.

cd — Displays the path of the current directory.

pwd — Creates a new directory.

ls — Navigates to the parent directory.

mkdir — Changes directories.

ls -A — Lists regular files in the current directory.

cd .. — Lists **all** files in the current directory.

Code Magnets Solution

We have all the steps listed to create a new folder, change to it, and initialize to create a new Git repository. Being diligent developers, we often check to make sure we are in the correct directory. To help our colleagues, we had the code nicely laid out on our fridge using fridge magnets, but they fell on the floor. Your job is to put them back together. Note that some magnets may get used more than once.

From page 16.

pwd is a great check to make sure we are always in the right place. Always good to check, right?

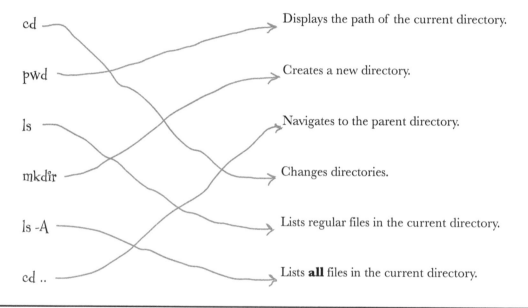

```
pwd
mkdir new-repository
cd new-repository
pwd
git init
```

BE Git Solution

Recall that any file in your working directory is either untracked or tracked. Also, a tracked file can be either staged, unmodified, or modified.

In this exercise, assume you just created a new repository. Can you identify the state of the files for each of the following steps?

From page 32.

You create a new file in the repository called Hello.txt.

Untracked	Tracked	Staged	Unmodified	Modified
X				

You add Hello.txt **to the index (using** git add**).**

Untracked	Tracked	Staged	Unmodified	Modified
	X	X		

You commit all the changes that you staged (using git commit**).**

Untracked	Tracked	Staged	Unmodified	Modified
	X		X	

You edit Hello.txt **with some new content.**

Untracked	Tracked	Staged	Unmodified	Modified
	X			X

Sharpen your pencil
Solution

From page 34.

Time to experiment. Navigate to the `headfirst-git-samples` directory, create a new directory called `play-with-index`, and then `cd` into this directory. Go ahead and initialize a new repository using `git init`. Using your text editor, create a new file in the `play-with-index` called `multiple-add.txt`. **After each step, draw what the working directory and the index look like**:

1. The initial contents of `multiple-add.txt` should be "`This is my first edit`". Be sure to save the file!

2. Switch back to the terminal, and use `git add multiple-add.txt` to the index.

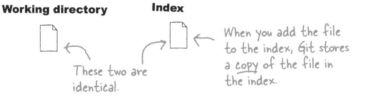

When you add the file to the index, Git stores a copy of the file in the index.

These two are identical.

3. Back in the editor, change the text in the file to "`This is my second edit`". Again, be sure to save.

The asterisk indicates the file is modified now.

These two no longer look the same.

4. Back at the terminal, add the file to the index again.

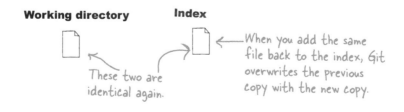

These two are identical again.

When you add the same file back to the index, Git overwrites the previous copy with the new copy.

Test Drive Solution

From page 40.

The `ch01_03` repository still has one untracked file, namely `Checklist.md`. Edit it to look like this.

"x" marks to-dos as done.

```
# Checklist

- [x] Create two files, README.md and Checklist.md

- [x] Add README.md and make a commit

- [ ] Update Checklist.md, then add it and make a commit
```

Checklist.md

Perform each of the steps below, each time noting the output of `git status`.

1 Add **Checklist.md** to the index.

```
File Edit Window Help
ch01_03 $ git add Checklist.md
ch01_03 $ git status
On branch master
Changes to be committed:
  (use "git restore --staged <file>..." to unstage)
        new file:   Checklist.md
```

2 Make a commit with the commit message "`my second commit`".

```
File Edit Window Help
ch01_03 $ git commit -m "my second commit"
[master 91c8746] my first commit
 1 file changed, 5 insertions(+)
 create mode 100644 Checklist.md
ch01_03 $ git status
On branch master
nothing to commit, working tree clean
```

Crossword Init Solution

You've done a lot in one chapter! Congratulations on getting started with Git. Time to relax with a crossword puzzle—you'll find all of the answers somewhere in this chapter.

From page 43.

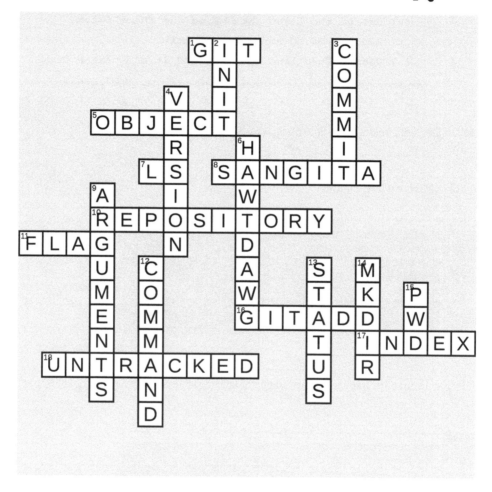

2 branching out

Multiple Trains of Thought

Now that we know what we need to do for our group project, I'm going to go get started on my own. We can catch up later. OK?

You can walk and chew gum at the same time. Git old-timers will tell you, as they recline in their lawn chairs (sipping their handcrafted green tea), that one of Git's biggest selling points is the ease with which you can create branches. Perhaps you have been assigned a new feature, and while you are working on it, your manager asks you to fix a bug in production. Or maybe you just got around to putting the finishing touches on your latest change, but inspiration has struck and you've just thought of a better way of implementing it. Branches allow you to work on multiple, completely disconnected pieces of work on the same codebase at the same time, independently of one another. Let's see how!

It all started with an email

Norm was completely immersed—his fingers flew frantically all over the keyboard, code appeared at a breathtaking pace on his screen, and everything just worked. He felt like Neo in the Matrix—he was the system, and the system was just an extension of him. He was so close to finishing up a complex change to the codebase that he could almost taste it.

Norm knew he wasn't done yet. But he committed his code anyway, and he started to tackle the bug. At the end of a long day, when he knew he had fixed that bug once and for all, he committed his work. This is what his commit history looked like now:

Exercise

Think about the commit history. See if you can figure out what Norm got wrong. Jot down your notes here:

_____

Answers on page 103.

But things didn't quite pan out...

Norm! All you were supposed to do was fix the bug! Why are we seeing new functionality in the app? And it doesn't even work right! Instead of fixing the bug, you ended up making a bigger mess!

So, what happened?

Norm failed to account for the fact that Git commits build on previous commits. When Norm made the commit for the bug fix, it was *after* he had committed his partially done work. This meant that the bug fix commit was derived from a commit that included incomplete work!

What else could I have done? Did they expect me to undo all my changes before I fixed the bug?

This commit introduces incomplete work.

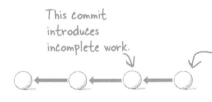

By fixing the bug after committing his work in progress, Norm accidentally included changes that he shouldn't have!

What would you do if you were Norm?

What were Norm's options here? Well, he could have painstakingly taken notes of all the changes he made across all his files, then undone all his changes. He could then fix the bug, commit the fix, and go back and reapply all of his previous work, hoping he doesn't miss anything. Seems painful, right?

At this point you are probably wondering if Git will come riding along and save the day. It will! Git allows you to "switch tracks" using a feature called *branches*. Branches allow you to keep your changes completely independent of one another.

Git allows multiple developers to contribute to the same project, also using branches. But that's a topic for another chapter.

One way to think about your commit history is to visualize your commits as buds on a tree branch. When you work on any branch, the commits are sequential, appearing one after the other.

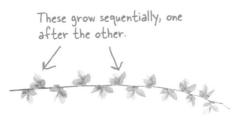

These grow sequentially, one after the other.

However, tree branches can fork off and grow in parallel. So can Git branches. What this means is that you can work on different things simultaneously without accidentally including things that you did not intend to (like Norm did).

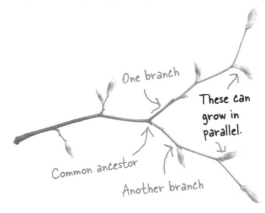

One branch

These can grow in parallel.

Common ancestor

Another branch

A commit represents a point in time, and a branch represents a series of commits. Recall that a series of commits is also the commit history. So branches are different commit histories, all in the same repository! At any point you can choose to create a new branch, switch between branches, discard a branch (that is, decide to abandon all the work you put into it), and even merge branches.

Updating the restaurant menu

Speaking of making choices, congratulations on your new job—managing the menu at the '80s Diner, where delightful recipes meet nostalgia.

Your role is to drum up exciting and nutritious dishes for the fall season. However, you need to get approval from the chef and the kitchen crew to make sure that they can actually prepare your delicious concoctions.

You are already familiar with using Git and Git repositories, so you take it upon yourself to bring the menu publishing system into the modern era. (Yeah, they don't call themselves the '80s Diner for no reason.) You decide to first take their existing menu and put it in a Git repository before you start on any new work.

The current menu of the '80s Diner.

The '80s Diner

Top Gumbo
You'll be ready to brave the heights after this hearty, spicy Southern-style seafood-and-okra stew.

Mac to the Future
Mix the '80s with the '50s with our classic baked mac and cheese, handmade with a five-cheese blend and topped with buttery breadcrumbs.

Raiders of the Lost Tarka Dal
Take a trip to India with Dr. Jones's favorite creamy lentils, fragrant with spices. Vegetarian!

Remember, instructions for the book downloads are in the introduction section of this book. You will find this menu in a file called menu.md in a folder called chapter02.

menu.md

First things first

Let's get the '80s Diner into the 21st century. We will start by putting their existing menu in a Git repository. This will give us a chance to practice some of our recently acquired Git skills.

Make sure you are following the instructions here. You are going to need this set up for the rest of the chapter.

1 Create a new directory called **80s-diner** inside the umbrella **headfirst-git-samples** and change to it using the cd command. Go ahead and initialize a new Git repository using git init.

If your terminal is still open from the last exercise in the previous chapter, be sure to use cd .. to go one level up.

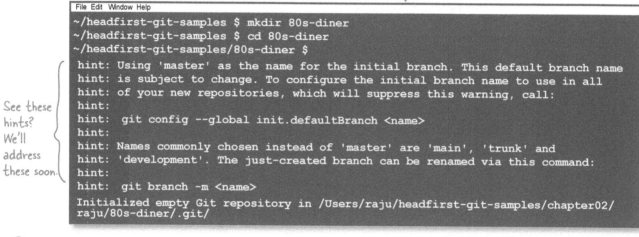

See these hints? We'll address these soon.

```
File Edit Window Help
~/headfirst-git-samples $ mkdir 80s-diner
~/headfirst-git-samples $ cd 80s-diner
~/headfirst-git-samples/80s-diner $
hint: Using 'master' as the name for the initial branch. This default branch name
hint: is subject to change. To configure the initial branch name to use in all
hint: of your new repositories, which will suppress this warning, call:
hint:
hint:   git config --global init.defaultBranch <name>
hint:
hint: Names commonly chosen instead of 'master' are 'main', 'trunk' and
hint: 'development'. The just-created branch can be renamed via this command:
hint:
hint:   git branch -m <name>
Initialized empty Git repository in /Users/raju/headfirst-git-samples/chapter02/
raju/80s-diner/.git/
```

2 Copy the **menu.md** file that you downloaded into the newly created 80s-diner folder.

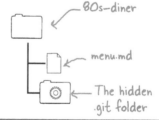

80s-diner

menu.md

The hidden .git folder

3 Next, add the file to the index and commit it to the 80s-diner repository using the commit message "add the main menu."

```
File Edit Window Help
~/headfirst-git-samples/80s-diner $ git add menu.md
~/headfirst-git-samples/80s-diner $ git commit -m "add the main menu"
[master (root-commit) ea6b05e] add the main menu
 1 file changed, 0 insertions(+), 0 deletions(-)
 create mode 100644 menu.md
```

You'll see a different commit ID. That's OK.

4 Finally, let's make sure git status reports that everything is fine.

This is exactly what you want to see.

```
File Edit Window Help
~/headfirst-git-samples/80s-diner $ git status
On branch master
nothing to commit, working tree clean
```

Every time I check the status of my repository, I see a reference to the "master" branch. Since we are talking about branches, is this related?

Very astute!

When we did our exercises with `git status` in Chapter 1, we asked you to ignore the branch details, because we were not ready to talk about branches just then.

It turns out that when you initialize a new Git repository and make your first commit, you are already working with branches! Git by default uses a branch called **master**, which explains why `git status` reported that you were on that branch.

So far, in the newly created `80s-diner` repository, you only have one commit. As long as you do not create another branch, every subsequent commit you make will be on this branch.

We'll just say it right here—*you are going to be using branches a lot when working with Git*. Although initially it may seem like more trouble than it's worth, you will soon see that creating, managing, and eventually integrating your work between branches is painless in Git. Not to mention that it gives you a ton of freedom as you work.

Serious Coding

There is nothing special about the default branch or the name `master`. This branch is no different from any branch that you can create. You can rename it if you choose, and in fact many teams do. If you were to go back and read the hints that `git init` provided on the previous page, you'll notice that Git provides you not only a way to change the name of `master` to something else, it tells you how to permanently set the name of the default branch for any repository that you might create going forward.

However, Git still defaults to `master`, and to avoid confusion, we are going to continue using the name `master` for the default branch throughout this book.

Choices...so many choices!

Managing branches in Git uses another command, appropriately named `branch`. You can use the `branch` command to create a new branch, list all the branches in your repository, and even delete branches. And, like everything you have done so far, all this happens in the terminal inside your working directory.

Let's start by creating a new branch. You can use the `branch` command, giving it the name of the branch you wish to create as an argument.

This is your sign to stop, grab a cup of your favorite beverage, and let the waves of Git knowledge wash over you. We will let you know when it's time to get some work done.

Invoke Git like we always do.

The branch command

The name of the new branch

`git branch my-first-branch`

Git does not report success or failure, but you can list all your branches by using the same `branch` command, except with no arguments.

The asterisk here marks the branch we are on.

Notice the asterisk does not move.

File Edit Window Help
```
$ git branch
* master
  my-first-branch
```

The output of the `git branch` command is a list of all the branches in the current repository. Git helpfully puts an asterisk next to the branch that we are currently using.

Creating a new branch does not mean you can start to use it immediately. You have to switch to it first.

Serious Coding

The Git `branch` command, with no arguments, is like the `git status` command, in that it is a "safe" command. It simply lists all the branches in your repository without changing anything. You can run it as often as you deem necessary.

there are no Dumb Questions

Q: Can I have whitespaces in my branch name?

A: No. If you want a multi-word branch name, use hyphens or underscores. If you attempt to put a space in your branch name, Git will report an `"is not a valid name"` error. Forward slashes (/) are allowed, though!

We'll talk more about branch names at the end of this book, so stay tuned for that.

Q: What happens if I try to create a branch with a name that already exists?

A: Just like with an invalid branch name, Git will error out, telling you that a branch with that name already exists. It's good to get in the habit of running `git branch` to list all the branches in your repository prior to creating a new one.

Q: How many branches can I have in my Git repository?

A: As many as you like! But as we will see soon, usually you will use a branch to work on a small, isolated change, then merge that into an "integration" branch when you are done, and then delete the branch. We'll dive into integration branches and deleting branches soon. This helps you keep a nice tidy repository.

Switching tracks

Now you know how to create branches, but you also just learned that creating a new branch does not mean you can start using it. To switch to another branch, you will use yet another Git command, aptly named `switch`, which takes one argument, namely the name of the branch you wish to switch to:

 *Nothing for you to do just yet.*

The switch command ↘ *The name of the branch you wish to use* ↙

git switch my-first-branch

This is how you know it worked. ↘

```
File Edit Window Help
$ git switch my-first-branch
Switched to branch 'my-first-branch'
```

You can use `git branch` to list all the branches again:

Now the asterisk points to the branch you just switched to. ↘

```
File Edit Window Help
$ git branch
  master
* my-first-branch
```

We realize that words like "fatal" can be scary, but worry not—over time you will get better at reading error messages.

there are no Dumb Questions

Q: What happens if I misspell the name of the branch?

A: No worries. Git will simply report an error like "`fatal: invalid reference`". We prefer to copy and paste the name we wish to use from the output of the `git branch` command. Typos begone!

Serious Coding

If you like performing remarkable feats at the command line, then you'll be happy to know that the `git switch` command lets you create a new branch and switch to it in one fell swoop. You can invoke the `git switch` command with the `-c` (or `--create`) flag, giving it the name of the branch you wish to create, like so:

```
git switch -c my-first-branch
```

This will prompt Git to create the branch called `my-first-branch` and switch to it immediately. However, since this is your first foray into Git, we'll continue using the `git branch` command to create new branches for the remainder of this book.

Back at the '80s Diner

You are feeling good. The '80s Diner menu is now being managed in a Git repository. And you have a new request—management are planning on introducing a special fall menu, and your task is to invent some spooky Halloween-themed specials. You take it upon yourself to binge-watch horror movies from the '80s to get in the right frame of mind, and you walk into work brimming with ideas for recipes.

Let's be diligent and create a branch so you can iterate over menu ideas. We will start in the terminal:

No rest for the weary! Be sure to follow the steps here in your terminal.

Recall that this means we have one branch and we are still using it.

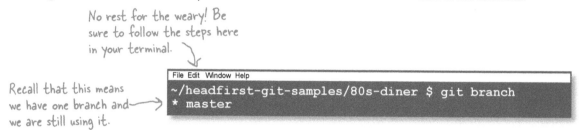

File Edit Window Help
```
~/headfirst-git-samples/80s-diner $ git branch
* master
```

Next, create a new branch named `add-fall-menu`, and switch to it.

Create the new branch.

File Edit Window Help
```
~/headfirst-git-samples/80s-diner $ git branch add-fall-menu
~/headfirst-git-samples/80s-diner $ git switch add-fall-menu
~/headfirst-git-samples/80s-diner $ git branch
* add-fall-menu
  master
```

The asterisk is next to the new branch. Brilliant!

Then switch to it.

You know the drill. Here is your checklist:

You can type this out, or just use the fall-menu.md file in the chapter02 directory that you downloaded.

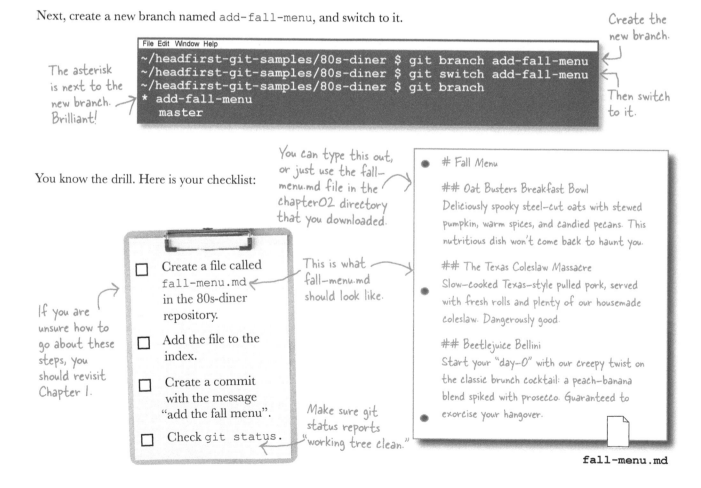

- ☐ Create a file called `fall-menu.md` in the 80s-diner repository.
- ☐ Add the file to the index.
- ☐ Create a commit with the message "add the fall menu".
- ☐ Check `git status`.

If you are unsure how to go about these steps, you should revisit Chapter 1.

This is what fall-menu.md should look like.

Make sure git status reports "working tree clean."

Fall Menu

Oat Busters Breakfast Bowl
Deliciously spooky steel-cut oats with stewed pumpkin, warm spices, and candied pecans. This nutritious dish won't come back to haunt you.

The Texas Coleslaw Massacre
Slow-cooked Texas-style pulled pork, served with fresh rolls and plenty of our housemade coleslaw. Dangerously good.

Beetlejuice Bellini
Start your "day-0" with our creepy twist on the classic brunch cocktail: a peach-banana blend spiked with prosecco. Guaranteed to exorcise your hangover.

fall-menu.md

Send it back!

Uh oh! You showed the cooking staff your newly created fall menu, but they're not thrilled with the new menu's lukewarm title. They need it to be a tad more exciting, so they ask you to change the heading from "Fall Menu" to "The Graveyard Shift."

This is not done!

We might as well make that change. Go back to your text editor and change the first line of the `fall-menu.md` file from "Fall Menu" to "The Graveyard Shift". Make sure to save the file before proceeding.

We will start by checking our Git status. Since we edited the `fall-menu.md` file, it should show up as "modified."

You're still playing along, right?

To save space, we are not displaying the directory name here. Just be sure to be in the 80s-diner directory.

```
File Edit Window Help
$ git status
On branch add-fall-menu
Changes not staged for commit:
  (use "git add <file>..." to update what will be committed)
  (use "git restore <file>..." to discard changes in working directory)
      modified:   fall-menu.md

no changes added to commit (use "git add" and/or "git commit -a")
```

Since you edited the file, git status tells you that it's modified.

Updated fall-menu.md. Notice the first line has been updated.

That looks good, so let's go ahead and commit it. We will start by adding the file to the index, and then committing it. Let's use the message "update heading":

> # The Graveyard Shift
>
> ## Oat Busters Breakfast Bowl
> Deliciously spooky steel-cut oats with stewed pumpkin, warm spices, and candied pecans. This nutritious dish won't come back to haunt you.
>
> ## The Texas Coleslaw Massacre

Commit your update of the fall-menu.md file.

```
File Edit Window Help
$ git add fall-menu.md
$ git commit -m "update heading"
[add-fall-menu 245482d] update heading
 1 file changed, 1 insertion(+), 1 deletion(-)
$ git status
On branch add-fall-menu
nothing to commit, working tree clean
```

Code Magnets

Oh dear! To help our fellow developers, we had carefully laid out all the commands needed to list all the branches in their (existing) repository, create a new branch, switch to it, and check to make sure that all is well. Alas! The magnets fell on the floor. It's your job to put them back together. Be careful; a few extra magnets got mixed in, and some get used more than once.

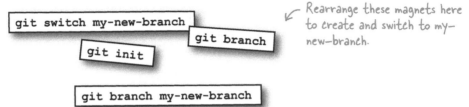

```
git switch my-new-branch
```

```
git branch
```

```
git init
```

```
git branch my-new-branch
```

Rearrange these magnets here to create and switch to my-new-branch.

Answers on page 103.

You've lost me. It seems like we're doing exactly what we've always done. What exactly did we achieve with branches?

Great question! It might not look like it right now, but branches offer you a ton of flexibility as you start to work with multiple requirements.

Right now, you have two branches: master and add-fall-menu. You initialized the repository, which put you on the master branch. You added and committed the existing menu on the master branch.

When you got the requirements for the fall menu, you chose to do all that work on a separate branch: namely the add-fall-menu branch.

These two branches represent two completely separate requirements. Remember, branches allow you to isolate parts of the work from one another. If tomorrow management were to come around and ask that you work on something totally unrelated (and most assuredly they will!), you simply create a new branch from master and get to work. All the work you did on the add-fall-menu branch remains undisturbed till you get a chance to get back to it.

The good news here is that working on a branch is not new to you—you've been working with branches all along! Other than having to create and switch branches, your workflow remains the same—you add or edit files, you add them to the index, and then you commit them.

Visualizing branches

So what happens when you make a commit on a branch? Perhaps it will help to recap what we have done so far, *after* initializing a repository in the 80s-diner folder:

* We added the menu.md file and committed it. Recall that this commit is on the default, that is, the master branch.

* We then created the add-fall-menu branch.

* We introduced the fall-menu.md file and committed it.

* We had to fix the heading, so we made a change to the fall-menu.md file and made a **second** commit.

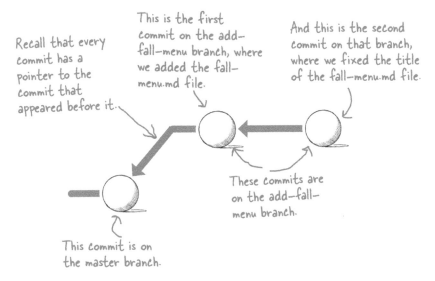

Recall that every commit has a pointer to the commit that appeared before it.

This is the first commit on the add-fall-menu branch, where we added the fall-menu.md file.

And this is the second commit on that branch, where we fixed the title of the fall-menu.md file.

These commits are on the add-fall-menu branch.

This commit is on the master branch.

As you can see, we did some work on the master branch, and now have work in the add-fall-menu branch.

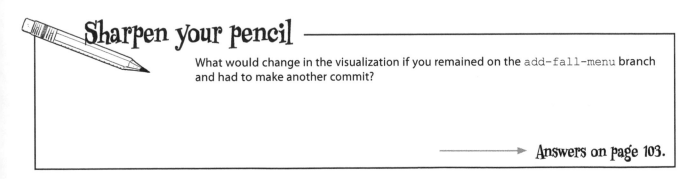

Sharpen your pencil

What would change in the visualization if you remained on the add-fall-menu branch and had to make another commit?

Answers on page 103.

Branches, commits, and the files contained within

We know that commits on a branch are "sequenced"—that is, they are like buds on a tree branch—one comes after the next. What does that mean for the files that each commit knows about? Recall that Git repositories default to the `master` branch. So, our first commit, which introduced the `menu.md` file, was on the `master` branch.

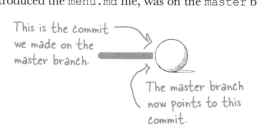

This is the commit we made on the master branch.

The master branch now points to this commit.

At this point we had one commit on the `master` branch. When we then created the `add-fall-menu` branch, Git used this commit as the starting point for the new branch. In other words, the `master` branch and the `add-fall-menu` branch both share this commit.

master branch   add-fall-menu branch

So far, we've only committed the `menu.md` file. Since both the `master` and the `add-fall-menu` branch point to the same commit, they both know about the same `menu.md` file.

We then introduced the `fall-menu.md` file on the `add-fall-menu` branch and committed it.

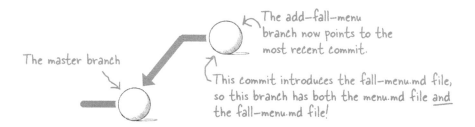

The add-fall-menu branch now points to the most recent commit.

The master branch

This commit introduces the fall-menu.md file, so this branch has both the menu.md file and the fall-menu.md file!

Since the `add-fall-menu` branch started with the commit that included the `menu.md` file and then introduced the `fall-menu.md` file, it now has both files in it. But the `master` branch has only the commit with the `menu.md` file, so the `master` branch only has the `menu.md` file in it.

BE Git

Spend a little time understanding how Git changes your working directory when you switch branches.

Start with your terminal—make sure you are in the `80s-diner` directory, and use `git branch` to ensure you are on the `add-fall-menu` branch.

To be safe, let's make sure we are in the right directory and the right branch.

```
File Edit Window Help
$ pwd
/headfirst-git-samples/80s-diner
$ git branch
* add-fall-menu
  master
```

Recall that ls "lists" all the files.

```
File Edit Window Help
$ ls
```

Now switch to the `master` branch. List the output of `git branch`:

```
File Edit Window Help
$ git branch
```

Write your results here.

List all the files again:

```
File Edit Window Help
$ ls
```

Finally, see if you can explain what you are seeing here.

Explanation goes here.

Answers on page 104.

Maddie   Guinevere   Armando

Cubicle Conversation

Maddie: I know you're waiting on the final approval for the fall menu, but I have something else I need you to take care of for me.

Guinevere: Wait, is this a new menu?

Maddie: Yep. We've decided to make a special menu for Thursday nights. The theme is '80s movies, so it stays on brand, and we are calling it...wait for it...Throwback Thursdays!

Guinevere: OK...but we are still in the middle of finishing up the fall menu.

Armando: It's fine, Guinevere. I'll create a new file in our repository, work in the new menu, and commit it.

Guinevere: Whoa! Hold on. If you commit now, you'll commit it on the `add-fall-menu` branch. We want to keep these changes independent of one another. Here, let me show you what will happen if you commit right now:

master branch

If we stick to the add-fall-menu branch, any new commits will show up on that branch. We certainly don't want that.

Armando: Then I'll just use the `branch` command to create a new branch. That should do the trick, right?

Guinevere: Well, we want to be sure we don't include any of the fall menu changes. We're currently on the `add-fall-menu` branch. If you create a new branch, it'll be based on the `add-fall-menu` branch. We want the new branch to be based on the `master` branch.

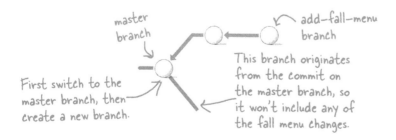

master branch

add-fall-menu branch

First switch to the master branch, then create a new branch.

This branch originates from the commit on the master branch, so it won't include any of the fall menu changes.

Armando: Ah! OK. So first, switch to the `master` branch, then use the `branch` command to create a new branch. That way we keep the fall menu changes completely independent of the Thursday menu changes. Got it!

Working in parallel

Let's see what it takes to start working on the menu for Throwback Thursdays. Make sure you are in the `80s-diner` directory, and that `git status` reports all is well.

Fire up your terminal and follow along with us.

Here's what we got. Looking good!

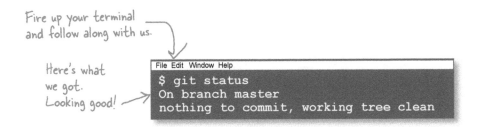

```
File Edit Window Help
$ git status
On branch master
nothing to commit, working tree clean
```

If you are not on the `master` branch, then your first action item is to switch to the `master` branch. This ensures that the new branch will be based on the `master` branch. We can then create our new branch and add the new Throwback Thursday menu. Let's call our new branch `add-thurs-menu`.

The new menu

If you don't feel like typing this out, you will find it in the chapter02 folder.

Create the new branch and switch to it.

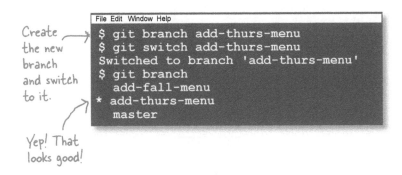

```
File Edit Window Help
$ git branch add-thurs-menu
$ git switch add-thurs-menu
Switched to branch 'add-thurs-menu'
$ git branch
  add-fall-menu
* add-thurs-menu
  master
```

Yep! That looks good!

The next steps are all you. Create a new file called `thursdays-menu.md` in the `80s-diner` directory with the menu as shown on the right, add it to the index, and commit it with the message "add thursdays menu". Be sure to check `git status` when you are done!

● # Throwback Thursdays

The Breakfast Club Sandwich

A club that breaks the rules: ham, bacon, turkey, and tomato plus a fried egg, all between layers of toast.

Footloose Burger

● A juicy grilled Black Angus quarter-pounder with American cheese and plenty of bacon.

Fried Green Tomatoes

OK, it's from 1991, but we bet you can't resist these tart, juicy slices of ● cornmeal-crusted Southern bliss.

thursdays-menu.md

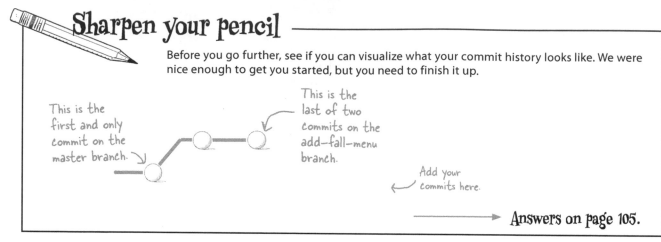

Sharpen your pencil

Before you go further, see if you can visualize what your commit history looks like. We were nice enough to get you started, but you need to finish it up.

This is the first and only commit on the master branch.

This is the last of two commits on the add-fall-menu branch.

Add your commits here.

Answers on page 105.

BE Git

Let's repeat our previous exercise of visiting all of the branches in our repository and listing the files that are present in each branch, except this time around, we have three branches. For each of the windows shown below, jot down the output of invoking `git branch`, and then list all the files in each branch:

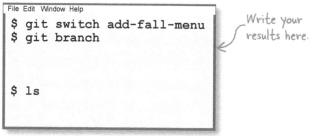

```
File Edit  Window Help
$ git switch add-fall-menu
$ git branch



$ ls
```

Write your results here.

```
File Edit  Window Help
$ git switch master
$ git branch



$ ls
```

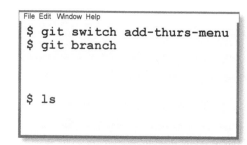

```
File Edit  Window Help
$ git switch add-thurs-menu
$ git branch



$ ls
```

Answers on page 105.

Brain Power

Imagine there was a way to combine the three different branches into one branch. What would your working directory look like? How many files would be there as a result of integrating the three branches into one?

What is a branch, really?

Say it with us—a branch is simply a reference to a commit. So what makes a branch a branch? Let's start with the role of a commit—a commit is a snapshot of the content you staged (that is, the files you added to the index). If you happen to be working on a task in which you have made two or more commits, then the commits are "strung" together. That is, every subsequent commit records the ID of the commit that came just before it.

We talked about this in Chapter 1.

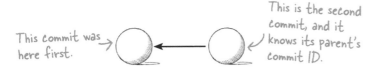

This commit was here first.

This is the second commit, and it knows its parent's commit ID.

Imagine you have a separate note for every branch in your repository. Every note has the name of the branch and the ID of the last commit on that branch. When you make a commit on a branch, Git first creates the commit. It then takes the "sticky note" representing that branch, erases the commit ID that was on it, and scribbles in the new one:

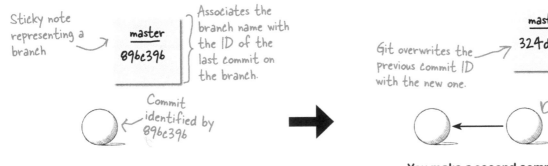

Sticky note representing a branch

master
896c396

Associates the branch name with the ID of the last commit on the branch.

Commit identified by 896c396

Git overwrites the previous commit ID with the new one.

master
324d769

ID: 324d769

Initially, there is only one commit on the master branch.

You make a second commit, which has ID 324d769.

A branch always points to the last commit on that branch, and every commit, in turn, points to another commit (its "parent" commit), and so on and so forth.

A branch is simply a reference to a commit via its ID. This reference is updated every time you make another commit on that branch.

Sharpen your pencil

Look at the hypothetical commit graph below, and fill in the sticky notes with the information needed to associate a branch name with the commit ID that it points to. Note that there might be more sticky notes than you might actually need.

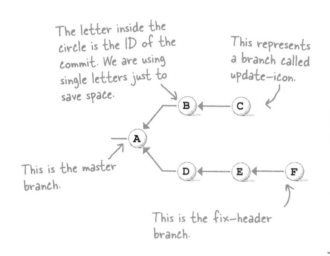

The letter inside the circle is the ID of the commit. We are using single letters just to save space.

This represents a branch called update-icon.

This is the master branch.

This is the fix-header branch.

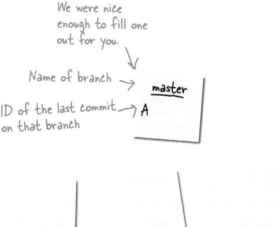

We were nice enough to fill one out for you.

Name of branch →

ID of the last commit on that branch →

master

A

Now suppose we were to switch to the fix-header branch, make some edits, and make another commit, which was given ID "G." Can you visualize what would change in the diagram above?

Draw the commit history and the updated sticky note here.

Answers on page 106.

Switching branches, or switching directories?

Remember all those exercises we made you do in which you switched branches and listed the files in your working directory? Well, all that hard work is about to pay off. You are about to understand what it means to switch branches.

Remember, branches are just pointers to commits. And a commit is simply a snapshot of everything you added to the index, along with some metadata including the commit message you provided when you created the commit. In other words, the commit remembers the state of the index at the time you made the commit.

Let's return to the commit graph you created for the '80s Diner. We have annotated it for you, showing you the files that you will find in each branch:

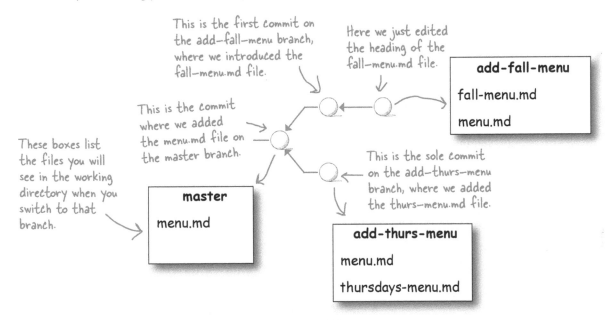

This is the first commit on the add-fall-menu branch, where we introduced the fall-menu.md file.

Here we just edited the heading of the fall-menu.md file.

This is the commit where we added the menu.md file on the master branch.

These boxes list the files you will see in the working directory when you switch to that branch.

This is the sole commit on the add-thurs-menu branch, where we added the thurs-menu.md file.

add-fall-menu
fall-menu.md
menu.md

master
menu.md

add-thurs-menu
menu.md
thursdays-menu.md

As you can see, every time you switch branches, you are potentially switching commits (unless the two branches in question point to the same commit). And a commit records the state of the index when you made the commit. Which means...

Every time you switch branches, Git rewrites your working directory to look like it did when you made the most recent commit on the branch you just switched to.

It's super important to wrap your head around this. So take a break, walk away, think about it, then come back to this book.

This is particularly important if you have files open in your editor. It's a good idea to either refresh the files in your editor or simply reopen the project after switching branches so you see the latest set of files.

I get it. When I switch branches, Git rewrites the working directory to represent the set of files to match what I last committed on that branch. But at some point, don't we want all files on one branch?

Yes, we have often been disappointed too. But let's not agonize over all those "Lost" hours.

Yes we do! Think of your favorite movie or TV show. Almost any scintillating story has a number of smaller storylines that support the main arc, and what makes for a truly satisfying ending is that all the subplots eventually tie up the primary narrative with a bow.

You can think of branches that you create to work on a particular task or story as subplots that eventually need to tie back into the main storyline. Think about the work you have done so far on the '80s Diner—you have ideas for different menus, but once everyone involved signs off, you want all three menus to be on the same branch. That is, you want to merge all three branches into one.

Some branches are more equal than others

We know having separate menus living on separate branches isn't what we want. That begs the question—*which* branch should everything live on?

Recall that when you initialize a new Git repository, you always start with a branch called `master`. Since this branch is created by default, it's always there! So many teams simply use the `master` branch as the branch that will hold the main storyline of their project.

This is often referred to as an "integration" branch—in that this is where you bring together all the different tasks you worked on in other branches.

Choosing `master` is often just a matter of convenience. You can choose to make **any** branch the integration branch. As long as you and your colleagues agree, it's all good.

While you are choosing branch names, you might as well choose a good name. One popular option is "main" instead of `master`.

So integration branches are where things come together. What does that make everything else? Other branches are often referred to as "feature" branches—essentially branches that serve to introduce one thing. These branches would serve to add a new feature, or fix a bug, or add and improve documentation. Essentially, they are one and done—for every separate task, there would be a different feature branch.

Serious Coding

"Feature" branches are often called "topic" branches. They are essentially the same.

Sharpen your pencil

We mentioned that many teams use names like main instead of master for integration branches. Can you think of any other names? List a few here (feel free to use your favorite search engine to get some ideas):

⟶ Ideas on page 107.

Brain Power

Let's say you have a bunch of pictures in one folder on your computer, and others in some other folder. Also, there are some duplicates between the two. Can you think of any issues you might face if you tried to combine all the files from both folders?

Bring it in!

Integration branches play a critical role in your Git repository. Remember, what makes a integration branch special is just convention; any branch can be made an integration branch that serves as the place where everything—big and small, features and bug fixes—comes together.

Bringing the work that was done in separate branches together is called ***merging***, and Git has a command specifically built in to do just that: merge. The git merge command allows you to combine the work done in different branches.

Merging in Git typically involves two branches—the branch that you are on (we'll refer to this as the "proposer") and the branch you wish to merge or "mix" in (we'll call this the "proposee").

Since we are so food obsessed, we are going to double down on it! Think about baking a cake. You can start preparing the icing as the cake has to cool after coming out of the oven. At some point, you want to "merge" the two together. Here, the cake would be the proposer, and the icing would be the proposee.

Let's continue with that analogy (oh yeah—we are doubling down on it!): let's say you had two branches in your repository—bake-cake and prepare-icing.

You are on the bake-cake branch.

```
File Edit Window Help
$ git branch
* bake-cake
prepare-icing
```

We then simply tell Git to merge the prepare-icing branch into the bake-cake branch, like so:

The argument to the merge command is the branch that is to be "mixed" into the branch you are on.

Invoke the merge command.

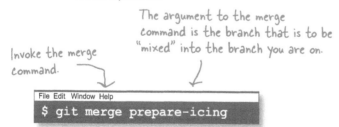

```
File Edit Window Help
$ git merge prepare-icing
```

Sounds complex? Don't worry—we will ease into it, one small step at a time.

Make it Stick

Roses are red, violets are blue,
Keep **feature branches** specific
To the **one thing** they do.

Roses are yours, violets are mine,
Use **integration branches**
When it's time to combine.

Sharpen your pencil

Let's say you attended a friend's wedding. You took some pictures on your phone, and a few days later, the wedding photographer asks you to send them the pictures you took. You make a copy of the wedding pictures on your phone and send them the copy so they could combine them with the ones they took.

Now take a few minutes to think about the following questions:

➤ Who has the "complete" set of pictures?

➤ Did either one of you lose any pictures?

Fill in your answers here.

➤ Which one of you is the "integration" branch in this scenario?

Answers on page 107.

All together now!

Read the #&$!@ manual (git branch edition)

Git tries to be super helpful, and it comes loaded with a full-on manual. The good news is that you don't have to remember every nuance of every Git command (and there are a **lot** of commands)—you can simply ask Git to help you out. If you are the kind of person who reads technical documentation for leisure, then you want to run "git <command> --help"—for example, git branch --help. This is the whole enchilada: everything you ever need to know about the branch command is listed here, including examples of usage! This is a page you'll want to come back to once you get some hands-on experience with Git.

> Apologies for the intermission, but this digression will help us in a few minutes.

> You can also use "git help <command>", which is an alias for "git <command> --help".

If you are in a hurry, or just a CliffsNotes kinda person, then the version you want is "git <command> -h" like so: git branch -h. This is a much shorter version of the help page. Of course, if something catches your eye but you don't understand what it does or how to use it, you can always use the longer version (--help) to get more details.

> Here is your memory trick of the day: "--help" has more characters in it than "-h", just as the --help page has more characters and details than the -h page.

Git by default uses a "pager" when displaying long outputs, you know, like help pages. A *pager* is simply a program that only displays one page of text at a time. You can use your cursor keys to navigate up and down the page one line at a time. Once you are done, hit the letter "q," which stands for "quit," and your terminal will be restored back to the prompt.

Exercise

In the 80s-diner directory, go ahead and run git branch --help (or git help branch—use either one), and find the section regarding the -v or --verbose flag. **Read up on what it does.**

Next, run git branch -v and record the branch name and the latest commit ID here. (You are going to need these for the next few sections in this chapter.)

add-fall-menu ———————————
add-thurs-menu ———————————
master ———————————

> Fill in your commit IDs here.

Answers on page 108.

Making the fall menu official

Back at the '80s Diner, after weeks of waiting, the chefs have signed off on your proposal for the fall menu. They love the new dishes you conjured up and are gearing up for the launch night. Seems like you are done with your work on that feature. So now what?

We'll be sticking to the standard convention of using the `master` branch as the integration branch. That means that all work needs to be merged into the `master` branch. So let's do just that.

Back in the terminal, `cd` into the `80s-diner` directory. First, a sanity check to make sure you are in a good place: `git status`.

Molto bene!

Follow along here. This will set you up for the next exercise.

Be sure to be in the right directory.

This is where we left things off in the last exercise.

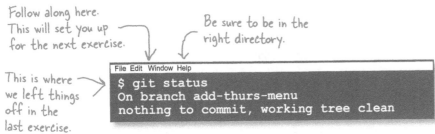

```
File Edit Window Help
$ git status
On branch add-thurs-menu
nothing to commit, working tree clean
```

Since `master` branch is the integration branch, you should merge the `add-fall-menu` branch *into* the `master` branch. You will have to first switch to the `master` branch, and then merge the `add-fall-menu` branch into it.

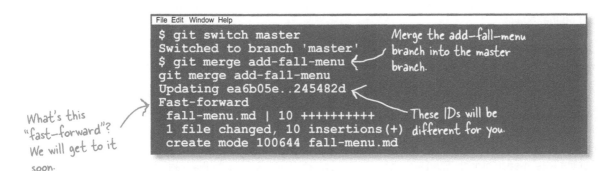

```
File Edit Window Help
$ git switch master
Switched to branch 'master'
$ git merge add-fall-menu
git merge add-fall-menu
Updating ea6b05e..245482d
Fast-forward
 fall-menu.md | 10 ++++++++++
 1 file changed, 10 insertions(+)
 create mode 100644 fall-menu.md
```

Merge the add-fall-menu branch into the master branch.

These IDs will be different for you.

What's this "fast-forward"? We will get to it soon.

Now, if you were to list all the files that are part of the `master` branch, you will see the `master` branch has two files: `menu.md` and `fall-menu.md`! That is, the `master` branch reflects the work that was done in the two branches separately.

```
File Edit Window Help
$ ls
fall-menu.md
menu.md
```

there are no Dumb Questions

Q: Why didn't we merge the `master` **branch into the** `add-fall-menu` **branch?**

A: You are absolutely right to ask that question. There are two separate issues here.

First, consider the intent—if the `master` branch is the integration branch, then everything should get merged *into* the `master` branch.

Second, merging means bringing together multiple different lines of work, which has an effect on the commit history of your project. *What* gets merged into what has deep implications on how the merge will happen, and what the final result will look like. Yes, that sounds nebulous—so we are going to be spending a lot of time in this chapter talking about exactly that. More in a few pages.

Q: OK, so you are telling me that the work we did in the `add-fall-menu` **branch is now merged into the** `master` **branch. So what happens to the** `add-fall-menu` **branch?**

A: For now, you can let it be. If you get another request to make additional changes to the fall menu, you would create a **new** branch based on `master`, make your changes, and when done simply merge back into `master`.

The answer to your question lies in deleting branches, which we will discuss at the end of this chapter.

Q: I got a `merge: not something we can merge` **error. Help!**

A: Make sure you get the name of the branch right! We highly recommend listing all your branches and copy-pasting the name to avoid such mistakes.

Exercise

Let's flex our command-line skills a bit more. You are going to repeat our previous exercise of listing the latest commit IDs on each branch. Recall that you can use `git branch -v` and see information about each of your branches. Go ahead and do that again:

add-fall-menu   _____   ←   *Just like last time, list*
add-thurs-menu   _____   *your commit IDs here.*
master   _____

Compare these with the ones you did the last time around. What changed?

Finally, list the files in each branch. Start with the `master` branch, then `switch` to the `add-fall-menu` branch and finally the `add-thurs-menu` branch, using `ls` to list the files you see in each branch:

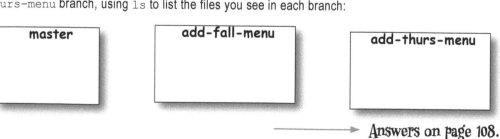

master	add-fall-menu	add-thurs-menu

Answers on page 108.

Some merges are straightforward

fast- (written above "straight", with "straight" crossed out)

When you merge two branches together, you are combining the work done in the individual branches: that is, you are bringing together two separate commit histories. You might have also noticed the "fast-forward" that appeared in your terminal output when you performed the merge between the `master` and the `add-fall-menu` branch. So what did Git actually do?

Let's start with the commit history, focusing only on `master` and `add-fall-menu`. For simplicity we'll use letters in alphabetical order to represent the commit IDs. It looks something like this.

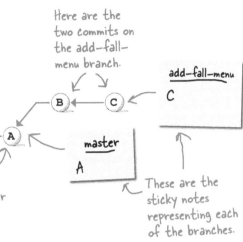

Here are the two commits on the add-fall-menu branch.

This is the only commit on the master branch.

These are the sticky notes representing each of the branches.

In this scenario, we have two sticky notes to represent the two branches, each one pointing to the latest commit on that branch. The thing to notice here is that the `add-fall-menu` branch is based on the latest commit on the `master` branch. The `master` branch has not changed (no new commits on it) since the inception of the `add-fall-menu` branch. In other words, the `add-fall-menu` branch has everything the `master` branch does! Which means, for Git to make `master` (the proposer) look like `add-fall-menu`, Git could simply move `master` to the same commit as the last commit on the `add-fall-menu` branch.

That is exactly what Git does. Git rewrites the `master` sticky note to point to the same commit that the `add-fall-menu` sticky note points to. This is referred to as a "fast-forward" merge—where a branch, in this case `master`, simply jumps forward.

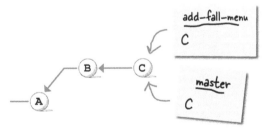

When merging, the fast-forward merge is the best-case scenario, since technically it's not a merge at all. It's simply one branch "catching up" with another.

Look back and study the commit IDs you listed on the previous page. Notice that the `add-fall-menu` branch and the `master` branch both point to the same commit after the merge.

Brain Power

Can you think of an analogy that can explain a fast-forward merge? Think of "merging" the color orange (made of yellow and red) and the color yellow. What does it mean to "merge" yellow into orange?

It doesn't quite work the other way

Let's think of a hypothetical—what if, instead of merging into the `add-fall-menu` branch into `master`, we attempted to merge `master` into the `add-fall-menu` branch? Turns out, while this may not be obvious, it ***absolutely*** matters how we perform the merge.

← This is a thought experiment!

First, a recap of what the setup would look like. This time around, `add-fall-menu` is the proposer and `master` is the proposee. So we would start by switching to `add-fall-menu`, then merge the `master` branch into `add-fall-menu`.

Here is how this would play out:

```
File  Edit  Window  Help
$ git switch add-fall-menu
Switched to branch 'add-fall-menu'
$ git merge master
Already up to date.
```

Womp womp. Not quite what you expected, huh? To understand what transpired here, we go back to the commit history. This is what the commit history looked like before we merged `add-fall-menu` into `master`.

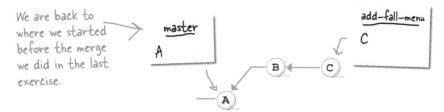

We are back to where we started before the merge we did in the last exercise.

Merging `master` into `add-fall-menu` is just another way saying "Hey Git, `add-fall-menu` should be the combination of `add-fall-menu` and `master`." Well, `add-fall-menu` is based on `master`, which means it already *has* everything that `master` has to offer.

Remember, master has no new commits on it since we created add-fall-menu branch.

So Git tells us that `add-fall-menu` is "Already up to date." Which is to say, `add-fall-menu` is already the combination of `add-fall-menu` and `master`. To put it in terms of the commit history, nothing changed since there was nothing to do.

Logically, the "direction" of the merge always results in two files (`menu.md` and `add-fall-menu.md`) being present in the working directory. Remember—the `add-fall-menu` branch, being based on `master`, already has the `menu.md` file in it because it started with it! But the order of the merge has a huge impact on your commit history, as we just saw. In one case, `master` fast-forwarded to the commit that `add-fall-menu` points to; in the other case, nothing changed.

A little more Git setup

Before we proceed with the rest of the chapter, we need to make one more configuration update to Git. You might recall that we, in Chapter 1, configured our name and email address, which is recorded in every commit *we* make. However, there are times when it's *Git* that needs to make a commit (we will see this scenario over the next few pages). But in order to do so, Git needs a commit message. So far it's just been you creating commits, and every time you did so, you supplied a commit message using the -m flag supplied to the `commit` command. However, if Git ever needs to create a commit, Git will present you with a text editor to type your commit message in. The question is—what editor should it use?

Git is configured to use a default editor, which is Vim. If you are familiar with using Vim, feel free to skip this page and go on to the next one. However, if you want to change to an editor you are more familiar with, then keep reading.

In the introduction of this book we recommended you install Visual Studio Code. If you *are* using Visual Studio Code, then fire up your terminal and run this little nugget of code.

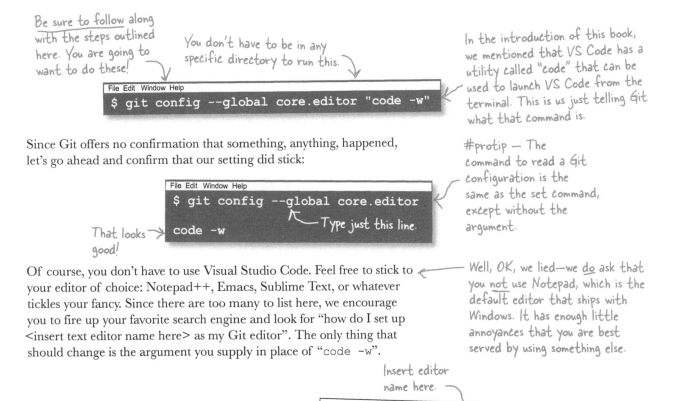

Be sure to follow along with the steps outlined here. You are going to want to do these!

You don't have to be in any specific directory to run this.

In the introduction of this book, we mentioned that VS Code has a utility called "code" that can be used to launch VS Code from the terminal. This is us just telling Git what that command is.

```
File Edit Window Help
$ git config --global core.editor "code -w"
```

Since Git offers no confirmation that something, anything, happened, let's go ahead and confirm that our setting did stick:

#protip — The command to read a Git configuration is the same as the set command, except without the argument.

```
File Edit Window Help
$ git config --global core.editor
code -w
```
Type just this line.

That looks good!

Of course, you don't have to use Visual Studio Code. Feel free to stick to your editor of choice: Notepad++, Emacs, Sublime Text, or whatever tickles your fancy. Since there are too many to list here, we encourage you to fire up your favorite search engine and look for "how do I set up <insert text editor name here> as my Git editor". The only thing that should change is the argument you supply in place of "code -w".

Well, OK, we lied—we <u>do</u> ask that you <u>not</u> use Notepad, which is the default editor that ships with Windows. It has enough little annoyances that you are best served by using something else.

Insert editor name here.

how do I set up _____ as my Git editor?

> I'm going to have to stop you here. You keep showing us these commit history graphs. Why are they so necessary?

Great question! The last few exercises have shown you how important it is to be able to visualize the commit history so you can understand why Git behaves the way it does.

Everything we have done so far, including creating commits and branches and merging branches together, has involved interacting with the commit history. New commits are chained together with their parent commits on the same branch; branches are sticky notes that point to commits; and merges serve to bring two branches (two separate commit histories) together.

Truly, Git enlightenment lies in understanding the commit history!

Furthermore, almost every subject we touch upon in this book will revolve around this graph.

There are a slew of graphical user interface (GUI) tools that let you work with Git. So far we have only used the Git command-line tools, but once you are far enough in your journey with Git, you might start to use GUI tools too. And guess what? They all show you the same commit history graph! You are just ahead of the class in that regard. Now aren't you glad you bought this book?

This is a screenshot from a popular free and open source tool called Sourcetree, from a company called Atlassian.

It shows a small piece of the commit history of a popular Ruby-based framework called Ruby on Rails.

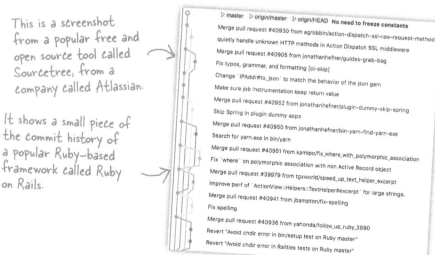

It's almost Thursday!

The newly christened fall menu is a hit. The '80s Diner has never seen so much foot traffic, and business is booming. Management wants to capitalize on all the buzz by starting Throwback Thursdays *now*.

We've decided to use the master branch as the integration branch. Now that the Thursday menu has gotten the sign-off, we are going to merge the add-thurs-menu branch into the master branch. But before you start, remember—the add-thurs-menu branch was created off the master branch. Merging the add-fall-menu branch into master resulted in a fast-forward merge—in other words, master simply moved forward to the latest commit on add-fall-menu.

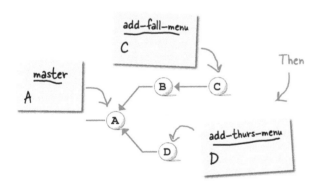

Commit graph when we created the add-thurs-menu branch

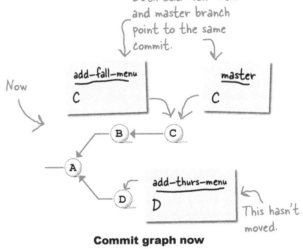

Both add-fall-menu and master branch point to the same commit.

This hasn't moved.

Commit graph now

You should already be on the master branch if you left things just the way they were after your last exercise, but to be sure:

This looks good. If you are not on the master branch, be sure to switch to it.

```
File Edit Window Help
$ git branch
  add-fall-menu
  add-thurs-menu
* master
```

You are ready to merge.

Brain Power

Leaving aside the technicalities of the merge, can you list the files that would result if you merged the add-thurs-menu branch into the master branch? How many files would you see in the working directory?

Wait! You moved?

It might be a tad surprising that although `add-thurs-menu` was based on the `master` branch, the `master` branch has since moved to a new commit. This is where it's important to realize that whenever you branch, you are actually creating a branch that points to a **commit**, not to another branch. Branches, being simple pointers to commits, offer an easy way to get to commits. Remember, the "basis" for the branch is *always* a commit.

You will often hear fellow developers say "Go ahead. Branch off master." What they are really saying is create a new branch that points to the same commit that master points to at that moment.

So what does it mean to merge `add-thurs-menu` into the `master` branch? The answer lies, of course, in the commit history.

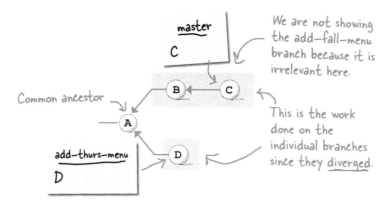

We are not showing the add-fall-menu branch because it is irrelevant here.

Common ancestor

This is the work done on the individual branches since they diverged.

add-thurs-menu

Notice that both the `master` branch and the `add-thurs-menu` branch share a common ancestor (in this case, the commit with ID "A"). When we merge the two branches together, we are attempting to combine the work done **after** that commit.

We want to combine the changes made in B and C with those in D.

This particular scenario is a great example of branches diverging from one another after starting at a common point in time. Think of it as being like two trains departing from one station, going on their individual routes, picking up passengers, and then converging (merging) at another station.

Looks like our commit history, right?

It's almost Thursday! (continued)

So you're all set up and ready to merge add-thurs-menu into master. You switched to the master branch, so let's go ahead and merge the add-thurs-menu branch into it:

Be sure to follow along with us here.

```
File Edit Window Help
$ git merge add-thurs-menu
hint: Waiting for your editor to close the file...
```

Your editor isn't always visible.

Every so often, your editor might be hidden behind other windows on your desktop, particularly if you have many applications open. If you don't see it, look around—it's there, we promise.

What happened? Git is trying to create a "merge commit" (more about this in a minute). Since this is a new commit, Git needs a commit message. So Git will attempt to bring up your default editor (the same one we configured a few pages ago) and prompt you to type in a commit message, like so:

This is Visual Studio Code.

Notice the window title.

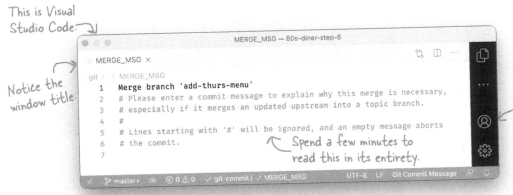

Spend a few minutes to read this in its entirety.

We will get to why this exhibits different behavior than your last merge in a minute.

Git very handily fills in a default commit message, and usually we prefer to just keep it that way. You are free to type in any commit message here. When done, save, and then **close** that window. Your terminal should report a successful merge.

If you read the text Git presents, you will know that anything preceded by a hash mark (#) is a comment and will be ignored.

This is not a fast-forward merge.

```
File Edit Window Help
$ git merge add-thurs-menu
Merge made by the 'recursive' strategy.
 thursdays-menu.md | 10 ++++++++++
 1 file changed, 10 insertions(+)
 create mode 100644 thursdays-menu.md
```

Yay! Another successful merge. Now all the work that is in the add-thurs-menu branch has been merged into the master branch. A quick listing of the files shows that this is indeed the case.

```
File Edit Window Help
$ ls
fall-menu.md
menu.md
thursdays-menu.md
```

Time to finally enjoy some good food and dance the night away!

there are no Dumb Questions

Q: Is the commit message that I supplied in VS Code any different from the commit messages we supply when we commit with the "−m" flag?

A: No. They are exactly the same. In fact, you could even have merged `add-thurs-menu` into the `master` branch using something like: `git merge add-thurs-menu -m "Merge branch 'add-thurs-menu'"`. We wanted to show you a scenario in which Git asks you to supply a commit message using your default editor.

As to why it behaved this way, well, we will see that in just a second.

Q: I got an error when trying to complete this. What did I do wrong?

A: If you got an error like "`error: Empty commit message`", then it means that you might have accidentally cleared out all the text in your merge editor window and then closed it. This supplies an empty message, and Git errors out. Git will inform you what to do, but the easiest way is to type `git commit` and hit Enter in the console window. This will bring up your editor once again. This time, type in your message, save the file, then close it. You should be good to go now.

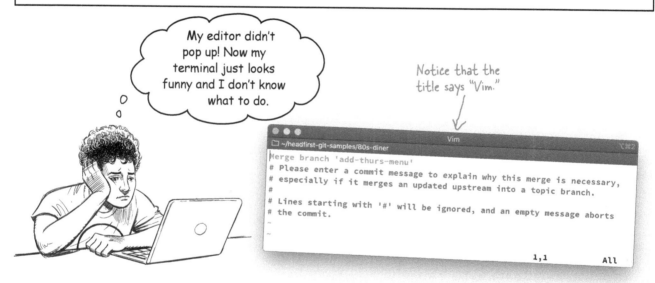

My editor didn't pop up! Now my terminal just looks funny and I don't know what to do.

Notice that the title says "Vim."

```
Merge branch 'add-thurs-menu'
# Please enter a commit message to explain why this merge is necessary,
# especially if it merges an updated upstream into a topic branch.
#
# Lines starting with '#' will be ignored, and an empty message aborts
# the commit.
~
~
                                              1,1          All
```

Uh oh! For some reason, setting your Git editor didn't quite work. So Git is using its default editor, Vim, which is a bit tricky. Here is what you do to get out of Vim. Start by hitting the Escape key on your keyboard, followed by this sequence of characters : wq.

Once you get past this, be sure to go back a few pages and configure your default editor.

That's a colon.

w stands for "write" (in other words, save).

| ESC | : | w | q |

And q stands for "quit."

It's either this or learn Vim. :)

It's a merge commit

We know, you are brimming with questions! Is this merge any different from our last merge? If it is, why? We have never seen an editor pop up to ask for a commit message before, so what's different now?

Let's go back to our color mixing analogy. (You did do that Brain Power exercise, right?) When you mix yellow into orange, you end up with ← orange. That's because orange already contains yellow. This, in Git world, would be analogous to a fast-forward merge. This is what we saw when we merged `add-fall-menu` into `master`.

But what if you attempt to mix two primary colors like red and blue? Well, you get a whole **new** color: purple!

What's this got to do with our latest merge exercise? Recall that before we merged `add-thurs-menu` and `master`, `master` had diverged away from `add-thurs-menu` because `master` had moved (fast-forwarded) to the commit that the `add-fall-menu` pointed to. When we try to merge `add-thurs-menu` into `master`, Git has to reconcile two *different* sets of changes into one. So Git pulls a fast one—it creates a **new** commit for us that represents the combined work from both branches. Here is what your commit history looks like before and after the merge:

Well, technically you end up with a lighter orange, but then again, every analogy eventually breaks.

Mixing yellow into orange essentially gives us orange.

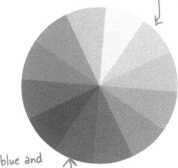

Mixing blue and red, on the other hand, produces a new color.

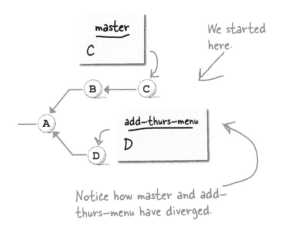

We started here.

Notice how master and add-thurs-menu have diverged.

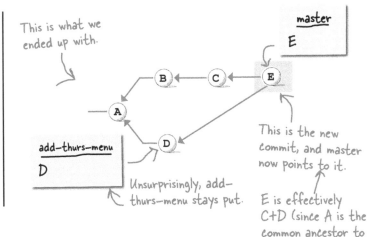

This is what we ended up with.

Unsurprisingly, add-thurs-menu stays put.

This is the new commit, and master now points to it.

E is effectively C+D (since A is the common ancestor to both branches).

Notice that `master` moves to point to the latest commit, identified by "E." This is expected—the `master` sticky note is updated to reflect the new commit on that branch, while `add-thurs-menu` stays put. This is called a **merge commit**, and it is comprised of all the changes that were introduced in the two separate branches.

However, every commit that we make in Git needs a commit message that describes what that commit contains. We usually do this explicitly with the "-m" flag. Since we did not supply Git with a commit message when we performed the merge, Git pops up our editor to give us a place to do just that!

Exercise

Another hypothetical commit history for your viewing pleasure. To elaborate upon how we got here:

* We started by making commit A on the `master` branch.
* We then created the `add-chat` branch and made another commit, B.
* We created the `add-emojis` branch based on commit B and proceeded to make two more commits on that branch, C and D.
* We then `switch`-ed back to the `add-chat` branch and made another commit, E.

Here is what the commit graph looks like:

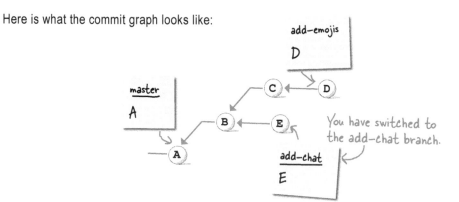

Now, we will attempt to merge the `add-emojis` branch into the `add-chat` branch. In other words, the `add-chat` branch is the proposer, and `add-emojis` is the proposee. Will this result in a fast-forward merge, or will this form a merge commit?

Finally, draw the resulting commit graph here.

Draw the updated commit history here.
↙

Answers on page 109.

Hint: Has add-chat diverged from add-emojis?

Merge commits are kinda special

A merge commit is like any other commit you have created so far. It records the work that resulted from bringing two branches together, along with some metadata. The metadata includes your name and email, the time when the commit was created, and the commit message you supplied when we performed the merge. Also, every commit (other than the very first one in a repository) records the ID of the commit that preceded it.

However, merge commits have a few interesting characteristics. For one thing, remember that you did not create this commit explicitly—rather, Git did, when it merged two branches that had diverged away from one another.

For another thing, a merge commit has *two* parents—the **first** parent is the last commit on the branch that is the proposer, and the **second** parent is the last commit from the proposee branch that was merged in. Looking back at the 80s-diner commit history:

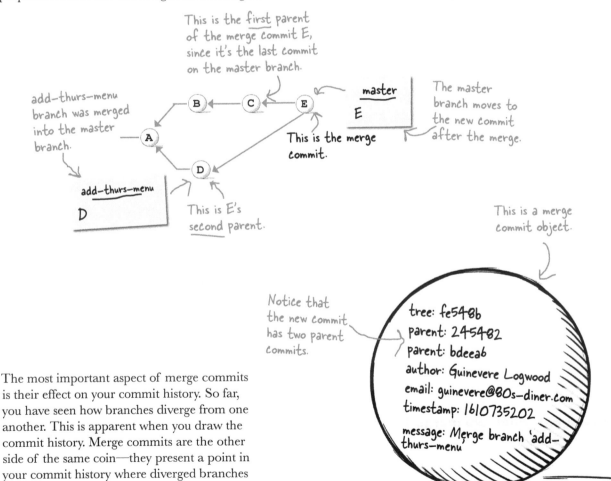

This is the first parent of the merge commit E, since it's the last commit on the master branch.

add-thurs-menu branch was merged into the master branch.

The master branch moves to the new commit after the merge.

This is the merge commit.

add-thurs-menu
D

This is E's second parent.

Notice that the new commit has two parent commits.

This is a merge commit object.

```
tree: fe548b
parent: 245482
parent: bdeea6
author: Guinevere Logwood
email: guinevere@80s-diner.com
timestamp: 1610735202
message: Merge branch 'add-
thurs-menu
```

The most important aspect of merge commits is their effect on your commit history. So far, you have seen how branches diverge from one another. This is apparent when you draw the commit history. Merge commits are the other side of the same coin—they present a point in your commit history where diverged branches come together.

Things don't always go so smoothly

Imagine the multiverse: you exist in multiple universes at the same time, living different lives. In one universe, you might be a humanitarian, intent on solving all human suffering. In another, you are a villain, laser-focused on world domination. Now suppose these two universes come crashing into one another. What happens? There can only be one of you—so which one will it be? The humanitarian or the villain? Or could you somehow be both?

In the '80s Diner repository, so far we have not needed to work with the same file in multiple branches. We had three branches, all of which introduced new files. But what if all three branches worked with the same file, modifying it in different ways? Perhaps you edited a file in one branch, and then edited the exact **same line** in the **same file** in another branch. That is, in one branch the file looks different than the same file in another branch.

Consider a repository with two branches —master and feat-a. The master branch has one commit on it, which introduces the notice.md file (commit A), which only has one line of text in it. We then create the feat-a branch, switch to it, edit the file, and make commit B. Finally, we switch back to the master branch, edit the file *again*, and make one final commit, C.

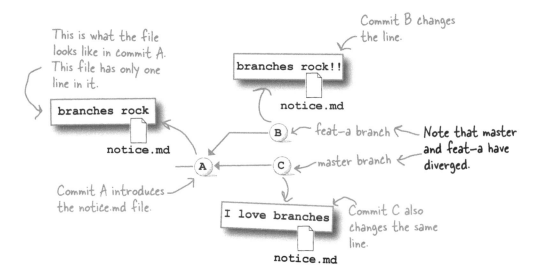

What happens when we merge these two branches?

I am so conflicted!

Merge conflicts result when we attempt to bring together commits that affect the same files in different ways. This is similar to our alternate universes crashing into one another—when that happens, how will you reconcile your humanitarian and villain selves?

Nothing for you to do just yet.

One such scenario is the one we just described—we have the same file in two different branches, continue to treat the `master` branch as the integration branch, and merge `feat-a` into the `master` branch. What happens?

Git throws its hands up in surrender! Git has absolutely no way of determining which version to keep, so it **stops** the merge midway and reports a merge conflict.

We know that sounds bad. Don't worry! One step at a time.

```
File Edit Window Help
$ git merge feat-a
Auto-merging notice.md
CONFLICT (content): Merge conflict in notice.md
Automatic merge failed; fix conflicts and then commit the result.
```

Git tells us about the merge conflict and the filename.

Git's `status` may look scary, but if we read it carefully, Git is doing its best to help us out. Let's take a look:

Git tells us that it could not merge some "paths," aka files.

The listing of files that failed to merge properly.

```
File Edit Window Help
$ git status
On branch master
You have unmerged paths.
  (fix conflicts and run "git commit")
  (use "git merge --abort" to abort the merge)

Unmerged paths:
  (use "git add <file>..." to mark resolution)
        both modified:   notice.md

no changes added to commit (use "git add" and/or "git commit -a")
```

This is your next action step.

Run this if you want to cancel the merge.

Git `merge` fails immediately, but it tries to be helpful by telling you which files have a merge conflict.

Git `status`, much like the `merge` command, also tells us that Git could not complete the merge for some files, and it lists them. It also tells us to fix the conflicts and then run the `git commit` command.

It might be confusing when Git says "both modified"—this means that **both** branches modified the same file.

You are in the middle of the merge process—and Git is asking for your help.

I am so conflicted! (continued)

The easiest way to resolve merge conflicts is to open the files that have merge conflicts in your editor. If you were to open `notice.md` in your text editor, this is what you would see:

Git rewrites the file, highlighting the section that has conflicting changes.

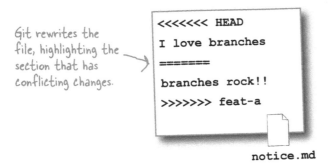

```
<<<<<<< HEAD
I love branches
=======
branches rock!!
>>>>>>> feat-a
```

notice.md

Linus Torvalds, who created Git, described it as "the stupid content tracker." In other words, Git does not aim to be smart. If it does not know what to do, it will simply stop and hand over control to you.

Looks pretty gnarly, huh? Don't worry—we will walk you through it, one step at a time. Just remember, there are **two** branches being merged, and each one is introducing its own change to the same file. Here is what those funny-looking markers mean:

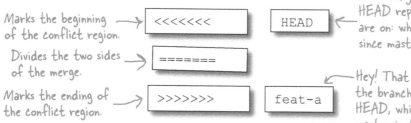

Marks the beginning of the conflict region. → `<<<<<<<` `HEAD`

Divides the two sides of the merge. → `=======`

Marks the ending of the conflict region. → `>>>>>>>` `feat-a`

For now, just remember that HEAD represents the branch you are on: which in this case is master, since master is the proposer.

Hey! That looks familiar. That's the branch we are merging *into* HEAD, which happens to be master in this case.

Now that you know that, here is the same file shown in its fully annotated glory:

This represents what the "current" branch (master in this case) changes in the file.

This divides the two halves.

This represents what the "other" branch (feat-a in this case) has changed.

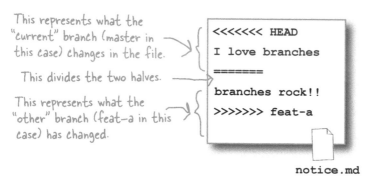

```
<<<<<<< HEAD
I love branches
=======
branches rock!!
>>>>>>> feat-a
```

notice.md

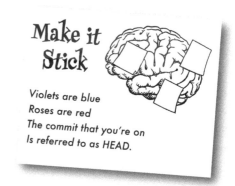

Make it Stick

Violets are blue
Roses are red
The commit that you're on
Is referred to as HEAD.

Now it's just a question of editing the files that have merge conflicts. You have four options....

I am so conflicted! (Ooof! Almost there)

When you have a merge conflict, you have four choices. You can pick the changes introduced in the `master` branch, the changes in the `feat-a` branch, pick both (in this particular case), or ignore both and write something new altogether! Remember that the markers that Git put in there are just to highlight the conflicts—they are just there to help you out.

Once you choose, this is what the file should look like:

Your options:

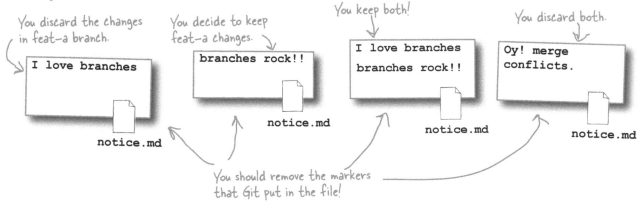

You discard the changes in feat-a branch.

```
I love branches
```
notice.md

You decide to keep feat-a changes.

```
branches rock!!
```
notice.md

You keep both!

```
I love branches
branches rock!!
```
notice.md

You discard both.

```
Oy! merge
conflicts.
```
notice.md

You should remove the markers that Git put in the file!

Of course, you may not be always be able to pick both changes, particularly if the final result is not syntactically valid. This is particularly true for source code, and then you would be forced to pick one or the other, or just ignore the changes on both sides and write something new altogether.

Once you make your choice and finish editing the file in your text editor, save the file.

Next, we just follow the instructions that `git status` offered us. We use `git add` to add the final result to the staging area, then follow that with `git commit`.

Reread the output of git status that we showed you a couple pages ago if you need to refresh your memory.

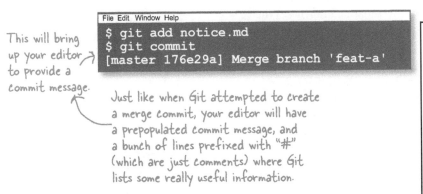

This will bring up your editor to provide a commit message.

```
File Edit Window Help
$ git add notice.md
$ git commit
[master 176e29a] Merge branch 'feat-a'
```

Just like when Git attempted to create a merge commit, your editor will have a prepopulated commit message, and a bunch of lines prefixed with "#" (which are just comments) where Git lists some really useful information.

Voila! Congratulations on resolving your first merge conflict!

there are no Dumb Questions

Q: What if I have conflicts in more than one file?

A: As you might expect, `git merge` will stop midway and list all the files that have conflicts in them. You can use your editor to resolve the conflicts, just like we did, then use `git add` for all the files that had a merge conflict in them. Finally, run `git commit`.

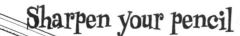

Sharpen your pencil

Can you visualize what the commit history would look like after merging the `feat-a` branch into the `master` branch? We got you started here—your mission is to finish the graph.

This is the feat-a branch. ↓

(B)

→ (A) ← (C)

↑ This commit is on the master branch.

Hint: B and C have diverged from one another.

→ **Answers on page 110.**

> There's no way you can convince me this happens regularly. I would remember editing a file in a branch. What are the chances I would touch the same file again in another branch?

Sounds improbable, right? Turns out, not so much. Most projects comprise dozens, if not hundreds, of files. It's not unusual to work on multiple tasks at the same time. And you might end up inadvertently touching the same file in two separate branches. When you get to merging those separate branches together, there is a potential for conflict.

The other scenario is when multiple people start to use Git as a collaboration tool. We haven't gotten to talking about that just yet, but it involves different people working on different branches. When two different people, working on two different tasks in two different branches in the same repository, affect the same file, they're likely to create a merge conflict.

Merge conflicts occur more than you think, so get comfortable with them. But don't you worry—the next exercise will make you an expert in conflict resolution.

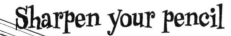

Sharpen your pencil

Navigate back to the `headfirst-git-samples` directory (or wherever you have been creating sample repositories), and follow along:

1. Create a new folder called `loving-git`.

2. Change directories into `loving-git`, and initialize a new Git repository.

3. Create a new file called `tribute.md` (using a text editor) with the following content:

> *tribute.md on the master branch*

```
# Tribute to Git
```

4. Add the file to the index, and then commit it. Use the commit message "A".

5. Create a branch called `improvisation`, `switch` to it, and then edit the `tribute.md` file to look like this:

```
# Tribute to Git
There's a version control tool called Git
When you feel like you just want to quit
Go and try something new
You can track what you do
Since you've got a great tracking kit.
```

← Your first edit on the improvisation branch

You'll find these files in the source for this chapter—look for the files called tribute-2.md and tribute-3.md.

6. Again, add and commit the file. Supply the commit message "B".

7. Switch back to the `master` branch again and edit the file to look like this:

Second edit to tribute.md on the master branch →

```
# Tribute to Git
There's a version-control tool called Git
For software it's an excellent fit
If your attitude ranges
Feel free to make changes
Since you've got a great tracking kit.
```

8. Once again, add and commit the file. This time use the commit message "C".

9. Merge the `improvisation` branch into the `master` branch. Resolve any conflicts as you see fit. **Be sure to read what information Git supplies when it brings up your editor to supply a commit message.**

What does the commit history look like after the merge?

Draw the commit graph here.

———————→ Answers on page 111.

Cleaning up (merged) branches

We have seen what a typical branching workflow looks like—you get a request for a new feature, or a jarring email regarding a bug that needs to be fixed stat. You create a branch, start your work, commit when necessary, and when you are ready, merge back into the integration branch.

This is our discussion phase. You'll get an exercise soon enough.

But after a while, you have all these branches sitting around in your Git repository, so it's time for a cleanup. Git allows you to delete branches, using the `git branch` command. First things first: **you can't delete the branch that you are on**! So if you happen to be on the branch you are about to delete, you need to switch to another branch.

Take this hypothetical repository as an example. It has two branches, `master` being the integration branch, and a feature branch, called `feat-home-screen`. `feat-home-screen` was just merged into `master`, so we can safely delete it.

We have two branches in this repository, and we are on the master branch. Spectacular!

```
File Edit Window Help
$ git branch
  feat-home-screen
* master
```

To delete a branch, we supply the -d (or --delete) flag to `git branch` along with the name of the branch we wish to delete, like so:

Invoke the branch command.

The -d flag follows the branch command.

Or you can use the --delete flag.

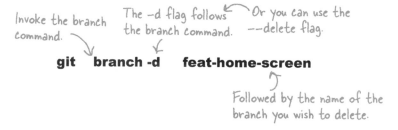

git   branch -d   feat-home-screen

Followed by the name of the branch you wish to delete.

Git will respond with a success message, like this:

Git reports the commit ID of the last commit on that branch.

```
File Edit Window Help
$ git branch -d feat-home-screen
Deleted branch feat-home-screen (was 64ec4a5).
```

Git always attempts to be as helpful as possible. This time it not only tells you that it deleted the branch but follows it up with the commit ID of the last commit on that branch. This is very useful in case you accidentally delete the wrong branch. If you suddenly realize you deleted the wrong branch, you can use a variation of the `git branch` command that lets you supply it the commit ID the branch should be based on, like so: `git branch <branch-name> <base-commit-id>`. This will allow you to undo an accidental delete.

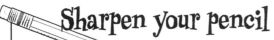

Sharpen your pencil

Your turn! Navigate to the `80s-diner` repository in your terminal, and do the following:

1. List the branches that you have:

2. Delete all branches except `master`. But first, list the steps you need to follow:

Answers on page 112.

Brain Power

We have compared branches to sticky notes. What do you think happens to these sticky notes when you delete branches in Git?

there are no Dumb Questions

Q: It seems that I can delete my branch as soon as I am done integrating my work. Should I wait a little bit longer?

A: Nope! You got it right the first time. Once you merge your branch into the integration branch, there is no reason to keep that branch around. Go ahead! Delete it.

Q: I got an error when deleting my branch.

A: If you got an error that looks like `error: branch not found`, then you either misspelled the name of the branch or are trying to delete a branch that you've already deleted. You can use `git branch` to list all your branches, verify that the branch exists, and make sure you get the name right.

Q: Why do I need to delete these branches? Why not just keep 'em around?

A: Branches are used to work on a single thing, away from other tasks you might have in flight. Think of them as single-use containers like a coffee cup from a drive-through—once you get your caffeine fix, you simply toss away the container.

Finally, if you don't delete branches you no longer need, your `git branch` list gets longer and longer over time, and it gets harder to figure out which branches are "active" and which ones have been merged and are no longer needed. And who doesn't like a nice clean repository?

Hold up a second. What happens to the commits on a branch after I delete it?

The answer to your question lies in the commit history.

When we talked about deleting branches, we specifically talked about deleting branches that have already been merged. Suppose you worked on a feature branch called `feat-a`, which you just merged into the `master` branch. Take a moment to think about what your commit history looks like after you finish merging:

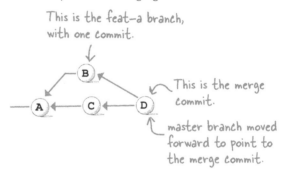

When you delete the `feat-a` branch, all Git does is to throw away the sticky note that represents the `feat-a` branch. As for commit "B": notice that the merge commit "D" has two parents, "C" and "B," **and** the `master` branch sticky note points to commit "D." So "B" sticks around because your commit history needs it. (Remember, it acts as the second parent of commit "D.")

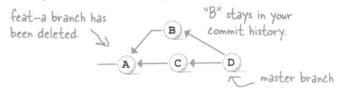

The thing to remember is that as long as a commit is "reachable"—that is, there is a reference to it (like a branch) or another commit pointing to it as a parent—it will stay in your commit history. In this case, the `master` branch points to commit "D," and "D" points to "B." So commit "B" stays. You can extend this logic to "A" as well—because it has two commits referencing it—"B" and "C."

Deleting unmerged branches

You now understand the impact of deleting branches. Which is, if the branch you are deleting has been merged, then your commit history does not change! Only the sticky note that represents the branch disappears. But what if you try to delete a branch that hasn't been merged yet? Let's look at another hypothetical commit history where we have two branches, `master` and `feat-b`, but we haven't merged them together yet.

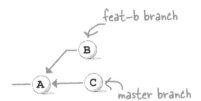

Notice that there is a commit "B" on the `feat-b` branch. Now, if we tried to delete the `feat-b` branch, this is what you'd see:

Git errors out when you attempt to delete an unmerged branch.

```
File Edit Window Help
$ git branch -d feat-b
error: The branch 'feat-b' is not fully merged.
If you are sure you want to delete it, run 'git branch -D feat-b'.
```

Git notices that if you were to delete the `feat-b` branch, commit "B" would not be reachable. In other words, there is nothing (a sticky note, or another commit) referencing it. And so it refuses to!

Now there is a chance that you created a branch just to try out an idea or approach a problem using a different tack, and you don't care for it anymore. You can supply the branch command with the -D (yep, uppercase D) flag to force its deletion.

Git will display the ID of the latest commit of the branch that you force deleted, so you can always recover it like we showed you a few pages ago.

> **Use the force delete flag with care.**
>
> *It's often tempting to run the command or use the option that Git offers you, especially if you are in the midst of something. But it is important to pay attention to what Git is trying to tell you—in this case, it's telling you that you **will** lose the work you made in one or more commits.*
>
> *So the next time Git doesn't do what you are asking of it, pause for a second, take a breath, and read Git's messages carefully. Then only proceed if you are sure that you know exactly what you want Git to do.*

A typical workflow

So far we have created branches to work on individual tasks, and merged them back into the integration branch. Here are a few of the practices that many developers adhere to when branching and merging:

1   **Typically, base your new branches on commits on integration branches.**
Integration branches reflect the work of all branches. This means that your new branch will have everything that has been completed so far, so you can work knowing that you have a good starting point.

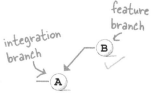

2   **Merge back into the integration branch once you are done.**
It's tempting to delay merging back into the integration branch, but once you think you are done with the task at hand, then merge. If you miss something, you can always create another branch based on the integration branch (which will now reflect the changes you merged earlier).

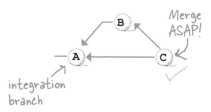

3   **Don't reuse branches.**
A typical workflow involves creating a new branch, getting your work done, merging into the integration branch, and then deleting the feature branch. Again, remember, you can always create a new branch if you need to.

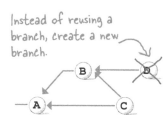

there are no
Dumb Questions

Q: How do I know when to create a new branch, and when to merge it?

A: Typically, create a new branch for any new "task." Let's say you are assigned a ticket to add a new feature, or fix a bug—that's your sign to create a new branch. Once your work meets the "definition of done" in the ticket, you should merge your work into the integration branch.

Q: I don't get it. Why shouldn't I reuse branches?

A: When you start work on a new task, you always want the freshest set of changes in that project, which is always reflected in the integration branch. Branches, on the other hand, can get "stale."

Secondly, branches are cheap in Git. They are simply references to commits in the directed acyclic graph. Use them, and once done with the task at hand, delete them!

Bullet Points

- Branches are one of Git's best features. Branches allow you to work on multiple tasks at the same time.

- When working in Git, you are *always* working on a branch. Every repository starts with a branch and defaults to the name `master`.

- The `master` branch is not special in any way. It's no different than any other branch you create. You can rename or even delete the `master` branch.

- The primary command to work with branches is `git branch`. You can use `git branch` to create, list, and delete branches.

- To create a branch called `update-profile`, supply the name to `git branch` like so:
  `git branch update-profile`

- `git branch` allows you to create branches, but to start using the new branch, use the `git switch` command. Supply it with the name of the branch you wish to start using, like so:
  `git switch update-profile`

- Think of a branch as a sticky note that contains the branch name and the commit ID of the last commit on that branch.

- Every time you make a commit on a branch, Git updates the sticky note that represents that branch, giving it the new commit ID. This is how a branch "moves."

- Since branches always point to commits, they offer an easy way to create other branches.

- Whenever you `switch` branches, Git rewrites the working directory to reflect the state captured in the latest commit on that branch.

- In a typical workflow, some branches (by convention) are treated as "integration" branches to collect the work done in other branches.

- In contrast, day-to-day work is done in "feature" branches. Each feature branch is to be used for one thing and one thing only: for example, to introduce a new feature, or fix a bug.

- To combine the work you've done in an integration branch, you *merge* the feature branch *into* the integration branch.

- The easiest kind of merge is called a "fast-forward merge," in which one branch simply "catches up" with another branch.

- The other kind of merge is when you merge two branches that have *diverged* from one another, in which case Git will create a merge commit.

- A merge commit is like any other commit, except it's created by Git and has not one but two parents—the first parent is the latest commit on the integration branch, and the second parent is the latest commit on the feature branch.

- Occasionally, the same line in the same file has been modified in the two branches being merged, causing a merge conflict. Git relies on you to resolve the merge conflict.

- You can delete a branch using the `git branch` command, along with the `-d` (or `--delete`) flag.

- If you attempt to delete a branch that has not been merged yet, Git will error out. If you are absolutely sure you want to delete an unmerged branch, you'll have to use the `-D` (uppercase "D") flag with the `git branch` command.

- A branch is always based on a commit. If you know the ID of the commit you want to use as the basis for a branch, you can supply it to the `git branch` command:
  `git branch branch-name commit-ID`

Git branch "crossword puzzle"

After all that branching and merging, are you feeling conflicted?
Take a break, branch out, and try this crossword puzzle.

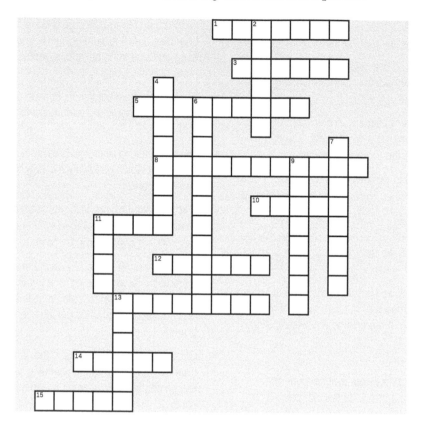

Across

1 You can see a graph of your branches in your commit _____

3 _____ Studio Code

5 These happen if you merge two branches that change the same line in the same file

8 An _____ branch is where it all comes together

10 Bring branches together using the git ___ command

11 The commit you're on right now

12 When you need to work on something separately, create one of these

13 Information recorded in your commit, like the ID and timestamp

14 A scary word that won't kill you

15 Get a taste of nostalgia at the '80s _____

Down

2 The git ___ command lets you hop from one branch to another

4 Every branch points to one of these identifiers (2 words)

6 A type of merge that "jumps ahead" (2 words)

7 In October, the '80s Diner will serve you a "Texas _____ Massacre"

9 Git creator Linus _____

11 This flag gives you lots of information about commands

13 Git's default name for your first branch

→ Answers on page 113.

Exercise Solution   From page 52.

Think about the commit history. See if you can figure out what Norm got wrong. Jot down your notes here:

Because Norm committed incomplete work prior to working on the bug, now the code in the last commit includes all of his half-baked changes!

Code Magnets Solution   From page 62.

Oh dear! To help our fellow developers we had carefully laid out all the commands needed to list all the branches in their (existing) repository, then create a new branch, switch to it, and check to make sure that all is well. Alas! The magnets fell on the floor. It's your job to put them back together. Be careful; a few extra magnets got mixed in, and some get used more than once.

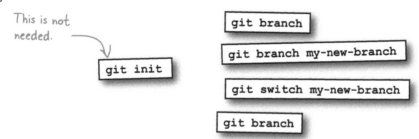

This is not needed.

```
git init
```

```
git branch
```

```
git branch my-new-branch
```

```
git switch my-new-branch
```

```
git branch
```

Sharpen your pencil Solution   From page 63.

What would change in the visualization if you remained on the `add-fall-menu` branch and had to make another commit?

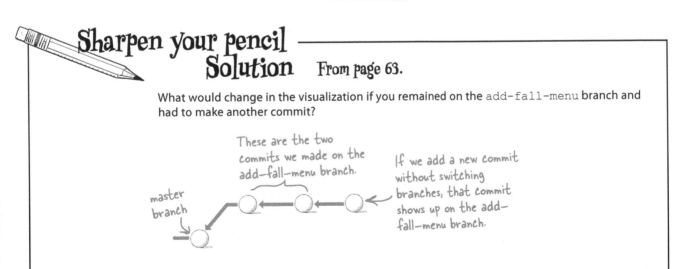

These are the two commits we made on the add-fall-menu branch.

If we add a new commit without switching branches, that commit shows up on the add-fall-menu branch.

master branch

BE Git Solution

Spend a little time understanding how Git changes your working directory when you switch branches.

From page 65.

Start with your terminal—make sure you are in the 80s-diner directory, and use git branch to ensure you are on the add-fall-menu branch.

```
File Edit Window Help
$ pwd
/headfirst-git-samples/80s-diner
$ git branch
* add-fall-menu
  master
```

Recall that ls "lists" all the files.

```
File Edit Window Help
$ ls
fall-menu.md
menu.md
```

Now switch to the master branch. List the output of git branch:

```
File Edit Window Help
$ git branch
  add-fall-menu
* master
```

Did you see these as well?

List all the files again:

```
File Edit Window Help
$ ls
menu.md
```

Finally, see if you can explain what you are seeing here.

The latest commit on the add-fall-menu branch committed the fall-menu.md file, but this branch started from the master branch, which already had the menu.md file. So the add-fall-menu has both files: menu.md and fall-menu.md. But the master branch has only one commit in it, with the menu.md file.

Sharpen your pencil Solution

From page 68.

Before you go further, see if you can visualize what your commit history looks like. We were nice enough to get you started, but you need to finish it up.

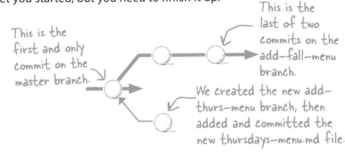

This is the first and only commit on the master branch.

This is the last of two commits on the add-fall-menu branch.

We created the new add-thurs-menu branch, then added and committed the new thursdays-menu.md file.

BE Git Solution

Let's repeat our previous exercise of visiting all of the branches in our repository and listing the files that are present in each branch, except this time around, we have three branches. For each of the windows shown below, write out what you think will be the output of invoking `git branch`, and what files will be listed in each branch:

From page 68.

```
File Edit Window Help
$ git switch add-fall-menu
$ git branch
* add-fall-menu
  add-thurs-menu
  master
$ ls
fall-menu.md   menu.md
```

Write your results here.

```
File Edit Window Help
$ git switch master
$ git branch
  add-fall-menu
  add-thurs-menu
* master
$ ls
menu.md
```

```
File Edit Window Help
$ git switch add-thurs-menu
$ git branch
  add-fall-menu
* add-thurs-menu
  master
$ ls
menu.md
thursdays-menu.md
```

Sharpen your pencil
Solution

From page 70.

Look at the hypothetical commit graph below, and fill in the sticky notes with the information needed to associate a branch name with the commit ID that it points to. Note that there might be more sticky notes than you might actually need.

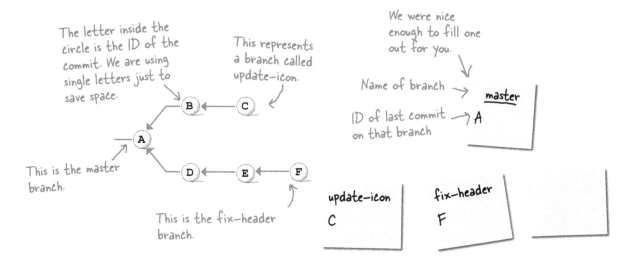

The letter inside the circle is the ID of the commit. We are using single letters just to save space.

This represents a branch called update-icon.

We were nice enough to fill one out for you.

Name of branch → **master**

ID of last commit on that branch → A

This is the master branch.

This is the fix-header branch.

update-icon
C

fix-header
F

Now suppose we were to switch to the `fix-header` branch, make some edits, and make another commit, which was given ID "G." Can you visualize what changes in the diagram above?

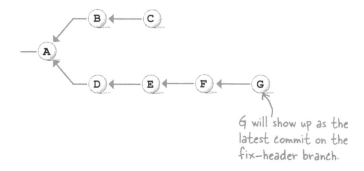

G will show up as the latest commit on the fix-header branch.

Sharpen your pencil
Solution

From page 73.

We mentioned that many teams use names like `main` instead of `master` to indicate integration branches. Can you think of any other names? List a few here (feel free to use your favorite search engine to get some ideas):

develop

latest

trunk

Sharpen your pencil
Solution

From page 75.

Let's say you attend a friend's wedding. You took some pictures on your phone, and a few days later, the wedding photographer asks you to send them the pictures you took. You make a copy of the wedding pictures on your phone and send them the copy so they could combine them with the ones they took.

Now take a few minutes to think about the following questions:

➤ Who has the "complete" set of pictures?

The photographer has the complete set of pictures, since they have their own set, and you sent them a copy of yours.

➤ Did either one of you lose any pictures?

No. Remember, you sent the photographer a copy of the photos you took.

➤ Which one of you is the "integration" branch in this scenario?

That would be the photographer, since they are "merging" their copy with yours.

Exercise Solution

In the `80s-diner` directory, go ahead and run `git branch --help` (or `git help branch`—use either one), and find the section regarding the `-v` or `--verbose` flag. **Read up on what it does**.

Next, run `git branch -v` and record the branch name and the latest commit ID here. (You are going to need these for the next few sections in this chapter.)

add-fall-menu   245482d update heading   } This is what we got.
add-thurs-menu   bdeea6f add thursdays menu   Remember, commit IDs
master   ea6b05e add the main menu   are unique. You will get a
                                                    different set of IDs.

From page 76.

Exercise Solution

Let's flex our command-line skills a bit more. You are going to repeat our previous exercise of listing the latest commit IDs on each branch. Recall that you can use `git branch -v` and see information about each of your branches. Go ahead and do that again:

add-fall-menu   245482d update heading   Notice that master changed for us from the
add-thurs-menu   bdeea6f add thursdays menu   previous exercise. Similarly, you should see
master   245482d update heading   the same commit ID for add–fall–menu and
                                                master.

Compare these with the ones you did the last time around. What changed?

Since we merged add–fall–menu and master, they point to the same
commit. add–thurs–menu remains unchanged.

Finally, list the files in each branch. Start with the `master` branch, then `switch` to the `add-fall-menu` branch and finally the `add-thurs-menu` branch, using `ls` to list the files you see in each branch:

master	add-fall-menu	add-thurs-menu
fall-menu.md menu.md	fall-menu.md menu.md	menu.md thursdays-menu.md

From page 78.

Exercise Solution

From page 88.

Another hypothetical commit history for your viewing pleasure. To elaborate upon how we got here:

✱ We started by making commit A on the `master` branch.
✱ We then created the `add-chat` branch and made another commit, B.
✱ We created the `add-emojis` branch based on commit B and proceeded to make two more commits on that branch, C and D.
✱ We then `switch`-ed back to the `add-chat` branch and made another commit, E.

Here is what the commit graph looks like:

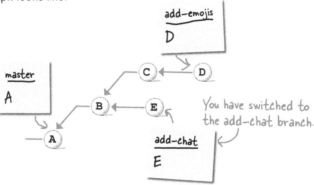

You have switched to the add-chat branch.

Now, we will attempt to merge the `add-emojis` branch into the `add-chat` branch. In other words, the `add-chat` branch is the proposer, and `add-emojis` is the proposee. Will this result in a fast-forward merge, or will this form a merge commit?

Looking at the commit graph, we see that both add-chat and add-emojis share a common commit (B), but they have diverged from one another (since they both have commits since B). So this will result in a merge commit.

Finally, draw the resulting commit graph here.

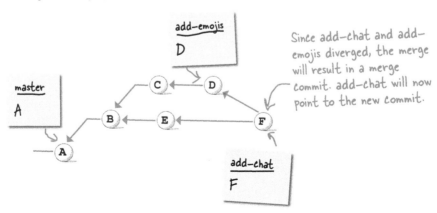

Since add-chat and add-emojis diverged, the merge will result in a merge commit. add-chat will now point to the new commit.

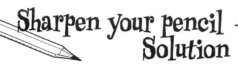

Sharpen your pencil
Solution

From page 94.

Can you visualize what the commit history would look like after merging the `feat-a` branch into the `master` branch? We got you started here—your mission is to finish the graph.

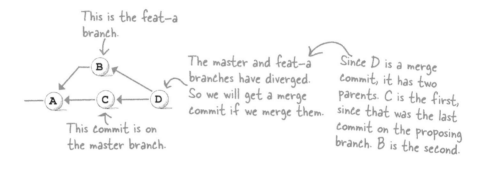

This is the feat-a branch.

The master and feat-a branches have diverged. So we will get a merge commit if we merge them.

Since D is a merge commit, it has two parents. C is the first, since that was the last commit on the proposing branch. B is the second.

This commit is on the master branch.

Sharpen your pencil
Solution

From page 95.

Navigate back to the `headfirst-git-samples` directory (or wherever you have been creating sample repositories), and follow along:

1. Create a new folder called `loving-git`.

2. Change directories into `loving-git`, and initialize a new Git repository.

3. Create a new file called `tribute.md` (using a text editor) with the following content:

> *tribute.md on the master branch*

```
# Tribute to Git
```

4. Add the file to the index, and then commit it. Use the commit message "A".

5. Create a branch called `improvisation`, `switch` to it, and then edit the `tribute.md` file to look like this:

```
# Tribute to Git
There's a version control tool called Git
When you feel like you just want to quit
Go and try something new
You can track what you do
Since you've got a great tracking kit.
```

← *Your first edit on the improvisation branch*

← *You'll find these files in the source for this chapter—look for the files called tribute-2.md and tribute-3.md.*

6. Again, add and commit the file. Supply the commit message "B".

7. Switch back to the `master` branch again and edit the file to look like this:

Second edit to tribute.md on the master branch →

```
# Tribute to Git
There's a version control tool called Git
For software it's an excellent fit
If your attitude ranges
Feel free to make changes
Since you've got a great tracking kit.
```

8. Once again, add and commit the file. This time use the commit message "C".

9. Merge the `improvisation` branch into the `master` branch. Resolve any conflicts as you see fit. **Be sure to read what information Git supplies when it brings up your editor to supply a commit message.**

What does the commit history look like after the merge?

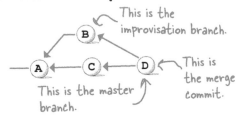

This is the improvisation branch.

This is the master branch.

This is the merge commit.

Sharpen your pencil

From page 97.

Your turn! Navigate to the `80s-diner` repository in your terminal, and do the following:

1. List the branches that you have:

       add-fall-menu

       add-thurs-menu

       * master ⟵ You should be on
                     the master branch.

2. Delete all branches except `master`. But first, list the steps you need to follow:

       git branch -d add-fall-menu

       git branch -d add-thurs-menu

Git branch "crossword puzzle" Solution

After all that branching and merging, are you feeling conflicted? Take a break, branch out, and try this crossword puzzle.

From page 102.

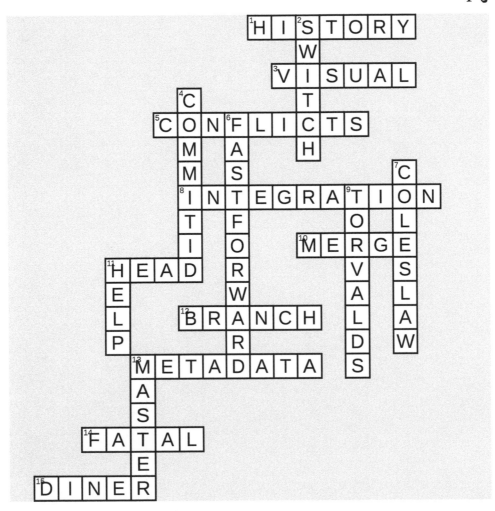

3 looking around

Investigating Your Git Repository

You ready to do some digging, Sherlock? As you continue to work in Git, you'll create branches, make commits, and merge your work back into the integration branches. Each commit represents a step forward, and the commit history represents how you got there. Every so often, you might want to look back to see how you got to where you are, or perhaps if two branches have diverged from one another. We'll start this chapter by showing you how Git can help you visualize your commit history.

Seeing your commit history is one thing—but Git can also help you see how your repository changed. Recall that commits represent changes, and branches represent a series of changes. How do you know what's changed—between commits, between branches, or even between your working directory, the index, and the object database? That's the other topic of this chapter.

Together, we will get to do some seriously interesting Git detective work. Come on, let's level up those investigative skills!

Brigitte's on a mission

Allow us to introduce you to Brigitte. Brigitte, after a much-needed vacation, is in the market for a new job. She needs a resume, and knowing that she'll probably go through a few iterations, she created a repository to work in, started working on a draft of her resume, and committed it.

She sent her resume draft off to a few friends from her previous job, who suggested some changes. Brigitte took her friends' advice to heart, and for every edit suggested, she made a new commit. Below is her commit history. We've annotated every commit with the commit ID and the commit message that Brigitte used when she made the commit. Note that she has three branches—master, add-skills, and edit-per-scotty.

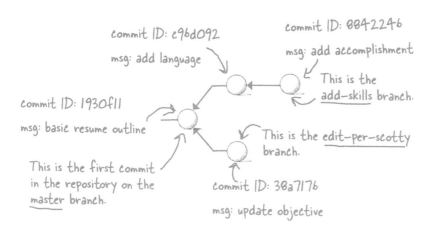

We are going to use Brigitte's repository to demonstrate some of the ideas in this chapter, so feel free to bookmark this page in case you need to jog your memory.

As Brigitte explores her future employment options, why don't you use some of the skills you've learned so far to explore another repository we've set up for you? Look to the next page.

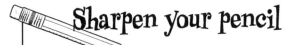

Sharpen your pencil

Answers on page 150.

Our friends at the '80s Diner are getting ready to submit their best sauce recipe for this year's Cilantro Fest. All the local restaurants compete to win, and it certainly makes for great publicity. Naturally, they've created a Git repository to keep track of the variations they try.

Well, we managed to get that repository, and you'll be using it for all your exercises in this chapter. You will find the repository in the source files you downloaded for this book, under `chapter03`, **called** `recipes`.

Open a new terminal window, and be sure to be in the `recipes` directory. See if you can answer the following questions. Important: make sure that you compare your answers with ours at the end of the chapter before you move on.

➢ What is the current status of the repository? List the command you are to use and its output here.

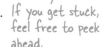

If you get stuck, feel free to peek ahead.

➢ How many branches are in this repository? List them here:

I think we need just a dash of salt and a jalapeño to spice things up!

➢ What branch are you currently on?

Anytime you see this image, it's your reminder to work in the recipes folder.

Commits aren't enough

Suppose Brigitte wants to inspect her commit history—how should she go about doing it? You see, committing your work to Git on a regular basis is a good idea. Commits, as you probably recall, are simply snapshots of the changes that you add to the index (or the staging area). Each commit represents the state of changes as they were when you made the commit.

This means that commits are snapshots taken at a particular time. Consequently, a commit in and of itself does not give us much insight into the history of a project. The project's history—its evolution over time—is baked into its commit history.

For Brigitte to visualize her commit history, Git provides us a command, called `log`, that does just that. By default the `git log` command lists all the commits in the current branch, with the latest commit at the top, followed by its parent, and so on:

Relax. It's not your turn yet.

Feel free to glance back to the previous page and see if you can align what you are seeing here with Brigitte's commit history. Note: this is the log of the edit-per-scotty branch.

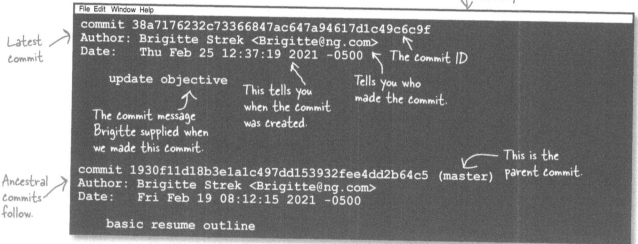

Latest commit

commit 38a7176232c73366847ac647a94617d1c49c6c9f
Author: Brigitte Strek <Brigitte@ng.com>
Date: Thu Feb 25 12:37:19 2021 -0500

    update objective

The commit ID

Tells you who made the commit.

This tells you when the commit was created.

The commit message Brigitte supplied when we made this commit.

Ancestral commits follow.

commit 1930f11d18b3e1a1c497dd153932fee4dd2b64c5 (master)
Author: Brigitte Strek <Brigitte@ng.com>
Date: Fri Feb 19 08:12:15 2021 -0500

    basic resume outline

This is the parent commit.

You might recall from Chapter 1 that a commit stores a bunch of metadata alongside a pointer to the changes that you committed. Well, the role of the `git log` command is to detail all that in a simple list.

We'll grant you that the log won't take your breath away. It's pretty plain and rather verbose. Worry not! We will see several ways to prettify the output so that not only does the log look nice, it gives us a ton more information about the history of our repository.

One final note before we move on. The `git log` command uses a pager, in case you have more commits to show than there is space for. Recall you can use the up and down arrow keys to navigate it; when you are done, simply hit the q (stands for "quit") key, which returns you back to the command prompt.

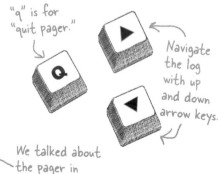

"q" is for "quit pager."

Navigate the log with up and down arrow keys.

We talked about the pager in Chapter 2 as well.

Exercise

⟶ Answers on page 151.

It's time to unleash your `git log` skills on the `recipes` repository. Open up your terminal (or just use the one from the last exercise). Make sure you are on the `spicy-version` branch. Using the `git log` command, see if you can answer the following questions for each of the three branches in the repository.

Remember to hit the "q" key to quit the git pager.

✱ How many commits are on the branch?

✱ List the **first seven characters** of each commit ID along with their respective commit messages in reverse chronological order (that is, the order they are presented to you).

> **Branch: spicy-version**
>
> Commit count:
>
> Commit listing:

> **Branch: different-base**
>
> Commit count:
>
> Commit listing:

Remember, this is your hint to be in the recipes folder.

> **Branch: master**
>
> Commit count:
>
> Commit listing:

Brain Power

Look over the commit IDs that you recorded in the last exercise. What happened in this repository? **Hint**: Start by listing all the branches in the repository, then look over the commits you recorded and see if there are any commits in common between the branches. That should give you a good starting point.

Use this space to take notes.

Mirror, mirror on the wall: who is the prettiest log of all?

> Let the waves of Git knowledge wash over you.

While the output of the `git log` command is exhaustive, it certainly leaves much to be desired, especially when it comes to discerning the history of our project. Fortunately, the `log` command offers flags to pretty up its output and make it more useful. Let's take a look at some of these flags and their effect on the output.

First up, let's truncate the commit ID. Recall that commit IDs are unique, and usually the first few characters are enough to identify a commit. The `abbrev-commit` flag only displays enough characters to identify a commit uniquely, which is usually what you want:

HEAD points to the commit you are on.

Note that Git still uses a pager. Striking the letter "q" will drop you back to the terminal.

Use the abbrev-commit flag to git log. Note the double hyphens.

```
git log --abbrev-commit
```

Git displays just enough characters of the commit ID to uniquely identify each commit.

```
File  Edit  Window  Help
commit 38a7176 (HEAD -> edit-per-scotty)
Author: Brigitte Strek <Brigitte@ng.com>
Date:     Thu Feb 25 12:37:19 2021 -0500

    update objective

commit 1930f11 (master)
Author: Brigitte Strek <Brigitte@ng.com>
Date:     Fri Feb 19 08:12:15 2021 -0500

    basic resume outline
```

Perhaps you don't care to see all the information about the author and the date. No problem! The `git log` command has you covered with the `pretty` flag. We are going to use a built-in formatting option called `oneline`:

Git has a handful of built-in formatting options like oneline that you can use, or you can write a custom one. As you get to know Git more, you can learn how to customize it to your heart's content. For now, oneline is a great start.

Notice how we supply the oneline option to the pretty flag.

```
git log --pretty=oneline
```

```
File  Edit  Window  Help
```
Commit ID   *Remember, HEAD tells you the commit you are on.*   *Branch name.*   *Commit message*
```
38a7176232c73366847ac647a94617d1c49c6c9f (HEAD -> edit-per-scotty) update objective
1930f11d18b3e1a1c497dd153932fee4dd2b64c5 (master) basic resume outline
```

Oops! Since we did not tell Git to --abbrev-commit, we are back to displaying the full commit ID.

Together now! You can combine many of the flags available in the `git log` command, so if you like the shorter commit IDs presented by the `abbrev-commit` flag but you also want the succinct view, use both!

Combine the two flags.

It does not matter in which order you supply these.

Just be sure to supply oneline to the --pretty flag.

```
git log --pretty=oneline --abbrev-commit
```

Best of both worlds!

Looking good, Scotty! Beam us up!

```
File  Edit  Window  Help
38a7176 (HEAD -> edit-per-scotty) update objective
1930f11 (master) basic resume outline
```

This combination is so popular that Git gives you a shortcut: the `--oneline` flag.

We know it's confusing, but --oneline is a flag just like --abbrev-commit. This is not the same as the "oneline" formatting option we supplied to the pretty flag.

```
git log --oneline
```

Produces the same output as --pretty=oneline --abbrev-commit.

We absolutely love this flag, and we are going to be using it going forward in this book. We highly recommend you do the same.

Brain Power

Go back to the output of `git log` without any flags. Now that you know that you can customize its output, is there any information that you would like to add (or not display)? Take your notes here. Once you get more comfortable, you will figure out how to customize `git log` to see exactly what you want.

Sharpen your pencil

Try putting the `git log` command through some paces in the `recipes` repository. Start with the terminal, and be sure to be in the `recipes` folder.

➢ **Start with the `different-base` branch.** Use `git log --oneline` and list what you see here:

➢ Next up is the `spicy-version` branch.

➢ Finally, the `master` branch.

→ Answers on page 152.

I've tried using the git log command with all the options you described. But I only see commits for a single branch. Something tells me I should be able to see the commits on **all** branches. Right?

Right! Every commit (excluding the very first commit in your repository) has a pointer to its parents (or, if it's a merge commit, to both of its parents). So, what happens when you run `git log`? Well, Git looks at the last commit you made and displays details about that commit per the flags you supplied. It then follows the pointer to the parent commit and repeats. Lather, rinse, repeat till it reaches a commit that has no parents.

But Git also knows how many branches you have in your repository! This implies that Git should be able to find the latest commit on *every* branch and trace the lineage of that commit simply by following the parent pointer.

Let's see how we can do that. We get the feeling you are going to be very pleased with the results.

How does git log work?

What happens when Brigitte looks at the log of her repository? Consider a hypothetical commit history—it is made up of three branches—master, feat-a, and feat-b. Suppose Brigitte is on the feat-a branch and executes the git log command:

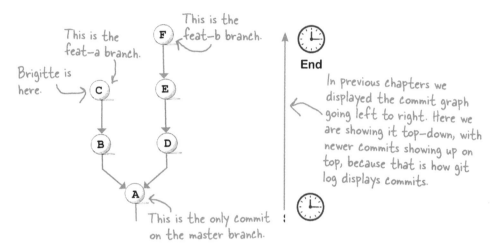

Since Brigitte is on the feat-a branch, which points to commit "C," the output of the git log command starts with C. It then reads and displays the details of that commit. It sees that "B" is C's parent, so it does the same for "B."

After displaying the details of commit "B," Git proceeds to commit "A" since that is the parent commit of "B." However, "A" is the first commit made in this repository, and it has no parent, so it stops.

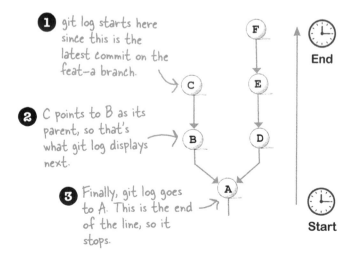

Making git log do all the work

Enough with the suspense! Let's see what it takes Brigitte to see **all her commits across all the branches** in her repository. If you guessed more flags, then ding, ding, ding—you win the prize! We know we like the --oneline flag—this time around we are going to add two more flags, namely --all and --graph. The --all flag does exactly what it says on the tin—it displays all branches in the repository. The --graph flag asks the git log command to display the commits as a graph. This is how we use it:

Nacho turn yet!

Recall that this displays abbreviated commits and single lines.

This displays all branches in the log.

This displays the log as a graph.

This graph is the "directed acyclic graph" that we mentioned in Chapter 1. We've come full circle!

```
git log --oneline --all --graph
```

This is the output.

Again, the order does not matter.

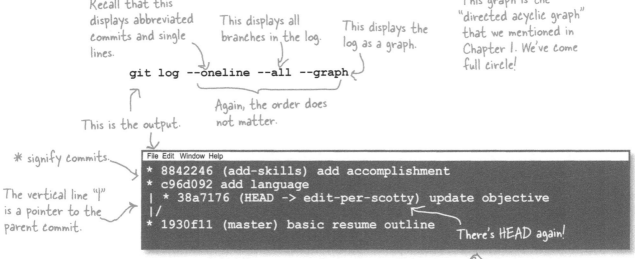

* signify commits.

The vertical line "|" is a pointer to the parent commit.

```
File Edit Window Help
* 8842246 (add-skills) add accomplishment
* c96d092 add language
| * 38a7176 (HEAD -> edit-per-scotty) update objective
|/
* 1930f11 (master) basic resume outline
```

There's HEAD again!

The output this time around is pretty, but terse. Git shows off the abbreviated commit IDs, along with branch names where appropriate. The order is still bottom to top, with newer commits showing up first. Let's contrast this with the format we have been using so far so you can see how to align the two.

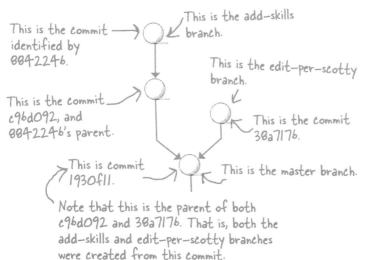

This is the commit identified by 8842246.

This is the add-skills branch.

This is the commit c96d092, and 8842246's parent.

This is the edit-per-scotty branch.

This is the commit 38a7176.

This is commit 1930f11.

This is the master branch.

Note that this is the parent of both c96d092 and 38a7176. That is, both the add-skills and edit-per-scotty branches were created from this commit.

In case you were wondering how we drew every commit graph that you have seen so far in this book, well, now you know. We are truly huge fans of the graph output, and this is our go-to way to view the history of any Git repository.

Take a breather here, maybe grab a cup of your favorite beverage while you ruminate over this for a bit. This book isn't going anywhere.

Exercise

You've seen enough Git commit graphs in this book. Now it's your turn to sketch the commit history of the `recipes` repository. Using the terminal, navigate to the `recipes` folder. Make sure you are on the **spicy-version** branch. Use our favorite `git log` combo of flags:

```
git log --oneline --all --graph
```

✱ Here is a console window for you to record the output, so you don't have to keep flitting back and forth.

```
 File  Edit  Window  Help




```

✱ Next, sketch out the Git commit history using our usual format. We got you started—your mission is to fill out the rest:

This is commit 5db2b68.   This is the only commit on the master branch.

Answers on page 153.

Great.... So I can visualize the commit history. And while I admit it is pretty, I am failing to see how it's useful. How does this help me when I use Git on a day-to-day basis?

In future chapters, we will see how we can use Git to collaborate with others. The git log command is particularly handy here so we can see how others have added to the history of the project as well.

Ah! Great question. The commit history of our repository reflects how the repository has evolved over time. As we progress with our work, we will be continuously making commits. These commits, in sequence, will represent the commit history of the branch we are working on. Maybe we will have multiple such branches in flight. Over time, we will create many such branches and then merge them into the integration branch. For projects that stick around for a while, it's easy to forget what happened when. This is where the `git log` command is handy—think of it as automatic note-taking for our project.

Also, we can easily answer questions like "Has my branch diverged away from the integration branch?" or "Will this be a fast-forward merge?" by looking at the commit history of our branch and the branch we intend to merge *into*.

Finally, recall that every commit we make reflects a set of changes that we added to Git's memory in the form of a commit. That is, each commit differs from another commit in some way. And every so often we might want to know the difference between two commits, or even two branches. So how would we do that? Well, in order to compare two commits, we will need:

1. A way to identify the things we wish to compare, namely the commit IDs. We know `git log` can help with this.

2. A way to compare the two—which is exactly the topic of our next discussion!

Brigitte's job hunt isn't going so well, so she decides to work with an independent career coach (also known as a recruiter). After a *really* personal conversation with the coach, she receives some edits.

> Hey! Based on our conversation, I have made some edits to your resume. Take a look and let me know your thoughts pronto! We should be able to land you an interview here real soon.

```
# Brigitte Strek

## Objective
To leverage my language skills as Chief Communications Officer


## Languages
English (native)
Romulan (beginner)  Klingon (fluent)


## Education
Starfleet Academy, San Francisco, CA
Valedictorian, Class of 2018


## Experience
2018-2020, Federation Starship Atlantis - Communications Ensign

                all
Routed ^ incoming subspace communications to the correct officer
```

resume.md

Brigitte's "independent career coach"

Brigitte takes her recruiter's handwritten notes and applies them to the `resume.md` file in her repository. Let's see how she can use Git to figure out the differences between her version and the edits the recruiter sent her.

What diff-erence does it make?

Take a sip of your favorite beverage. We'll have an exercise for you soon.

Since we are on the topic of finding differences, let's first talk about what we mean when we say "different."

The role of a Git repository—any Git repository—is to track the content of your files. You may create new files or edit or move or delete existing files as you progress with your work, maybe committing along the way. So what constitutes a difference?

Well, if Git knows what a file (or a set of files) looks like, and you make a change to it, now Git can help you figure out *what* changed. And remember—Git only knows what a file looks like if it's *tracking* the file, in that, at some point, you either added a particular file to Git's index, or committed it.

We talked about untracked and tracked files in Chapter 1.

Let's make this a bit more concrete—say this is the status of Brigitte's repository after she edited her resume:

```
File Edit Window Help
$ git status
On branch edit-per-scotty
Changes not staged for commit:
  (use "git add <file>..." to update what will be committed)
  (use "git restore <file>..." to discard changes in working directory)
        modified:    resume.md
```

Git tells us the file is not staged.

To help jog your memory, there are various states Git assigns to your files as they move from the working directory to the index, and finally, when you commit them.

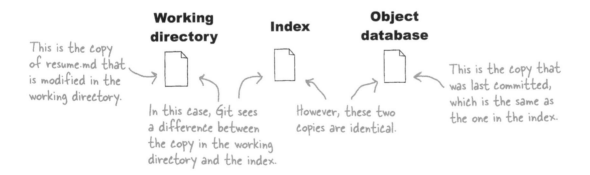

Working directory   **Index**   **Object database**

This is the copy of resume.md that is modified in the working directory.

In this case, Git sees a difference between the copy in the working directory and the index.

However, these two copies are identical.

This is the copy that was last committed, which is the same as the one in the index.

We can infer a couple of things from the Git status report—for one, that the file is being "tracked" by Git (since it is not marked as "untracked"). Git also reports that the file has been modified but isn't staged—so this file was previously committed, but Brigitte has edited it since then. However, she hasn't added it to the index yet.

But in what *way* did the file change? That's where the `git diff` command comes into play.

Visualizing file differences

The `git diff` command is short for "difference." This command can be used to find the difference—in other words, compare—between all kinds of things in Git. If Brigitte were to execute the `git diff` command in her repository, this is what she would see:

Like git log, git diff will use the pager. Hit "q" to get out of it.

```
File  Edit  Window  Help
diff --git a/resume.md b/resume.md
index 73d57b6..b179a00 100644
--- a/resume.md
+++ b/resume.md
@@ -5,7 +5,7 @@ To leverage my language skills as Chief Communications Officer

   ## Languages
  English (native)
-Romulan (beginner)
+Klingon (fluent)

   ## Education
  Starfleet Academy, San Francisco, CA
@@ -14,4 +14,4 @@ Valedictorian, Class of 2018
   ## Experience
  2018-2020, Federation Starship Atlantis - Communications Ensign

-Routed incoming subspace communications to the correct officer
+Routed all incoming subspace communications to the correct officer
```

See how this line starts with "@@"? This is a "hunk" header.

More about this in a second.

This is called a "hunk."

Notice how some lines are prefixed with "+"s and "−"s.

This is another hunk header. (Note the "@@" at the beginning.)

Before we jump into the details, let's see what Git is doing from a big-picture perspective. Running `git diff` in a repository compares the version that Git has in its *index* with the version of the file in the *working directory*. This ordering is important! You can think of it as the version in the index being the "old" version and the version in the working directory being the "new" version.

Why is the version in the working directory the "new" version? Because you just edited the file in the working directory, making that version the "new" version.

Since Brigette edited her resume (per the recommendations her recruiter made) but hasn't added it to the index yet, the `git diff` command sees and highlights those differences.

Just bear in mind that while Brigitte has only one file in her repository, many repositories contain lots of files with lots of changes. So Git shows us all the differences for a file, followed by the next file. Even within a file, it tries to show us one area—or one "hunk"—at a time.

To put a button on it—the `git diff` command's output is one file at a time, divvied up into separate areas of changes, each called a *hunk*. Next, let's zoom in.

Visualizing file differences: one file at a time

Whenever Git sees variation between a file in the index and the version of that file in the working directory, Git displays information about the differences between them:

This is how we know the names of the files that Git is currently comparing. →

```
diff --git a/resume.md b/resume.md
```

Git is telling you that it's comparing the resume.md file (in the index) with the resume.md file in the working directory. Here, version "a" is the version of the resume.md file in the index (the old version) being compared with the new (indicated by "b") version of the resume.md file.

This is followed by a weird sequence of characters:

You can ignore this line—you will probably never need this on a day-to-day basis. →

```
index 73d57b6..b179a00 100644
```

Next up on the agenda are two lines that you can think of as a legend—the git diff command output is telling us that if we see a line prefixed with a "-", that line belongs to the "a" (old) version of the resume.md file. And any line prefixed with a "+" is from the "b" (new) version of the file.

This is another important bit. Git is telling you that any line prefixed with a minus ("−") is a line from the version "a", which in this case is the version in Git's index. Similarly, any line prefixed with a plus ("+") is a line in the version in the working directory.

```
---    a/resume.md
+++    b/resume.md
```

Think of this as a legend.

All of this sets up the backdrop. We know we are looking at the "diff" of the resume.md file, with any changes that were introduced in the file since we last added it to the index. The changes that Git knows about—that is, the changes stored in the index—will be prefixed with a "-", and the changes we just introduced in the file in the working directory will be prefixed with a "+".

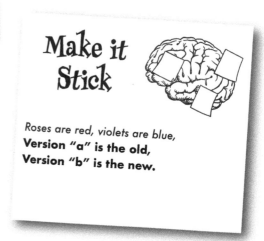

Make it Stick

Roses are red, violets are blue,
Version "a" is the old,
Version "b" is the new.

Visualizing file differences: one hunk at a time

Now let's take a look at the rest of the output and tease it apart, bit by bit. Git does not display the entire file in the output of the `git diff` command—that wouldn't be particularly useful if the file had a few thousand lines in it, would it? Instead it chooses to display only the parts of the file that have changed (hunks). To provide some context, it tells us the starting line number (5, in this case), and how many lines are being displayed in this hunk (7). It tries to show some text from surrounding lines so we can attempt to discern how this change fits into the big picture.

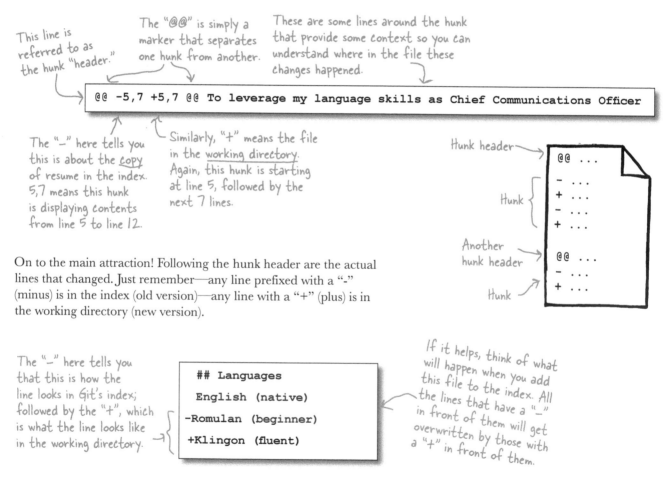

This line is referred to as the hunk "header."

The "@@" is simply a marker that separates one hunk from another.

These are some lines around the hunk that provide some context so you can understand where in the file these changes happened.

`@@ -5,7 +5,7 @@ To leverage my language skills as Chief Communications Officer`

The "−" here tells you this is about the copy of resume in the index. 5,7 means this hunk is displaying contents from line 5 to line 12.

Similarly, "+" means the file in the working directory. Again, this hunk is starting at line 5, followed by the next 7 lines.

Hunk header → `@@ ...`

Hunk { `- ...` `+ ...` `- ...` `+ ...`

Another hunk header → `@@ ...`

Hunk → `- ...` `+ ...`

On to the main attraction! Following the hunk header are the actual lines that changed. Just remember—any line prefixed with a "-" (minus) is in the index (old version)—any line with a "+" (plus) is in the working directory (new version).

The "−" here tells you that this is how the line looks in Git's index; followed by the "+", which is what the line looks like in the working directory.

```
## Languages
English (native)
-Romulan (beginner)
+Klingon (fluent)
```

If it helps, think of what will happen when you add this file to the index. All the lines that have a "−" in front of them will get overwritten by those with a "+" in front of them.

Git will **only** display as many hunks as it needs to show us the differences in different parts of the file. That means that on one side, if we have just one change in a big file, we will see only one hunk. Alternatively, we'll see many more hunks if the file we're diffing is long and has a bunch of changes.

If you look back at the diff output, you will notice that Git used two hunks to display all the differences.

Dumb Questions

Q: I am used to visual diffing tools. Why can't I just use something I am familiar with here?

A: There are a bunch of tools available that can show diffs in a visually appealing way, and Git supports using many of these. It has a command called `difftool` that shows changes using external diff tools. It also allows you to configure which tool it should use to compare files. You can use `git difftool --tool-help` to see the flags available, and also to configure Git to use a particular tool to display diffs. However, in this book we are going to stick to the tools that Git gives you out of the box.

Another reason you want to get used to the output of the `git diff` command is that depending on the context you may not always have all the tools you are used to available. Perhaps you are working on a server, or a colleague's machine. However, you know that `git diff` will always be available.

Q: Is it just me, or is the diff output a lot more verbose than it needs to be?

A: We can empathize with this sentiment. It takes a while to get used to the output of the `git diff` command, and it certainly seems complicated. However, it helps to look one bit at a time. Git collating the output in separate hunks is certainly helpful. This will get easier—we promise.

Making diffs easier on the eyes

Most Git commands offer several flags. We've already seen a few that are available for the `git log` command. There is one flag you might want to consider that makes looking at diffs easier:

```
git diff --word-diff
```
This shows how individual words differ rather than how lines differ.

```
diff --git a/resume.md b/resume.md
index 73d57b6..b179a00 100644
--- a/resume.md
+++ b/resume.md
@@ -5,7 +5,7 @@ To leverage my language skills as Chief Communications Officer

## Languages
English (native)
[-Romulan (beginner)-]{+Klingon (fluent)+}

## Education
Starfleet Academy, San Francisco, CA
@@ -14,4 +14,4 @@ Valedictorian, Class of 2018
## Experience
2018-2020, Federation Starship Atlantis - Communications Ensign

Routed {+all+} incoming subspace communications to the correct officer
```

All the header information remains the same.

Notice how Git shows word changes next to each other.

Again, the diff is shown at the word level.

Feel free to pick whichever flag works best for you. Personally, we like both—we aren't picking sides here.

Exercise

Why don't you make some changes to the sauce recipe so you can play with the diff command? Start with the `recipes` repository, and make sure you are on the `spicy-version` branch.

When we last tried the recipe, we felt that the sauce needed a little punch, so we are offering these changes to the `saucy.md` file:

These are the edits we recommend to the saucy. md file.

```
# Spicy Green Mean Machine


## Ingredients
1/2 cup - Plain yogurt
3-4 cloves - Garlic
2 cups - Chopped cilantro
1/4 cup - Olive oil
1/4 cup - Lime juice
1 pinch - Salt    2 pinches - Salt
1 - Jalapeno, deseeded    2 - Jalapenos, deseeded


## Instructions
                                      desired consistency
Add all ingredients to a blender. Mix until smooth_
```

saucy.md

Your first task is to apply these changes to the `saucy.md` file in your repository. Make sure to save the file once you are done, and then proceed to the next page.

continued on the next page...

Exercise

On the previous page, you edited the `saucy.md` file in the recipes repository. Below, we have provided you with the output of `git diff`. Your job is to annotate it and highlight what the diff output is trying to tell you. (Don't worry—we got you started.)

```
diff --git a/saucy.md b/saucy.md

index 20b7e5a..8d49c34 100644

--- a/saucy.md

+++ b/saucy.md

@@ -6,8 +6,8 @@

 2 cups - Chopped cilantro

 1/4 cup - Olive oil

 1/4 cup - Lime juice

-1 pinch - Salt

-1 - Jalapeno, deseeded

+2 pinches - Salt

+2 - Jalapenos, deseeded


 ## Instructions

-Add all ingredients to a blender. Mix until smooth.

+Add all ingredients to a blender. Mix until desired consistency.
```

We are comparing the version of saucy.md *in the index with the version in the working directory.*

"a" represents the copy in the index, while "b" represents the copy in the working directory.

Answers on page 154.

Brain Power

The `git diff` command tells us the difference between what we previously put in the index (and potentially committed) and what we have in the working directory. If you were to add the `saucy.md` file to the index and then run `git diff` in the recipes repository, what would you expect the output to be?

That recruiter totally nailed it. My resume looks so much better now. Heading out to buy some books on interview prep so I can get a head start. Wish me luck!

Quick update on Brigitte's job hunt—she really likes the updates the recruiter (er, independent career coach) sent her. So she uses the `git add` command to add the `resume.md` file to the index. She's ready to commit, but she really wants to be sure that she is only committing the changes her recruiter suggested. But when she tries `git diff`, she gets no output!

Uh oh!

Well, let's find out what's going on with her repository and see if we can help Brigitte out. She has a ton of interview prep to do, just in case that phone rings.

Diffing staged changes

The default behavior of the `git diff` command is to compare the contents of the files in the index with the contents of the working directory and show you the differences. Now, Brigitte has already added all the files in the working directory to the index. This is the state of the files in her repository:

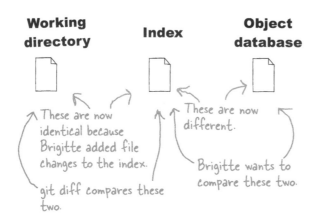

Working directory **Index** **Object database**

These are now identical because Brigitte added file changes to the index.

git diff compares these two.

These are now different.

Brigitte wants to compare these two.

Diffing staged changes (continued)

Because the contents of the working directory and the index are identical since Brigitte added all the files to the index, the `git diff` command reports no difference. So how does she know what she is going to commit?

Brigitte can still use the `git diff` command to compare the contents she had in her last commit with the index, except this time she will need to supply the "--cached" flag:

`git diff --cached` ← This tells Git to compare the contents of the object database with those of the index.

Serious Coding

Git diff offers another flag, `--staged`, which you will see referenced in many a tutorial or blog post online. `--staged` is just a synonym for `--cached`. Feel free to use whichever appeals to you more.

When she runs this, the output she gets is shown below.

```
diff --git a/resume.md b/resume.md
index 73d57b6..b179a00 100644
--- a/resume.md
+++ b/resume.md
@@ -5,7 +5,7 @@ To leverage my language skills as Chief Communications Officer


 ## Languages
 English (native)
-Romulan (beginner)
+Klingon (fluent)

 ## Education
 Starfleet Academy, San Francisco, CA
@@ -14,4 +14,4 @@ Valedictorian, Class of 2018
 ## Experience
 2018-2020, Federation Starship Atlantis - Communications Ensign


-Routed incoming subspace communications to the correct officer
+Routed all incoming subspace communications to the correct officer
```

Here "a" marks the contents of the object database. "b" marks the contents in the index.

The line previously committed is prefixed with a "−" and the line in the index is prefixed with a "+".

Notice that the output isn't so different from the first time she ran `git diff` (with no flag). The most significant difference between `git diff` and `git diff --cached` is that in the case of the former, we are comparing the index with the working directory; in the second, we are comparing the *previously committed version with the index*.

After seeing this diff, Brigitte is happy with the changes she is about to commit. So she does just that, using the `git commit` command and the message "edit per recruiter." All right! Now where's that book on interview prep?

Sharpen your pencil

In the last exercise, you edited the `saucy.md` file. Now go ahead and add the `saucy.md` file to the index (make sure you are on the **spicy-version** branch).

➤ Start by visualizing the state of the working directory, the index, and the object database. We've got you started—your job is to finish it.

Working directory   **Index**   **Object database**

This is the saucy.md file. →

➤ Run `git diff`. Is there a difference between the files? Why or why not? Jot down your explanation here:

➤ Run `git diff --cached`. Is there a difference between the files? Again, why or why not?

⟶ **Answers on page 155.**

Exercise

To make things easier in the following sections, go ahead and commit the changes in the index (again, be sure to be on the `spicy-version` branch). Use the message "add punch." Remember to check the `git status` prior to and after committing! Here's some blank space—use it as a scratch pad to write down the commands you are going to use in the order you are going to use them:

⟶ **Answers on page 155.**

Diffing branches

Brigitte's been studying pretty hard so she can nail the interview when the time comes. Brigitte was super excited about the edits her recruiter suggested. She happily made the changes to her resume, which she then committed on the edit-per-scotty branch with the commit message "edit per recruiter". She now has three branches—add-skills, edit-per-scotty, and master. What if she wants to find out what changed between, say, the add-skills and the edit-per-scotty branches?

Once again, git diff to the rescue! You can use the git diff command to compare two branches.

Exercise coming soon! Nothing for you to do here.

We are using git log --oneline --all --graph.

```
File Edit Window Help
* 846c398 (HEAD -> edit-per-scotty) edit per recruiter
* 38a7176 update objective
| * 39afa28 (add-skills) add accomplishment
| * 585bd1c add language
|/
* 1930f11 (master) basic resume outline
```

Notice Brigitte's latest commit.

Brigitte is on the edit-per-scotty branch (she used git branch to make sure). She is ready to merge the add-skills branch into the edit-per-scotty branch, but she wants to be sure she knows what the final result will be. She can compare edit-per-scotty with the add-skills branch like this:

We made this commit in a copy of the original resume folder, called resume-final. You will find resume-final in the directory you downloaded for this book.

Supply the names of the two branches you wish to compare as arguments to the git diff command.

```
git diff edit-per-scotty add-skills
```

This is often referred to as the "target."

This is the "source."

If Brigitte wants to merge the add-skills branch *into* the edit-per-scotty branch, then it makes sense to have the add-skills branch as a "source" and the edit-per-scotty branch as the "target." To compare the two, specifying edit-per-scotty *first* makes it the target, and add-skills second makes it the source.

But before we perform the diff, let's make sure we know exactly what we are comparing...

As you might have guessed, you can use the --word-diff flag here as well.

Diffing branches (continued)

A branch is used to capture a single unit of work. Often, you'll make several commits on the same branch before you are ready to merge your work into another branch. So what does it mean when Brigitte compares the `add-skills` branch to the `edit-per-scotty` branch?

When you compare two branches, Git simply compares the latest commits on each branch—often referred to as the *tips* of the branches. This is what comparing the two branches looks like:

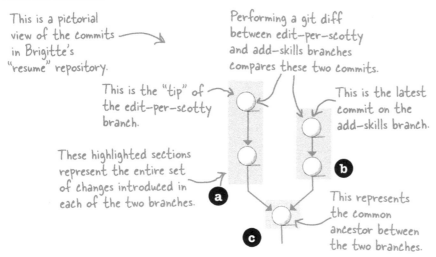

This is a pictorial view of the commits in Brigitte's "resume" repository.

Performing a git diff between edit-per-scotty and add-skills branches compares these two commits.

This is the "tip" of the edit-per-scotty branch.

This is the latest commit on the add-skills branch.

These highlighted sections represent the entire set of changes introduced in each of the two branches.

a

b

This represents the common ancestor between the two branches.

c

Every commit in a branch builds on top of the commits that came before it. Which means that when you compare the tips of two branches, you are actually comparing the entire set of changes introduced in each of the branches. In the picture above, the changes introduced by the `edit-per-scotty` branch are indicated by the letter "a," and all the changes in the `add-skills` branch are marked by "b." Notice that both branches originate from `master`. This set of changes is therefore common between the two, marked by "c." Here is the result of the `git diff` command represented as a Venn diagram:

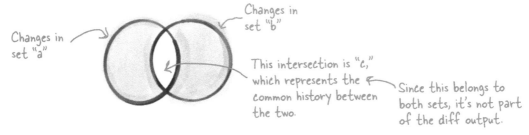

Changes in set "a"

Changes in set "b"

This intersection is "c," which represents the common history between the two.

Since this belongs to both sets, it's not part of the diff output.

Now you know what the output of the `git diff` command represents. Next, let's take a look at what we get when we actually run the `git diff` command in Brigitte's repository.

Diffing branches (we are there!)

As a gentle reminder, this is the command Brigitte executed:

```
git diff edit-per-scotty add-skills
```

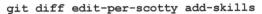

Since we are supplying edit-per-scotty first, that would be represented by "a."

This is the target.

Subsequently, add-skills would be represented by "b."

This being the second argument makes it the source.

And this is what she would see:

"a" represents the changes in the edit-per-scotty branch.

"b" represents the changes in the add-skills branch.

Any change in the edit-per-scotty branch will be prefixed by a "-".

Any change in the add-skills branch will be prefixed by a "+".

```
diff --git a/resume.md b/resume.md
index b179a00..384caab 100644
--- a/resume.md
+++ b/resume.md
@@ -1,11 +1,12 @@
 # Brigitte Strek

 ## Objective
-To leverage my language skills as Chief Communications Officer
+To leverage my skills as Chief Communications Officer
```

Notice that the header info hasn't changed from our previous experiments with the diff command.

This is what the line looks like in the edit-per-scotty branch.

And this is what it looks like in the add-skills branch.

There you have it. Finding the differences between two branches isn't that different from comparing the index to the working directory, or the object database with the index.

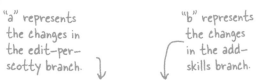

Brain Power

What would change in the output of `git diff` if you were to swap the order of the branch names? You can even give it a try if you like. Did you get it right?

there are no Dumb Questions

Q: I recall seeing the "a" and "b" file markers in our earlier experiments with the `git diff` command. Do those represent sets of changes as well?

A: Yes! Whenever you run the `git diff` command, you always have two "sets" of changes that you are comparing. When you run `git diff` (with no arguments) you are comparing the index (marked as "a") with the working directory (marked as "b"). Similarly, when you run `git diff --cached`, the object database is marked as "a" and the index marked as "b."

Feel free to revisit our earlier experiments with `git diff` and `git diff --cached` and see how the Venn diagram analogy works there as well.

Q: Does the `git` command help me figure out if there is going to be a merge conflict when I do actually merge the two branches?

A: It doesn't. Remember, diff stands for "difference." Comparing two branches shows you how they differ from each other. A merge, on the other hand, is a union. The difference tells you *how* the branches look different from one another, which is probably a good thing to know prior to merging them together.

To answer your question: the best way to know if you are going to see a merge conflict is to, well, merge.

Be careful when you compare branches!

The `git diff` command does not need to be supplied two separate branch names. You can simply supply it the name of a single branch, and it will seem to work. But Git pulls a fast one when you do this, and the results can be confusing. Suppose you run this:

`git diff add-skills`   **as compared to**   `git diff edit-per-scotty add-skills`

Since Git was only supplied one branch in the version on the left, it assumes you want to compare that branch with the working directory! That is, you are no longer comparing two branches. Instead, you are comparing the branch you supplied with the current state of your working directory. Furthermore, the order is now flipped!

Git assumes that your implied second argument is the working directory.

`git diff add-skills <working-directory>`

This time around add-skills is "a."

This is now the target.

And the working directory is "b."

And this is the source.

This is even more confusing if you have modified files in your working directory or the index, since those differences will show up in the diff output.

As you can tell, the pluses (+) and minuses (-) will be reversed since the order of the arguments is reversed. It's best to be explicit with the arguments you supply to the `git diff` command, so you know exactly what you are comparing.

Sharpen your pencil

Head over to the recipes folder. In an earlier exercise we committed our changes to the saucy.md file on the spicy-version branch. Here is the output of the following command. Your job is to annotate the output:

git diff spicy-version different-base

```
diff --git a/saucy.md b/saucy.md
index 8d49c34..3f421be 100644
--- a/saucy.md
+++ b/saucy.md
@@ -1,13 +1,12 @@
-# Spicy Green Mean Machine
+# Call me Cilly

  ## Ingredients
-1/2 cup - Plain yogurt
+1/2 cup - Sour cream
  3-4 cloves - Garlic
  2 cups - Chopped cilantro
  1/4 cup - Olive oil
  1/4 cup - Lime juice
-2 pinches - Salt
-2 - Jalapenos, deseeded
+1/2 pinch - Salt

  ## Instructions
-Add all ingredients to a blender. Mix until desired consistency.
+Add all ingredients to a blender. Mix until smooth.
```

→ Answers on page 156.

I can use the git log command to find commit IDs in my repository. Could I supply two commit IDs to the git diff command and compare them?

Ding ding ding! The `git diff` command is truly as versatile as a multitool pocketknife. We have seen how to compare the working directory with the index, and the index with the object database. We then saw how to compare two branches.

The thing is, you can use the `diff` command to compare just about anything, including two different commits.

So, the question is—why would you ever do that? Well, suppose you are furiously working on a branch, and have made a series of commits. Perhaps you want to see what you've changed between two commits on a branch. Or perhaps you just want to compare two arbitrary commits.

Serious Coding

There are many more Git commands than any one book could possibly teach you. As you progress through your journey with Git and learn more advanced commands (`git cherry-pick` comes to mind, which allows you to move commits from one branch to another), this ability to compare commits will come in handy. Take a sneak peek at the appendix if you would like to know more about cherry-picking commits.

Diffing commits

Brigitte is curious about what changed between her latest commit on the `edit-per-scotty` branch and the commit that came just before it. Here is Brigitte's commit log:

This is the output of git log --oneline --graph --all.

There are the commit IDs that we so yearn for.

```
File Edit Window Help
* 846c398 (HEAD -> edit-per-scotty) edit per recruiter
* 38a7176 update objective
| * 8842246 (add-skills) add accomplishment
| * c96d092 add language
|/
* 1930f11 (master) basic resume outline
```

Brigitte wants to compare the commit with ID `846c398` with the commit that came just before it (`38a7176`). It's important she get the order of the commits right—if the intent is to find what changed since the last commit, then the latest commit should be the "source," like so:

This is the "target."

Notice that the latest commit is the second argument, that is, the "source."

Changes in 38a7176.

Changes in 846c398.

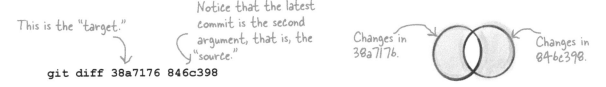

```
git diff 38a7176 846c398
```

Think about it—changes in the target (the left-hand side of the Venn diagram) always show up as minuses (-) and changes in the source (right-hand side) show up as pluses (+). In order to see what was "added" in the latest commit, you would want to put that commit ID second, since its diffs will show up with the plus prefix. The output is very similar to the output of every other `diff` command we have seen so far, so we are going to skip showing it again.

Using the `diff` command, Brigitte can compare any two commits in her repository. They don't have to be parent and child, or even on the same branch!

Serious Coding

We've mentioned this before, but like the `git status` and `git branch` commands (with no arguments), both the `git log` and `git diff` commands are safe. That is, they only "ask" your repository for information—they don't change it in any way. So use them as often as you like.

What does the diff for a new file look like?

Suppose Brigitte creates a new file, calls it `cover-letter.md`, and adds it to the index. What would the output of `git diff --cached` look like? Recall that the `cached` flag compares the last committed version with the version in the index:

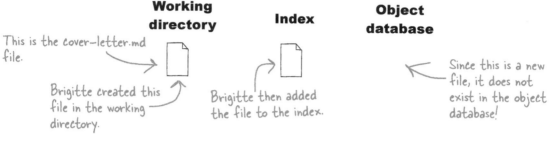

Working directory

Index

Object database

This is the cover-letter.md file.

Brigitte created this file in the working directory.

Brigitte then added the file to the index.

Since this is a new file, it does not exist in the object database!

Here's the output of `git diff --cached`:

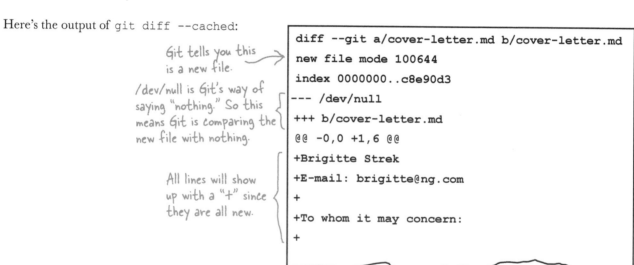

Git tells you this is a new file.

/dev/null is Git's way of saying "nothing." So this means Git is comparing the new file with nothing.

All lines will show up with a "+" since they are all new.

```
diff --git a/cover-letter.md b/cover-letter.md
new file mode 100644
index 0000000..c8e90d3
--- /dev/null
+++ b/cover-letter.md
@@ -0,0 +1,6 @@
+Brigitte Strek
+E-mail: brigitte@ng.com
+
+To whom it may concern:
+
```

Since Git has nothing to compare the file with (Brigitte has just created it and added it to the index), Git compares the file with nothing—which it marks as `/dev/null`. This also means that all the lines in the file will be prefixed with a "+" since they are all new!

You'd get a similar output if you were to compare two commits, or two branches, where one commit or branch introduces a new file.

Serious Coding

We mentioned in Chapter 2 that when you switch branches, Git rewrites your working directory to look like it did when you made the most recent commit on that branch. Well, it also updates the index to look the same! How else would the `git diff` command work? See, if you update a file in the working directory after switching branches, Git needs to have the previous version in the index with which to be able to compare it!

I am both nervous and excited about starting a new chapter in my career. I feel like I'm going where no one has gone before.

We are always looking for folks with an adventurous palate. If that's you, feel free to send us a resume!

That's it for this chapter! Let's wish Brigitte the very best in her job hunt. As for the folks at the '80s diner, we certainly hope they win the competition at the Cilantro Fest. If you get a chance to try out the cilantro sauce recipe at home, be sure to let us know if you come up with any modifications!

Bullet Points

- The `git log` command shows us the commit history of our repository.

- The `git log` command, by default, lists all the commits, along with the commit metadata, for the current branch.

- Flags like `--abbrev-commit`, `--pretty` with the `oneline` option, or the `--oneline` flag make it easier to visualize the commit history of a single branch.

- Using the `--all` and `--graph` flags with the `git log` command allow us to visualize the history of every branch in our repository.

- Git tracks changes—between the working directory and the index, and index and the object database.

- To find out what changed between the index and the working directory, use the `git diff` command. The default behavior of the `git diff` command is to compare the index and the working directory.

- The output of the `git diff` command starts by telling you which file's differences are currently being displayed. Typically, one set of changes is prefixed with "a," and the other is marked by "b":

```
diff --git a/resume.md b/resume.md
```

- This is followed by a legend that tells how the log output will differentiate between lines that exist in "a" versus "b":

```
--- a/resume.md
+++ b/resume.md
```

The legend is followed by a series of "hunks" that allow you to see the changes in bite-sized pieces. Each hunk has lines prefixed with a minus (meaning it comes from the version of the file prefixed with "a/"), or a plus (meaning it is present in the file prefixed with version "b/").

- Git will display as many, and only as many, hunks as needed to display all the differences. This makes it easier to compare large files.

- The `--cached` (or `--staged`) flag for the `diff` command allows us to compare the changes that we last committed: that is, the changes in Git's object database with the changes added to the index.

- We can supply the `git diff` command with two branch names. In such a case, `git diff` will compare the differences between the "tips" of the two branches.

- The `git diff` command is always comparing two sets of changes, which can be visualized by a Venn diagram. The first argument is the set on the left (always indicated by "a/") and prefixed with a minus ("-"). The second argument is the set of the right, indicated by "b/", and prefixed with a "+".

- Swapping the order of the arguments swaps the left-hand and right-hand sides of the Venn diagram.

- We can use the `git log` command to identify commit IDs, which in turn we can supply to the `git diff` command to compare two disparate commits.

A Diff-icult Crossword

Is there a difference in your Git vocabulary now that you've read this chapter? Find out with this crossword.

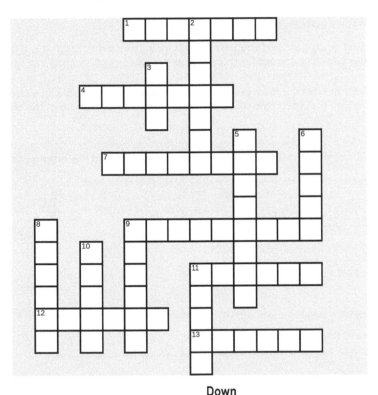

Across

1 Files move from the _____ directory to the index

4 Formatting flag that tells git log to put everything in a single line

7 Kind of sauce the chefs are making

9 Brigitte compares this branch with the edit-per-scotty branch (2 words)

11 Command that lists the commits you've made on a branch (2 words)

12 Flag that tells Git to compare what's in the index and what's in the object database

13 Flag to clean up formatting in git log

Down

2 Brigitte is fluent in this language

3 Flag that tells git log to show every branch in the repository

5 She's working on her resume in Git

6 List of differences between files output by the git diff command

8 Committing moves files from the index to the _____ database

9 The --_____-commit flag displays shortened commit IDs in your Git log

10 The new branch for our recipe is called _____-version

11 Flag that tells git log to draw a diagram of your commit history

———————➤ Answers on page 157.

Sharpen your pencil
Solution

From page 117.

Our friends at the '80's Diner are getting ready to submit their best sauce recipe for this year's Cilantro Fest. All the local restaurants compete to win, and it certainly makes for great publicity. Naturally, they've created a Git repository to keep track of the variations they try.

Well, we managed to get that repository, and you'll be using it for all your exercises in this chapter. You will find the repository in the source files you downloaded for this book, under `chapter03`, **called** `recipes`.

Start a new terminal window, and be sure to be in the `recipes` directory. See if you can answer the following questions. Important: make sure that you compare your answers with ours at the end of the chapter before you move on.

➤ What is the current status of the repository? List the command you use and the output here.

```
File Edit Window Help
$ git status
On branch spicy-version
nothing to commit, working tree clean
```

This is what we got. Did you?

➤ How many branches are in this repository? List them here:

```
File Edit Window Help
$ git branch
  different-base
  master
* spicy-version
```

➤ What branch are you currently on?

spicy-version

Exercise Solution

From page 119.

It's time to unleash your git log skills on the `recipes` repository. Open up your terminal (or just use the one from the last exercise). Make sure you are on the `spicy-version` branch. Using the `git log` command, see if you can answer the following questions for each of the three branches in the repository.

* How many commits are on the branch?
* List the **first seven characters** of each commit ID along with their respective commit messages in the reverse chronological order (that is the order they are presented to you).

Branch: spicy-version

Commit count: 3

Commit listing:

8d670e9 – update recipe name

4cca5a7 – make it spicy

5db2b68 – first attempt

Branch: different-base

Commit count: 3

Commit listing:

0065b8a – cut down salt

549e0da – use sour cream

5db2b68 – first attempt

Branch: master

Commit count: 1

Commit listing:

5db2b68 – first attempt

Sharpen your pencil
Solution

From page 122.

Try putting the `git log` command through some paces in the `recipes` repository. Start with the terminal, and be sure to be in the `recipes` folder.

➤ **Start with the `different-base` branch.** Use `git log --oneline` and list what you see here:

> 0065b8a (HEAD -> different-base) cut down salt
>
> 549e0da use sour cream
>
> 5db2b68 (master) first attempt

➤ Next up is the `spicy-version` branch.

> 8d670e9 (HEAD -> spicy-version) update recipe name
>
> 4cca5a7 make it spicy
>
> 5db2b68 (master) first attempt

➤ Finally, the `master` branch.

> 5db2b68 (HEAD -> master) first attempt

Exercise Solution

From page 126.

You've seen enough git commit graphs in this book, and now it's your turn to sketch the commit history of the `recipes` repository. Using the terminal, navigate to the `recipes` folder. Make sure you are on the **spicy-version** branch. Use our favorite `git log` combo of flags:

```
git log --oneline --all --graph
```

✱ Here is a console window for you to record the output so you don't have to keep flitting back and forth.

```
File Edit Window Help
* 8d670e9 (HEAD -> spicy-version) update recipe name
* 4cca5a7 make it spicy
| * 0065b8a (different-base) cut down salt
| * 549e0da use sour cream
|/
* 5db2b68 (master) first attempt
```

✱ Next, sketch out the Git commit history using our usual format. We got you started—your mission is to fill out the rest:

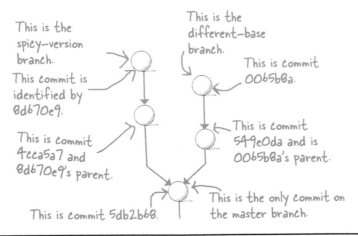

This is the spicy-version branch.

This commit is identified by 8d670e9.

This is commit 4cca5a7 and 8d670e9's parent.

This is commit 5db2b68.

This is the different-base branch.

This is commit 0065b8a.

This is commit 549e0da and is 0065b8a's parent.

This is the only commit on the master branch.

Exercise Solution

From page 135.

On the previous page, you edited the the `saucy.md` file in the recipes repository. Below, we have provided you with the output of `git diff`. Your job is to annotate it and highlight what the diff output is trying to tell you. (Don't worry—we've got you started.)

```
diff --git a/saucy.md b/saucy.md
index 20b7e5a..2f27db3 100644
--- a/saucy.md
+++ b/saucy.md
@@ -6,8 +6,8 @@
 2 cups - Chopped cilantro
 1/4 cup - Olive oil
 1/4 cup - Lime juice
-1 pinch - Salt
-1 - Jalapeno, deseeded
+2 pinches - Salt
+2 - Jalapenos, deseeded

 ## Instructions
-Add all ingredients to a blender. Mix until smooth.
+Add all ingredients to a blender. Mix until desired consistency.
```

We are comparing the version of saucy.md in the index with the version in the working directory.

This tells us that a line from version "a" (that is, the index) will be prefixed with a "–". Similarly, any line in the working directory will have a "+".

"a" represents the copy in the index, while "b" represents the copy in the working directory.

We replaced these two lines in the index...

with these two lines.

This line is from the index.

And this is the replacement in the working directory.

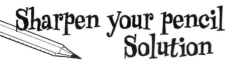

Sharpen your pencil
Solution

From page 138.

In your last exercise, you edited the saucy.md file. Now go ahead and add the saucy.md file to the index (make sure you are on the **spicy-version** branch).

➤ Start by visualizing the state of the working directory, the index, and the object database. We got you started—your job is to finish it.

Working directory   **Index**   **Object database**

This is the saucy.md file.

Since we added the file to the index, the contents of the working directory and the index are the same.

➤ Run git diff. Is there a difference between the files? Why or why not? Jot down your explanation here:

git diff by default compares the working directory with the index, so in this case, there will be no difference.

➤ Run git diff --cached. Is there a difference between the files? Again, why or why not?

git diff with the --cached flag, on the other hand, compares the index with the object database. Since we added the file to the index but haven't committed it yet, git sees a difference between the index and the last time we committed this file.

Exercise
Solution

From page 138.

To make things easier in the following sections, go ahead and commit the changes in the index (again, be sure to be on the spicy-version branch). Use the message "add punch". Remember to check the git status prior to and after committing! Here's some blank space—use it as a scratch pad to write down the commands you are going to use in the order you are going to use them:

Always start and end with git status.

```
git status
git add saucy.md
git commit -m "add punch"
git status
```

Sharpen your pencil
Solution

From page 143.

Head over to the `recipes` folder. In an earlier exercise we committed our changes to the `saucy.md` file on the `spicy-version` branch. Here is the output of the following command. Your job is to annotate the output:

```
git diff spicy-version different-base
```

Since we supply spicy-version first, that represents set "a" in this Venn diagram.

And different-base will be set "b.".

Use all this space to scribble away!

```
diff --git a/saucy.md b/saucy.md
index 8d49c34..3f421be 100644
--- a/saucy.md
+++ b/saucy.md
@@ -1,13 +1,12 @@
-# Spicy Green Mean Machine
+# Call me Cilly

  ## Ingredients
-1/2 cup - Plain yogurt
+1/2 cup - Sour cream
  3-4 cloves - Garlic
  2 cups - Chopped cilantro
  1/4 cup - Olive oil
  1/4 cup - Lime juice
-2 pinches - Salt
-2 - Jalapenos, deseeded
+1/2 pinch - Salt

  ## Instructions
-Add all ingredients to a blender. Mix until desired consistency.
+Add all ingredients to a blender. Mix until smooth.
```

Here "a" represents all the changes in the spicy-version branch and "b" is the set of changes in the different-base branch.

Lines introduced in spicy-version are prefixed with a "−".

Anything different in different-base branch are prefixed with a "+".

This is a line in the spicy-version branch.

And this line is from the different-base branch.

Here, two lines are in the spicy-version branch.

This comes from the different-base branch.

Lastly another line from the spicy-version branch.

This final line comes from the different-base version.

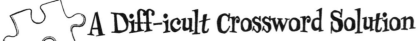

A Diff-icult Crossword Solution

Is there a difference in your Git vocabulary now that you've read this chapter? Find out with this crossword.

From page 149.

4 undoing

Fixing Your Mistakes

We all make mistakes, right? Humans have been making mistakes since time immemorial, and for a long time, making mistakes was pretty expensive (with punch cards and typewriters, we had to redo the whole thing). The reason was simple—we didn't have a version control system. But now we do! Git gives you ample opportunities to undo your mistakes, easily and painlessly. Whether you've accidentally added a file to the index, made a typo in a commit message, or made a badly formed commit, Git gives you plenty of levers to pull and buttons to push so that no one will ever know about that little, ahem, "slip-up."

After this chapter, *if* you trip up, it won't matter what kind of mistake you've made, you'll know exactly what to do. So let's go make some mistakes—and learn how to fix 'em.

Planning an engagement party

Love is in the air, and we've got some news to share with you. Gitanjali and Aref are newly engaged! They want to throw an engagement party with their closest friends, and to make sure they get it right, they've decided to hire Trinity, an event planner.

Trinity and her partner Armstrong are true professionals—and huge proponents of Git. All of their ideas for invitation cards, guests, and gift lists are always tucked away in a Git repository that they create specifically for that client. This way, they can always use Git as their second (or third, in this case) brain. This is particularly useful, since Trinity and Armstrong are all about helping their clients figure out all their options—plans do change, and Git is a tool that allows Trinity and Armstrong to iterate quickly.

Trinity just finished a conversation with Gitanjali and Aref. She initialized a new Git repository almost as soon as she put the phone down: she wanted to capture her notes about their guest list and gift registry ideas right away. She created two files, `guest-list.md` and `gift-registry.md`, and committed them on the `master` branch.

Her mind was racing with ideas for their invitation card, so she created a file called `invitation-card.md` and jotted down some ideas, along with a tentative date for the festivities. She committed that as well. This is what her commit history looks like:

This is Trinity's second commit, with the first draft of the invitation-card.md file

This is the master branch.

This represents the first commit in Trinity's repository, where she committed the guest-list.md and gift-registry.md files.

Armstrong

Trinity

As you can see, Trinity's repository contains one branch, `master`, and the two commits she has made so far. This engagement party is off to a great start! Now Trinity and Armstrong need to brainstorm some party themes.

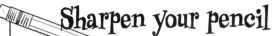

Sharpen your pencil

Trinity has made two commits in her repository. The first commit added two files, `guest-list.md` and `gift-registry.md`, and the second commit introduced the first draft of the `invitation-card.md` file. Without peeking, list all the files in the `gitanjali-aref` repository. How many files in total are in this repository? Explain your answer.

————————▶ Answers on page 202.

Exercise

Time to use the skills you acquired in Chapter 3. Navigate to the location where you downloaded the source code for this book, and in the `chapter04` folder you will find a directory called `gitanjali-aref-step-1`.

Using our favorite version of the `git log` command (which would be `git log --oneline --all --graph`), investigate Trinity's repository and identify the commit IDs of each of her commits, along with the commit message she supplied when she created each commit. Here is her commit history again. Annotate away!

————————▶ Answers on page 202.

An error in judgment

Trinity has just realized something: she made a scheduling error! Gitanjali and Aref suggested July 3 for the engagement party date. There were many things to discuss, so Trinity simply made the change to the `invitation-card.md` file, and they moved on to other topics.

But July 4 is the US Independence Day, a bank holiday, full of traffic and people headed to picnics. Oops! Trinity called the couple and brought this to their attention. They agreed it probably wasn't the best weekend for *their* celebration, so they decided to keep the date they'd originally agreed on. Except they couldn't remember what the original date was!

Fortunately, Trinity had not committed her changes yet. She used the `git diff` command to compare the changes in her working directory with the state of the index in the `gitanjali-aref` repository (which, as you know, contains a copy of the file from her first commit). This is the output she saw when she ran `git diff`:

> Relax. It's not your turn yet.

If you are wondering how Trinity would have fixed this if she had already committed her changes, worry not! We will see how to fix commits as well in this chapter.

As a reminder, git diff, by default compares the index with the working directory.

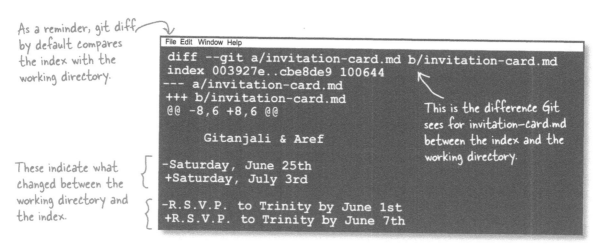

```
File  Edit  Window  Help
diff --git a/invitation-card.md b/invitation-card.md
index 003927e..cbe8de9 100644
--- a/invitation-card.md
+++ b/invitation-card.md
@@ -8,6 +8,6 @@

         Gitanjali & Aref

-Saturday, June 25th
+Saturday, July 3rd

-R.S.V.P. to Trinity by June 1st
+R.S.V.P. to Trinity by June 7th
```

This is the difference Git sees for invitation-card.md between the index and the working directory.

These indicate what changed between the working directory and the index.

The `git diff` command, by default, compares the working directory with the index. Here is the state of the `invitation-card.md` file in the three regions of Git:

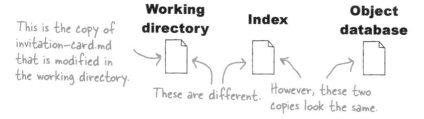

This is the copy of invitation-card.md that is modified in the working directory.

Working directory   **Index**   **Object database**

These are different.   However, these two copies look the same.

So how does Trinity recover from this?

Cubicle conversation

Armstrong: Good thing we use Git for all of our ideas. It's so easy to see what changes we've made. Do you want me to just use the output of the `git diff` command and use that to bring back all the changes?

Trinity: You could do that, and in this case, it's only two changes, so it's certainly possible. But here's something even better: we can ask Git to undo our change for us.

Armstrong: Really? How?

Trinity: Git is our memory store. We already committed `invitation-card.md`. This means there is a copy of this file in the index *and* in the object database. We can ask Git to replace the copy in the working directory with the one in the index.

Armstrong: OK, I get that. But how do I get the copy from the index into the working directory?

Trinity: The answer lies in a command called `git restore`. Here, take a look at the output of `git status` and see what it's telling you:

```
File Edit Window Help
$ git status
On branch master
Changes not staged for commit:
  (use "git add <file>..." to update what will be committed)
  (use "git restore <file>..." to discard changes in working directory)
      modified:   invitation-card.md

no changes added to commit (use "git add" and/or "git commit -a")
```

This is Git telling us how to use the restore command.

Armstrong: Ah! I see. Git is telling us we can supply the file path to the `git restore` command, and that will discard any changes in the working directory.

Trinity: Yep. `git restore` is the opposite of `git add`. It takes the copy of a file in the index and moves it back into the working directory.

Armstrong: Cool! Can we do that now?

Brain Power

What would you do if you made lots of changes in lots of files that you had previously committed? How would you compare versions? Take your notes here:

Undoing changes to the working directory

Trinity has to undo the changes she made to the working directory, by replacing her changes with the ones in the index. She can use the `git restore` command, supplying it the path to the file that is to be put back.

Nacho turn yet!

Invoke the git restore command.

Supply the path of the file to be put back.

git restore invitation-card.md

If all goes well, Git will not report anything. The only way to find out is to resort to our good friend, `git status`.

```
File Edit Window Help
$ git status
On branch master
nothing to commit, working tree clean
```

The working directory is clean. Brilliant!

The git restore command is relatively new.

If you get an error like `restore is not a git command`, *be sure to check the version of Git you have installed using the* `git version` *command. You need to have version 2.23.0 or greater.*

The `git restore` command's default behavior, as you can see, is the exact opposite of the `git add` command. The `add` command takes the version of a file that's in the working directory and makes a copy of it in the index, overwriting the previous version. The `restore` command, on the other hand, takes the version of the file stored in the index, and overwrites the version in the *working directory*.

The Git restore command moves the file from the index to the working directory.

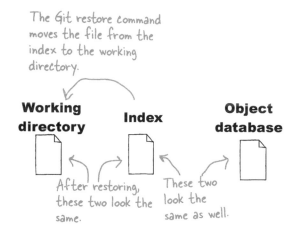

Working directory   **Index**   **Object database**

After restoring, these two look the same.

These two look the same as well.

Git will report an error if you get the filename wrong.

If you make a typo when supplying the name of a file to the `git restore` *command, Git will report* `error: pathspec did not match any file(s) known to git`. *We suggest you use the output of* `git status` *and just copy-paste the names of the files.*

there are no Dumb Questions

Q: Why can't I just use my editor's undo function to fix these kinds of mistakes?

A: You can. But many editors only keep the undo stack as long as you are using the editor. If you were to close your editor at the end of today, you probably wouldn't be able to use your editor to undo your changes tomorrow. And if you switch editors, your new editor will certainly not have the old one's undo stack available.

Git, on the other hand, can detect differences because it stores your changes on disk. This allows you to use Git even if your editor loses its undo stack.

Q: The output of the `git diff` command shows me all the things I have changed. Why not just copy and paste them back in my editor? Wouldn't that have the same effect?

A: You could, but it would be a lot more work—and because it's manual, you run the risk of introducing errors or missing something, especially if you've made a bunch of changes across several files. The `git restore` command uses Git's ability to detect differences between the index and the working directory, so we know that it will find everything. In other words, the `git restore` command ensures that you don't miss a spot.

Q: What if I want to restore changes in multiple files?

A: A great starting point is the output of the `git status` command, since it lists all files that have been modified. The `git restore` command can take one or more file paths, so you can supply them all at the same time, as arguments to the `git restore` command, and undo all those changes in one fell swoop:

```
git restore file-a file-b file-c
```

This will restore `file-a`, `file-b`, and `file-c`. Done!

Exercise

Your turn to try restoring files. Pretend you are Trinity's intern, working at her laptop, and help her fix her issue. Like the last exercise, go to the location where you downloaded the exercises for this book and then open the `chapter04` folder. Inside that you will find the `gitanjali-aref-step-2` folder.

Start with `git status` and `git diff` to be sure you can identify which file was modified, and the difference between the working directory and the staging area.

➤ Your task is to restore the modified files in the repository to the version last committed. List the command you will run here:

➤ Execute the command, then write the output of `git status` here:

➤ Answers on page 203.

Undoing changes in the index

When Trinity fixed her error, she had not yet added the `invitation-card.md` file to the index. But what if she had? How would she go about restoring her changes?

When a file is added to the index, Git makes a copy of the file in the working directory and places it in the index. This is what the state of the working directory would look like for Trinity if she *had* added `invitation-card.md` to the index.

Let the waves of Git knowledge wash over you.

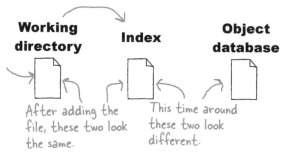

When you add a file to the index, Git puts a copy of the file in the index.

Working directory   **Index**   **Object database**

Trinity modified the invitation-card.md file in the working directory.

After adding the file, these two look the same.

This time around these two look different.

The answer lies in the output of `git status`:

```
File Edit Window Help
$ git status
On branch master
Changes to be committed:        ── Boom! There it is.
  (use "git restore --staged <file>..." to unstage)
      modified:   invitation-card.md
```

Git tells us exactly what to do to fix this. We can use the same `restore` command, except this time we have to give it the `--staged` flag, followed by the filename, like so:

Invoke the restore command.

Supply the --staged flag.

Followed by the name of the file to be restored.

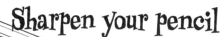

git restore --staged invitation-card.md

Sharpen your pencil

What command would you use to see what has changed in `invitation-card.md`? Feel free to flip back to Chapter 3 if you need a refresher. List that command here:

Answers on page 203.

Undoing changes to the index (continued)

The `git restore` with the `--staged` flag is the command you can use to restore files in the index to their previous state. But what does this command actually do? You know `git restore` (without any flags) replaces the contents of the working directory with the contents held by the index.

When the `git restore` command is supplied with the `--staged` flag, Git takes the content of the file in the object database, specifically the contents as they were *last* recorded in a commit, and overwrites the contents of the file in the index with that content. This is what it looks like:

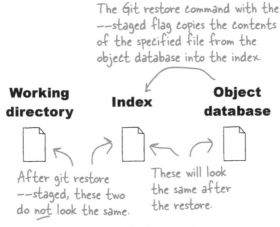

The Git restore command with the `--staged` flag copies the contents of the specified file from the object database into the index.

Working directory   **Index**   **Object database**

After git restore `--staged`, these two do *not* look the same.

These will look the same after the restore.

Earlier we discussed that `git restore` is the opposite of `git add`—the latter copies the contents of a file from the working directory into the index, the former copies from the index into the working directory. You can think of `git restore` with the `--staged` flag as having the opposite effect on your files as the `git commit` command. The `git commit` command, as you know, takes the contents of the index and stores them in the object database. The `git restore` command takes the previously committed contents of a file and overwrites the index with them.

Note: git restore with the `--staged` flag is not undoing the commit! It's simply copying the contents of the file as they were *last* committed into the index.

The git commit command copies the contents of the index into the object database.

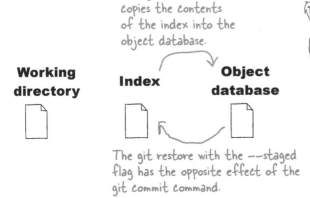

Working directory   **Index**   **Object database**

The git restore with the `--staged` flag has the opposite effect of the git commit command.

Brain Power

Say you have a clean working directory—that is, `git status` tells you `nothing to commit, working tree clean`. You edit a file, then use the `git add` command to add it to the index. But then you change your mind! You use `git restore --staged` to recover the contents of the file from the object database. What will `git status` report?

Sharpen your pencil

Back to work! This time around, you're going to work with the folder named `gitanjali-aref-step-3`, inside the `chapter04` folder. Navigate to that folder and see if you can help Trinity restore a file she accidentally added to the index.

✱ As always, start with `git status` and `git diff --cached` and see if you can spot what changed between the object database and the index.

✱ Next, use what you just learned to recover the contents of the index. List the command you will use here first:

✱ Next, look at the output of `git status`. What do you see? Explain your answer here by describing the state of `invitation-card.md` in terms of the differences between the working directory, index, and the object database.

Working directory	Index	Object database

This represents the invitation-card.md file. → 📄 📄 📄

→ Answers on page 204.

Who Does What?

We had our Git commands all figured out, and then they got all mixed up. Can you help us figure out who does what?

git status   Compares the index and the working directory

git diff   Displays the branches in your repository

git restore --staged Recovers files from the object database into the index

git diff --cached Recovers files from the index into the working directory

git branch   Displays the state of the working directory and the index

git restore   Compares the object database with the index

→ Answers on page 204.

Deleting files from Git repositories

"Huh. Well, that's a first," thought Trinity, as she read Gitanjali's email informing her that the engaged couple have decided not to set up a gift registry for their engagement party. Instead, they want to set up a "home fund" to allow their families and friends to contribute money directly toward their first home.

However, in previous discussions, Gitanjali and Aref did have some ideas for gifts, which Trinity listed in a file called `gift-registry.md` and committed on her `master` branch. Here is the list of files in the `master` branch:

Trinity would rather not have superfluous files in her repository, so she needs to delete the gift registry. But how?

Git has a command for this—`git rm`. Just like the `git restore` command, the `git rm` command takes the paths of one or more *tracked* files and removes them from the working directory *and* the index. To remove the `gift-registry.md`, this is what Trinity would use:

git rm gift-registry.md

And this is the state of Trinity's repository after she runs this command:

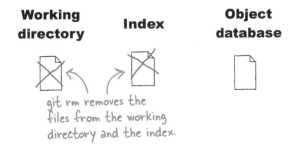

Note that the object database is **not** affected. The question is—what is the status of the repository after we run the `git rm` command?

Committing to delete

What does the `git rm` command really do? Its role is to remove ("rm") tracked files. After running `git rm gift-registry.md`, when Trinity lists the files in her working directory, this is what she sees:

Relax. It's not your turn yet.

```
File Edit Window Help
$ ls
guest-list.md          invitation-card.md
```
↑ gift-registry.md is gone.

As you can see, one effect of the `git rm` command is to delete the file from the working directory. It also removes the file from the index, as `git status` highlights:

Git tells us that you need to commit the deletion of the file. →

```
File Edit Window Help
$ git status
On branch master
Changes to be committed:
  (use "git restore --staged <file>..." to unstage)
        deleted:    gift-registry.md
```
↑ Git informs us that it deleted the file from the index.

The output of the `git status` command is something you haven't seen before. It's telling us that a file was deleted, and that if you are indeed sure that this is what you want, you should commit these changes.

In other words, this commit will record the fact that a previously added and committed file is being deleted! That's different from what you have done so far in this book, where you have always committed new or edited files.

At this point you can choose to make a commit with an appropriate message or use the `restore` command to undo the deletion.

There are two things to note here. First, you can only use the `git rm` command to delete *tracked* files. If you've only added a new file to the working directory (that is, it's an "untracked" file), you can just delete it like you would any other file: by moving it to the Trash (Mac) or the Recycle Bin (Windows).

Second, the `git rm` command only deletes files from the working directory and the index. Versions of the file that were previously committed remain as they were in the object database. This is because a commit represents the changes you made at the time of the commit. If a file existed at the time a commit was made, the commit will remember that for as long as the repository exists.

Read that again! You can use the git restore command to get back a file that you just deleted but haven't committed yet. Super handy if you make a typo in the filename and accidentally remove the wrong file.

This may sound surprising. However, a commit is a snapshot in time. Think of those childhood photos of you with a weird haircut. Just because you are sporting a trendy haircut now doesn't mean that was always the case. And we have pictures to prove it!

there are no
Dumb Questions

Q: **Why can't I just delete files using Finder or File Explorer?**

A: Remember that any changes you make, like adding, editing, or deleting files, only affect the working directory. In order to commit the deletion, you also need to remove the file from the index, because a commit only records changes in the index. If you choose to use the Finder (for Mac) or File Explorer (for Windows) to delete a file, you will then have to run the `git add` command with a special flag, `-u` or `--update`, to tell Git to record the name of the deleted file in the index:

```
git add -u gift-registry.md
```

The `git rm` command, as we have seen, updates the working directory *and* the index for us, saving us from having to run

the `git add` command again. We feel it's far more convenient to use the `git rm` command.

Q: **Why can't I use the `git rm` command to delete untracked files?**

A: Git commands can only be used for files that Git knows about: that is, they can only operate on tracked files. For any file that Git does not know about, you'll have to use your operating system's traditional mechanisms, like Finder or File Explorer, for deleting, renaming, and so on.

Q: **You mentioned that deleting a file does not remove it from the object database. Is there any way I *can* delete files from the object database?**

A: Recall that every commit records everything in the index, along with some metadata (like your name and email address) and the commit message. All this information is used to calculate the commit's ID. Furthermore, this commit ID may be recorded as the parent of one or more child commits. In other words, removing one or more files from a commit involves recalculating that commit's ID, as well as those of any child commits.

Git does offer some advanced mechanisms to do this, but they fall well outside the scope of this book.

Exercise

Answers on page 205.

It's time for you to practice removing tracked files. Navigate to the `gitanjali-aref-step-4` folder inside the `chapter04` directory.

* Start by listing the files in the working directory:

File Edit Window Help

* Use the `git rm` command to remove the `gift-registry.md` file. Be sure to check the status of the repository.
* List the files again in the working directory:

File Edit Window Help

* Finally, commit your changes using the message "delete gift registry".

Serious Coding

When you tell Git to remove a file, it only has to delete the file. However, in order to delete a directory, Git has to remove all the files (or subdirectories) included within the directory you specify. In that case, the `git rm` command has to be supplied the `-r` (for recursive) flag, which gives Git permission to recursively delete all the files in the directory you specify.

Renaming (or moving) files

Let's look at another operation that's closely related to deleting files—renaming or moving files. Git affords you another command—the `git mv` command. The `git mv` command has all of the same characteristics as the `git rm` command—the `git mv` command only works with tracked files, and like the `git rm` command, the `git mv` command renames or moves the files you tell it to in both the working directory and the index. Let's say you have a file called `file-a.md` and you want to rename it to `file-b.md`:

Invoke the mv command.

The name of the file you wish to rename

git mv file-a.md file-b.md

The new name of the file

`git status` will report the file rename:

```
File Edit Window Help
$ git status
On branch master
Changes to be committed:
  (use "git restore --staged <file>..." to unstage)
      renamed:    file-a.md -> file-b.md
```

Git informs us that it has renamed the file.

As with removing files, you can always choose to rename files using the Finder or File Explorer, but you'll still have to update the index to reflect the new filenames. However, like the `git rm` command, the `git mv` command not only updates the working directory for you, it also updates the index to reflect the change—so you're just one step away from committing your changes.

Editing commit messages

The engagement-party planning is in full swing, with Gitanjali and Aref bouncing ideas off Trinity. One thing they feel all their friends will enjoy is spending time in nature, so on their last call they suggested a camping party. The plan is simple—everyone can bring a tent and contribute supplies like food and drinks, cooking supplies, and plasticware. They'll make s'mores over the campfire and celebrate under the stars.

Trinity realizes that this is just one of many ideas that she's going to be working with, so she creates a branch in her repository called `camping-trip`. She creates a new file called `outdoor-supplies.md` to draft a checklist of guests and supplies. She adds the file to the index, then commits it with the commit message "final outdoors plan".

Trinity knows she's messed up as soon as she hits the Return key. Gitanjali and Aref are still coming up with ideas and have yet to iron out all the details. They'll probably ask for changes or even switch plans altogether, so the commit message "final outdoors plan" seems a little premature.

Trinity is nothing if not a stickler for details. She is going to have to edit that commit message.

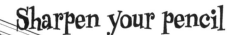

Sharpen your pencil

Let's make sure you understand Trinity's commit history so far. Go ahead and navigate to the `gitanjali-aref-step-5` folder inside the `chapter04` folder.

➤ Start by listing the branches and indicate the branch you are on right now.

➤ Use the skills you acquired in Chapter 3 to sketch out Trinity's commit history. The command to use is `git log --oneline --all --graph`.

Answers on page 205.

Editing commit messages (continued)

It's a good thing Trinity caught the bad commit message as soon as she made it. Git allows for editing commit messages using the `git commit` command, with a special flag called `--amend`.

> Take a sip of your favorite beverage. We'll have an exercise for you soon.

The first thing to check is that you are on the same branch as the commit you wish to edit. The next thing, and this is super important, is that you want to have a **clean working directory**. You can verify both of these with our good friend the `git status` command.

Next, you can amend the last commit on the branch:

```
File Edit  Window Help
```

Invoke the git commit command.

Use the --amend flag.

Supply the new commit message just like you always do.

Git reports the new commit ID just like any other commit.

```
$ git commit --amend -m "initial outdoors plan"
[camping-trip 5e44107] initial outdoors plan
 Date: Sat Mar 13 14:48:54 2021 -0500
 1 file changed, 16 insertions(+)
 create mode 100644 outdoor-supplies.md
```

After this, Git will record a commit replacing the one you had, except this time it will reflect the new commit message. This commit will have all the same changes as the original commit, including all the same metadata, like your name and email and the timestamp (which will also be the same). In other words, the only difference between the previous commit and the amended commit is the commit message.

Watch it!

Be sure to have a clean working directory when amending commits.

When amending commits, you should have a clean working directory. Specifically, you want no uncommitted changes in the index, or else the changes you've staged will be part of the amended commit! That is, you might accidentally add more changes to the commit than you intended to. Make it a practice to always check the `git status` *prior to amending commits.*

But what if you have have already staged changes? The easiest thing to do here is to use the `git restore` *command with the* `--staged` *flag for every file you have in the index, so that Git puts them back in the working directory. Only then should you amend the latest commit.*

there are no
Dumb Questions

Q: **Can I amend any commit in my repository?**

A: No. Git only allows you to amend the latest commit on any branch, which we've referred to as the "tip" of the branch.

Q: **Can I amend a commit more than once, like if I make a typo while amending a commit?**

A: Absolutely. Feel free to amend again and again to your heart's content.

Exercise

Will you help Trinity fix the error in her commit message? Switch to your terminal. Navigate to the `gitanjali-aref-step-5` directory in the `chapter04` folder. Make sure you're on the `camping-trip` branch.

✱ Use the `git commit` command with the `--amend` flag to edit the last commit on the `camping-trip` branch. Change the commit message to be "initial outdoors plan" (instead of "final outdoors plan"). Jot down the first command you are going to use here, then give it a try:

✱ Next, use `git log --oneline --all --graph` to make sure that you can see the amended commit in your history.

✱ Has the commit ID changed? Explain why or why not.

→ Answers on page 206.

> Earlier you said that Git replaces the previous commit. Does that mean the old commit is still hanging out somewhere in my repository?

Aren't you the observant one!

When you ask Git to amend a commit, Git pulls a fast one. It essentially looks at the commit you are appending and **copies** all the changes you made in that commit back into the index. *It leaves the original commit as is.* It then runs `git commit` again, this time with the new commit message, which records the changes put in the index by the commit you are amending.

You see, Git commits are *immutable*. That is, once you create a commit, that version of the commit is preserved. Any edits to the commit (like amending it) will create a new commit that *replaces* the old commit in your history. Think of it as like writing in pen versus pencil: with a pen, you can cross out your mistakes, but you can't erase them. Immutable commits are one of Git's biggest strengths, and a lot of the power in Git comes from this simple idea.

Git copies all the changes recorded in the original commit into the index.

Finally Git records a new commit that has a copy of everything in the index, but with the new message.

Index

This is the commit you are amending.

This is the commit you will see in your Git log from now on. It has all the same metadata as the commit you amended, including the author info, timestamp, and the same parent commit.

This is yet another instance of Git's cautious nature. By keeping old commits around for a while, it gives you even more chances to recover. How you would go about doing that goes beyond the scope of the book. And don't worry about those commits lying around—Git is very good at housekeeping.

This is why you should always check the status of your repository **before** you amend a commit. If by chance you've added files to the index and you proceed to amend a commit, all of the files in the index will show up in the new commit. That is, the new commit will record more changes (both the files you had in the index and the files Git added from the amended commit).

As for the commit you amend? Git keeps it around for a while, but will eventually delete it from your repository.

Renaming branches

Trinity finds herself bemused: Gitanjali and Aref have just informed her that their outdoors engagement party isn't just camping—it's "glamping," short for "glamorous camping." "Glamping" still involves spending time with nature, but with all the comforts of home and then some: electricity, a roof over your head, and some fabulous furniture and decorations.

Trinity is always keen to learn new things, and she wants to get the details right. The branch name "camping-trip" seems incorrect now that she knows about glamping. She's going to have to rename that branch.

There are plenty of reasons you might want to rename branches like Trinity did. Perhaps you don't like the name "master" and you want to use "main" instead. Perhaps you made a typo in the name of your branch. No matter the reason, Git aims to please.

> *Yep, we hate tpyos too!*

In Chapter 2, as you probably recall, you learned that a branch works like a sticky note that records the name of the branch and the ID of the latest commit on that branch. Creating a branch is simply creating a new "sticky note."

Renaming the branch is just as easy. Git simply grabs the "sticky note" that represents the branch and overwrites the name!

To rename a branch, you use the `git branch` command—except this time, you supply the -m (or --move) flag.

Trinity wants to rename `camping-trip` to `glamping-trip`. There are **two ways** she can go about this.

① Switch to the branch you wish to fix, then rename:

The -m flag must follow the branch command. *Or you could use --move.* *Last argument is the new name.*

git branch -m glamping-trip

————— **OR** —————

② Rename a branch without switching:

First argument is the name of the branch you wish to correct. *Last argument is the new name.*

git branch -m camping-trip glamping-trip

> *Most Git commands offer different ways of achieving the same thing. Having a consistent way of always doing something frees up your brain so you can think of more important things in life—like, is it a good idea to smear avocado on fruit? What does it mean to put fruit on fruit?*
>
> *Didn't realize avocado is a fruit, did ya? See what we mean by more important things in life?*

The second option works regardless of what branch you are currently on—the command works even if the branch you are attempting to rename is the current branch. This is why we always prefer using the second option.

Exercise

Why don't you take a few minutes to help Trinity rename the `camping-trip` branch? Navigate to `gitanjali-aref-step-6` inside the `chapter04` folder.

✱ Your first action step is to ensure you are on the `camping-trip` branch. Write the command you will use to list the branches in the repository.

✱ Next, `switch` to the `camping-trip` branch and rename it to `glamping-trip`. Use this space to list the command you are going to use.

✱ Finally, list the branches again:

```
File  Edit  Window  Help


```

✱ Next, you are going to rename `master` to `main`, *without switching to master*. Note the command you are going to use here first:

✱ Just to be sure you got it right, jot down the branches in your repository again.

```
File  Edit  Window  Help


```

→ Answers on page 207.

Making alternative plans

When Trinity plans big events, she likes to have several ideas in her back pocket, just in case something falls through. Gitanjali and Aref are huge board-game fans with a massive collection of games. The second idea they've been throwing around is to celebrate their engagement doing what they love: strategizing, rolling the dice, and bonding with their friends over board games!

To capture this idea, Trinity creates a new branch based on `main`, which she calls `boardgame-night`. She next creates a file called `indoor-party.md` and takes notes about which games are on the list, then commits it. Gitanjali, Aref, and Trinity also discuss potential venues to host the party, which Trinity puts in a file called `boardgame-venues.md`. She adds a note about venue selection to `indoor-party.md` and makes another commit.

Trinity feels good now. Gitanjali and Aref have two strong party ideas—one outdoors event, and one indoors.

Exercise

Why don't you spend a little time looking over Trinity's repository? Start by navigating to the `gitanjali-aref-step-7` folder inside the `chapter04` directory.

✱ List the branches in the repository and note the branch you are on:

```
File Edit Window Help
$
```

✱ Use `git log --oneline --all --graph` to sketch out Trinity's commit history:

Draw the commit history here.

You aren't done yet! Look to the next page.

→ Answers on page 208.

Exercise

Next, look at the changes Trinity made in her latest commit: she added a new file and edited an existing file. Here is the command she runs now:

```
git diff 3e3e847 39107a6
```

And here is the output. Your job is to annotate it. (Remember, she added a new file, and edited another.) We've got you started:

```
diff --git a/boardgame-venues.md b/boardgame-venues.md
new file mode 100644
index 0000000..c3684a0
--- /dev/null
+++ b/boardgame-venues.md
@@ -0,0 +1,6 @@
+# A list of potential game-cafe venues for board-game night
+
+- Winner's Game Cafe
+- Rogues and Rangers Tavern
+- Natural 20 Games & Coffee
+- Bottleship Gaming Bar
diff --git a/indoor-party.md b/indoor-party.md
index 2064ec5..6ca6def 100644
--- a/indoor-party.md
+++ b/indoor-party.md
@@ -16,5 +16,6 @@ Here are just a few of the games we can play:
 * Exploding Kittens


 Feel free to bring your favorite games.
+Venue decision will probably happen at the roll of a 20-sided die!
 And remember, as long as we are together, we're all winners.
```

This tells us that this is a new file being introduced.

We spoke of this in Chapter 3. The /dev/null means Git has nothing to compare this with.

Answers on page 209.

It seems every time I need to find the difference between two commits, it involves running the git log command and copy-pasting commit IDs, which is getting annoying fast. Is there another way to reference commits?

Turns out there is! Its name is HEAD. You've seen HEAD before. In fact, in Chapter 2 we even gave you a rhyme to help you remember what it means. Here it is again:

Make it Stick

Violets are blue
Roses are red
The commit that you're on
Is referred to as *HEAD*.

If you've ever used a smartphone with a map application, then you already know what HEAD is. It's the pin that shows you exactly where you are on the map.

Similarly, if you can visualize your commit history as a series of different timelines (branches), then HEAD marks your current location. Furthermore, HEAD knows about the "stops" you made along the way, also known as commits, so you can use HEAD to reference commits in relation to your current location and even to hop between commits.

HEAD Tells All

An exclusive interview

Head First: Welcome, HEAD! We realize you're super busy out there, what with playing a role in every Git repository, so we're glad you took the time to speak with us.

HEAD: No problem. You're right, I have a lot riding on my shoulders. *Every* Git repository uses me *all* the time. It's kind of a lot to handle!

Head First: That's impressive, given that you're just a reference.

HEAD: Well, sure, but I'm the user's compass as they navigate their commit history. Without me, they would be lost. And hey, I'm so important, I'm in the title of this book!

Head First: Ahem. Moving on, we know you have an especially large role to play when our readers use the git log command. Care to tell us a little bit more about that?

HEAD: You bet. Every time your readers view their Git log, there I am, standing right next to the branch that they're currently on. Here's a picture of me on the red carpet in a recent appearance:

```
97a2899 (HEAD -> boardgame-night)
```

Head First: Looking good there, HEAD! Any other recent appearances that you want to share with us?

HEAD: My talent agent sure has my calendar full. I make a cameo experience every time your readers use the git branch command to list all the branches in their repository.

Head First: Really? How does that work?

HEAD: You know that asterisk that shows up in the branch list? Yeah, that's me! It took me months of training to get into character, but it was totally worth it.

Head First: So that's it? Your role centers around telling our readers where they are in the commit history.

HEAD: That's it? You don't know anything about me, do you? My role isn't just to tell your users where they are in the commit history. Git itself needs me. It can't work correctly without me. Did you know that?

Head First: Wow. You got me.

HEAD: Your readers know that every time you make a commit, the new commit has a reference to the parent commit.

Head First: Sure. That's how the commit history is built over time.

HEAD: How do you think Git knows what the parent commit is?

Head First: Huh. That's interesting.

HEAD: I don't get enough credit for that role. I think that's what will get me the Oscar nomination. You see, when your readers make a new commit, Git looks to me first to see which commit I'm pointing to. It then records *that* commit ID as the parent of the new commit.

Head First: Impressive! That's a pretty important role. Are you proud of the work you're doing there?

HEAD: Absolutely! The commit I am pointing to will always be the parent commit of the next commit in the repository. That's HUGE!

Head First: Well, thank you so much for your time.

HEAD: Wait, I haven't told you about my upcoming role in this superhero—

Head First: We'll have to leave it here. Looking forward to next time. Thanks for joining us, HEAD!

The role of HEAD

Every time you switch branches, HEAD moves to reflect the branch you switched to. Consider a hypothetical commit history. Let's say you are on the master branch, so HEAD points to the latest commit on that branch. When you switch branches, HEAD moves to the new branch:

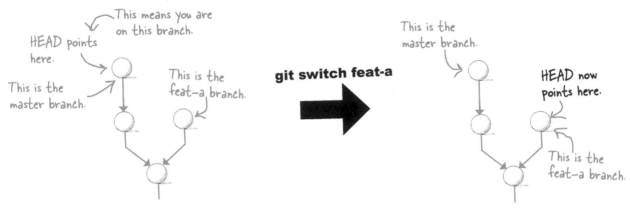

HEAD is simply a reference, like branches are. This difference is that a Git repository can have many branches, but there is only one HEAD. HEAD also serves as the launch point to decide how the commit history will change, in that the commit that HEAD points to **will be** the parent of the next commit—it's how Git knows *where* to add the new commit in the commit history.

Recall that every time you make a commit on a branch, Git rewrites the branch sticky note to point to the new commit on that branch. Well, there is one more thing that happens—Git moves HEAD to the new commit as well.

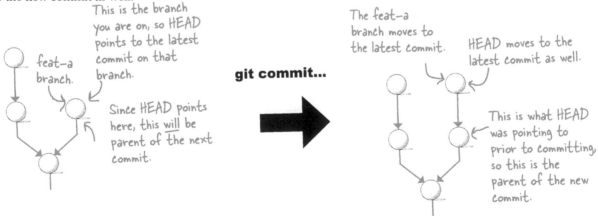

In Chapter 2, we spoke of merging branches. We referred to the branch you are on as the proposer, and the branch that is being merged in as the proposee. Once you merge the two branches, the proposing branch moves to reflect the merge—in the case of a fast-forward merge, the proposing branch moves to the latest commit on the proposee branch. In the case of a merge that creates a merge commit, again, the proposing branch moves to the merge commit that is created. In both cases, HEAD moves as well.

Sharpen your pencil

Why don't you try tracking HEAD? You're going to use the `gitanjali-aref-step-7` folder inside the `chapter04` folder.

➤ Start by using `git log --graph --oneline --all`, and notice where HEAD is. List it here. What does that tell you about which branch you are on right now?

➤ Next, switch to the `glamping-trip` branch, and use `git log --graph --oneline --all` again to see where HEAD is at.

➤ Switch to the `main` branch (remember, you renamed `master` to `main` in an earlier exercise). Repeat the above exercise. Once again, jot down where HEAD is at.

➤ **Super important!** Switch back to the `boardgame-night` branch, and you should be all set for the exercises to come.

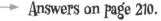 Answers on page 210.

Serious Coding

So far we have described HEAD as pointing to the latest commit on a branch. In reality, HEAD usually points *to a branch*, which as you know, always points to the latest commit on that branch. That is, HEAD is an indirect reference to a commit. This distinction usually doesn't matter since you will almost always be working on a Git branch, so we can assume that both HEAD and the branch sticky note both point to the same commit.

There is a scenario where HEAD points to a commit that isn't the latest commit on a branch, but some arbitrary commit in your commit graph. This is called a "detached HEAD" state. We'll revisit this in future chapters. Don't touch that dial!

Referencing commits using HEAD

Given that HEAD points to the commit you are on, you can reference other commits relative to HEAD. Git offers a special operator, the tilde (~), that allows you to do this. Consider this hypothetical commit history:

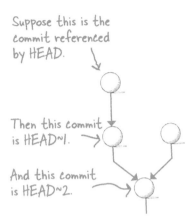

Suppose this is the commit referenced by HEAD.

Then this commit is HEAD~1.

And this commit is HEAD~2.

A number n following the tilde operator represents the nth generational ancestor. For example, HEAD~1 references the first parent of the commit you are on. HEAD~2 means the parent of the parent of the commit you are, and so on and so forth.

So how does this help you? Suppose you want to find the difference between the commit you are on and the previous commit, using the git diff command. Instead of having to look up commit IDs, here is how you would go about doing it:

This is the parent commit.

This represents the current commit.

git diff HEAD~1 HEAD

HEAD~1   HEAD

As a reminder, this means that changes in the parent commit will show up with a "−" (minus) and changes in the current commit will show up as a "+" (plus).

Serious Coding

HEAD~ is an alias for HEAD~1. We prefer to be explicit, but feel free to use one or the other.

Traversing merge commits

Merge commits, as we discussed in Chapter 2, are special. They have more than one parent. So how do you go about navigating from HEAD to the first parent? Or the second parent? Recall that the first parent is the latest commit on the proposing branch, and the second commit is the latest commit from the proposee branch.

Git offers another operator that works with HEAD: the caret (^), which helps when you're navigating from commits with multiple parents. Take a look to see how that works for this hypothetical commit graph:

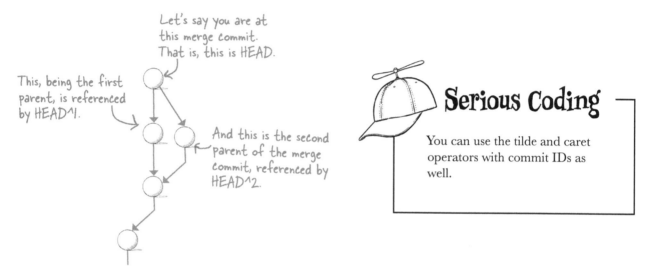

Let's say you are at this merge commit. That is, this is HEAD.

This, being the first parent, is referenced by HEAD^1.

And this is the second parent of the merge commit, referenced by HEAD^2.

Serious Coding

You can use the tilde and caret operators with commit IDs as well.

Like the tilde operator, the caret operator uses a number to figure out which parent of a merge commit you want to reference.

Finally, you can combine the ~ operator and the ^ operator. Here is how HEAD^1~2 would traverse the commit history:

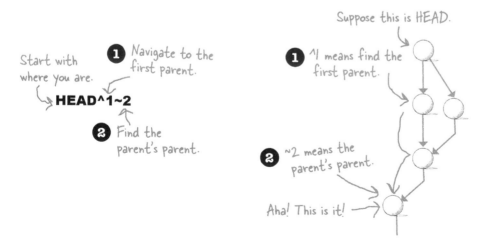

Start with where you are.

HEAD^1~2

1 Navigate to the first parent.

2 Find the parent's parent.

Suppose this is HEAD.

1 ^1 means find the first parent.

2 ~2 means the parent's parent.

Aha! This is it! →

Don't get carried away with lookup patterns.

Using the lookup operators is nifty, but it's easy to get carried away and attempt to reference a commit that does not exist. If you do, Git will report a `fatal: ambiguous argument: unknown revision or path not in the working tree` *error. Our recommendation is to use the lookup operators when the lookup pattern is relatively short. Otherwise, you might be better off just referencing a commit using its ID.*

there are no Dumb Questions

Q: What does HEAD~1 mean for a merge commit?

A: That's a great question. As you know, a merge commit has two parents. If you ask Git to look up `HEAD~1` for a merge commit, which translates to the merge commit's parent, Git will follow the path of the first parent. Essentially, `HEAD~1` for a merge commit is the same as `HEAD^1`.

Q: All the operators you told me about only navigate back through the commit history. Is there any way to go forward?

A: No. Remember that commits point to their parents. However, commits have no idea how many children they have. The two operators we spoke of, namely ~ and ^, are simply following the parent pointer recorded in the commits themselves.

Q: Would you suggest I always be explicit and use commit IDs, or always use the operators? Is one better than the other?

A: The operators you just learned about are simply a different way to reference a commit, so feel free to use whichever is easier. We routinely use the `HEAD~1` operator with the `git diff` command, but again, use whichever is more convenient for you. Our recommendation—if the pattern you are using looks complicated, it's complicated—just use commit IDs.

Sharpen your pencil

Take a little time to practice your newly acquired commit history navigation skills. Here is a hypothetical commit history. We have marked the commits with letters for IDs.

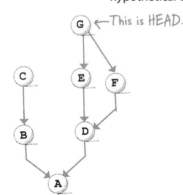

←This is HEAD.

Your job is to identify which commit is being referenced.

HEAD~1 ___E___

HEAD~3 _____

HEAD^1 _____

HEAD^2~1 _____

HEAD^2 _____

HEAD^1~2 _____

→ Answers on page 211.

Undoing commits

Turns out, all the scouting Trinity did to find a place to host board-game night was in vain. Gitanjali and Aref have decided it will be much easier to host the party at their home. This way, if the party goes on late into the night, the guests won't have to drive back home—they can just crash there for the night.

Unfortunately, Trinity has already committed the `boardgame-venues.md` file (with options for venues) in her repository. She also hinted at a possible venue selection coming soon in the `indoor-party.md` file she created for board-game night. Here is Trinity's commit history:

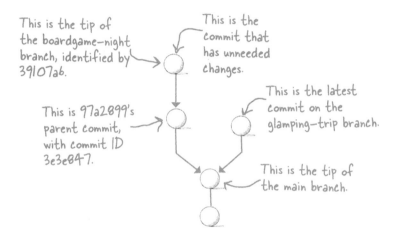

This is the tip of the boardgame-night branch, identified by 39107a6.

This is the commit that has unneeded changes.

This is 97a2099's parent commit, with commit ID 3e3e847.

This is the latest commit on the glamping-trip branch.

This is the tip of the main branch.

As you can see, Trinity has a commit on the `boardgame-night` branch that is no longer needed. And now she has to figure out how to get rid of it.

Brain Power

So far in this book, you have used the `git diff` command to see the differences between two commits. You also know how to remove a file from the repository using the `git rm` command. Can you think of how you would go about resolving Trinity's dilemma by getting rid of her unneeded commit? What would your commit history look like if you managed to pull this off?

Removing commits with reset

How does Trinity undo a commit? She has two options. The first option is to simply move the board-game branch back one commit. If she could do this, all her problems would be gone. Essentially, after moving the branch back, her commit graph would look like this:

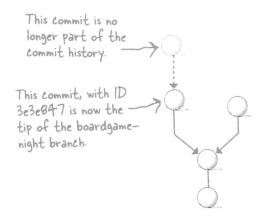

This commit is no longer part of the commit history.

This commit, with ID 3e3e847 is now the tip of the boardgame-night branch.

In other words, you want to move HEAD to HEAD~1. The command that allows you to do this is the git reset. You can supply git reset with a reference to a commit, either a commit ID or using one of the operators we spoke of, namely tilde (~) or caret (^).

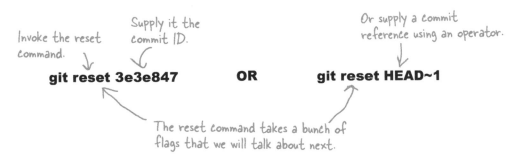

Invoke the reset command.

Supply it the commit ID.

Or supply a commit reference using an operator.

git reset 3e3e847   **OR**   **git reset HEAD~1**

The reset command takes a bunch of flags that we will talk about next.

The git reset command has two immediate effects—it moves the HEAD *and* the branch to the commit you specify. But every commit that you make in a repository records a set of changes—you might have added or removed files, or edited existing files, or both. So what happens to those changes?

Well, that's the million-dollar question, isn't it?

The three types of reset

Git has three distinct places where changes can live—the working directory, the index, and the object database. Therefore, the `git reset` command offers three options to undo a commit, each option doing different things with regards to the changes that you are undoing and how it affects each of the three areas of Git.

Bear in mind that the one thing the `git reset` command *always* does is to move the HEAD *and* the branch to the commit you specify. The only question we are aiming to answer is, what happens to the changes you had committed? Let's say your repository had two commits—a commit with ID B, and its parent A.

This is the commit you want to undo.

git reset --soft

The `git reset` command can be given the `--soft` flag. This flag takes the edits you committed and **moves** them back into the index, and then from the index it copies those changes into the working directory.

In other words, the edits you had committed (in commit B) are gone from the object database. It's like you never made the commit to begin with! But because they are in the index, you're just one `git commit` command away from committing them back. Those changes are still available to you—in the index and the working directory. HEAD now points to commit A.

Git <u>moves</u> the changes from commit B into the index <u>and</u> the working directory.

Supply the --soft flag to reset.

git reset --soft A

OR

git reset --soft B~1

That is, index and working directory look identical.

Working directory

Index

Object database

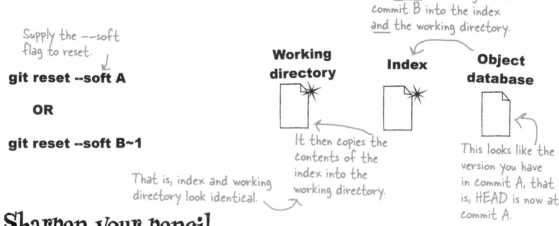

It then copies the contents of the index into the working directory.

This looks like the version you have in commit A, that is, HEAD is now at commit A.

Sharpen your pencil

Suppose you had a clean working directory before you ran `git reset --soft A`. What would `git status` report?

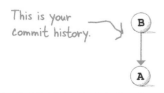

This is your commit history.

Hint: Think back to Chapter 3. What is the difference between the working directory and the index, and the index and the object database?

Answer on page 211.

Using git reset (or git reset --mixed)

The `git reset` command's default mode is `--mixed`, so you can invoke `git reset` or `git reset --mixed` with the same results. This is how to use it:

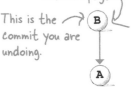

We're showing this diagram again so you don't have to flip back and forth between pages.

This is the commit you are undoing.

git reset A   **OR**   **git reset --mixed A**

The `--mixed` mode does a bit more work than the `--soft` mode does. It has two steps:

1 First, it moves the changes in commit B (the commit you are undoing) into the index, and then copies those changes from the index into the working directory, **just like --soft mode does**.

2 It then **copies** the contents of **commit A** into the index. That is, the index now looks exactly like the commit you just reset to.

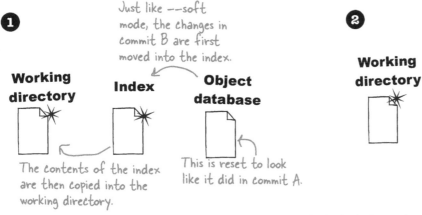

1

Just like --soft mode, the changes in commit B are first moved into the index.

Working directory   **Index**   **Object database**

The contents of the index are then copied into the working directory.

This is reset to look like it did in commit A.

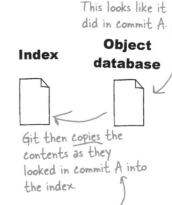

2

This looks like it did in commit A.

Working directory   **Index**   **Object database**

Git then copies the contents as they looked in commit A into the index.

That is, HEAD points to A and the index looks like HEAD.

Contrasting the soft and mixed behavior: `--soft` mode leaves both the index and the working directory changed. But `--mixed` mode only leaves the working directory changed. With mixed mode, the changes you committed in "B" reside only in the working directory—the index looks like the changes in commit "A.".

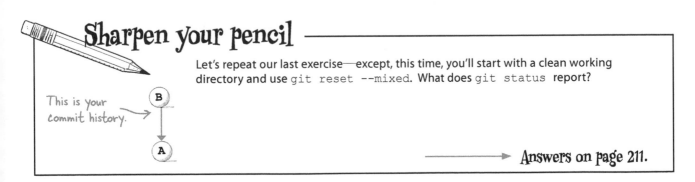

Sharpen your pencil

Let's repeat our last exercise—except, this time, you'll start with a clean working directory and use `git reset --mixed`. What does `git status` report?

This is your commit history.

B
↓
A

Answers on page 211.

git reset --hard

Finally, the third flag that reset offers is --hard. Remember, the intent is to undo the changes in a commit. --soft mode moves the changes in the commit you are undoing and puts them in both the index and the working directory. --mixed mode on the other hand puts the changes in the commit you are undoing ("B") into the working directory, but the index and the object database look like the commit you reset to ("A"). Effectively, --mixed mode takes the changes you had in the commit that you just undid, and makes them appear in the working directory.

Finally, the --hard mode takes what the --mixed mode does to its logical end. In mixed mode, the second step copies the contents commited in "A" into the index, and stops there. --hard mode does not. It takes the contents of the index (which have the changes as they are in commit A) and overwrites the working directory. This means that the object database, the index, and the working directory all look the same. It's as if commit B never happened! After a hard reset, the working directory, the index, and HEAD all look like commit "A."

We know, we are really nice. Save you a page flip.

This is the commit you are undoing.

B

A

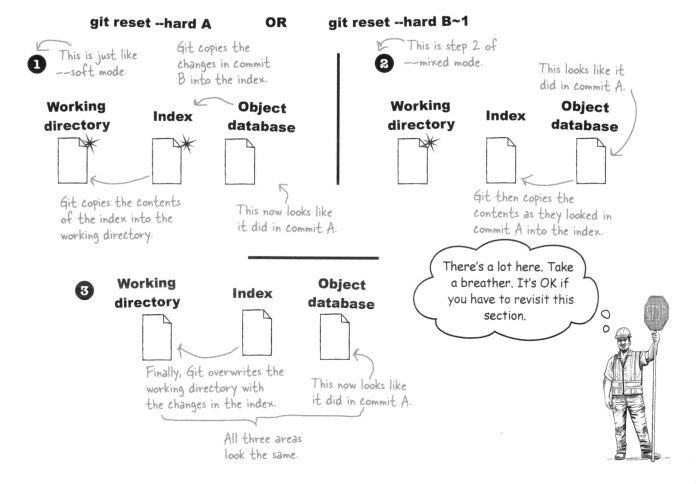

git reset --hard A   OR   **git reset --hard B~1**

① This is just like --soft mode.

Git copies the changes in commit B into the index.

Working directory   **Index**   **Object database**

Git copies the contents of the index into the working directory.

This now looks like it did in commit A.

② This is step 2 of --mixed mode.

This looks like it did in commit A.

Working directory   **Index**   **Object database**

Git then copies the contents as they looked in commit A into the index.

③ **Working directory**   **Index**   **Object database**

Finally, Git overwrites the working directory with the changes in the index.

This now looks like it did in commit A.

All three areas look the same.

There's a lot here. Take a breather. It's OK if you have to revisit this section.

Q: **This all seems really confusing. Can you distill it down for me?**

A: We understand. Remember, the intent of the `git reset` command is to undo a commit. The only question is—what do you want to do with the changes you made in that commit? If you want them to appear in the index (so they appear as "Changes to be committed"), use `--soft`. If you want them to appear in the working directory (as "Changes not staged for commit"), use `--mixed`. If you don't want to see them at all, use `--hard`.

Q: **You mentioned that the reset command can take a commit reference. So can I reset to any commit, instead of just the parent commit?**

A: Yes, you can. For example, if you invoke `git reset HEAD~3`, you are asking that Git take you back three commits. Git will then collect the changes you made in all three commits (that you are undoing), and depending on the mode you specify (`--soft`, `--mixed`, or `--reset`), Git will place those changes in the index, working directory, or throw them away.

But baby steps, right? Let's take it one step at a time.

Q: **How is using `git reset --mixed` different than `git restore` with the `--staged` flag? They both copy the content of the object database into the index, right?**

A: First, the `git restore` command works at the file level, that is, it only works with one file at a time. The `git reset` command works at the commit level, effectively undoing all the changes committed. This might be more than one file that you potentially added, edited, or modified in the commit you are undoing.

Second, the `git restore` command with the `--staged` flag takes the contents of the file you specify as they were last committed, and copies that into the index, effectively making the file in the index look exactly like it did since you last committed. It does not, however, move the HEAD—the `git restore` command does **not** modify your commit history.

In contrast, while `git reset --mixed` does copy all of the files as they were last committed and move them into the index, it also moves the HEAD to the commit you specify. When you use the `git reset` command, you're rewriting history by erasing history!

Q: **Can I reset a merge commit?**

A: Yes, you can. But remember, a merge commit has two parents. And the `git reset` command needs to know which commit to reset HEAD and the corresponding branch to. So, if you are going to reset a merge commit to one of its parents, you will need to supply which parent you wish to reset to using the caret (^) operator.

Using git reset with the --hard flag is destructive!

*Take a look at the previous section, and you'll notice that `--soft` and the default mode, `--mixed`, do **not** throw away the changes from the commit that was undone. On the other hand, the `--hard` option does throw them away. So be very careful with the `--hard` flag. We highly recommend using the default mode (`--mixed`) most of the time. You're better off reviewing the changes manually, and then, if you are absolutely sure you no longer need those changes, you're a `git restore` away from a clean working directory.*

Also: if you search for "How do I undo a commit in Git?" in your favorite search engine, you'll find a lot of results that recommend the `--hard` option. You've been warned!

Exercise

Take a few minutes and help Trinity undo her latest commit on the `boardgame-night` branch. Navigate to the `gitanjali-aref-step-7` folder inside the chapter04 directory. You should be on the `boardgame-night` branch. Switch to it if you need to.

Here is Trinity's commit history:

This is the boardgame-night branch.

HEAD points here.

This is the commit, with ID 3910726, that you are going to undo. Remember, it adds a new file called boardgame-venues.md and edits the indoor-party.md file.

This is the glamping-trip branch.

This is the parent commit, with ID 3e3e847.

This is the main branch.

✱ You're going to undo the latest commit on the `boardgame-night` branch using Git operators: specifically, the tilde (~) operator and `--mixed` mode. List the `git reset` command you will use here:

✱ Run `git status`, then explain what you see:

✱ Restore `indoor-party.md` to undo any edits, and delete the `boardgame-venues.md` file. Run `git status` to make sure you've cleaned everything up.

✱ Finally, run `git log --graph --oneline --all` again, and make sure that HEAD points to the commit with ID 3e3e847.

⟶ Answers on page 212.

Congratulations, you time traveler, you!

Seriously. You just traveled through time. It's been quite a journey, but for the first time, you've used Git's time-traveling abilities. The `git reset` command sets the state of the working directory and the index to one that you had recorded in a previous commit! That is, the `git reset` command rewrites your history! Remember, with great power comes great responsibility. We will talk of the potential pitfalls with this approach in future chapters, but for now, sit back and bask in your newfound powers.

Another way to undo commits

When we started talking about undoing commits, we mentioned that Trinity has two options. The first approach is using the `git reset` command.

However, Git offers us another approach, but before we get to that, let's take a minute to talk about what a commit is. A commit records a set of changes—you might have edited a bunch of files, maybe added or deleted a few. You'll see these changes if you use the `git diff` command to compare a commit with, say, its parent. They appear as a set of pluses ("+") and minuses ("-"). This is referred to as the "delta," or the variation between two commits.

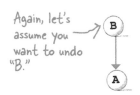

Again, let's assume you want to undo "B."

Another approach to undoing a commit is as simple as negating a commit—for every file added, you could delete it, and vice versa. For every line in every file that was added, you delete it, and for every line that was deleted, bring it back.

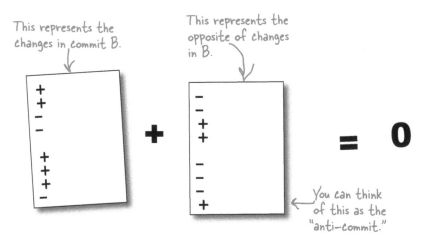

This represents the changes in commit B.

This represents the opposite of changes in B.

You can think of this as the "anti-commit."

Given that Git can calculate the differences introduced by a commit, it can also calculate the reverse of the differences, or if you like, the "anti-commit." And you can use this to "undo" a commit.

If it helps, think of matter and anti-matter coming in contact with each other. End result: complete annihilation!

Reverting commits

You can create "anti-commits" by using the `git revert` command. The revert command, like the `reset` command, can be given a commit ID or a reference to a commit. There is a big difference, though—the `git revert` command is to be given the ID or reference of the commit you want to undo. Consider our hypothetical repository again—let's say you want to undo commit B. This is how you would use the git revert command:

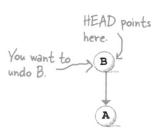

HEAD points here.

You want to undo B.

The argument identifies the commit you wish to undo.

Invoke the revert command.

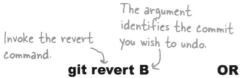

git revert B   **OR**   **git revert HEAD**

This is super convenient if you want to undo the latest commit.

Notice that for revert you supply the ID of the commit <u>you want to undo</u>, as opposed to reset where you supply the commit ID of the <u>commit to reset to!</u>

Git looks at the changes introduced in B and calculates the anti-commit. This is an actual commit that Git will prepare. Now just like any other commit, this commit needs a commit message. So Git will use your preconfigured editor and bring it up, prompting you to supply a message for the newly created commit:

We have seen this before, in Chapter 2: when we merge two branches, that results in an merge commit. Recall that Git brings up your editor and prompts you for a commit message.

This is VS Code.

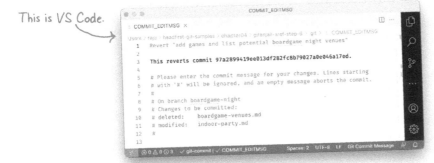

We usually prefer to keep the message as is. Once you close the editor, Git will confirm creating a new commit. So what is the effect of a revert? This is what your commit history will look like after a revert:

HEAD now points here.

This is the commit you are undoing.

This is the new anti-commit: that is, the opposite of the changes introduced in B.

Like the `git reset` command, the `git revert` command moves the HEAD and the branch, except in this case, you are not erasing commits. Rather, you are adding new commits. However, both commands allow you to "undo" commits.

Tonight's talk: **The RESET and REVERT commands answer the question: "Who's the better undoer?"**

The RESET command:

Look, I have incredible powers. I mean, come on: I have the ability to erase history! I am absolutely what everyone should be using to undo bad commits.

The REVERT command:

Yeah, but you're so negative. Going back in time? Really? I'm a glass-half-full kind of person—I let folks undo their mistakes by *adding* to their commit history. This keeps their commit history intact. Not to mention I'm a lot easier for people to wrap their heads around.

So two wrongs make a right, huh? No way! I allow for a clean commit history. If you've mistakenly committed some work, why would you want a constant reminder?

Sure. But you *are* more complicated to use. There's the "soft" mode, and then there's the "mixed" mode. Not to mention "hard" mode, which is destructive. People can lose their changes if they accidentally run you in hard mode!

It's called flexibility! I give the people what they want— choices. What do you do? Create a commit that's the exact opposite of the commit to be undone. Pfft! Our readers could do that manually. So what good are you?

Undoing commits by hand can involve hundreds of files or changes. It's so tedious, not to mention error-prone. I automate that away. Isn't that what computers are for?

Fine. Whatever.

I'm just going say one last thing, so listen up: once our readers learn how to use Git as a collaboration tool, they won't need you. Maybe you should consider another line of work.

Ha! We'll see about that.

We will be revisiting this topic in Chapter 5. Stay tuned!

Sharpen your pencil

Your next task is to help Trinity fix her latest commit again, except this time you are going to use the `git revert` command. Navigate to the `gitanjali-aref-step-8` folder in the `chapter04` directory to get started.

This repository has the same history as your previous exercise. Here it is again:

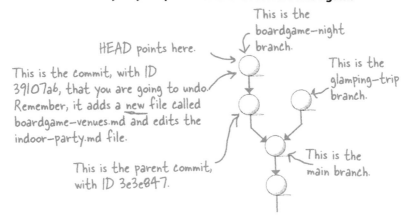

➤ You are going to revert `HEAD`. Start by listing the command you are going to use here:

➤ Next, execute the command. (Keep an eye out: your editor should pop up.) Leave the message as it is and close the editor.

➤ Run `git log --graph --oneline --all`, and explain what you see:

➤ How is this different from your previous attempt in `gitanjali-aref-step-7`?

—————▶ Answers on page 213.

Aaaaand that's a wrap!

Trinity is so excited for Gitanjali and Aref—all the effort that she put into planning their party paid off. Everyone had a wonderful time celebrating their engagement. She wishes them the very best in their life together.

Trinity's commit history looks clean: just the way she likes it. She still has some cleanup to do, so she merges the `boardgame-night` branch into the `master` branch. She also deletes the unmerged `glamping-trip` branch. Planning the ← glamping trip was indeed a lot of work, but hey! As long as her clients are happy, Trinity's happy.

We talked about cleaning up your branches (merged and unmerged) in Chapter 2.

Not to mention, Gitanjali now wants Trinity to plan the wedding, too! She wants something really exotic. (The South Pole has been mentioned once or twice—Trinity may have to talk her out of that one. Or not!) Oh well. Time to create another repository.

As for you, well done! It was quite a journey learning how to undo your work in Git. Just remember: Git, for the most part, is not destructive when you undo. In other words, you can undo an undo if you need to, so breathe easy.

Bullet Points

- Git offers you several ways to undo your changes.

- The `git restore` command allows you to undo changes to one or more files—both in the working directory and the index. You can supply `git restore` with a list of file paths.

- The `git restore` command, by default, undoes changes in the working directory by replacing them with the version of the file that was last added to the index.

- To undo changes to files that have been already added to the index, you can also use the `git restore` command. However, you will need to supply it with the `--staged` flag.

- The `git restore --staged` command will replace the contents of the files in the index with the version that was last committed.

- You can delete files that you previously committed to Git with the `git rm` command.

- The `git rm` command, like the `git restore` command, takes a list of file paths. It then removes the files from the working directory and the index.

- You are still required to make a commit to record the fact that you deleted one or more files. That is, removing files is a two-step process—`git rm` removes the files from the working directory and the index, and the subsequent commit records the deletion.

- You can edit commit messages with the `git commit` command along with the `--amend` flag.

- You should only amend the tips of branches.

- When you amend a commit, you are not actually changing a commit. Git records a new commit with the new commit message and replaces the previous commit in your commit history. Git will eventually delete the older commit.

- Git allows you to rename branches by using the `git branch` command with the `-m` (or `--move`) flag.

- The commit you are on is referred to as HEAD. HEAD is a reference to a commit.

- HEAD is how Git knows which branch you are on; it's a lot like the pin in a map that shows your location. HEAD is updated every time you switch or merge branches.

- The commit that HEAD points to **will be** the parent of the next commit in the repository.

- Git offers two operators to reference ancestor commits relative to HEAD. You have the tilde (~) operator to reference parents of the current commit. HEAD~2, for example, takes you back two generations: it represents the grandparent of the current commit.

  You can use the caret (^) operator to reference the parents of a merge commit. HEAD^1 points to the first parent, and HEAD^2 points to the second.

- The tilde and caret operators make it easier to supply commits to commands like `git diff`, saving you from having to copy-paste commit IDs.

- Git offers two different ways to undo commits. The `git reset` command moves the HEAD and the branch "sticky note" to a different commit.

  The `git reset` command has three different modes—`soft`, `mixed`, and `hard`. Each one has a different effect on the changes that were recorded in the commit that was undone.

- Be warned! The `git reset` command in "hard" mode is destructive: if you use it, you will lose your changes. **So don't use it.**

- `git reset` allows you to "time travel," in effect, because it moves you to a previous commit.

- Another way to undo a commit is with the `git revert` command, which creates an "anti-commit"—a commit that introduces a set of changes that are the exact opposite of the commit that you wish to undo.

Undo Crossword

Here's a bonus tip for undoing your errors: solve this crossword using a pencil.

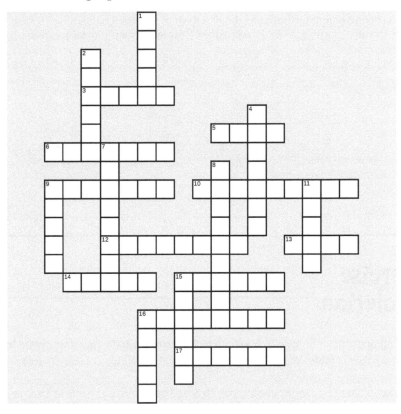

Across

3 Git reset modes include soft, ___, and hard

5 The -m flag is short for this

6 Command to compare the index's contents with the working directory (2 words)

9 The git ___ command replaces the version of the file in the working directory with the version in the index

10 She's getting married to Aref

12 Character that appears in the git branch output to tell you where HEAD is

13 This chapter is all about ___-ing your mistakes

14 Before you edit a commit, make sure your working directory is ___

15 Flag used with the git restore command to retrieve the last contents of your files as they were in the last commit

16 Fancier version of camping

17 The -u flag to the git add command is short for this

Down

1 Character used with HEAD to reference a commit's parent

2 The git ___ command copies the contents of the index into the object database

4 It's a fruit!

7 Deleting a file won't remove it from the object ____

8 A piece of metadata that tells you when the commit was made

9 The git ___ command moves HEAD and a branch to a specific commit

11 Flag that lets you fix a mistake in a commit message

15 Use the git ___ command to check the state of your Git repository

16 The ___ ___ command removes tracked files from the working directory and the index (2 words)

Answers on page 214.

Sharpen your pencil
Solution

Trinity has made two commits in her repository. The first commit added two files, `guest-list.md` and `gift-registry.md`, and the second commit introduced the first draft of the `invitation-card.md` file. Without peeking, list all the files in the `gitanjali-aref` repository. How many files in total are in this repository? Explain your answer.

Three. Commits build on the commits that came before them. Since the first commit introduced two files, and the second commit added another, you end up with three files.

This is the second commit, which added the invitation-card.md file, so you end up with three files.

The first commit introduced two files—guest-list.md and gift-registry.md.

From page 161.

Exercise
Solution

Time to use the skills you acquired in Chapter 3. Navigate to the location where you downloaded the source code for this book, and in the `chapter04` folder you will find a directory called `gitanjali-aref-step-1`.

Using our favorite version of the `git log` command (which would be `git log --oneline --all --graph`), investigate Trinity's repository and identify the commit IDs of each of her commits, along with the commit message she supplied when she created each commit. Here is her commit history again. Annotate away!

This is the second commit with ID 8d704f8, and message "first cut at invitation card".

This is the first commit with ID 6e16680, and message "initial set of guests and gift registry".

From page 161.

Exercise Solution

Your turn to try restoring files. Pretend you are Trinity's intern, working at her laptop, and help her fix her issue. Like the last exercise, go to the location where you downloaded the exercises for this book and then open the `chapter04` folder. Inside that you will find the `gitanjali-aref-step-2` folder.

Start with `git status` and `git diff` to be sure you can identify which file was modified, and the difference between the working directory and the staging area.

✱   Your task is to restore the modified files in the repository to the version last committed. List the command you will run here:

Invoke the restore command.

Supply the path of the file to restore.

`git restore invitation-card.md`

✱   Execute the command, then list the output of `git status` here:

On branch master

nothing to commit, working tree clean

Perfect! You have a clean working directory.

From page 165.

Sharpen your pencil Solution

From page 166.

What command would you use to see what has changed in `invitation-card.md`? Feel free to flip back to Chapter 3 if you need a refresher. List that command here:

git diff --cached

We mentioned this in Chapter 3, but you can also use the --staged flag here.

Sharpen your pencil
Solution

From page 168.

Back to work! This time around, you're going to work with the folder named `gitanjali-aref-step-3`, inside the `chapter04` folder. Navigate to that folder and see if you can help Trinity restore a file she accidentally added to the index.

➤ As always, start with `git status` and `git diff --cached` and see if you can spot what changed between the object database and the index.

➤ Next, use what you just learned to recover the contents of the index. List the command you will use here first:
git restore --staged invitation-card.md

➤ Next, look at the output of `git status`. What do you see? Explain your answer here by describing the state of `invitation-card.md` in terms of the differences between the working directory, index, and the object database.

git restore with the --staged flag copies invitation-card.md as it was last committed to the index.

Working directory   **Index**   **Object database**

This represents the invitation-card.md file.

After restoring, these two no longer look the same.

Who Does What?
Solution

From page 168.

We had our Git commands all figured out, and then they got all mixed up. Can you help us figure out who does what?

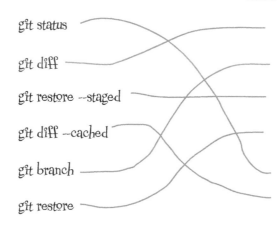

git status — Compares the index and the working directory

git diff — Displays the branches in your repository

git restore --staged — Recovers files from the object database into the index

git diff --cached — Recovers files from the index into the working directory

git branch — Displays the state of the working directory and the index

git restore — Compares the object database with the index

Exercise Solution

From page 171.

It's time for you to practice removing tracked files. Navigate to the `gitanjali-aref-step-4` folder inside the `chapter04` directory.

✱ Start by listing the files in the working directory:

> File Edit Window Help
>
> **gift-registry.md   guest-list.md   invitation-card.md**
>
> ↖ *There it is.*

✱ Use the `git rm` command to remove the `gift-registry.md` file. Be sure to check the status of the repository.
✱ List the files again in the working directory:

At this point gift-registry.md was removed from the working directory and the index. →

> File Edit Window Help
>
> **guest-list.md   invitation-card.md**

✱ Finally, commit your changes using the message "delete gift registry".

Sharpen your pencil Solution

From page 173.

Let's make sure you understand Trinity's commit history so far. Go ahead and navigate to the `gitanjali-aref-step-5` folder inside the `chapter04` folder.

➤ Start by listing the branches and indicate the branch you are on right now.

    * camping-trip ⟵ *You are on the camping-trip branch.*
    master

➤ Use the skills you acquired in Chapter 3 to sketch out Trinity's commit history. The command to use is `git log --oneline --all --graph`.

This is the latest commit on the camping-trip branch, identified by efa799d. → ◯

This is the last commit on the master branch, with ID 8d704f8. ◯

This is the very first commit, with ID be1b680. ⟵ ◯

Exercise Solution

From page 175.

Will you help Trinity fix the error in her commit message? Switch to your terminal. Navigate to the `gitanjali-aref-step-5` directory in the `chapter04` folder. Make sure you're on the `camping-trip` branch.

✱ Use the `git commit` command with the `--amend` flag to edit the last commit on the `camping-trip` branch. Change the commit message to be "initial outdoors plan" (instead of "final outdoors plan"). Jot down the first command you are going to use here, then give it a try:

git commit --amend —m "initial outdoors plan"

✱ Next, use `git log --oneline --all --graph` to make sure that you can see the amended commit in your history.

This is the modified commit. It now has a new ID, cf5e718, with the commit message "initial outdoors plan".

Remember, your commit ID will be different than ours.

These two commits remain unaffected.

✱ Has the commit ID changed? Explain why or why not.

When you amend a commit, Git creates a new commit. This commit records the same changes as the one you are amending. It also has the same metadata—the author name and email, as well as the timestamp. However, the commit message is different, which, along with everything else, is something Git uses to calculate the commit ID. New message, therefore new commit ID.

Exercise Solution

From page 178.

Why don't you take a few minutes to help Trinity rename the `camping-trip` branch? Navigate to `gitanjali-aref-step-6` inside the `chapter04` folder.

✱ Your first action step is to ensure you are on the `camping-trip` branch. Write the command you will use to list the branches in the repository.

> git branch

✱ Next, `switch` to the `camping-trip` branch and rename it to `glamping-trip`. Use this space to list the command you are going to use.

> git branch —m "glamping-trip"   *You are renaming the current branch here.*

✱ Finally, list the branches again:

```
File Edit Window Help
* glamping-trip    ← That's correct.
  master
```

✱ Next, you are going to rename `master` to `main`, *without switching to master*. Note the command you are going to use here first:

You can use —m or --move here.   *"move" the master to main.*

> git branch —m master main

✱ Just to be sure you got it right, jot down the branches in your repository again.

```
File Edit Window Help
* glamping-trip
  main    ← Yep! It worked!
```

Exercise Solution

From page 179.

Why don't you spend a little time looking over Trinity's repository? Start by navigating to the `gitanjali-aref-step-7` folder inside the `chapter04` directory.

✱ List the branches in the repository, and note the branch you are on:

```
File Edit Window Help
$ * boardgame-night
  glamping-trip
  main
```

✱ Use `git log --oneline --all --graph` to sketch out Trinity's commit history:

This is the latest commit on the boardgame-night branch, with ID 39107ab.

This is the only commit on the glamping-trip branch, identified by cf5e718.

This is 39107ab's parent, with ID 3e3e847.

This is the last commit on the master branch, with ID 8d704f8.

Initial commit with ID be16680.

You aren't done yet! Look to the next page.

Exercise Solution

From page 180.

Next, look at the changes Trinity made in her latest commit: she added a new file and edited an existing file. Here is the command she runs now:

```
git diff 3e3e847 39107a6
```

And here is the output. Your job is to annotate it. (Remember, she added a new file, and edited another.) We've got you started:

```
diff --git a/boardgame-venues.md b/boardgame-venues.md
new file mode 100644
index 0000000..c3684a0
--- /dev/null
+++ b/boardgame-venues.md
@@ -0,0 +1,6 @@
+# A list of potential game-cafe venues for board-game night
+
+- Winner's Game Cafe
+- Rogues and Rangers Tavern
+- Natural 20 Games & Coffee
+- Bottleship Gaming Bar
diff --git a/indoor-party.md b/indoor-party.md
index 2064ec5..6ca6def 100644
--- a/indoor-party.md
+++ b/indoor-party.md
@@ -16,5 +16,6 @@ Here are just a few of the games we can play:
 * Exploding Kittens

Feel free to bring your favorite games.
+Venue decision will probably happen at the roll of a 20-sided die!
And remember, as long as we are together, we're all winners.
```

You are comparing the version of boardgame-venues.md in commit ID 3e3e847 with the changes in commit ID 39107a6.

boardgame-venues.md is a new file.

Here is the beginning of another hunk.

"a" are the changes in commit 3e3e847. "b" are in commit 39107a6, prefixed with "+".

This is showing the differences in the indoor-party.md file.

This line was added in commit 39107a6.

Sharpen your pencil
Solution

Why don't you try tracking HEAD? You're going to use the `gitanjali-aref-step-7` folder inside the `chapter04` folder.

➤ Start by using `git log --graph --oneline --all`, and notice where HEAD is. List it here. What does that tell you about which branch you are on right now?

> I see this: "HEAD -> boardgame-night," which tells me that I am on the boardgame-night branch. The output of the git branch command can be used to verify this.

➤ Next, switch to the `glamping-trip` branch, and use `git log --graph --oneline --all` again to see where HEAD is at.

> This time I see "HEAD -> glamping-trip," which tells me I am on the glamping-trip branch now.

➤ Switch to the `main` branch (remember, you renamed `master` to `main` in an earlier exercise). Repeat the above exercise. Once again, jot down where HEAD is at.

> Now I see "HEAD -> main", which means I am on the main branch.

➤ **Super important!** Switch back to the `boardgame-night` branch, and you should be all set for the exercises to come.

From page 184.

Sharpen your pencil
Solution

Take a little time to practice your newly acquired commit history navigation skills. Here is a hypothetical commit history. We have marked the commits with letters for IDs.

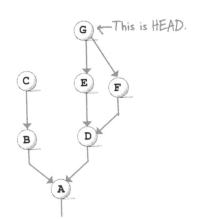

←This is HEAD.

Your job is to identify which commit is being referenced.

HEAD~1 *E (immediate parent)*

HEAD~3 *A (parent's parent's parent)*

HEAD^1 *E (G is a merge commit, so this is its first parent)*

HEAD^2~1 *D (G's second parent's parent)*

HEAD^2 *F (G's second parent)*

HEAD^1~2 *A (G's first parent's parent's parent)*

From page 187.

Sharpen your pencil
Solution

Suppose you had a clean working directory before you ran `git reset --soft A`. What would `git status` report?

This is your commit history. →

B
↓
A

In the "soft" mode, the git reset command takes the changes that were committed in commit B and copies them into the index and the working directory. At this point the index and the working directory look identical. So there is no difference between the working directory and the index, but there is a difference between the index and the object database. So git status will report that there are changes that need to be committed.

From page 190.

Sharpen your pencil
Solution

Let's repeat our last exercise—except, this time, you start with a clean working directory and use `git reset --mixed`. What does git status report?

This is your commit history. →

B
↓
A

This time around, Git first takes the changes committed in B into the index, and then into the working directory (just like soft mode). But it then copies the changes in A into the index. Which means the object database and the index look the same. However, the index and the working directory do NOT look the same (working directory has changes that were in B, and index looks like A). So Git will ask you to stage your changes.

From page 191.

Exercise Solution

From page 194.

Take a few minutes and help Trinity undo her latest commit on the boardgame-night branch. Navigate to the gitanjali-aref-step-7 folder inside the chapter04 directory. You should be on the boardgame-night branch. Switch to it if you need to.

Here is Trinity's commit history:

HEAD points here.

This is the boardgame-night branch.

This is the commit, with ID 39107a6, that you are going to undo. Remember, it adds a new file called boardgame-venues.md and edits the indoor-party.md file.

This is the glamping-trip branch.

This is the parent commit, with ID 3e3e847.

This is the main branch.

➤ You're going to undo the latest commit on the boardgame-night branch using Git operators: specifically, the tilde (~) operator and --mixed mode. List the git reset command you will use here:

> git reset --mixed HEAD~1   OR   git reset HEAD~1

The default mode is --mixed.

➤ Run git status, then explain what you see:

> Git reset in mixed mode only affects the working directory. Commit (ID 39107a6) introduced a new file, called boardgame-venues.md, AND modified the indoor-party.md file. So after the reset, boardgame-venues.md shows up as an "untracked file" (new file) and indoor-party.md shows up as modified. It's like you had never made the commit to begin with.

➤ Restore indoor-party.md to undo any edits, and delete the boardgame-venues.md file. Run git status to make sure you've cleaned everything up.

> 1. Delete the boardgame-venues.md file using Finder or File Explorer.
>
> 2. git restore indoor-party.md

➤ Finally, run git log --graph --oneline --all again, and make sure that HEAD points to the commit with ID 3e3e847.

Sharpen your pencil
Solution

From page 198.

Your next task is to help Trinity fix her latest commit again, except this time you are going to use the `git revert` command. Navigate to the `gitanjali-aref-step-8` folder in the `chapter04` directory to get started.

This repository has the same history as your previous exercise. Here it is again:

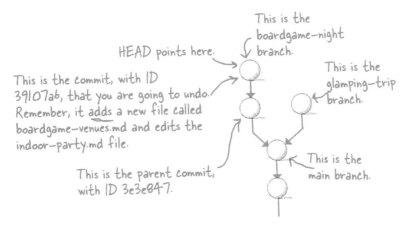

➤ You are going to revert `HEAD`. Start by listing the command you are going to use here:

> git revert HEAD

➤ Next, execute the command. (Keep an eye out: your editor should pop up.) Leave the message as it is and close the editor.

➤ Run `git log --graph --oneline --all`, and explain what you see:

> I see a new commit, which is a child of the commit with ID 39107ab, with the commit message 'Revert "add games and list potential boardgame night venues"'.

➤ How is this different from your previous attempt in `gitanjali-aref-step-7`?

> When you reset the commit, the commit with ID 39107ab is no longer in the commit history. It's like it never happened. When you revert, commit ID 39107ab is still in the graph, but its effects are negated with the new commit that the revert command created.

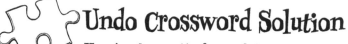

Undo Crossword Solution

Here's a bonus tip for undoing your errors: solve this crossword using a pencil.

From page 201.

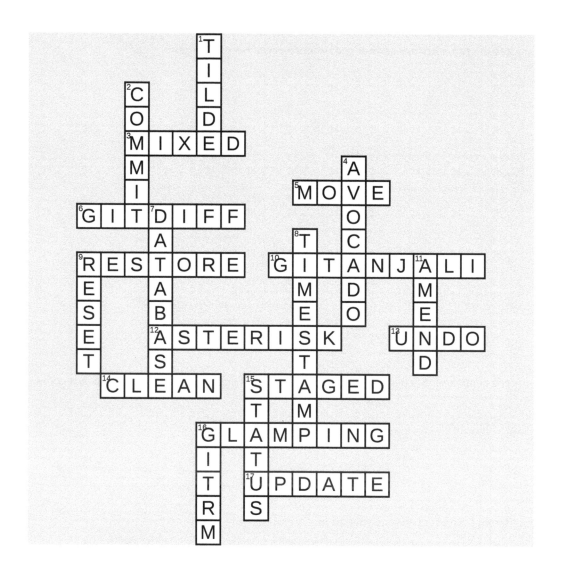

5 collaborating with Git - part I

Remote Work

I've got it now! We are so in sync.

Working by yourself can get dull quickly. So far in this book, we have learned a lot about how Git works, *and* how to work with Git repositories. The repositories we used are ones that we initialized locally using the `git init` command. Despite that, we've managed to get a lot done—we created branches, merged them, and used Git utilities like the `git log` and `git diff` commands to see how our repository evolved over time. But most projects aren't like that. We often work in teams or with friends or colleagues. Git offers a very powerful collaboration model—one in which we can all share our work using a single repository. It all starts by making our repository "publicly available," which makes the commit history of the project a "shared" history. In a public repository we can do everything we've learned so far, just as we've always done (with a few exceptions). We can create branches and commits and add to the commit history, and so can others; everyone can see and add to that history. That's how we collaborate with Git.

But before we start collaborating, let's spend some time together to understand how public repositories work and how to get started with them. Go team!

Another way to a Git repository: cloning

In Chapter 1 we talked about the `git init` command, which converts a folder on your computer into a Git repository. Git offers you another way to create a repository locally: you can use one that was created elsewhere.

How would such a situation come about? Imagine your friend is working on an open source project and asks for your help. They can create a Git repository and share it with you. Now the two of you can work on it together.

Think of the millions of open source projects out there (some of which you've probably used!). Most, if not all, rely on the work of dozens of collaborators. You might decide to help out one such project by fixing a bug or adding a much-needed feature. But to do that, you're going to need the code. How can you get it?

Git is a powerful collaboration tool, connecting people from all walks of life, dissolving political and cultural boundaries, and allowing people to come together and bring their ideas to life.

You'll use another Git command: `clone`. As the name suggests, the `git clone` command allows you to create a copy (a "clone") of an existing repository. The clone command expects to get a special URL as its argument:

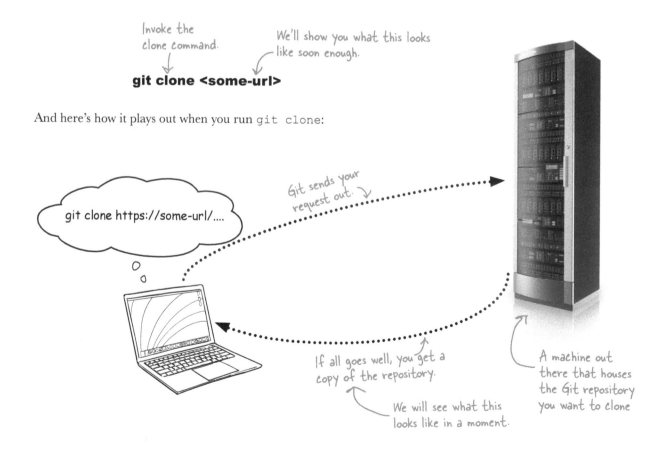

Invoke the clone command.

We'll show you what this looks like soon enough.

git clone <some-url>

And here's how it plays out when you run `git clone`:

git clone https://some-url/....

Git sends your request out.

If all goes well, you get a copy of the repository.

We will see what this looks like in a moment.

A machine out there that houses the Git repository you want to clone

Hosting a Git repository

When you clone a repository, you are asking Git to make a copy of a repository that already exists elsewhere. So what does "elsewhere" mean? That would be any other computer that you can access—that is, a computer that you can connect to over a network, like the internet, and that you have permissions to clone repositories from.

Where can you host Git repositories? There are plenty of options. You *could* set up a personal server, but that's a lot of work: you'd have to find a place to run it and learn about Git administration. The easiest option is to use a service that allows you to host a Git repository with minimal fuss. (Yes, we are all about that!)

Perhaps you've heard of GitHub, owned by Microsoft. Or GitLab. Or Bitbucket, owned by Atlassian. All of these services allow you to host repositories and make it easy to get started. All you need is a login. For the purposes of this book, we decided to show you GitHub—but for the most part, everything you learn about GitHub will work with similar sites out there, albeit with minor variations. GitHub offers a generous free plan for personal projects, so you won't need to worry about pricing.

We mentioned that you are going to need a GitHub login in the book introduction. If you haven't done so, head back there and follow the instructions. We'll wait right here.

We are listing three—but there are lots of other options out there.

These are often referred to as "repository managers."

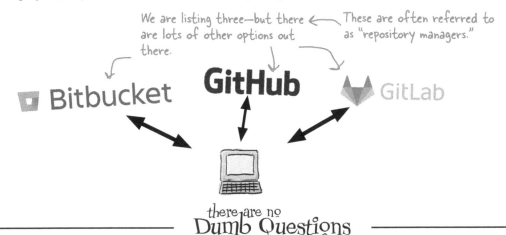

there are no Dumb Questions

Q: My company uses GitHub as a collaboration tool, so I already have a login. Do I need to create another login?

A: We are big fans of separating business from pleasure. (Go ahead, admit it—reading this book has been a real pleasure!) If you're using your company email to log into GitHub, we suggest you create an account with your personal email address.

Q: I would rather run my own server than use a third-party service. Change my mind.

A: Hosting a Git repository isn't just about setting up a server! You'll also need to set up a way to serve up the Git repository over the network, potentially protect it behind an authentication mechanism, and manage the server over its lifetime. It's a commitment!

Our objective in picking GitHub is just to show you how to use Git as a collaboration tool, so we are going to keep it simple. One thing at a time, right?

Setting up: forking repositories (a sidebar)

We realize that this seems a tad jarring—weren't we just talking about cloning? We'll clarify in a minute—just bear with us while we get you set up for this chapter.

Before you get started, you are going to need to do a little bit of setup. Head to this URL in your browser: *https://github.com/looselytyped/working-with-remotes*. At the top right-hand corner, you should see a "Fork" button.

Be sure to follow along here.

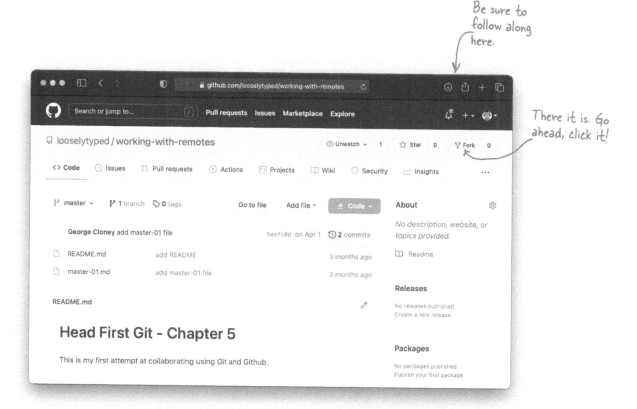

There it is. Go ahead, click it!

When you click that button, GitHub will prompt you to log in, if you haven't already. It will then copy the repository we set up under *your account* in GitHub.

Pay close attention to the address bar in your browser after this completes. It will change to https://github.com/your_account_name/working-with-remotes. (Might wanna bookmark that.)

So what just happened? The repository *we* created is under our account, which means that while *you* can see it, you can't modify it. *Forking* is a **GitHub feature** that makes it easy to copy our repository (or any other publicly available repository) to your account.

Not to beat a dead horse, but there is no such feature as "forking" in Git itself. Forking is a feature GitHub offers to make it easier to collaborate.

Cloning? Forking? This is a lot. My head hurts. I'm not sure what just happened here. Why we are even talking about this?

We can empathize. We will start by saying that forking isn't a Git feature: it is a *GitHub* feature. So why did we just make you do the last exercise? This book is about Git, not GitHub, right?

Think about how you've worked the exercises for Chapters 1 to 4: you downloaded a zip file with all of the exercises. That is, you got a *copy* of the exercises we created for you, available locally on your hard drive. This allowed you to play with them to your heart's delight.

For this chapter, we've done something a little different. We created a Git repository for you—it's called `working-with-remotes`. We uploaded it to GitHub, but it lives under *our* account. In order to modify our repository (or any other repository you don't own), the owner would need to give you explicit permissions to do so. In GitHub, this means you would have to send us your GitHub login so we could add you as a "collaborator" on our repository.

Now, as much as we love you (and you know we do), we are hoping that we will have thousands of readers. Not only would adding each and every one of you become tedious, but you would all end up stepping on each other's toes as you made changes.

Forking a repository simply gives you your *own copy* of that repository, under your own account, so you can play with it, again, to your heart's delight. It's a lot like how you downloaded our repository for the other chapters, except this time you're downloading to your GitHub account instead of your hard drive.

So how do you get it onto your hard drive? You *clone* it.

---

there are no
Dumb Questions

Q: **Can I clone a repository without forking? If so, what does that mean?**

A: Absolutely. You could visit github.com right now, peruse any one of the millions of repositories available, and clone any one of them.

However, if you wanted to collaborate on that project, you'd have to ask the owner of that repository for permissions. Throughout this chapter you are going to be making changes to the `working-with-remotes` repository. By forking it, you get a copy of our repository under your account in GitHub, and you can do with that whatever you like without us granting any additional permissions. Certainly makes things easier all around.

Ready, set, clone!

You are now set up for the next few exercises. If you navigate to your account in GitHub, you should see the `working-with-remotes` repository. GitHub gives you an easy way to clone this repository and put a copy on your local machine. First, you need that special URL we mentioned, which you'll supply to the `git clone` command.

Sit back and just soak it in. You will have a chance to do this on your own soon enough.

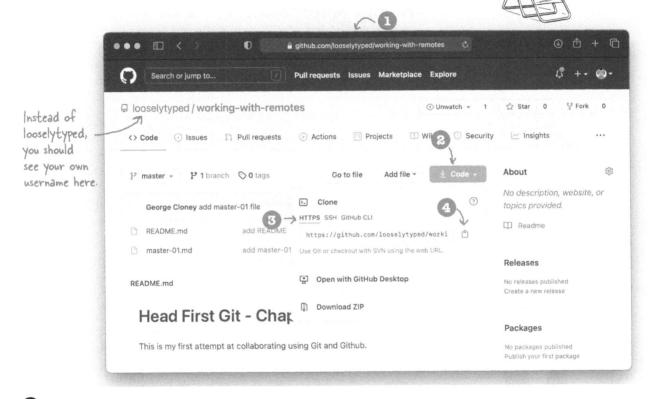

Instead of looselytyped, you should see your own username here.

1 **Make sure your username is in the URL.**
Notice that our URL has `looselytyped` in it, which happens to be our username. Yours will have *your* GitHub username in it.

2 **Click on the green "Code" button.**
This will reveal a pop-up with three tabs—`HTTPS`, `SSH`, and `GitHub CLI`.

3 **Make sure you select the HTTPS tab.**
The URL underneath will switch to something that starts with `https` and ends with `.git`.

4 **Copy the URL that is revealed.**
You can click on the icon next to the URL to copy the URL to your clipboard.

Unless you have a clipboard manager, be sure not to copy anything else after this, or you will lose the URL and have to do this all over again.

Ready, set, clone! (continued)

You now have the URL that the `git clone` command needs. Let's look closely at it for a moment.

Nothing for you to do here. Exercise coming up soon, though.

This tells you that you are using a secure protocol over HTTP.

This is the host.

This is the username on GitHub. Remember, yours will be different.

This is the name of the repository.

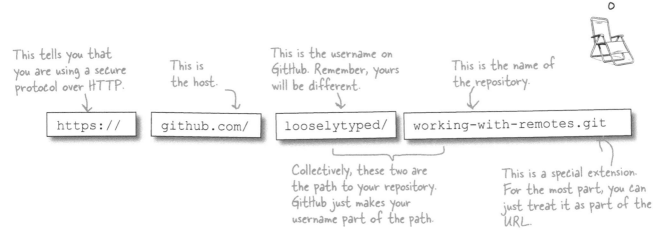

```
https://      github.com/      looselytyped/      working-with-remotes.git
```

Collectively, these two are the path to your repository. GitHub just makes your username part of the path.

This is a special extension. For the most part, you can just treat it as part of the URL.

You can supply this to the `git clone` command, and it will copy the repository from your account in GitHub. We cloned this repository inside a folder called `chapter05`. Here's how that looks:

```
File  Edit  Window  Help
$ pwd
/Users/raju/headfirst-git-samples/chapter05
                    ⮤ Make sure we are in        When you do this exercise, remember
                      the right directory.        this will be your username.
$ git clone https://github.com/looselytyped/working-with-remotes.git
Cloning into 'working-with-remotes'...
remote: Enumerating objects: 10, done.
remote: Counting objects: 100% (10/10), done.
remote: Compressing objects: 100% (7/7), done.
remote: Total 10 (delta 0), reused 10 (delta 0), pack-reused 0
Receiving objects: 100% (10/10), done.

$ ls
working-with-remotes  ← Woot! There it is.
```

Invoke the git clone command.

Git reports doing a bunch of work.

Notice that, by default, Git creates a folder with the same name as the repository you are cloning, then proceeds to create the repository inside that folder.

There you go: now you know another way to get a Git repository on your workstation.

Exercise

By now you should have forked our repository to your account. Now's your chance to clone it. Using your browser, log into GitHub and go to the `working-with-remotes` repository. To make things easier, here is the URL:

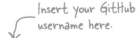

Insert your GitHub username here.

https://github.com/your-GitHub-username/working-with-remotes

✱ Follow the instructions from a few pages ago to find the clone URL.

✱ List the command you are going to use to clone your repository here:

✱ Using a terminal, go to the location where you have downloaded the other exercises for this book and clone the `working-with-remotes` repository. (Just so you know, we prefer to create a folder called `chapter05` first, and then clone the repository inside the `chapter05` folder. It just keeps things organized.)

✱ Spend a few minutes looking around the repository. List the files in your working directory here:

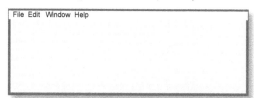

File Edit Window Help

✱ Next, list all the branches. Take a note of where your HEAD is:

File Edit Window Help

✱ Use `git log --graph --oneline --all` to inspect the commit history. Sketch out your commit history graph here.

Answers on page 261.

---

there are no
Dumb Questions

Q: **You made us fork the repository first, *then* clone it. Is this a usual workflow?**

A: That depends. For a project at work, you will most likely be made a collaborator on that project, which automatically gives you permissions to modify the repository. This means you wouldn't have to fork the repository—you could simply clone it and start collaborating with your colleagues.

However, if you want to play around with or contribute to an open source project, you'll most likely need to fork the project. This makes it easier for the people managing the open source project, because they don't have to explicitly add you as a collaborator.

Q: **You pointed out that the `git clone` command, by default, creates a folder with the same name as the repository I'm cloning. What if I want to change the name? Can I do that?**

A: Sure! That's just the default behavior. The name of the folder Git creates really has nothing to do with the clone operation. To change the name of the folder, you can supply the name you want as a second argument to the clone command:

```
git clone <url> name-of-folder-to-be-
created
```

Alternatively, you can rename the folder after cloning—it's just the name of the directory. All the information Git needs is safely tucked inside the hidden `.git` folder. However, we usually prefer to keep the name of the directory the same as the repository we are cloning, unless it collides with something we already have, like an existing folder with the same name that happens to be in the same directory.

It's just another Git repository

The `working-with-remotes` repository that you cloned from GitHub and that resides on your hard drive isn't any different from any other repository you've seen so far. Everything you've learned to do in this book, every Git command you've learned, you can use in this repository—as you saw in the last exercise.

Full disclosure—there is one teeny-tiny difference, which we will explain soon.

> I'm just a regular old Git repository, folks. Move along, nothing special to see here.

Serious Coding

You've probably noticed that our remote URL starts with `https`, which stands for Hypertext Transfer Protocol Secure. Git supports various other protocols to communicate with the server, like SSH, which stands for Secure Shell. However, SSH is a bit involved since it requires you to set up your public and private SSH keys, and upload keys to GitHub. If you haven't worked with SSH before, be sure to look up GitHub's documentation on how you can use it.

What happens when you clone?

If you wish to clone a repository, your starting point is always another repository, which is referred to as the **remote**. And much like any repository you've worked with so far, the repository you clone consists of commits, branches, HEAD, commit history, and anything else a repository can have in it.

When you clone such a repository, Git does a few things:

1 Git first creates a folder in the directory where you ran the git clone command; the folder will have the same name as the repository you are cloning (unless you specify a different name). Inside that, it creates a .git folder.

2 It then copies the entire commit graph, including all commits, branches, and a few other things, from the repository you are cloning into the .git folder it just created.

3 Finally, it uses the git switch branch to check out the same branch that was checked out in the original (the one you are cloning from).

This would be the same commit as HEAD points to.

You know from Chapter 2 that when Git switches branches, it rewrites the working directory to look exactly like it did when you made the last commit on that branch.

master branch

HEAD

Start here

git clone

This is called the remote.

Git creates the necessary folders.

This is the .git folder.

Git pulls down the commit history in the .git folder.

master branch

HEAD

Finally, Git switches to the branch that HEAD points to in the remote.

I understand that I have a clone of the remote available locally. But are they connected somehow? If I make a change to my local copy, will it show up in the remote?

Brilliant question! The remote repository and the local copy are completely independent of one another (although the local copy knows *where* it was cloned from). You can make any number of changes to your local copy, and the remote would be completely unaware of those changes.

Think about it this way—suppose you create a funny meme using one of the many meme generator sites online and share it on your favorite social media site. You probably don't know how many people see it (hopefully more than a few), but everyone who sees it knows it came from you. In this scenario, you are the "remote"— lots of folks saw ("cloned") your meme and they know it came from you.

When you clone a repository, the remote repository does not know you cloned it. However, your local copy knows about the remote repository that it "originated" from. This is how clones differ from the other repositories you've created so far in this book, in that your local repositories don't have a "remote" counterpart. (More about this in a bit.)

Let's take the analogy a bit further—your friends might decide to share your funny meme to their followers. Those followers will consider your friends the "origin" of that meme, right?

Similarly, you could share your fork, or even your local repository, with other users, and the repositories cloned from your copy would treat your copy as *their* remote.

All this stems from a particular characteristic of Git: it's a distributed version control system.

Git is distributed

Git belongs to a family of version control systems that are referred to as "distributed." In a distributed system, everyone who clones a repository gets a full copy of the repository. Every commit, every branch—we mean *everything*. So, if you have a full copy of the original, what differentiates your copy from the original?

Nothing.

Others who can access your copy can now treat it as the original, or "source of truth." In other words, everyone who clones a repository is equal. The first benefit of this is that if something were to happen to the original remote, everyone could switch to using another clone as their remote and continue working.

If you've ever used or heard of Subversion or CVS—these are examples of centralized version control systems.

The original source goes away.

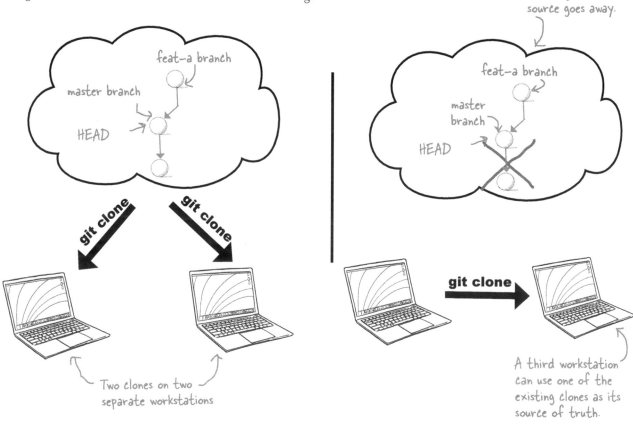

Two clones on two separate workstations

A third workstation can use one of the existing clones as its source of truth.

There is another huge benefit to this model: your local copy is completely disconnected from the remote. You can perform pretty much any operation—branch, commit, merge, view the commit history using the `git log` command, and see differences using the `git diff` command—all of it locally, without the remote knowing about it. There is **no server communication** going on while you get your work done locally. This means you can still work even if you aren't connected to the internet (like on a plane).

You can try this right now! Disconnect your laptop from the internet and try viewing your commit log.

there are no Dumb Questions

Q: Git is distributed. I get that. So why use a service like GitHub or GitLab?

A: First and foremost, GitHub keeps things easy. It offers a very convenient way to host a Git repository, with facilities like authentication built in. These services make operationalizing a Git server easy.

They also offer high availability. If you were to host a Git repository on, say, your laptop, it might be unavailable if you turned off your computer on vacation, or if your machine has a catastrophic failure.

What's more, these services are easy to find (you just navigate to GitHub.com or GitLab.com using your browser) and easy to access (you just need to have a login). They also make it easy for the repository owner to add collaborators, using their email or login ID.

Finally, if you are going to collaborate with your colleagues on projects, you all need to decide what the "source of truth" is going to be: the place where everyone's work comes together. All these benefits make picking a service like GitHub an easy choice.

All that said, there isn't anything stopping you from running your own hosting solution. Everything we discuss in this book will work no matter which route you take.

Exercise

Let's get you warmed up for the upcoming sections. Your task is to make a couple of changes to the repository you cloned. Time to fire up your terminal.

✳ Start by navigating to the location where you cloned the `working-with-remotes` repository.

✳ Check to make sure you are on the `master` branch, and that the status of the working directory is clean. List the commands you are to use here:

✳ Open the `master-01.md` file in your text editor and add a second line, so that the file looks like this after your edit:

You are going to add the <u>second</u> line. →

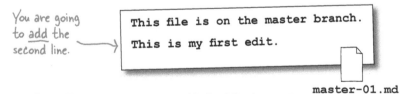

```
This file is on the master branch.
This is my first edit.
```

`master-01.md`

✳ Add another file, called `master-02.md`, with the following contents:

This is a new file that <u>you</u> are to create. →

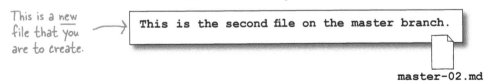

```
This is the second file on the master branch.
```

`master-02.md`

✳ Finally, add both files to the index. Make a commit with the message "my first commit on master".

← Whitespace for your notes

➤ **Answers on page 262.**

OK. So I've made some changes locally to my repository. Something tells me that if the git clone command copies the remote's commit history to my local workstation, there must <u>be</u> a way for me to push my changes up to the remote. Right?

You just answered your own question.

The answer lies in a Git command called `git push`. It allows you to take any new commits that you've created in your local repository, and push them to the remote. In other words, the `git push` command allows you to synchronize your local changes with the remote.

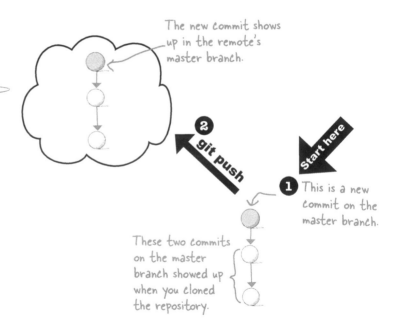

The new commit shows up in the remote's master branch.

git push ②

Start here

① This is a new commit on the master branch.

These two commits on the master branch showed up when you cloned the repository.

Just to be clear, you'll need to have connectivity to the remote for this to work. You can't perform a push while being disconnected.

It's easier to think of a remote repository as just another copy of your commit history, with the caveat that any changes you make to your local copy *eventually* need to be synchronized with the remote. The push command allows you to do just that.

Think of it as a remote backup!

Another bit of Git configuration

Before we get to pushing our changes to the remote repository, we need to run through just a bit of configuration. So far, your `working-with-remotes` repository has only one branch, which showed up when you cloned the repository the first time around. Now, when you push, Git will attempt to update the `master` branch in the remote with any changes that you've made to your local `master` branch. That is, Git will update the remote `master` branch to look like your local `master` branch.

But what if you've created a new branch in the meantime? If you decided to push the changes in the new branch, where would those changes go? To the `master` branch? Should Git create a new branch in the remote with the same name as the local branch, and then update it to reflect your local changes? Or should it just error out?

For now, we are going to keep it simple and just tell Git to error out if it doesn't know what to do. Once you get more comfortable with Git and working with remotes, you can choose a different behavior for Git.

We'll make these configuration changes in much the same way you made changes to Git in Chapters 1 and 2. You are going to be using your terminal for this. Here is what you have to do:

Fire up your terminal
and follow along here.

This affects the global Git
configuration, so you don't have
to be in any particular directory.

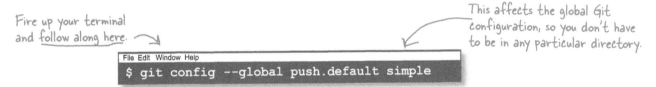

```
File  Edit  Window  Help
$ git config --global push.default simple
```

Git does not confirm that this actually did anything, but you can verify whether your changes did indeed stick by asking Git:

Git will respond with
the value for push.
default, which we
just set to "simple."

```
File  Edit  Window  Help
$ git config push.default

simple                    ← Let's ask Git.
```

Painless, right? Now we're all set, so let's see what it takes to push our changes to the remote.

Serious Coding

The "simple" push configuration is often referred to as the "seat belt" option, in that it's the safest choice of all the options that Git allows when it comes to configuring how `git push` will behave (there are four other options, in case you're curious).

Also, Git defaults to the simple push configuration for new installations. So why did we make you do this exercise? Well, first, we wanted to show you how to do it. Second, in the rare chance that you had this configuration set to a different value, this setup ensures that we're all on the same page. Better safe than sorry.

Pushing changes

All this business about Git being distributed is fine and dandy, but at the end of the day, you want to do your work, make some commits on a branch, and push your changes to the remote. That way, if someone were to clone that repository, they would clone everything, including the commits you just made and pushed to the remote. So how do you go about doing that? We've already spoken of the `git push` command, so let's see it in practice.

Let's say you've just made a commit on the `master` branch and you want to push it up to the remote. You would use the `git push` command. However, since GitHub needs to make sure you have the right access to write (there's a mouthful, huh?) to the repository, it will prompt you to log in:

You know it! Nothing for you to do here but sip your favorite beverage.

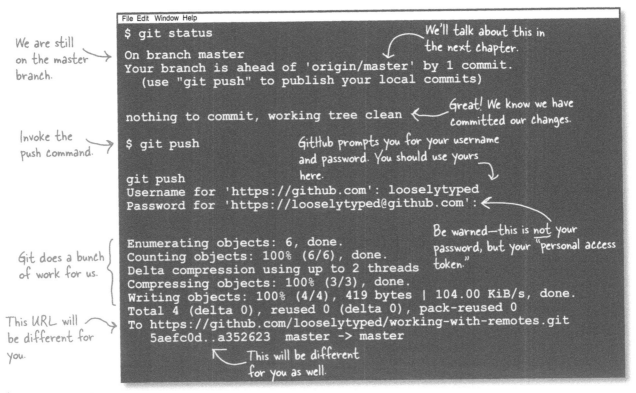

We are still on the master branch.

Invoke the push command.

Git does a bunch of work for us.

This URL will be different for you.

```
File Edit Window Help
$ git status

On branch master
Your branch is ahead of 'origin/master' by 1 commit.
  (use "git push" to publish your local commits)

nothing to commit, working tree clean

$ git push

git push
Username for 'https://github.com': looselytyped
Password for 'https://looselytyped@github.com':

Enumerating objects: 6, done.
Counting objects: 100% (6/6), done.
Delta compression using up to 2 threads
Compressing objects: 100% (3/3), done.
Writing objects: 100% (4/4), 419 bytes | 104.00 KiB/s, done.
Total 4 (delta 0), reused 0 (delta 0), pack-reused 0
To https://github.com/looselytyped/working-with-remotes.git
   5aefc0d..a352623  master -> master
```

We'll talk about this in the next chapter.

Great! We know we have committed our changes.

GitHub prompts you for your username and password. You should use yours here.

Be warned—this is not your password, but your "personal access token."

This will be different for you as well.

As you can see, GitHub prompts for the username and password here. Be sure to use your own username here. It is a tad confusing because although it says "password," what it's really asking for is your "personal access token." We told you how to set this up in the introduction of this book, but if you've somehow misplaced your token, you can always generate another one using the "Personal access tokens" panel under your profile in GitHub. Also, when you enter your token, you don't actually see what you type (for security reasons), which *can* be a little unnerving. Be sure to get it right!

Git then does a bunch of work to send your commits to the remote, and if all goes well, you won't see any errors. That's a good sign. But can you confirm if it *really* worked? Let's find out.

Verifying if the push worked

Pushing your changes takes the changes you made locally and sends them over to the remote. So how do you know if it worked?

For starters, if Git does not report an error in the console, then you know all went well. Another way to check is to take a look at the remote, which in this case is GitHub.

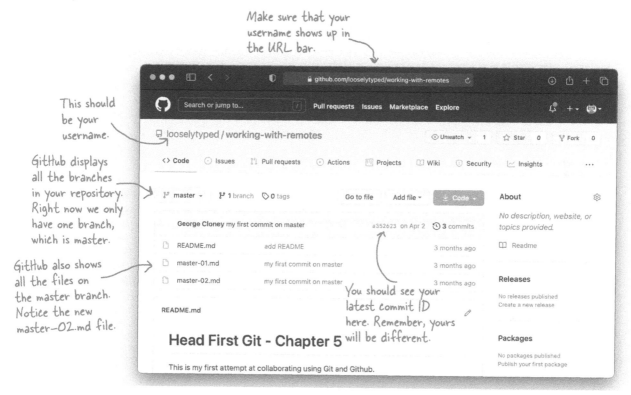

Make sure that your username shows up in the URL bar.

This should be your username.

GitHub displays all the branches in your repository. Right now we only have one branch, which is master.

GitHub also shows all the files on the master branch. Notice the new master-02.md file.

You should see your latest commit ID here. Remember, yours will be different.

GitHub displays a wealth of information about your repository, including a drop-down menu that lists all the branches that GitHub knows about, as well as the commit ID of the latest commit on each branch. You can also click on each of the files and see the contents as they were committed.

This is kinda nice, because you can use GitHub's interface to navigate your repository just like you would using your terminal and your favorite text editor: you can "switch" branches, click on files to see their contents—all that good stuff.

And you know how to do all this using the terminal as well! Look at you, you terminal ninja!

Using the interface is another way to check that your changes really did make their way up to GitHub and the push succeeded. It's worth doing this after pushing, at least till you get more familiar with working with remotes.

Watch it!

Be sure to get the password (ahem, token) right!

When you attempt to supply a password to GitHub using the prompt, you might see something like this:

```
File Edit Window Help
$ git push
Username for 'https://github.com': looselytyped
Password for 'https://looselytyped@github.com':
remote: Support for password authentication was removed on August 13, 2021.
Please use a personal access token instead.
remote: Please see https://github.blog/2020-12-15-token-authentication-
requirements-for-git-operations/ for more information.
fatal: Authentication failed for 'https://github.com/looselytyped/test.
git/'
```

Whoops! This is GitHub rejecting your credentials.

If so, it means one of two things has happened—either you mistyped your access token, or you're accidentally using your GitHub password. Either way, make sure that you are using your token, and that you got it right. It might be easier to paste in your access token instead of typing it in.

*Also know that GitHub will prompt you for your credentials **every** time you attempt to push to your repository. Many operating systems have a credentials helper: for example, the Credentials Manager in Windows or the Keychain Access on the Mac. Consider storing your GitHub personal access token there so you don't have to keep copy-pasting it every time.*

Just remember: whatever route you choose, keep those credentials secure!

Serious Coding

Remember how we told Git our name and email address (`user.name` and `user.email`) in the first chapter, and how we configured `push.default` to `simple` a couple of pages back? Git offers another configuration, called `credential.helper`, that you can configure to use one of the credential managers that your operating system supports. Once you've had some experience using Git, check it out.

there are no Dumb Questions

Q: I'm pretty sure I typed my token in correctly. But I still keep getting authentication failures. Help!

A: GitHub only shows you your personal access token at the time you generate it, so there is no way to verify if what you have is correct. Probably the best course of action for you is to just generate a new one and try again. Be sure to delete the other one if you know you no longer need it!

Exercise

Ready to push some commits?

✱ First, be sure to navigate to the location where you cloned the `working-with-remotes` repository, if you are not there already. Be sure to be on the `master` branch. Then use the `git log` command to record the commit ID of your latest commit here:

✱ List the command you are going to use to push your latest commit to your repository in GitHub (remember, always check what branch you are on first):

✱ Perform the push.

✱ Visit your repository on github.com. Do you see your new commit ID? (Check out the screenshot two pages back to see where GitHub displays it.)

✱ Finally, browse the `master-01.md` and `master-02.md` files on github.com and make sure you see your edits there.

──────────▶ Answers on page 263.

there are no Dumb Questions

Q: Why doesn't Git automatically update the remote when I commit?

A: There are several reasons for this. First, Git is very deliberate in the choices it makes; if there is any doubt, it defers to you. We saw in Chapter 2 that when a merge results in a conflict, Git simply throws up its hands and asks you to resolve it. We also know that pushing changes updates the remote. So, once again, Git will just sit back and wait for you to explicitly tell it to update the remote repository by doing a `git push`.

The second possible reason is that you might not be online. If Git attempts to push changes while you're, say, on a plane with no connectivity, the push would fail. Once again, Git defers to you to decide when to push.

Another reason is that Git allows you to undo typos in commit messages by amending them and to reset commits with the `git reset` command (we spoke of both of these in Chapter 4). So it waits till you are absolutely sure you're good and ready to go.

Also, your repository doesn't always have a remote! Up until now in this book, you have worked with standalone repositories created locally on your machine. For those kinds of repositories, it doesn't even make sense to push, does it?

Finally, Git encourages experimenting with branches. You might have created a branch to play with an idea or approach, and maybe you aren't ready to share that with the world. Git separates the act of making a commit from pushing those commits to a remote, thus allowing you to choose when and how that happens. You're the boss!

Q: What happens if I push a branch that I've already pushed?

A: No worries. If you push a branch and then push it again, Git will simply respond with an `Everything up-to-date` message. No harm done.

Let's take a moment to stop here and realize the importance of commit IDs, now that you know you can get commits from a remote and push them back. You know that Git is transporting your commit history back and forth, while keeping the commit IDs the *same*! This has pretty big implications, which we'll be talking more about soon.

The thing is, when you are working locally, Git does not care whether you create a commit yourself or get it as part of a repository you clone. Any and all commits in your commit history are the same, as far as Git is concerned.

Why does this matter? You already know that there are some Git operations that can change commit IDs (remember amending commit messages?) and modify commit histories (the `git reset` command). So what does this mean when working with remote repositories? Glad you asked—we gotta cover a bit of ground before we get there, but keep this in the back of your mind as you proceed through the rest of this book.

Test Drive

Why don't you spend a little time comparing the commit IDs between your local copy and the remote? Navigate to the location where you cloned the `working-with-remotes` repository. Then use the `git log --oneline` command combination to see your commit history.

Next, navigate to your repository on github.com and click on the commit count, shown here:

> *Note: we are only listing the commits on the master branch here.*

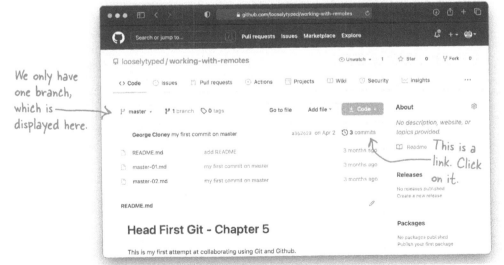

We only have one branch, which is displayed here.

This is a link. Click on it.

GitHub will reveal a page that displays the commits **on the `master` branch**. See if the commit IDs you see on GitHub line up with the commit IDs you see locally.

→ This is one of the exercises with no solution shown.

Knowing where to push: remotes

You now know you can push your changes to the remote. But how does Git know where to push? We mentioned earlier that when you clone a repository, the clone knows the location of the remote repository. If you're ever curious about the remote repository's location, you can ask Git with the `remote` command:

Feel free to play along with us here.

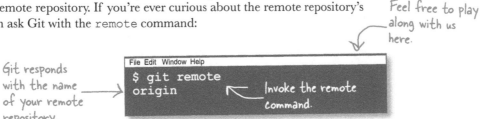

Git responds with the name of your remote repository.

```
File Edit Window Help
$ git remote
origin
```

Invoke the remote command.

Bit of a letdown, huh? The `git remote` command, by default, lists the "alias" that Git gives the remote, which, by default, is "origin." (This is just a label—you can change the name if you prefer.) To get a little more information, you can ask the `git remote` command to be more *verbose* with the `-v` (or `--verbose`) flag.

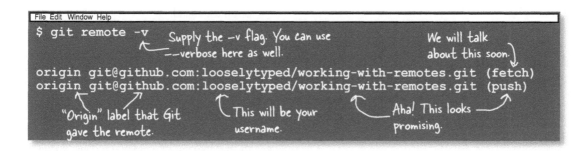

```
File Edit Window Help
$ git remote -v
origin git@github.com:looselytyped/working-with-remotes.git (fetch)
origin git@github.com:looselytyped/working-with-remotes.git (push)
```

Supply the -v flag. You can use --verbose here as well.

We will talk about this soon.

"Origin" label that Git gave the remote.

This will be your username.

Aha! This looks promising.

This looks a lot better. The `git remote` command in verbose mode provides more information. The second line is of particular interest—this is how Git knows what to do when you perform a `git push`. It looks at the URL next to the `origin` remote and sends over your changes to that location.

When you invoke the `git push` command, Git is actually performing `git push origin`. This, in turn, pushes your changes to the URL listed in the "push" entry when you run the `git remote` command.

git push = **git push origin**

You can use either one. As you might have guessed, we prefer the shorter option.

This is assuming you haven't changed the name of your remote from "origin" to something else.

Bullet Points

- `git init` is one of two ways to initialize a Git repository on your workstation. You can also initialize a repository by cloning an *existing* repository using the `git clone` command.

- The `git clone` command takes a URL as its argument, which it obtains from the original repository.

- To make a repository shareable, you can use a Git repository manager. There are several available, including GitHub, GitLab, and Bitbucket.

- When you clone an existing repository:

  - Git creates a folder that houses the repository on your machine and, by default, has the same name as the repository you are cloning.

  - Git then pulls the entire commit history of the original repository into the newly created folder, including all the branches.

  - Finally, Git switches to the "default" branch in the repository. This makes all the files in the default branch available to you in your working directory.

- We refer to the original repository as the "remote" and the local copy as the "clone."

- The remote and the clone are completely disconnected.

- You can work in the clone like you would in any other repository—you can commit, create new branches, you name it—because Git is a distributed version control system.

- In a distributed version control system, there is no *original* copy, since every clone has everything the origin does. If the original copy were to go away, you could treat any clone as the source of truth.

- Because the remote is completely independent of the clone, work you do on the clone will not be automatically reflected in the remote.

- If you create new commits on a branch that the **clone knows about** and you want to synchronize the commit histories of the remote and the clone, you have to explicitly tell Git to do so.

- In order to push new commits on a branch that exists on both the clone and the remote, you have to use the `git push` command.

- You can verify if your push has worked by visiting the location where the remote exists. Git repository managers like GitHub will list all of the branches and the individual commits on each branch.

- Git knows where to push because the clone records the URL of the remote.

- You can use the `git remote` command in a clone to see details about the remote.

- When you clone a repository, Git names the remote "origin" by default.

No photographs, please: public versus private commits

You started this chapter by cloning a repository. (Well, OK, you first forked, then cloned.) That pulled down a preexisting commit history that we prepared for you, in that we created and authored those commits. You then proceeded to make a new commit, which you added to the commit history of the `master` branch. For this new commit, though, *you* are the creator and author. Just remember, as far as Git is concerned, there is no difference between our commits and yours.

However, there is one semantic difference between the commit you created locally and the one you pushed. The local commit is private—only you know it exists, and you can do with it whatever you desire. You could choose to amend the commit message, which (as you might recall from Chapter 4) would change the commit ID. You could use `git reset HEAD~1` and undo the commit. You could decide not to push the commit at all, leaving it on your local `master` branch copy forever. But you pushed.

So what happens when you push? Git attempts to reconcile what you have locally with what's out there on the remote. In your case, it sees the new commit on the `master` branch and adds it to the remote's `master` branch (because that's the only change).

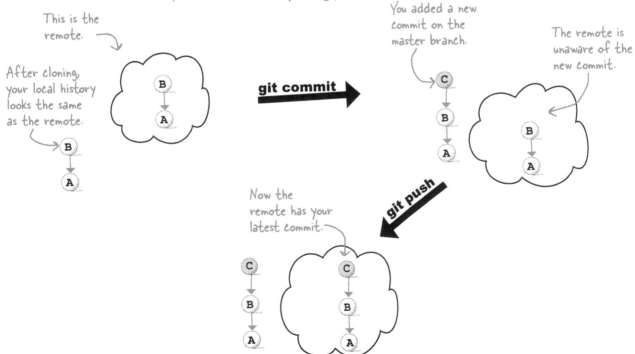

However, as soon as you push the commit to the remote, it's public! It's out there now. The world knows about it. Which means you have to be careful with what you do with it.

Public versus private commits (continued)

Commits that only exist in your local repository are a lot like a tweet that you are drafting, or a video that you just recorded on your phone but haven't published anywhere. You are free to edit the commit, undo it, or add more to it—it's private to you.

Pushing it to the remote makes it public. The world can see it now. Why is this important?

Well, remember that when you push, you are pushing your commit history, including commit IDs. So if you do something that changes the ID of a commit that is now public, what will happen when you push and the IDs don't match?

We don't mean to alarm you. Since you are the only contributor on this repository, this does not mean much. In the next chapter we'll talk about multiple collaborators working on the same repository. That's when public versus private becomes really important.

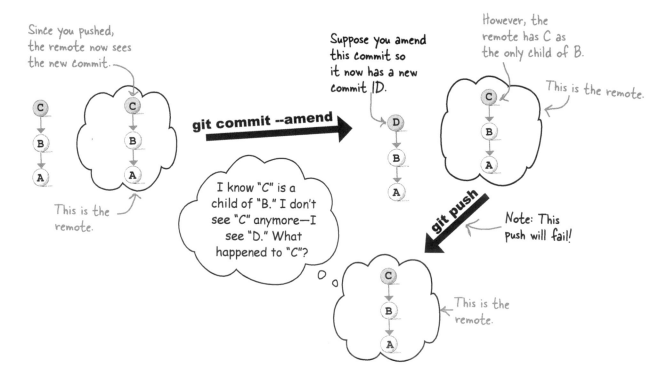

Since you pushed, the remote now sees the new commit.

This is the remote.

Suppose you amend this commit so it now has a new commit ID.

git commit --amend

I know "C" is a child of "B." I don't see "C" anymore—I see "D." What happened to "C"?

However, the remote has C as the only child of B.

This is the remote.

git push

Note: This push will fail!

This is the remote.

Git will reject your push, telling you (in complicated jargon that we will unravel soon enough) that the two commit histories don't line up.

Just remember, sharing is caring. Once you share your commit with the outside world, treat it with care.

If you are wondering how to avoid this conundrum, fear not! We'll get to this soon enough. We just have a few more things to talk about first.

Brain Power

You have a pretty good understanding of how to work with remotes—you now know that pushing your commits to the remote makes them "public." Why do you think it is important to treat public commits with care?

Hint: What if one of your friends or colleagues had cloned the same repository? How would changing the ID of a public commit affect them?

Standard operating procedure: branches

It doesn't really matter whether you create your Git repository locally using the `git init` command or by cloning it using the `git clone` command. Git repositories are Git repositories, and everything you have learned so far in this book applies—including how to work with branches. You learned about the workflow we recommended in Chapter 2: you always work in a branch, and when you're done, you merge that branch *into* an integration branch.

Similarly, for a cloned repository, you (and perhaps your team) decide which branch will play the role of integration branch, where everyone's work comes together.

This means that anytime you want to do some work, you should create a branch from the integration branch. Remember, the remote is completely unaware of the work you are doing. You can create a branch, add commits, rename branches, even delete them: as far as the remote is concerned, none of this matters. Just like the commits you prepare are private, so are the branches you create locally.

You already know one way to incorporate your changes into an integration branch—you simply merge your branch into it. But now that you have a remote, what does that mean for integrating your changes? Is it different, and if so, how? So let's start there. (We have a surprise waiting for you at the end of that discussion. Stay tuned!)

Exercise

✳ Fire up your terminal and navigate to the location where you cloned the `working-with-remotes` repository. Use the `git status` command to be sure you are still on the `master` branch and that you have a clean working directory.

✳ Use the `git branch` command to create a new branch called `feat-a`, and switch to it.

✳ Using your text editor, create a new file called `feat-a-01.md` and type in the following contents:

Only one line in this new file. →

> **This file is on the feat-a branch.**
>
> `feat-a-01.md`

Some whitespace to list out the commands you are going to use.

✳ Add `feat-a-01.md` to the index. Commit it with the message "my first commit on feat-a".

✳ Switch back to the `master` branch and create another file (call it `master-03.md`) that looks like this:

Add this file on the master branch. →

> **This is the third file on the master branch.**
>
> `master-03.md`

✳ Add this file to the index and commit it with the message "my second commit on master".

Answers on page 264.

Brain Power

In the previous exercise, you created a new branch called `feat-a` and committed a new file. You then switched back to the `master` branch, introduced another file, and committed that as well.

Now flex your brain: if you were to merge the feat-a branch into the `master` branch, would that be a fast-forward merge? Or would Git create a merge commit?

Hint: Think of the commit history. Have the two branches diverged from one another?

Merging branches: option 1 (local merges)

Good news: if you want to follow the standard model of merging into integration branches, you don't need to do anything different. If you are done with your work in a feature branch, merge into an integration branch (like `master`) and then push the `master` branch back to the remote.

Now that you've done the last exercise, this is what your commit history looks like:

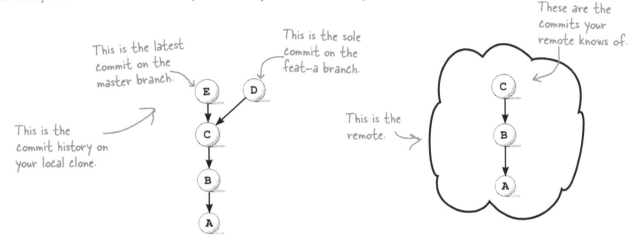

This is the latest commit on the master branch.

This is the sole commit on the feat-a branch.

These are the commits your remote knows of.

This is the commit history on your local clone.

This is the remote.

Remember, this repository is no different than the ones you have worked on in the past. You know how to merge your feature branch (`feat-a`) into the `master` branch. So how do you update the remote? You guessed it—you can use the `git push` command to push the `master` branch to the remote!

This is the what the master branch looks like in the remote after you push.

This is the merge commit.

The master branch sticky note moves to the new commit.

This is the feat-a branch.

git push

And the remote now has all your new commits!

One thing to note here is the remote only has the merge commit "F," as well as both its parents: "E" (on the `master` branch) and "D" (on `feat-a` branch). It does **not**, however, have the `feat-a` branch! Remember, you only pushed the `master` branch. The `feat-a` branch is still local to your repository.

Sharpen your pencil

You've already set up the branches and are ready to merge into `master`. Ready to do just that? Using your terminal, navigate to the location where you cloned the `working-with-remotes` repository.

➤ Start by making sure you are on the `master` branch. What command will you use?

➤ Now merge the `feat-a` branch *into* the `master` branch. This **will** create a merge commit, which means Git will prompt you for a commit message using your configured text editor. We suggest you leave the default merge message as is.

➤ List the command to push the `master` branch to the remote here. Then use it to push.

Use this space to list the commands you are going to use.

➤ Visit **your** repository page on GitHub. You should see **six** commits listed (as in the screenshot below). Can you explain what you are seeing here? Feel free to use `git log --oneline` in your terminal and compare notes.

Remember, this only displays the commit history of the branch you are on, which in this case is master.

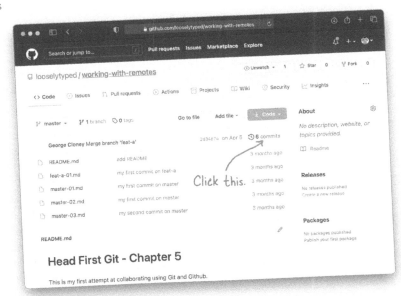

→ **Answers on page 265.**

there are no Dumb Questions

Q: I have merged my code into the `master` branch and pushed. So what do I do with my feature branch now?

A: Delete it! Your work has been incorporated into the integration branch, so there is no reason to hold onto the feature branch.

Q: What if I forget to push the `master` branch to the remote after merging my integration branch?

A: To be honest, this is probably the most common mistake newcomers make when working with remotes (though, let's be honest, even experienced users like us forget to push on occasion).

This takes us back to Git's distributed nature. Remember, the remote is completely unaware of your branching and merging efforts. If you decide not to (or worse, forget to) push the `master` branch back upstream to the remote, the remote will never know.

If you intend to push a branch, just do it as soon as you finish merging. Later, if you aren't sure, you can always push again. Git will do what it does best—send your commits up to the remote. Remember, though: if you push a branch twice in a row and nothing has changed, Git simply responds with `Everything up-to-date` and does nothing.

A quick note on GitHub's interface

You've probably noticed by now that when you navigate over to view the commits, GitHub will display all the commits that are "reachable" from a specific branch.

We talked about "reachable" commits at the end of Chapter 2.

This is the view in GitHub that lists all the commits for a particular branch.

You used this in the last exercise.

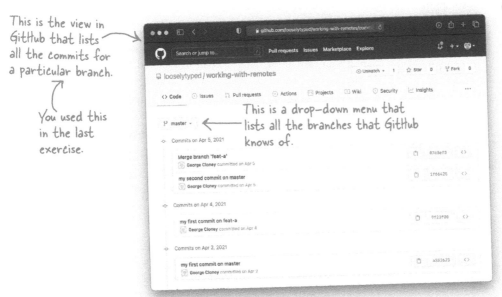

This is a drop-down menu that lists all the branches that GitHub knows of.

You can always use the drop-down menu to see the commit history for other branches (assuming you have any), but at the time of this writing, there is no way to see the entire commit history of your repository at once. This is why we taught you how to use the `git log` command and its various flags in Chapter 3! Using the terminal to read and understand the commit history is a necessary skill, so keep practicing.

I feel good about pushing the master branch. But what if I want to push my feature branch to the remote? Can I do that? I mean, a branch is a branch is a branch, right?

Sure! Git's strength lies in the ability to create branches easily (and cheaply). The workflow we recommend involves creating feature branches for any and all work, then merging back into integration branches when you are done.

There are many reasons you might want to push a feature branch up to the remote. For example, you might want a remote backup of your work, in case something were to happen to your workstation.

Or perhaps you'd like a colleague or a friend to look at your changes. If your branch is available in GitHub (or any other Git repository manager), they can look over your changes using their browser. (We will be diving into collaborating over Git and GitHub in the next chapter.)

Remember that surprise we mentioned earlier when we spoke about integrating your changes? Here it is—you can use repository managers like GitHub to perform merges!

We're getting carried away. Let's get your question answered—how do we push local feature branches to the remote?

Pushing local branches

The `working-with-remotes` repository that we created for you had just one branch, `master`, with two commits on it. When you cloned this repository at the beginning of this chapter, the `master` branch, both of those commits came along for the ride. Since the remote already knew about `master`, Git allowed you to push back to that branch using the `git push` command. Git knows there is a `master` in the remote, so it syncs up the remote `master` branch with any commits that appeared in your local `master` branch.

Relax. Enjoy the ride. Nothing for you to do here.

But if you've just created a new feature branch locally (like the one you created in the last exercise), the remote doesn't know about it. What happens if you push it?

Create a new branch.

Switch to it.

Try pushing it.

Eek! Git is not happy with us.

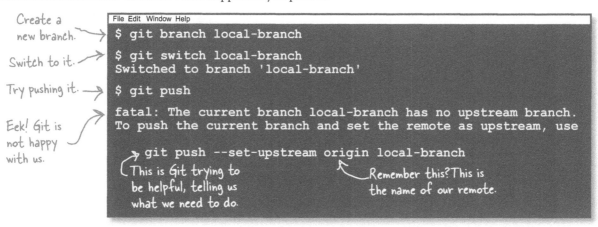

```
File Edit Window Help
$ git branch local-branch

$ git switch local-branch
Switched to branch 'local-branch'

$ git push

fatal: The current branch local-branch has no upstream branch.
To push the current branch and set the remote as upstream, use

    git push --set-upstream origin local-branch
```

This is Git trying to be helpful, telling us what we need to do.

Remember this? This is the name of our remote.

Well, that certainly didn't go as planned. What happened?

When you attempt to push a branch to the remote, Git tries to figure out exactly which remote branch it should update. But if the branch is brand new, Git won't see a counterpart in the remote. It doesn't know what to do, so it simply throws up its hands and asks! You need to explicitly tell Git the name of the branch in the remote it should update with the commits in your clone. Following Git's advice makes it all work:

```
File Edit Window Help
$ git push --set-upstream origin local-branch
Total 0 (delta 0), reused 0 (delta 0), pack-reused 0
remote:
remote: Create a pull request for 'local-branch' on GitHub by visiting:
remote: https://github.com/looselytyped/working-with-remotes/pull/new/local-branch
remote:
To github.com:looselytyped/working-with-remotes.git
 * [new branch]      local-branch -> local-branch
Branch 'local-branch' set up to track remote branch 'local-branch' from 'origin'.
```

We will be talking about this in a few.

Aha! That looks promising.

Pushing local branches (continued)

After you push a local branch up to the remote, you can verify that all has gone well by visiting your repository on GitHub to see if your new branch shows up in the branch menu:

This is a drop-down menu.

And there it is!

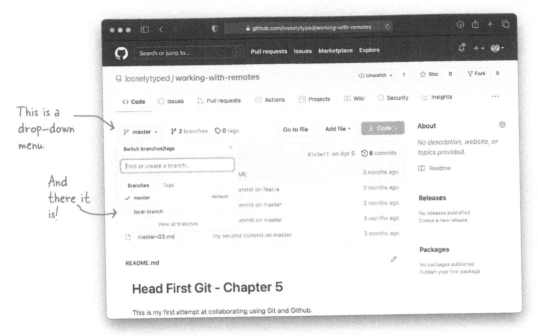

And that's how you push a newly created local branch up to the remote!

> **Heads up! You can use the -u flag instead of --set-upstream with git push if you like. They mean the same thing.**

Serious Coding

You might be wondering why you need to specify the name of the remote (`origin`) when you set the upstream destination for a branch. Git already knows about the remote, right? So why do we have to explicitly specify it?

Because Git allows your local repository to talk to multiple remotes. You might clone one repository but decide to push your changes to another.

Why? Well, that's a discussion for another book. For now, just know that when you set the upstream for a branch, you need to tell it *which* remote to push to. For us, that will always be "origin."

 Test Drive

Why don't you try pushing a local branch to the remote? Go back to your terminal; be sure you change directories to the location where you cloned the `working-with-remotes` repository.

➤ Check to make sure you are on the `master` branch. Use the `git branch` command to create another branch. Call it `feat-b` and switch to it.

➤ Using your text editor, create a new file called `feat-b-01.md` that looks like this:

This file only has one line in it.

This file is on the feat-b branch.

feat-b-01.md

We've provided all these files in the source code you downloaded for this book. Feel free to copy those files over if you don't feel like typing all this out.

➤ Add the `feat-b-01.md` file to the index and commit it using the message "my first commit on feat-b".

➤ Attempt to push the `feat-b` branch to the remote. **This will fail!** Follow the advice that Git offers you to fix the issue.

➤ **Visit your repository in GitHub.** Make sure you see the `feat-b` branch in the branch drop-down menu.

➤ Back to your clone! Using your terminal, switch back to the `master` branch. Create and save a file called `master-04.md` with the following contents:

Again, just a single line to keep things simple.

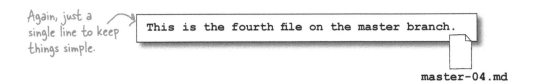

This is the fourth file on the master branch.

master-04.md

➤ Again, add the `master-04.md` to the index. Commit it. Use the message "my third commit on master".

➤ Push the `master` branch to the remote as well.

➤ Be sure to check your repository on GitHub to make sure that all has gone well. You can use the `git log --oneline --all --graph` to look up commit IDs. Check to make sure those show up on GitHub as well.

⟶ This is one of the exercises with no solution shown.

there are no Dumb Questions

Q: Why do we "set upstream"? Is that the same as the remote?

A: The terms *upstream* and *downstream*, while commonly used, are a bit confusing when you're working with a distributed system like Git. When we clone a repository and it gets data and puts it onto our local machine, the local is *downstream*.

When we push, or send data from the local to the remote, the remote is *upstream* from us. And yes, in our case, setting upstream is the same as setting the remote.

Q: Do I have to set the upstream every time I push a local branch?

A: Once you set the upstream for a local branch, you never have to do it again *for that branch*.

However, if you create *another* local branch and you want to push it, you *will* have to set the upstream for that branch.

Sharpen your pencil

➤ Take a moment to stop and think about your commit graph. Can you visualize it? Try to sketch it out from memory:

Nothing like a good whiteboarding session to get those creative juices flowing. Right?

➤ Once you're done, use `git log --oneline --all --graph` to confirm if you got it right.

➤ In the previous exercise you pushed both the `feat-b` and the `master` branches. What do you think the commit history in the remote looks like after that push? Take your notes here.

Answers on page 266.

Merging branches: option 2 (pull requests)

Sit back and read. We'll get to the exercise.

You know that you can create a branch, make some commits, merge into your integration branch, and push the integration branch back to the remote. Done!

But there is another way. Repository managers like GitHub offer much more than simply housing Git repositories. You've already seen how you can navigate files using your browser, list the branches you've pushed to the remote, and view all the commits for each of those branches.

But GitHub and other repository managers also allow you to manage your Git repository using your browser, including performing merges! This comes with a surprisingly useful feature called *pull requests*. If your team or company has chosen to collaborate using GitHub, chances are you'll use pull requests for merging. Let's get you prepared to hit the ground running!

Bitbucket also refers to this feature as "pull requests," but GitLab calls them "merge requests." Same difference—they all work in a similar fashion.

In your last exercise, when you pushed your `feat-b` branch to the remote, GitHub informed you that you can create a pull request in the command prompt. Here is the console output from the last exercise:

```
File Edit Window Help
$ Enumerating objects: 4, done.
Counting objects: 100% (4/4), done.
Delta compression using up to 16 threads
Compressing objects: 100% (2/2), done.
Writing objects: 100% (3/3), 313 bytes | 313.00 KiB/s, done.
Total 3 (delta 1), reused 0 (delta 0), pack-reused 0
remote: Resolving deltas: 100% (1/1), completed with 1 local object.
remote:
remote: Create a pull request for 'feat-b' on GitHub by visiting:
remote:      https://github.com/looselytyped/working-with-remotes/pull/new/feat-b
remote:
To github.com:looselytyped/working-with-remotes.git
 * [new branch]       feat-b -> feat-b
Branch 'feat-b' set up to track remote branch 'feat-b' from 'origin'.
```

Right here. Just remember—your URL will be different.

Don't worry if you closed or cleared your console. There are other ways to get to that URL.

Let's see two more ways you can create a pull request—even if you've already closed your console.

Creating pull requests

The first option for creating pull requests is easy—simply type out the URL in your browser window. Here it is, in its fully annotated glory:

This should be your username.

Name of the repository

"new pull" request

This is the name of the branch you wish to merge.

```
https://github.com/looselytyped/working-with-remotes/pull/new/feat-b
```

Relax. It's not your turn yet.

This can be cumbersome—who wants to type out long URLs by hand? Alternatively, if you visit your GitHub repository right after pushing a branch to the remote, you'll see that GitHub offers you a nice banner to get you started, no typing required. This is what it looks like:

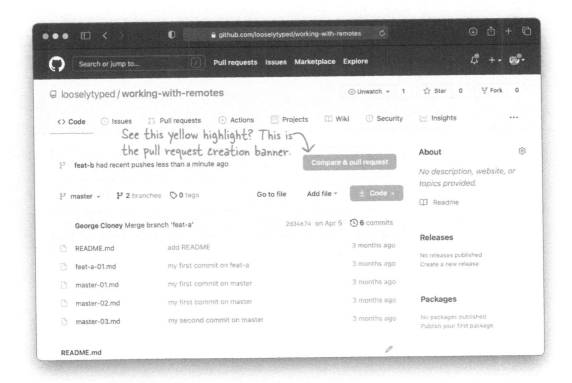

This banner is transient, so if you visit your GitHub repository page soon after pushing, you might not see it. Thus, let's look at yet another way to create pull requests....

Creating pull requests (continued)

If you visit your GitHub repository page, you should see a "Pull requests" tab on top:

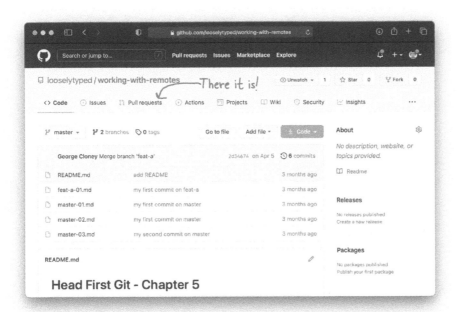

This will take you to another page that lists all the pull requests in your repository. Given that this is our first foray into working with pull requests, there's not much here. No worries—we're going to fix that. See the button to create a new pull request?

Creating pull requests (Yep! Almost there)

Clicking on the "Create pull request" button will finally lead you to something interesting: the screen that allows you to pick which branch to merge (the *source*) and which branch to merge it *into* (the *target*).

This is the source: the branch you want to merge. We used the drop-down menu to change this to feat-b.

This is the base, or target: the branch to merge into.

If GitHub asks you to "Choose a Base Repository," be sure to pick the one with your username!

The "Comparing changes" screen allows you to pick the branches you want to merge. Just know that what we call the *target* in this book, GitHub calls the *base*: that is, the branch that you wish to merge into. In the screenshot above, we have left master as the base and picked feat-b as the source. Clicking the "Create pull request" button leads to a screen that lets you add some information about your new pull request.

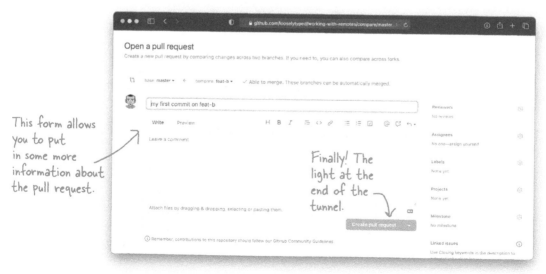

This form allows you to put in some more information about the pull request.

Finally! The light at the end of the tunnel.

A brand-new, shiny pull request

Finally! Here you are—the first pull request in the `working-with-remotes` repository. We'll soon talk about what this means and what you can do with it, but for now, why don't you take a minute to stop and breathe? It's been a long journey.

The pull request informs you about the target and source branches.

Along with how many commits and files have changed.

Test Drive

It's time for you to create a new pull request for yourself.

➤ Navigate to your repository on GitHub. Use the "Pull requests" tab to create a new pull request.

➤ Be sure to leave `master` as the base, and use the "compare" pull-down menu to pick the `feat-b` branch (from your previous exercise) as the source.

➤ You can leave the default settings as they are in the pull request creation form.

⟶ This is one of the exercises with no solution shown.

Brain Power

Spend a little time looking around your newly minted pull request. In GitHub, click on the "Pull requests" tab at the top, then click on the solitary pull request you just created. Pay close attention to the "Commits" and "Files changed" tabs. What do you notice?

Pull requests or merge requests?

A pull request is a way to request that your code be merged into another branch, typically an integration branch like `master`. Consider this—suppose you're working with several colleagues, sharing the same Git repository, which you've chosen to host on GitHub (like we did). Your repository's integration branch is `master`. You are all working independently of one another, in your own clones and your own feature branches.

When you're done, you want to merge your work back into `master`. Now, remember, your colleagues are doing the exact same thing—creating branches based on the integration branch before they start their work. In other words, when you incorporate your work into an integration branch, your changes affect everybody else working on the same repository! With lots of people, this can get tricky.

> We covered this workflow at the end of Chapter 2. Feel free to flip back to it and refresh your memory if you need to.

So instead of merging your local branch directly into `master`, you push the branch to the remote and create a pull request. This tells your colleagues that you wish to merge some work and displays the commits and the files changed, so they know what changes you've made. The pull request also gives your colleagues a way to make suggestions on how you could change or improve your work. Once they approve your pull request, you can go ahead and merge your changes. You're done!

You could think about pull requests as "merging in public"—your colleagues get a chance to review your work before it becomes part of the whole.

> Thank you for issuing a pull request. Now I can see the changes you made and we can discuss any improvements publicly using GitHub's web interface.

It might help to think of pull requests as merge requests, which is what they are—a request to merge the code in one branch into another branch.

Sangita

Q: It's just me working in this repository. What do I gain from making a pull request? Does it make sense for me to use them?

A: Good point. Pull (or merge) requests are really useful when you have more than one collaborator on a project. You can get their input on your changes and notify them that you're getting ready to merge your code.

To be completely honest, for solo projects, we prefer to just merge into our integration branch locally and push the integration branch to the remote. We believe that practice makes perfect, though, so you should practice issuing pull requests a few times just to get the hang of it.

When we're working on teams, it's a different story: we use pull requests. We are huge fans of collaboration and clear communication, and pull requests are great for both.

Q: Let's say I issue a pull request. Whose job is it to merge it?

A: That depends on the workflow you and your team settle on—different teams tend to work very differently in this regard.

One approach is to designate one or more members of your team—perhaps those with more experience who can make sure that all the i's are dotted and the t's are crossed before they merge the pull request.

Other teams often set a constraint that at least two other members must look at the pull request and give their approval before the pull request is merged.

Remember, the role of a pull request is to allow for communication, collaboration, and often knowledge sharing. Whatever works best for you and your team is what you should be doing. There are no wrong answers here.

Q: The pull request creation form asks for a title and a description. What's all that about?

A: Since pull requests are about communication and collaboration, these mechanisms encourage you to be explicit about what changes you are introducing and why.

Sometimes we have to try one or more different ways to solve a problem. We've found that the description is a good place to lay out how we've tried to solve the problem at hand and why we chose the approach we did. Providing a good description allows anyone looking over your pull requests to understand why you did what you did.

Finally, this is a good place to put useful links: for example, if you use a ticketing system in your work, you might link to the relevant ticket.

Q: You mentioned that the pull request allows others to review my work and suggest changes. If I've already issued the pull request and someone catches a typo in a comment or recommends renaming a variable, how do I implement the change?

A: Great question! You can simply open up your editor, make the suggested changes to your local branch, commit, and push again. The push will take your latest commit and update the remote. The pull request will **automatically** update to reflect all commits on the branch, so your colleagues can take a look at it again or follow along if they like.

Merging a pull request

There is so much more we could say about pull requests. They allow for a conversation around the changes introduced—you can apply labels and assign specific reviewers to pull requests.

But, since you are reading *Head First Git* and not *Head First GitHub*, we're going to show you how to merge code using merge requests, then leave the rest for you to discover on your own. Merging a pull request is easy: you simply visit the pull request page, and you should see a button that allows you to merge.

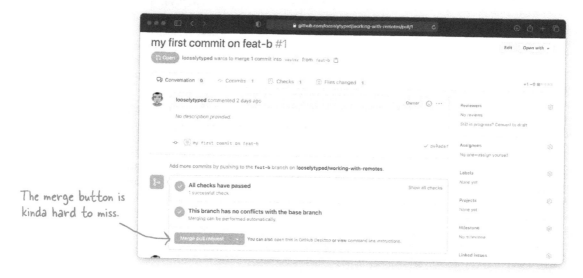

The merge button is kinda hard to miss.

Since you are merging code, GitHub **will create a merge commit**. And since every commit needs a commit message, when you choose to merge the pull request, GitHub will present you with another form that allows you to supply a commit message. Once you do that and confirm the merge, you are done!

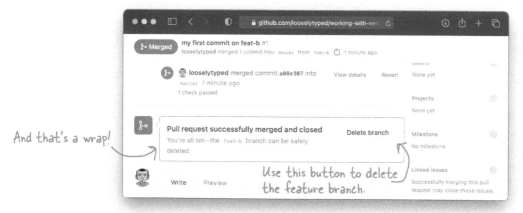

And that's a wrap!

Use this button to delete the feature branch.

Once you merge, you should clean up—GitHub gives you a button to delete the feature branch you just merged.

Q: You said that GitHub will always create a merge commit. But what if it's a fast-forward merge?

A: GitHub's default behavior is to always create a merge commit. GitHub uses a special flag when merging that forces Git to create a merge commit.

GitHub does offer other ways to merge branches that don't create a merge commit, but that's a conversation for another time. For now, just remember that using the defaults in GitHub will create a merge commit.

Q: I get that GitHub will always create a merge commit. I still don't get why.

A: A merge commit represents the joining of two branches. Having a merge commit show up in your commit history can make it easier to discern when a merge happened (since commits record the timestamp when they were created). Also, since a merge commit has two parents, it's easy to spot in the Git log output.

Q: What happens if merging two branches results in a merge conflict?

A: How very astute of you to ask! If GitHub detects a conflict between the two branches being merged, GitHub will defer to you to resolve it. GitHub, like Git, aims to be as helpful as possible, so it displays all the steps you need to take to resolve the conflict.

Of course, you can always choose to merge the branch locally, resolve any conflicts (like we did in Chapter 2), and then push the merge commit upstream, just like any other push you have done so far. While pull requests are a way to perform a merge, merging locally is always an option available to you.

By the way, we'll be talking about ways to avoid this in the next chapter. (Who says cliffhangers have to be relegated to the realm of the suspense genre?)

Test Drive

It's time to exercise your pull-request merging skills. Visit your fork of the `working-with-remotes` repository on GitHub, and navigate to the list of pull requests via the "Pull requests" tab at the top of the page. You should only see one pull request. Click on it, and click the "Merge pull request" button.

Once you get the confirmation banner, be sure to click the "Delete branch" button to delete the `feat-b` branch.

⟶ **This is one of the exercises with no solution shown.**

What's next?

It's been one major milestone after another, hasn't it? You created your first pull request a few pages back. Then, in your last exercise, you merged it in! Giant strides for one chapter.

But there are some loose ends that need tying up. Recall that GitHub offers you a button to delete the feature branch after you merge it in. In our last exercise, that was the `feat-b` branch. We deleted that branch—but only in the remote! What about your local clone? Here's how things stand right now:

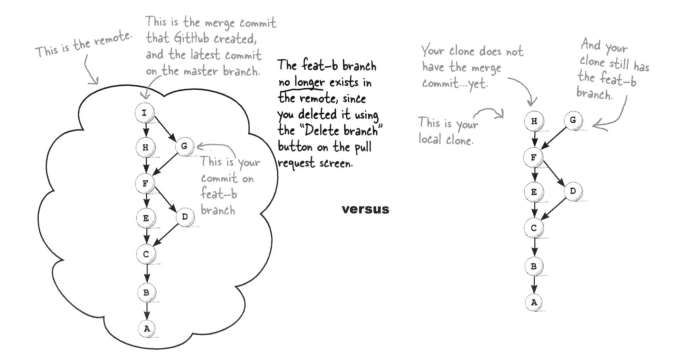

This is just a characteristic of the distributed nature of Git—when you perform an operation on the remote, like merging two branches or deleting branches, your local clone is completely unaware that anything has happened.

We know how to update the remote with new commits or new branches, using variations of the `git push` command. But how do we synchronize the local with changes that happened in the remote? How do you get the merge commit down to your remote? Well, that's the topic of our next chapter.

Another cliffhanger! Oh, the suspense.

Sharpen your pencil

Let's spend a little time thinking about the difference between the remote and the clone—you've merged the `feat-b` branch into `master` using a pull request, and deleted the `feat-b` branch in the remote. So now, will Git let you delete the `feat-b` branch in your clone? Compare the commit histories on the previous page to see if you can figure this one out. Here's a hint: think about the "reachability" (see the end of Chapter 2 when we spoke about deleting branches if you need a refresher) of commit "G" if you were to delete the `feat-b` branch.

Answers on page 266.

Bullet Points

- When you push your commits to the remote, Git synchronizes the commit history between the clone and the remote. This includes all commits and their commit IDs.

- Any commits that are pushed to the remote are now public commits. Once you push, you should refrain from performing any operation that changes this history: for example, don't do a `git reset` or amend a commit message (which would change the commit ID).

- Working with a clone is no different than working with any other Git repository. If you are working on a new feature or fixing a bug, you should create branches based on an integration branch, like `master`.

- Once you are done working on a branch, you have two options to merge your code into an integration branch:

  - The first option is to merge into an integration branch locally, then push the integration branch to the remote.

  - The second option is "merging in public," where you use the Git repository to perform a merge. GitHub offers "pull requests" to perform merges. Other repository managers offer similar facilities.

- If you choose to use pull requests, you will start by pushing the feature branch to the remote.

- To push a (new) local branch that the remote does not know about, you will use the `git push` command, paired with the `set-upstream` (or its shorter version, `-u`) flag. This lets you specify the name of the remote and the name of the branch that you want to create in the remote.

- After a local branch has been pushed to the remote, you can issue a pull request, where you pick the target (or base) branch—that is, the branch to merge into—and the source, or the branch that you wish to merge.

- A pull request (or merge request) allows fellow collaborators to review the changes you wish to merge. You can even start a conversation about them.

- GitHub's web interface allows you to merge your changes into the integration branch and delete the feature branch. (Don't forget to delete the feature branch!)

- Since the remote is unaware of the clone, deleting a branch in the remote does not delete the local branch in the clone. You have to do this yourself.

 A Pushy Puzzle

Now that you know how to work with remotes, test yourself with this "pushy" crossword.

Across

5 The ___ ___ command synchronizes your local changes with the remote (2 words)

7 To copy a repository to your own GitHub account, ____ it

9 Among git push configurations, this is the "seat belt" option

10 Popular repository manager owned by Atlassian

11 Pushing upstream sends your changes to the ___ repository.

13 To allow someone to change your repository on GitHub, make them a ___

16 Popular repository manager owned by Microsoft

⟶ Answers on page 267.

Down

1 Type of URL you should select when cloning

2 GitHub, GitLab, and a personal server are all places to ___ a repository

3 To copy a repository to your hard drive, ___ it

4 Subversion and CVS are examples of ___ version control systems

6 The git push command sends your changes in this direction

8 Everyone can see a ___ repository

12 You'll need to give GitHub your username and ___

14 Default name for the remote repository

15 A shared repository has a ___ commit history

Exercise Solution

From page 222.

By now you should have forked our repository to your account. Now's your chance to clone it. Using your browser, log into GitHub and go to the `working-with-remotes` repository. To make things easier, here is the URL:

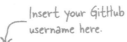

Insert your GitHub username here.

https://github.com/your-GitHub-username/working-with-remotes

✱ Follow the instructions from a few pages ago to find the clone URL.

✱ List the command you are going to use to clone your repository here:

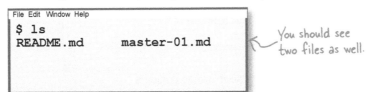

Your URL will have your username in it.

git clone https://github.com/looselytyped/working-with-remotes.git

✱ Using a terminal, go to the location where you have downloaded the other exercises for this book, and clone the `working-with-remotes` repository. (Just so you know, we created a folder called `chapter05` first, and then cloned the repository inside the `chapter05` folder. It just keeps things organized.)

✱ Spend a few minutes looking around the repository. List the files in your working directory here:

```
File Edit Window Help
$ ls
README.md        master-01.md
```

You should see two files as well.

✱ Next, list all the branches. Take a note of where your HEAD is:

Seems we only have one branch. So HEAD is pointed to it.

```
File Edit Window Help
$ git branch
* master
```

✱ Use `git log --graph --oneline --all` to inspect the commit history. Sketch out your commit history graph here.

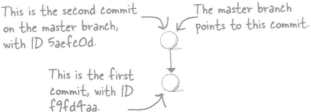

This is the second commit on the master branch, with ID 5aefc0d.

The master branch points to this commit.

This is the first commit, with ID f9fd4aa.

Exercise
Solution

From page 227.

Let's get you warmed up for the upcoming sections. Your task is to make a couple of changes to the repository you cloned. Time to fire up your terminal.

✱ Start by navigating to the location where you cloned the `working-with-remotes` repository.

✱ Check to make sure you are on the `master` branch, and that the status of the working directory is clean. List the commands you are to use here:

> git branch
>
> git status ⟵——— Remember, git status also tells
> you what branch you are on.

✱ Open the `master-01.md` file in your text editor and add a second line, so that the file looks like this after your edit:

You are going
to add the
second line. ⟶

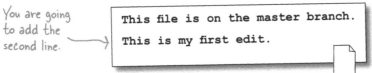

```
This file is on the master branch.

This is my first edit.
```

master-01.md

✱ Add another file, called `master-02.md`, with the following contents:

This is a new
file that you
are to create. ⟶

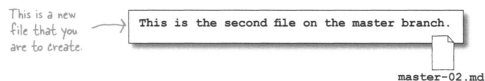

```
This is the second file on the master branch.
```

master-02.md

✱ Finally, add both files to the index. Make a commit with the message "my first commit on master".

First, add both
files to the index.

> git add master-01.md master-02.md ⟵
>
> git commit —m "my first commit on master"
>
> git status ⟵——— Always check the status to be sure
> you are in a good place.

Exercise
Solution

From page 233.

Ready to push some commits?

✻ First, be sure to navigate to the location where you cloned the `working-with-remotes` repository, if you are not there already. Be sure to be on the `master` branch. Then use the `git log` command to record the commit ID of your latest commit here:

a352623 ⟵   *Your commit ID*
                will be different.

✻ List the command you are going to use to push your latest commit to your repository in GitHub (remember, always check what branch you are on first):

     git branch ⟵ *It's always a good idea to check what branch you are on prior to pushing.*

     git push ⟵ *This will take any new commits on the branch and send them to the remote.*

✻ Perform the push.

✻ Visit your repository on github.com. Do you see your new commit ID? (Check out the screenshot two pages back to see where GitHub displays it.)

✻ Finally, browse the `master-01.md` and `master-02.md` files on github.com and make sure you see your edits there.

Exercise Solution

From page 240.

✱ Fire up your terminal and navigate to the location where you cloned the `working-with-remotes` repository. Use the `git status` command to be sure you are still on the `master` branch and that you have a clean working directory.

✱ Use the `git branch` command to create a new branch called `feat-a`, and switch to it.

> git branch feat-a
>
> git switch feat-a

✱ Using your text editor, create a new file called `feat-a-01.md` and type in the following contents:

Only one line in this new file. →

> **This file is on the feat-a branch.**
>
> **feat-a-01.md**

✱ Add `feat-a-01.md` to the index. Commit it with the message "my first commit on feat-a".

> git add feat-a-01.md
>
> git commit —m "my first commit on feat-a"

✱ Switch back to the `master` branch and create another file (call it `master-03.md`) that looks like this:

Add this file on the master branch. →

> **This is the third file on the master branch.**
>
> **master-03.md**

✱ Add this file to the index and commit it with the message "my second commit on master".

> git add master-03.md
>
> git commit —m "my second commit on master"

Sharpen your pencil
Solution

From page 242.

You've already set up the branches and are ready to merge into `master`. Ready to do just that? Using your terminal, navigate to the location where you cloned the `working-with-remotes` repository.

➤ Start by making sure you are on the `master` branch. What command will you use?

git branch ← *If you are not on the correct branch, you can use git switch to switch branches.*

➤ Now merge the `feat-a` branch *into* the `master` branch. This **will** create a merge commit, which means Git will prompt you for a commit message using your configured text editor. We suggest you leave the default merge message as is.

git merge feat-a ← *Since you are on the master branch, this will merge the feat-a branch into the master branch.*

➤ List the command to push the `master` branch to the remote here. Then use it to push.

git push

➤ Visit **your** repository page on GitHub. You should see six commits listed (as in the screenshot below). Can you explain what you are seeing here? Feel free to use `git log --oneline` in your terminal and compare notes.

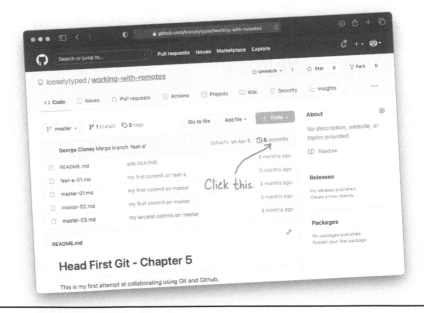

Sharpen your pencil
Solution

From page 248.

Take a moment to stop and think about your commit graph. Can you visualize it? Try to sketch it out from memory:

This is the last commit on the master branch where you committed the master-04.md file. →

← This is the only commit on the feat-b branch that introduced the feat-b-01.md file

This is the (merge) commit that Git created when you merged feat-a into master. →

➤ Once you're done, use `git log --oneline --all --graph` to confirm if you got it right.

➤ In the previous exercise you pushed both the feat-b and the master branches. What do you think the commit history in the remote looks like after that push? Take your notes here.

Since you just pushed both the feat-b branch and the master branch, all the commits on both branches are now in the remote. Which means the commit history in the remote should look just like what you see in your clone. You are all synced up!

Sharpen your pencil
Solution

From page 259.

Let's spend a little time thinking about the difference between the remote and the clone—you've merged the feat-b branch into master using a pull request, and deleted the feat-b branch in the remote. So now, will Git let you delete the feat-b branch in your clone? Compare the commit histories on the previous page to see if you can figure this one out. Here's a hint: think about the "reachability" (see the end of Chapter 2 when we spoke about deleting branches if you need a refresher) of commit "G" if you were to delete the feat-b branch.

Git will NOT let you delete the feat-b branch without using the -D (force) option to the branch command. This is because although feat-b was merged into the master branch in the remote, your clone is unaware of that! So if you were to delete the feat-b branch in your clone, commit "G" has no other references to it, making it unreachable. If you could fetch the merge commit from the remote first, then commit "G" will be reachable even after feat-b is deleted.

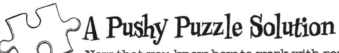

A Pushy Puzzle Solution

Now that you know how to work with remotes, test yourself with this "pushy" crossword.

From page 260.

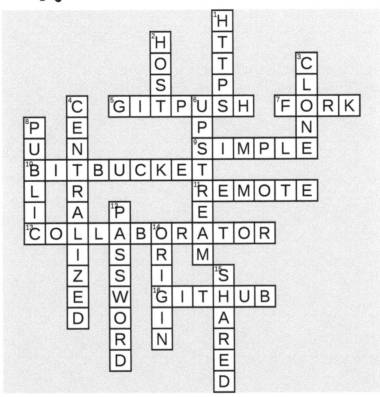

6
collaborating with Git - part II
Go, Team, Go!

Ready to bring in the team? Git is a fantastic tool for collaboration, and we've come up with a brilliant idea to teach you all about it—you are going to pair up with someone else in this chapter! You'll be building on what you learned in the last chapter. You know that working with a distributed system like Git involves a lot of moving parts. So what does Git offer us to make this easier, and what do you need to keep in mind as you go about collaborating with others? Are there any workflows that can make it easier to work together? Prepare to find out.

Ready. Set. Clone!

Cubicle conversation

The initial reviews for our HawtDawg dog dating app are looking great. But we still need an FAQ page and sample profile so we can onboard customers quickly. I think this will be a quick win with a huge impact on the customer journey. It'll help us find synergy and alignment with the ecosystem. Remember, content is king!

In case you're wondering, we searched for "most annoying buzzwords."

HawtDawg project manager

Addison: Apparently we need to find "synergy" here. Got any ideas?

Sangita: I know exactly what to do. I've been reading *Head First Git* to learn about collaborating using Git. Let's start with a shared repository in GitHub, and then you and I can use it to collaborate. Hey, Marge! Can you help us create a repository on GitHub?

Marge: Oh yeah, no worries. Easy peasy. I'll let you know when it's ready.

Sangita: Thanks, Marge. You good with that, Addison?

Addison: You showed me how to work with a remote before, so I think I know what to do there—clone the repository, create a branch off `master`, and get to work.

Sangita: Yep! You got it. Why don't you take on the FAQ, and I will work on the sample profile page?

Addison: That works. But what should I do when I'm ready to merge my work into `master`? Can I just merge it?

Sangita: Remember, we will ***both*** be working on clones of the ***same*** repository. There are a few more things I'll need to show you so we don't end up stepping on each other's toes.

Addison: I guess I can start working for now.

Sangita: We can "circle back" when you're in a good place.

Working in parallel

Building a car involves a bunch of complex pieces coming together. Imagine if one person had to work on all the different pieces in a car one by one, in sequence. They'd have to start by building the chassis, then the engine block, then the transmission block, and so forth. Seems kinda slow, huh?

Of course, that isn't how it's done in real life. That's why assembly lines were invented. To make things go faster, we have one team work on the chassis while another team puts the engine together and the transmission team works on the powertrain and gear box in their own little corner. It's a lot more efficient to work in parallel!

Of course, at some point, things have to come together. Given the transmission team spends most of its time in a heated debate discussing the differences between all-wheel drive and four-wheel drive (seriously, though—if all does not mean four, then does that mean there are cars out there with more than four wheels?), the engine team might be done. So then we can put together the chassis and the engine. When the transmission team is ready, they will have to figure out how to integrate their work with everything that has already been assembled.

Automotive experts—we realize that this isn't an accurate description of how cars are built. We've simplified it for the sake of analogy. Don't @ us!

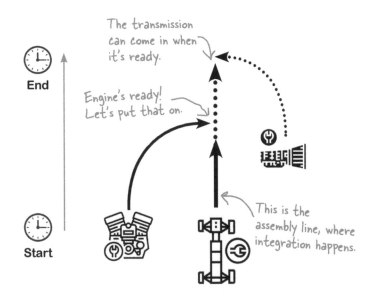

The transmission can come in when it's ready.

Engine's ready! Let's put that on.

This is the assembly line, where integration happens.

End

Start

The same logic is applicable in a variety of situations. Different teams work on different parts of a project—maybe a software development team cranks out new features while the graphic designers are busy creating images and icons. These teams can work in parallel and integrate their work when they are ready.

We already know how to work on different tasks simultaneously in Git—we use branches. Speaking of which...

Working in parallel...in Gitland

So how does all this play out with Git? You already know the secret sauce—shared repositories! You can use any repository manager out there, like GitHub, to share a repository between all the collaborators. Each member gets a copy of the repository by cloning it. Then they start to work in parallel, just like the car assembly line, and integrate when ready.

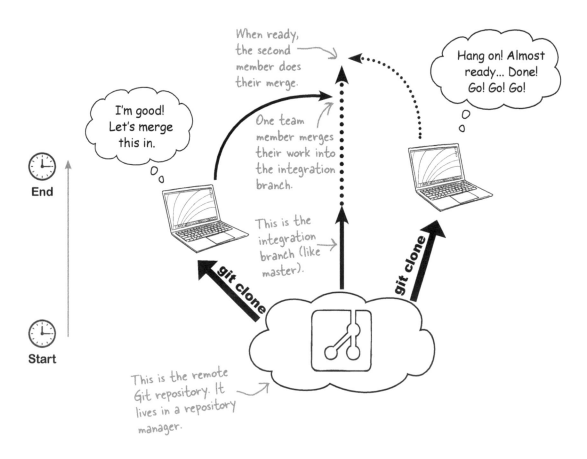

After cloning the repository, every collaborator proceeds to follow the workflow we've used throughout this book—first create a branch based on an integration branch, then get to work. When they are ready to integrate their work, they can either merge their work into the integration branch, or push their branch up to the remote and issue a pull request.

Naturally, when multiple members collaborate on a distributed version control system, there are challenges. We'll spend some time talking about those, but worry not! By the end of this chapter, you'll be a commit-wielding collaboration ninja!

Test Drive

Are you ready to put the pedal to the metal? We've created a repository for you to practice with.

➤ Your first task is to fork our repository, so you get a copy of it under your account in GitHub. Navigate to *https://github.com/looselytyped/hawtdawg-all-ears* using your favorite browser, log in (if you haven't already), and then click the Fork button at the top:

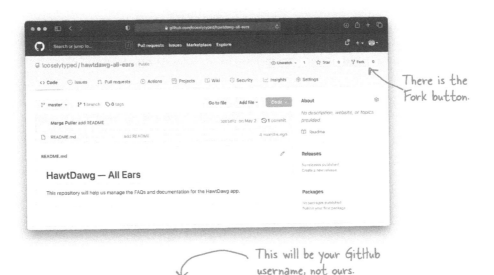

There is the Fork button.

This will be your GitHub username, not ours.

➤ The URL will look like *https://github.com/looselytyped/hawtdawg-all-ears*, but with your username. Jot it down here, just so you have it.

⟶ This is one of the exercises with no solution shown.

Cubicle conversation (continued)

Marge: I've created the repository on GitHub. Feel free to clone it when you're ready to work.

Addison: Thanks, Marge! I've been told they need this done pronto, so I'll get started right away.

Sangita: That was quick. I'll try to get to it soon. We're still drumming up ideas for the sample profile. Anyway, really appreciate it, Marge!

Collaborating, Git style

This is probably a good time to tell you that this chapter is going to be a **lot** more fun if you can find someone to work through it with you. It is a chapter about collaboration, after all! You and your partner will play the roles of Addison and Sangita to help us demonstrate how two different contributors—each working at their own pace—can collaborate effectively using Git. Each player works on their own workstation—one plays Addison and the other, Sangita.

Ask your spouse or partner, bribe your kid, trick your coworker, dupe a relative—it's all good. We can all use a little Git in our lives, right?

To start, we are going to ask that you create **two clones** of the `hawtdawg-all-ears` repository that you just forked. If you've found a willing partner (or an unwitting one—we aren't picky), each of you should clone the `hawtdawg-all-ears` repository **on your respective workstations**, thus making two clones total. Decide who will play which role.

If you're going solo instead, you'll have to clone the repository twice (don't worry—we will show you how). You will play **both** Addison and Sangita.

Just to keep things clear, we'll designate the person playing Addison as Player One and the person playing Sangita as Player Two. Each exercise has an icon that tells you which player should do the exercise.

The one-finger symbol means this exercise is for Player One (Addison). If you're playing solo, switch to the directory that represents Addison's clone. (We'll remind you.)

Any time you see the two-finger symbol, it's Player Two's (Sangita) turn to do the exercise.

Write your names next to the roles here, so you don't forget who's playing who.

_____ plays Addison.

_____ plays Sangita.

For exercises that involve both players, you'll see both images—that's the cue for everyone to get to work.

Now, even when it's not your turn, you should still be paying attention! **Be sure to read through all the exercises** so you know what the other player is up to.

All this may sound daunting, but don't worry—we will be right here, guiding you through it all.

Let's do this!

The setup for two collaborators on GitHub

We certainly hope you've found someone to collaborate with on this chapter—we promise, it *will* be a better experience! If you are going to go through this chapter on your own, though—that is, you are playing both Addison and Sangita—you can skip this section.

As a reminder, when you forked `hawtdawg-all-ears`, GitHub created a copy of that repository under *your* account. Now, if you are going to collaborate with someone on your forked copy, you will need to add them as a collaborator on GitHub. This allows them to push branches and commits to the repository under *your* account. To get started, browse to your fork of our repository on *GitHub.com*.

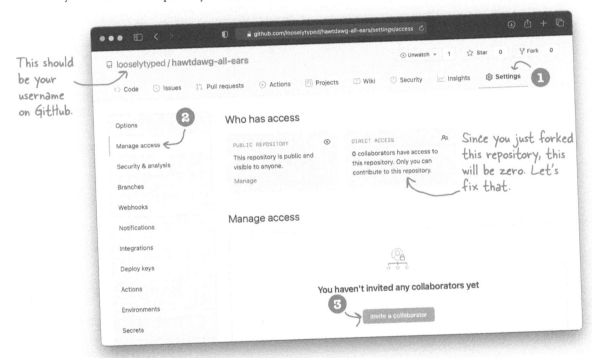

① **Start by clicking on the "Settings" tab.**

This will open up a panel where GitHub gives you tons of dials and levers to manage your repository. For now, we'll just focus on adding collaborators.

② **Click on the "Manage access" menu item on the left.**

Since you just forked this repository, you'll have 0 collaborators.

③ **Click on the green "Invite a collaborator" button.**

When you click on this, GitHub will (most likely) prompt you for your password again. Type that in, then turn the page...

The setup for two collaborators on GitHub (continued)

You're almost ready to play! GitHub makes it easy to search for collaborators—you can use your co-conspirator's GitHub username or email, and there's an autocompleting drop-down list so you can find them faster:

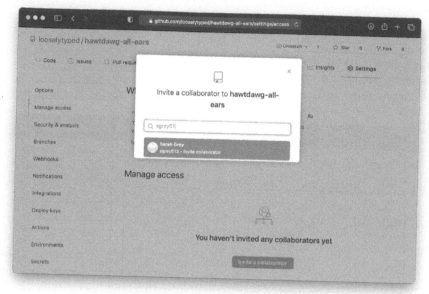

Make sure you get the name right! Once you select your collaborator, GitHub shows you a list of the collaborators on your repository so you can confirm that all went well:

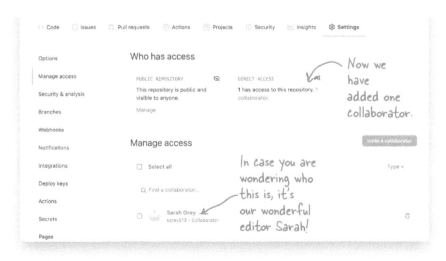

Remember—only <u>one</u> of you has to fork our repository. The two of you will collaborate on the <u>same</u> repository.

There you have it. Both you and your partner can push branches and commits to your fork of the `hawtdawg-all-ears` repository. Time to get to work.

Test Drive

This is for both players. If you're playing solo, you will do this exercise twice. Don't fret—we've made it pretty easy.

➤ First things first—locating the clone URL for the repository. You can do this by navigating to the forked repository on GitHub. Be sure to pick the HTTPS URL!

Remember, this has to be the username of whoever forked our repository.

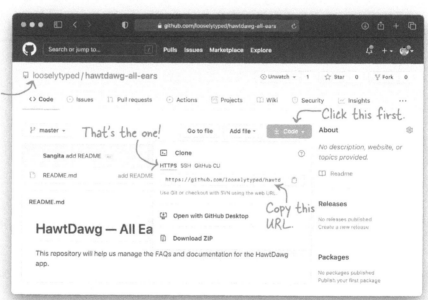

➤ Start with the terminal and navigate to the location where you store your files for all the other exercises for this book. (We created a folder called `chapter06` to use for all exercises in the chapter, but you do you!)

You have all you need to get started, but you aren't done with this exercise. Turn the page.

continued on the next page...

Test Drive

Recall that when you clone a repository, Git creates a folder with the same name as the remote. To avoid any confusion and make it easier for those playing solo, we are going to rename the folder that Git creates to indicate whose clone it is. For example, Addison's clone will be in a folder called `addisons-clone`. To make this happen, we're going to use a special variant of the `git clone` command:

We mentioned this variant of the git clone command in passing in Chapter 5.

This will be your username.

Supply the name of the folder to create.

```
git clone https://github.com/username/hawtdawg-all-ears.git    folder-name
```

If this is a two-player game for you, then this is for Player One, that is, the player role-playing Addison. If you are playing solo, then you should do this exercise.

➤ Ready Player One? You are going to clone the recently forked `hawtdawg-all-ears` repository locally. Here is the command to use:

Insert your GitHub username of the player who forked our repo.

git clone https://github.com/username/hawtdawg-all-ears.git addisons-clone

Name the folder appropriately.

Important! If you are playing solo, do **not** change directories just yet—you still have one more clone to go.

This is for Player Two. If you are playing solo, this applies to you as well.

➤ Player Two! You are going to clone the remote to a folder called `sangitas-clone`, like so:

Be sure to use the username of whoever cloned the repo.

Name it correctly for Player Two.

git clone https://github.com/username/hawtdawg-all-ears.git sangitas-clone

⟶ This is one of the exercises with no solution shown.

Our setup so far

Wow! You've accomplished a lot here, so let's take a step back to see where things stand. We are going to split this conversation into two parts: we'll start by looking at what happened with the two-player version, then with the solo version.

Two-player setup

One of you started by forking the `hawtdawg-all-ears` repository that we created for you, which you then cloned to your respective workstations: one in the `addisons-clone` folder, one in the `sangitas-clone` folder. This is how it looks:

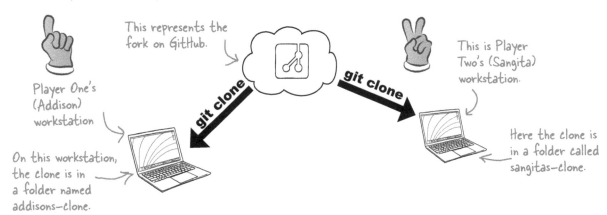

One-player setup

You forked the `hawtdawg-all-ears` repository and then proceeded to clone the repository *twice*—once in the `addisons-clone` folder, and then again in a sibling folder called `sangitas-clone`:

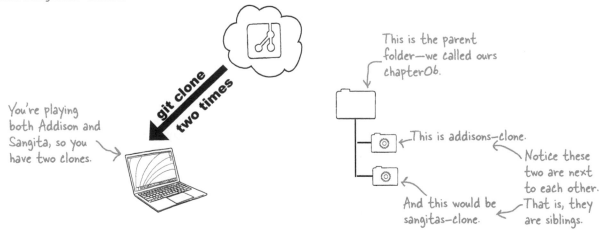

Exercise

This exercise is for both players.

You are going to spend a little time looking around the repository you cloned. Each player should navigate to the location where they have their respective clones. **For those playing solo**, navigate to `addisons-clone` for this exercise.

✱ Start by using `git log --graph --oneline --all` to inspect your repository's history. Use the space provided below to sketch it out:

→ Answers on page 332.

Brain Power

So far, there exist two clones of the same repository. If this is a two-player game for you, then each player has a clone on their individual workstation. If you're on your own, then you have two separate clones in two different directories on your machine.

Will the histories of the two clones look the same? Explain your answer.

there are no Dumb Questions

Q: This may be off-topic, but is it usual to rename the folder when you clone?

A: We'll admit it is a tad unusual. We usually prefer to keep the name of the folder that we clone the same as the name of the remote.

The only time we've found a good reason to rename the clone folder is if we have a conflict. That is: somehow, the folder in which we are about to clone a repository happens to contain another directory with the same name as the repository. As you can imagine, this is very rare.

However, in this chapter we used the special variant of the `git clone` command to help you discern between the two clones—that's it.

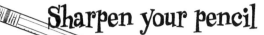

Sharpen your pencil

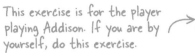

This exercise is for the player playing Addison. If you are by yourself, do this exercise.

➤ Player One, it's time for you to make some edits to the repository. Using your terminal, navigate to the location that contains `addisons-clone`. First, create a new branch based on the `master` branch. Call the new branch `addison-first-faq`. Use the following space to list the commands you will use. (**Hint:** Always be sure to check the status and verify what branch you are on before creating new branches.)

➤ Using your text editor, create a new text file called `FAQ.md` with the following contents:

This is what the FAQ.md file should look like.

You can find this file in the code you downloaded for this book under chapter06 in a file called FAQ-1.md. Be sure to rename it to FAQ.md!

```
# FAQ


## How many photos can I post?


We know you want to show off your fabulous furry face, so we've given you
space to upload up to 15 photos!

For those who are camera-shy, we recommend posting at least one to bring
your profile some attention.

Showcase your best self—whether that means a fresh-from-the-groomer glamour
shot or an action shot from your last game of fetch.
```

FAQ.md

➤ Save the file, add `FAQ.md` to the index, and then commit it with the message "addison's first commit".

➤ Using `git log --graph --oneline --all`, sketch out your commit history here:

➤ If you were to merge the `addison-first-faq` branch into `master`, would that create a child commit or a fast-forward merge? Explain your answer here:

➤ Answers on page 333.

Cubicle conversation (continued)

Addison: Hey, Sangita! I cloned the repository you shared with me and made an edit to the FAQ page. I'm done with this change. What's next?

Sangita: Wow! That was quick. All I've managed to do is clone the repository. I don't want to hold you up. Go ahead and merge it into the `master` branch and then push the `master` branch to the remote. I'm still stuck in meetings all day, but I'll try to get some of the sample profile done tomorrow.

Addison: Will do. Thanks, Sangita.

Exercise

This exercise is for Player One (Addison) and for solo players.

Your task this time around is to make the work that Addison did on the `addison-first-faq` branch available on the remote. As we showed you in Chapter 5, you can do this in one of two ways: merge locally and then push the integration branch, or push the `addison-first-faq` branch to the remote and then issue a pull request on GitHub. We're going to keep it simple and do the merge locally for this exercise. (In general, though, if you're working with a team, be sure to conform to the established conventions.)

✳ Start by merging the `addison-first-faq` branch into the `master` branch. It might help to list the commands you are going to use before you do the merge. (**Hint:** Always check your status. Remember, you **will** need to switch to the `master` branch because you are merging `addison-first-faq` *into* the `master` branch.)

Note that this was a fast-forward merge.

✳ Next, push the `master` branch to the remote using the `git push` command.

Use this space to list the commands you are going to use.

✳ Since your work in the feature branch has been merged into master, you can safely delete the `addison-first-faq` branch.

Answers on page 334.

Falling behind the remote

Git is distributed. The remote is unaware of any changes you make to your clone, like creating a branch or making commits. Turns out that's a double-edged sword! If a collaborator pushes a commit to a branch (say, an integration branch like `master`), your clone isn't informed in any way. That's exactly how things have transpired so far in the `hawtdawg-all-ears` repository. Let's take a look to see where things stand:

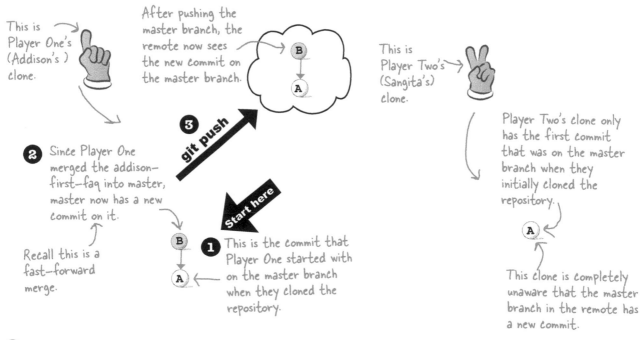

This is Player One's (Addison's) clone.

After pushing the master branch, the remote now sees the new commit on the master branch.

This is Player Two's (Sangita's) clone.

3 git push

2 Since Player One merged the addison—first—faq into master, master now has a new commit on it.

Recall this is a fast—forward merge.

Start here

1 This is the commit that Player One started with on the master branch when they cloned the repository.

Player Two's clone only has the first commit that was on the master branch when they initially cloned the repository.

This clone is completely unaware that the master branch in the remote has a new commit.

1 **Player One cloned the hawtdawg-all-ears repository.**
Cloning the `hawtdawg-all-ears` repository brought along with it one commit on the `master` branch ("A").

2 **Player One introduced a new commit on master.**
Player One started to work on their clone—they created a branch based on `master`, made a commit, and then merged that branch back into `master`. Now their `master` branch points to the new commit ("B").

3 **Player One pushed the master branch to the remote.**
Player One updated the remote by pushing the `master` branch to the remote. After the push, the remote also has the new commit ("B") as the only child of the original commit ("A").

All along, while Player One (Addison) has been busy at work, all Player Two (Sangita) has done is to clone the repository. Which means that, while Player Two's clone has the initial commit that was there on the `master` branch ("A") when they cloned the repository, it doesn't have the latest changes that have shown up on the remote!

Cubicle conversation (continued)

Addison: Hey, Sangita! I haven't seen you all week. Busy in meetings, huh? Anyway, just wanted to let you know—I merged my changes into the `master` branch and pushed.

Sangita: Nice work. I have some time today, so I will get started with the sample profile. I probably should make sure I have all the latest commits in the remote, including the changes you pushed to the `master` branch.

Addison: So, if I pushed, do you have to *pull*?

Sangita: Yes, exactly! You've been reading up on Git?

Addison: Uh, no! I was just being facetious.

Sangita: Funny how that works out sometimes. Git offers a command called `pull`, which lets you catch up with changes in the remote. Using the `git pull` command, I can update my local copy of the `master` branch with the commits that you pushed to the remote.

Addison: Mind if I sit with you and see how to do this?

Sangita: Of course! Let's do it right now.

Catching up with the remote (git pull)

How does one "catch up" with changes that appear in the remote? The answer is another Git command: pull. The role of the `git pull` command is to check if any new commits have appeared on the remote repository *for a particular branch*, and if so, retrieve those commits and update your local branch with the new commits.

Say this is your local master branch, which only has one commit.

Another collaborator pushes a new commit to the master branch.

This is the new commit.

git pull

Git fetches the new commit and adds to the commit history of the master branch in your clone.

The `git pull` command attempts to find the remote counterpart of the branch you are on, then asks the remote if there are any new commits on that branch. If there are, it will fetch those commits and add them to your local history.

Catching up with the remote (git pull, continued)

Let's see what Git does when you invoke the `git pull` command. Remember, you always pull the changes for a *particular* branch, so it's best to start by making sure you are on the right branch.

> Sit back and just soak it in. We'll have an exercise for you soon enough.

```
File Edit Window Help
$ git branch
* master          ←  Make sure you are on the correct
                      branch.

$ git pull    ←  Ask Git to pull the latest commits.
remote: Enumerating objects: 4, done.
remote: Counting objects: 100% (4/4), done.
remote: Compressing objects: 100% (3/3), done.
remote: Total 3 (delta 0), reused 0 (delta 0), pack-reused 0
Unpacking objects: 100% (3/3), 518 bytes | 259.00 KiB/s, done.
From github.com:looselytyped/hawtdawg-all-ears
   32b1d92..1975528  master      -> origin/master
Updating 32b1d92..1975528
Fast-forward
 FAQ.md | 7 +++++++
 1 file changed, 7 insertions(+)
 create mode 100644 FAQ.md
```

Git fetches new commits in the remote.

Ignore this for now.

Ah! Looks like we have the FAQ.md file now.

That was easy! Now the latest commit on the `master` branch in the remote will show up in the clone's commit history.

Exercise

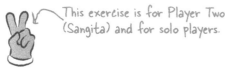 This exercise is for Player Two (Sangita) and for solo players.

✳ Let's make sure Sangita's clone has all the commits Addison pushed up to the remote's `master` branch. Navigate to `sangitas-clone` in your terminal. Write down the commands you will use to update your local `master` branch with the commits on the remote.

Hint: Always be sure to check what branch you are on before pulling!

✳ Next, run the commands you listed to update your local `master` branch.

Answers on page 335.

there are no
Dumb Questions

Q: There's the `git pull` **command, and there are pull requests—these sound pretty similar. Are they connected in any way?**

A: No. We realize it's confusing, but they are two different things. Pull requests are a GitHub feature that can be thought of as a "merge request," as we described in the last chapter. They offer a mechanism to tell fellow collaborators that you have some changes in a branch you wish to merge into another branch, usually an integration branch. All this is happening in GitHub—that is, in the remote.

The `git pull` command, on the other hand, allows you to update a branch *in your clone* with any commits that might have shown up on its counterpart branch in the remote repository.

Q: **How do I know that the remote has anything new for me to pull?**

A: You don't. However, if you issue the `git pull` command and there is nothing new to pull, Git will simply report `Already up to date`. No harm done.

Q: **This seems silly—why can't Git inform me that something in the remote changed? Isn't that the role of computers—to automate away the mundane?**

A: That's a fair point. If you recall, we warned you in the previous chapter—one of the most common things users forget to do is to push commits that they want to make available in the remote. The reason for that lies in Git's distributed nature—the system is designed so that the remote *is* unaware of any changes, such as any new branches or commits you've made in your clone.

The same reason applies to changes in the remote. The repository could have any number of clones, so expecting the remote to inform every clone that something has changed isn't very feasible.

So why doesn't Git have your clone automatically check the remote every so often to see if anything new has arrived? Well, you might not care about what changes have occurred in the remote. You might care about commits that show up on some branches and not others. You might care about new branches that somebody else has pushed to the remote, or you might not.

By handing over control to you, Git eliminates the guesswork. If and when you are interested in getting updates for any branch, you explicitly invoke the `git pull` command.

Q: **Is the** `git pull` **command the opposite of the** `git push` **command?**

A: It certainly seems that way, doesn't it? The `git push` command takes your local commits and sends them to the remote, and the `git pull` command brings remote commits and updates your local branches. However, they are not quite opposites.

Soon we will explain exactly what happens when you do a `git pull`, but for now, as long as you understand what the `git pull` command does, you are good to go.

Serious Coding

Git offers a multitude of ways to configure its behavior. In Chapter 5, for example, we set the `push.default` configuration to `simple`. This makes it so that when you push or pull a branch, *only the branch you are on* gets pushed (or pulled). As you get more experienced with Git, feel free to look at the documentation to see other options are available.

But if you ask us, we *always* use the `simple` option because we feel it's the least confusing *and* least surprising. We suggest you keep it as is.

> Every time I perform a git push or a git pull, I see references to "origin/master." "Origin" is the name of my remote, so I'm thinking this has something to do with the remote, right?

Right! These references that you see every time you check your status are a ***super important*** part of understanding how to work with remotes. So, yes! You are absolutely right in thinking these have to do with the remote.

We are going to be spending a lot of time discussing these references in detail, but for now, here's a high-level look at their role in your repository:

1 They are Git's bookmarks, so Git knows what to do when you push a branch to the remote.

2 They help you get updates that happen in the remote, so you're always working from the most up-to-date version.

3 They can tell you that you have commits in your clone that aren't in the remote—that is, you need to push.

4 They offer a safe way to "catch up" with the remote.

They seem pretty useful, right? Gosh! We can't wait to tell you all about these useful little things. Do you feel the energy yet? What are you waiting for? Look to the next page already!

Introducing the middlemen, aka remote tracking branches

You already know what happens when you clone a Git repository—Git creates the necessary folders, copies the commit history into your local .git directory, and finally switches to the default branch.

Flip back to Chapter 5 if you need a reminder on the details here.

And it does one more thing.

It creates a set of branches that have the same name as the branches in the remote, except they have the name of the remote (origin by default) prefixed to the name of the branch. For example, if the repository you cloned had a master branch, your local clone will have an origin/master branch. After the cloning is complete, your local master branch, the origin/master branch, and the remote's master branch all point to the same commit ID.

Recall that you can find the "name" of your remote using the git remote -v (or -vv) command. By default this is always "origin."

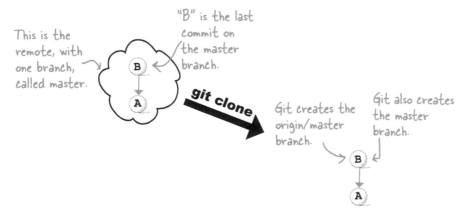

This is the remote, with one branch, called master.

"B" is the last commit on the master branch.

git clone

Git creates the origin/master branch.

Git also creates the master branch.

Let it wash over you. There's an exercise just around the corner.

These branches that Git creates when you clone (prefixed with the name of the remote) are called ***remote tracking branches***. Git hints at their presence in the output of many commands—you've probably seen references to remote tracking branches when you check the status of your repository. For example:

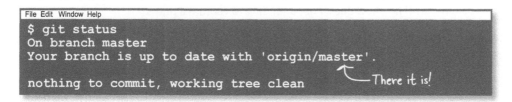

```
File Edit Window Help
$ git status
On branch master
Your branch is up to date with 'origin/master'.

nothing to commit, working tree clean
```
There it is!

Remote tracking branches are different from the branches that you've worked with so far—you can't switch to them, you can't create or delete them. In fact, you have no control over these branches. They are meant to be managed by Git. On the prevous page, we listed several of the roles these remote tracking branches play. Now let's dive into the details.

This is an important point!

Reason 1 for remote tracking branches: knowing where to push

Nothing for you to do just yet.

The first reason for remote tracking branches is so Git knows what to do when you perform certain Git operations, like pushing or pulling. Git can tell you which branches in your local clone are connected to branches in the remote. You can ask it using the `git branch` command, like so:

Invoke the git branch command with the -vv (very verbose) flag.

You've used the -v flag with the branch command in Chapter 2.

There is no -vvv option. But nice try. ;-)

```
File Edit Window Help
$ git branch -vv        This is the letter "v"
                        repeated twice.
* master 1975528 [origin/master] add first FAQ
        The master branch is connected to the
        master branch in the remote (origin).
```

You might recall (from Chapter 2) that the `branch` command has a flag called `verbose` (longhand for `-v`) that displays detailed information about your branches. The `git branch` command also supports the double-v (`-vv`) flag, which stands for *very verbose*. Using this option reveals even more information about your branches, which includes the name of the remote tracking branch associated with a branch (if it has one). The next time you push (or pull), Git knows that the local `master` branch's counterpart in the remote (named `origin`) is a branch called `master` (hence `origin/master`). This means that the next time you push, Git will update the remote's `master` branch with any new commits you added on your local `master` branch.

Brain Power

Our discussion on remote tracking branches does beg a question—what if you created a new branch in your clone? Does it have a remote? If not, how does it get one? Care to venture a guess?

We'll give you a hint—in Chapter 5, we showed you that when you attempt to push a **brand-new branch** (say, `feat-a`) to the remote, the push fails the first time. Git asks that you "set" the "upstream," like so:

```
git push --set-upstream origin feat-a
```

Remember that --set-upstream is just the longhand version of the -u flag.

What do you think the `--set-upstream` (or `-u`) flag does? Why? Take your notes here:

Reason 1 for remote tracking branches: knowing where to push (continued)

Now that you understand *one* reason why remote tracking branches exist, the question remains, what about new branches? How does Git know where to push a newly created branch? Well, if you attempted to answer the last Brain Power, then perhaps you have the answer (or a glimpse of it, anyway). Let's unravel the mystery behind the `--set-upstream` flag once and for all. Consider the repository we've been working in this chapter. It has only one branch, called `master`.

> Soak it in. We'll let you know when it's your turn.

We talked about this in Chapter 5.

List the branches in verbose mode.

Create a new branch.

Inspect our branches again.

Switch to the new branch.

Attempt to push. We know from Chapter 5 that this fails.

Set the upstream when we push.

List the branches again, in very verbose mode.

```
File  Edit  Window  Help
$ git branch -vv
* master 1975528 [origin/master] add first FAQ

$ git branch feat-a

$ git branch -vv
  feat-a 1975528 add first FAQ
* master 1975528 [origin/master] add first FAQ

$ git switch feat-a
Switched to branch 'feat-a'

$ git push
fatal: The current branch feat-a has no upstream branch.
To push the current branch and set the remote as upstream, use

    git push --set-upstream origin feat-a

$ git push --set-upstream origin feat-a
Total 0 (delta 0), reused 0 (delta 0), pack-reused 0
To  github.com:looselytyped/hawtdawg-all-ears.git
 * [new branch]      feat-a -> feat-a
Branch 'feat-a' set up to track remote branch 'feat-a' from 'origin'.

$ git branch -vv
* feat-a 1975528 [origin/feat-a] add first FAQ
  master 1975528 [origin/master] add first FAQ
```

We only have one branch with a remote tracking branch.

Notice that our new branch does not have a remote tracking branch just yet.

Git very nicely tells us what to do.

Now, THAT sounds promising!

Now our new branch has a tracking branch.

We realize there is a lot going on here, so take a moment to breathe and let it marinate. We aren't going anywhere.

When we "set" the "upstream" for a branch—`origin feat-a` like we did in this example—we are telling Git that the branch it should be tracking in the remote (`origin` in this case) is a branch called `feat-a`.

So what does the commit history of your repository look like after you push? Up next!

Remote tracking branch after you push

When you push, you are asking Git to synchronize the commits on your local branch with its counterpart in the remote. In other words, the remote branch will point to the same commit your local branch does. But where does that leave the remote tracking branch? Let's continue the discussion from the previous page:

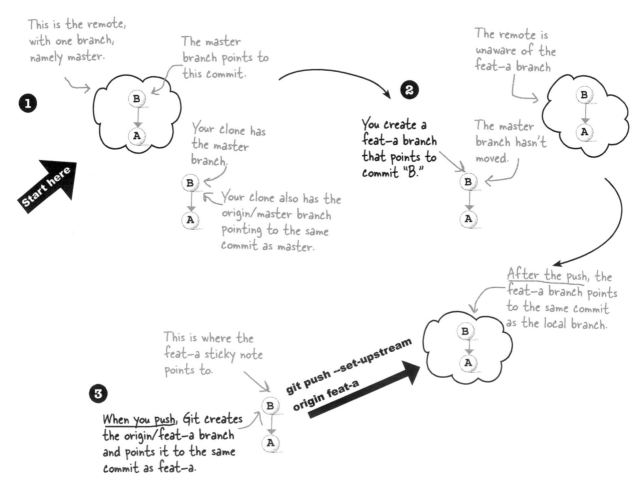

As you can see, **as soon as you push**, your local branch, its counterpart in the remote, and the newly created remote tracking branch (origin/feat-a, in this case) all point to the same commit ID. Recall that once you set the upstream for a branch, you *never have to do it again*—and now you know the reason. Git records *where* to push a branch with the help of the remote tracking branch.

That explains one reason why Git creates tracking branches, and how you would go about setting the remote for a new local branch.

There's more to remote tracking branches. But first, why don't you spend a little time with remote tracking branches?

Exercise

This exercise is for Player One; if you're playing solo, then it applies to you, too.

✱ It's time for you to spend a little time investigating how remote tracking branches work in your respective clones. Using your terminal, navigate to `addisons-clone`. List all your branches and their respective remote tracking branches (if any) using the `git branch` command with the `-vv` (double-v) flag:

```
File Edit Window Help



```

✱ Create a new branch called `addison-add-faqs` based on `master` and switch to it. We've provided this space so you can list out the commands you are going to use:

✱ Edit the `FAQ.md` file in the repository and **add** a second FAQ, like so:

Add this entry to the FAQ.md file.

Or you can use the FAQ-2.md file we provided in the source code for Chapter 6. Be sure to overwrite the existing FAQ.md.

```
## Where do I list my favorite treats?


Open the Hawt Dawg app and click on "Edit Profile."

Scroll down to the section called "Passions" and tell
potential mates and friends all about the treats and toys
that make your tail wag.

When you're done, click "Save Changes" to show the world.
```

✱ Add the `FAQ.md` file to the index and commit it with the commit message "add second FAQ".

FAQ.md

continued on the next page...

Exercise

Still Player
One! Solo
players, too.

✱ Use the `git branch` command with the `-vv` flag and write out what you see. (Note: you will not see the remote tracking branch for the newly created `addison-add-faqs` branch just yet.)

File Edit Window Help

✱ Next, push the `addison-add-faqs` branch to the remote. List the command you are going to use here:

✱ Use the `git branch` command again, with the "very verbose" flag. Do you see the remote tracking branch?

File Edit Window Help

Lightning Round!

Tick-tock!
Tick-tock!

✱ How many branches (including remote tracking branches) are in your repository?

✱ How many branches are there in the remote?

✱ True or false? Your local `addison-faq-branch`, `origin/addison-faq-branch`, and the remote's `addison-faq-branch` all point to the same commit.

✱ Does Sangita's clone know of the newly created `addison-add-faqs` branch?

→ Answers on page 337.

Exercise

This exercise is for Player Two, or if you are playing solo.

If you are playing solo, these steps might seem repetitious, but don't skip them. This is setting you up for the discussion to follow.

✱ Just like Player One, you, too, are going to spend a few minutes investigating how remote tracking branches work. Since you are playing Sangita, using your terminal, navigate to `sangitas-clone`. Using the `git branch` command with the `-vv` (double-v) flag, list your branches and their respective remote tracking branches, if any:

```
File  Edit  Window  Help



```

✱ Create a new branch based on `master`, call it `sangita-add-profile`, and switch to it. List out the commands you are going to need here:

✱ Using your text editor, create a new file in `sangitas-clone` called `Profile.md`. Add the following contents:

We've provided this in a file called Profile-1.md in the source code for chapter06. Be sure to rename it Profile.md!

```
# Profile

Name:  **Roland H. Hermon**

Age:  **3**

Breed:  **Beagle**

Location:  **Philadelphia**
```

Profile.md

✱ Add the `Profile.md` file to the index and commit it with the message "add sample profile".

continued on the next page...

Exercise

Yep! Still Player
Two and solo
players!

✱ Use the `git branch` command along with the "very verbose" (`-vv`) flag to inspect all your branches and their remote tracking branches (if any) again. (Pay attention to the newly created `sangita-add-profile` branch.)

```
File Edit Window Help



```

✱ Push the `sangita-add-profile` branch to the remote. Start by listing the command you are going to use to do that:

✱ Finally, use the `git branch` with the `-vv` flag again. Does your newly created `sangita-add-profile` branch now have a remote tracking branch?

```
File Edit Window Help



```

Lightning Round!

If you are playing solo, you can skip these. You've already answered these for addisons-clone.

Then again, practice does make perfect....

✱ How many branches (including remote tracking branches) are in your repository?

✱ How many branches are there in the remote?

✱ True or false? Your local `sangita-add-profile`, `origin/sangita-add-profile`, and the remote's `sangita-add-profile` all point to the same commit.

✱ Does Addison's clone know of the newly created `sangita-add-profile` branch?

⟶ **Answers on page 338–339.**

there are no
Dumb Questions

Q: We have tracked files in Git, and now we are talking about (remote) tracking branches. Any relation?

A: No. We realize this is confusing (like `git pull` and pull requests), but these are not related in any way. A "tracked" file is a file that Git knows about—at some point you added this file to the index.

Remote tracking branches, as we have seen, are to help Git know where to push. You can think of them as "bookmarks"— they help Git remember how to associate a branch locally with its counterpart in the remote. In short, they help track branches.

Q: I think I'm missing something— why does Git even need "bookmarks"? I mean, wouldn't I *always* want to push my local master branch to the remote's master branch? Seems rather obvious.

A: Recall that the name of the remote tracking branch has two parts to it. Consider `origin/master`—"origin" here stands for the default name that Git gives your remote when you clone (as shown by the output of the `git remote -v` command). We mentioned in Chapter 5 that you can change the name of the remote to something other than `origin`. Let's say you called it `upstream`. If you had done so, then the name of the remote tracking branch would be `upstream/master`. As you can see, it's not obvious what the remote's name would be.

Also, there is no mandate that you have to push your local `master` branch to the remote's `master` branch. Remember that when you set upstream, the second argument is the name of the branch in the remote—which means you could set the remote branch for your local `master` branch to some other branch! However, this is not something you do often— typically, you'll push your local branch to a branch with the same name in the remote.

Q: I get that when I push, Git updates the remote, and it also updates my remote tracking branch to point to the new commit. But what about `git pull`? Does it affect the remote tracking branch?

A: Great question! Yes, it does. When you do a `git pull`, Git fetches any new commits it sees in the remote for *that particular branch* and updates the remote tracking branch. It then proceeds to update your branch to point to the same commit that the remote tracking branch points to.

In other words: after you invoke the `git pull` command, the remote branch, your remote tracking branch, and your local branch will all point to the same commit ID.

Who Does What?

→ Answers on page 340.

You've built quite the repertoire of Git commands so far! Let's see if you can match each command to its description:

clone   Displays details about the remote

remote   Shows a list of all your branches.

branch   Lists all branches along with their remote tracking branches (if any)

push   Is another way to initialize a Git repository

branch -vv   Updates the remote branch with any new commits you made locally

Pushing to the remote: summary

Phew! That was quite the exercise. Let's do a quick recap to make sure we are all on the same page.

Player One (Addison), working in `addisons-clone`, created a new branch called `addison-add-faqs` based on `master`, made a commit, and pushed that branch to the remote.

Meanwhile, Player Two (Sangita), working in `sangitas-clone`, created a new branch called `sangita-add-profile`, added a sample profile page, made a commit, and pushed that to the remote.

All said and done, this is where things stand:

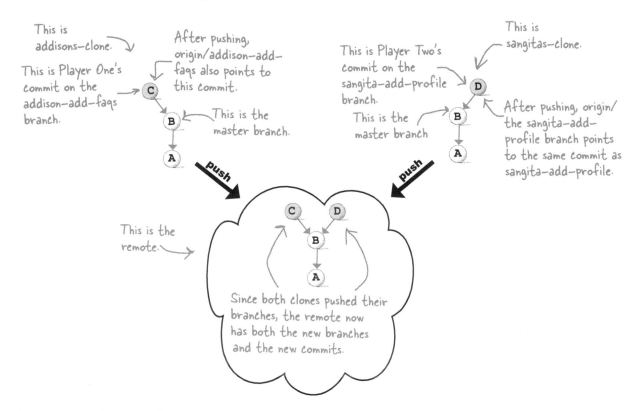

As you can see, the remote has the complete commit history now that both clones have pushed their respective changes. However, Player One's clone does not have Player Two's changes, and vice versa. But what if Player Two (playing Sangita) wants to see what Player One (playing Addison) did on their branch? How would they go about getting the `addison-add-faqs` branch from the remote?

The answer to that question alludes to the second reason that Git has remote tracking branches.

Fetching remote tracking branches

Git shines when it comes to collaboration. Branching is cheap! Branches are simply sticky notes that point to commits in your commit history. They allow you to experiment, introduce new features, and fix bugs without disturbing integration branches till you are ready to merge. Branches can be kept private or made public as soon as you push them to the remote.

You already know how to push a local branch to the remote. But how does another collaborator get that branch? The answer lies in another Git command, called `fetch`. The role of the `git fetch` command is to download all new commits and branches from the remote. But it does so with a twist! The `git fetch` command updates your clone *without affecting any of your local branches*. How, you ask? It updates the remote tracking branches.

Consider a hypothetical repository where you only have one branch, called `master`. You just invoked the `git pull` command, so your clone is caught up with the remote.

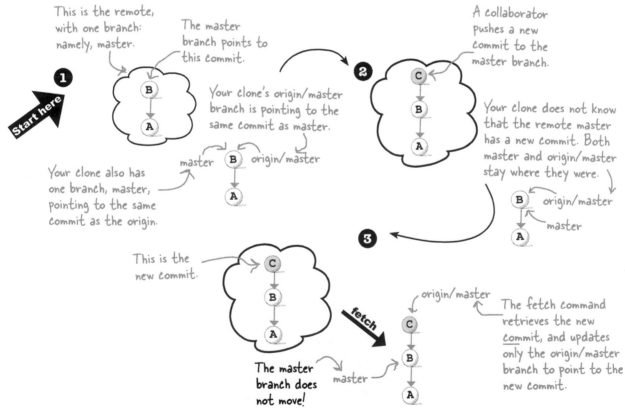

When you perform a `fetch`, much like `pull`, your clone gets the latest commits. But this is where the behavior of `fetch` is different from `pull`—fetch **only** updates the remote tracking branches, whereas `pull`, as you know, updates *both* the remote tracking branch *and* your local branch.

Reason 2 for remote tracking branches: getting (all) updates from the remote

Relax. It's not your turn yet.

You understand what the `git fetch` command does—it fetches any changes in the remote and updates your tracking branches to reflect those changes. But there is one important characteristic of `fetch` that we haven't told you about.

When you invoke the `git fetch` command, it will get **all** new commits and branches from the remote and update your clone with those changes. What does that mean in practice? Let's say a collaborator creates a new branch in their clone, makes some commits, and pushes those commits up to the remote. If you were to `fetch` now, you would get that new branch with all of its commits as part of the fetch, except it would be "tracked" in your clone as a remote tracking branch.

Let's say you are Sangita, happily working in `sangitas-clone`. In the meantime, Addison pushed her `addison-add-faqs` branch to the remote. This is what you will see if you do a `git fetch` in `sangitas-clone`:

Invoke git fetch.

Git does a bunch of work.

```
File Edit Window Help
$ git fetch
remote: Enumerating objects: 5, done.
remote: Counting objects: 100% (5/5), done.
remote: Compressing objects: 100% (3/3), done.
remote: Total 3 (delta 1), reused 0 (delta 0), pack-reused 0
Unpacking objects: 100% (3/3), 508 bytes | 254.00 KiB/s, done.
From github.com:looselytyped/hawtdawg-all-ears
 * [new branch]      addison-add-faqs -> origin/addison-add-faqs
```

There it is!

You can use the `git branch` command with the `-a` flag (shorthand for `--all`) to see a listing of **all** the branches in your repository: that is, the entire list of local and remote tracking branches.

```
File Edit Window Help
$ git branch -a
  master
* sangita-add-profile
  remotes/origin/HEAD -> origin/master
  remotes/origin/addison-add-faqs
  remotes/origin/master
  remotes/origin/sangita-add-profile
```

You can also use --all here if you prefer to be explicit.

And here is the addison-add-faqs branch.

As you can see, fetching gets you all the new commits and branches that are in the remote but aren't present in your clone. Just remember, though, your local branches remain unaffected. Only the remote tracking branches get updated.

Sharpen your pencil

Answers on page 341.

Each player will do this exercise in their respective clone. You're ready! We know it!

If you are playing solo, you will do this exercise twice— once in each clone.

Let's practice the `git fetch` command and see its effects on the remote tracking branches in your repository. To recap, the remote has *both* the `addison-add-faqs` and the `sangita-add-profile` branches.

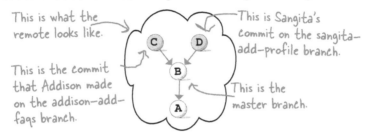

This is what the remote looks like.

This is Sangita's commit on the sangita-add-profile branch.

This is the commit that Addison made on the addison-add-faqs branch.

This is the master branch.

➤ Using your terminal, navigate to your clone—if you are Player One, that would be `addisons-clone`; if you are Player Two, that would be `sangitas-clone`. If you're playing solo, start with `addisons-clone`, followed by `sangitas-clone`. List all the branches in your repository using `git branch --all` (or `git branch -a`) and write them here:

File Edit Window Help

➤ Use the `git fetch` command to fetch anything new in the remote.
➤ Ask your Git repository to list all of its branches again. Write them here and note what has changed.

File Edit Window Help

there are no
Dumb Questions

Q: When I invoke `git pull`, I know I should be on the branch that needs to be updated. Do I need to be on any particular branch when I do a `git fetch`?

A: No. Remember that `git fetch` retrieves *any and all* new branches and commits that are in the remote but aren't present in your clone. Furthermore, `fetch` only updates the remote tracking branches—it leaves your local branches alone.

All this means that it does not matter what branch you are on when you fetch.

In fact, we recommend you get in the habit of fetching often when working in a clone. There is no downside to it. If there's nothing new in the remote, no harm done. And if there is, your local branches don't get affected—so again, no harm done.

Git branch flag soup

Git commands offer a ton of flags that do different things. Listed here are the flags for the `git branch` command that you've seen so far in this book, plus an added surprise!

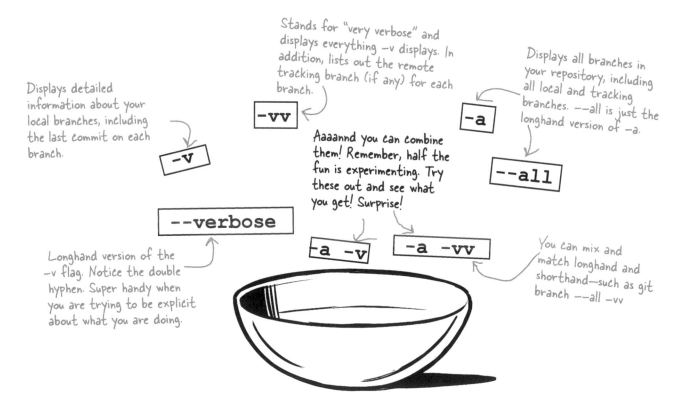

Displays detailed information about your local branches, including the last commit on each branch.

`-v`

Stands for "very verbose" and displays everything -v displays. In addition, lists out the remote tracking branch (if any) for each branch.

`-vv`

Aaaannd you can combine them! Remember, half the fun is experimenting. Try these out and see what you get! Surprise!

Displays all branches in your repository, including all local and tracking branches. --all is just the longhand version of -a.

`-a`

`--all`

`--verbose`

Longhand version of the -v flag. Notice the double hyphen. Super handy when you are trying to be explicit about what you are doing.

`-a -v`   `-a -vv`

You can mix and match longhand and shorthand—such as git branch --all -vv

Cubicle conversation (continued)

Addison: Good thing I managed to catch you today—I am really stuck. I've run out of ideas for the FAQs.

Sangita: I can take a look at it if you want. It's not like I'm making a whole lot of progress on the sample profile. Let's do this—let's swap for today. You take on the sample profile, and I'll tackle the FAQs. Maybe a fresh set of eyes will get the ball rolling.

Addison: That would be swell! I've already committed and pushed my branch to the remote. But I'm not sure how I would get to work on the branch that *you pushed*. I did learn about the `git fetch` command, so I did that. That gets me everything in the remote, right?

Sangita: Exactly. Except `fetch` does not update your local branches—it only updates the remote tracking branches in your clone.

Addison: Yeah, I understand that. I am still not clear how I can help you with your profile. My understanding is that you can't add to the commit histories of remote tracking branches. I mean, I didn't even create them—Git created them.

Sangita: Ha! Well, Git does allow you to switch to them. Like so:

```
git switch sangita-add-profile
```

> If the name of the remote is
> origin/sangita-add-profile, you
> skip the "origin/" part.

Sangita: See how you give it the name of the branch you want to switch to without the name of the remote, just like you would switch to any other branch? When you do that, Git will create a local branch with the same name as the remote tracking branch. And this new branch is just like any other branch that you've worked with so far—you can make commits, you can push and pull it.

Addison: That's easy. Let me try that, and hopefully we'll knock this out in no time.

> About time! My dating profile could use a little oomph. This should help. Let's go, people!

Collaborating with others

We are still talking about Reason 2 for remote tracking branches.

Nothing for you to do here just yet.

By fetching all new commits and branches, the `git fetch` command opens up a way to collaborate. Think about it—if your colleague is working on a task or attempting to fix a bug, using the workflow we shared with you in Chapter 2, they will create a branch based on an integration branch, like `master`.

But what if they want you to take a look at their changes or help out with a tricky issue? Well, you could walk over to their workstation and look over their shoulder.

Or they could push their branch to the remote. On your end, you would do a `git fetch`, which would fetch all remote branches, along with all their commits. Next, you'd switch to it, just like you would any other branch. Voilà—you have a local branch you can look at and work with.

Let's say you are Sangita, and you want to take a look at the changes Addison has introduced in the `addison-add-faqs` branch. Addison has already pushed the `addison-add-faqs` branch to the remote, and you've performed a `fetch`. This is where things stand now:

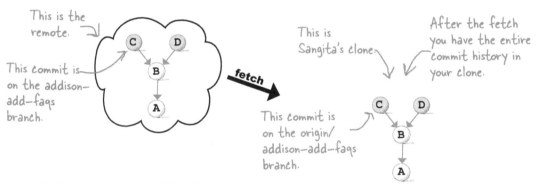

After you fetch, your clone has Addison's new branch and commits, except they are on the remote tracking branch (`origin/addison-add-faqs`). If you want a local copy of that branch, just switch to it:

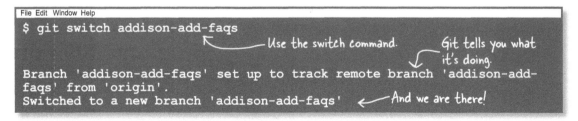

```
$ git switch addison-add-faqs
```
— Use the switch command.   Git tells you what it's doing.
```
Branch 'addison-add-faqs' set up to track remote branch 'addison-add-faqs' from 'origin'.
Switched to a new branch 'addison-add-faqs'
```
← And we are there!

Notice that you skip the "origin/" in the name. Git recognizes that you have a remote tracking branch with that name, so it simply creates a local branch called `addison-add-faqs`. Its remote tracking branch is automatically set to `origin/addison-add-faqs` (since that's where it originated from).

Collaborating with others (continued)

Switching to a branch with the same name as a remote tracking branch is enough to tell Git what to do—create a new local branch with the same name as the remote tracking branch, pointing to the same commit as the remote tracking branch, with its remote tracking branch set. This is what your repository looks like after the switch:

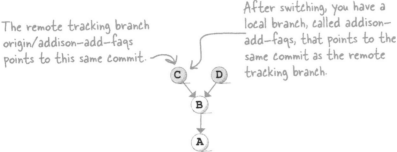

The remote tracking branch origin/addison-add-faqs points to this same commit.

After switching, you have a local branch, called addison-add-faqs, that points to the same commit as the remote tracking branch.

Now that you have a local branch, it's no different from any other branch in your repository. You can add commits, switch away to another branch and come back, or push or pull this branch. You can verify this by using the `git branch -vv` command:

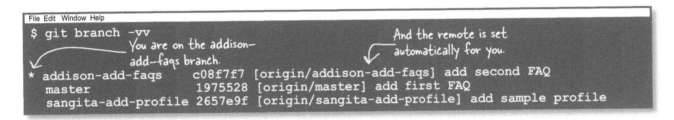

```
$ git branch -vv
                    You are on the addison-           And the remote is set
                    add-faqs branch.                   automatically for you.
* addison-add-faqs      c08f7f7 [origin/addison-add-faqs] add second FAQ
  master                1975528 [origin/master] add first FAQ
  sangita-add-profile 2657e9f [origin/sangita-add-profile] add sample profile
```

Git push/pull and remote tracking branches

Let's compare how remote tracking branches work for branches that you create versus those created by your collaborators. If you create a new branch, *you have to set the upstream* when you push, which creates a remote tracking branch in your clone.

A local branch that you created. → `feat-a` **git push --set-upstream origin feat-a** → `origin/feat-a`

Contrast that with `fetch`, which retrieves any new branches and commits from the remote and *creates* the remote tracking branch reference in your clone for you:

A branch somebody else pushed to the remote. → `feat-b` **git fetch** → `origin/feat-b`

Git creates the remote tracking branch in your clone in both cases.

Sharpen your pencil

This is for Player One (Addison).

And if you are by yourself, then you're up!

Player One, you are going to lend Sangita a hand with her sample profile. In your last exercise, you invoked the `git fetch` command in your clone, so you are caught up with the remote. You are going to add some helpful content to the sample profile she started working on in her `sangita-add-profile` branch.

➤ You are going to switch to the `sangita-add-profile` branch (the one that Sangita pushed to the remote). Start by listing the command you are going to use.

➤ Next, use the `--vv` flag with the `git branch` command, and jot down what you see here:

```
 File Edit Window Help




```

➤ Update the `Profile.md` file you see in your clone, and **add** the following line to the bottom of the file:

Add this line to the bottom of the `Profile.md` file.

We've provided this in a file called `Profile-2.md` in the source code for chapter06. Be sure to rename it `Profile.md`!

> Skills: Following scent trails, digging holes, treeing squirrels, looking after small children, guarding the pack, stealing chimkin when the little humans isn't looking

`Profile.md`

➤ Add the `Profile.md` file to the index, and then commit it using the commit message "update profile".

➤ Can you describe what you just accomplished? Take your notes here:

⟶ Answers on page 342.

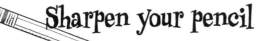
Sharpen your pencil

This is for Player Two.

And if you are by yourself, then yeah, you should do this exercise.

Just like Player One, you are going to extend yourself, and help Addison out by adding a new question to the FAQ.md file that she's been working on. You've already fetched all the remotes in your last exercise, so you are going to switch to the addison-add-faqs branch first and then make some edits to the FAQ.md file.

To get started, switch to the addison-add-faqs branch. (Yep, the one that Addison pushed to the remote.) Start by listing the command you are going to use.

➤ Next, use the `--vv` flag with the `git branch` command, and jot down what you see here:

```
File  Edit  Window  Help




```

➤ You are now going to add a new question in the FAQ.md file that you see in your clone:

Add this line to the bottom of the FAQ.md file.

Feel free to use the FAQ-3.md file that we've put in the source code for this chapter. Just be sure to rename it to FAQ.md.

```
## Photos are nice and all, but I don't see very well. How can
I smell the other dogs?


We regret that we are unable to offer our customers smell-o-
vision at this time.

As soon as human technology catches up to dog noses, we'll be
sure to add a scent feature to the app.

In the meantime, why not meet up at the dog park to get a whiff
of your new friend?
```

FAQ.md

➤ Add the FAQ.md file to the index, and commit it with the message "add third FAQ".

➤ Take a moment to think about what just happened. Take your notes here:

→ **Answers on page 343.**

Collaborating with others: summary

You just did something you hadn't before in this book—you made some commits on a branch that a collaborator created.

Player One (Addison) first switched to sangita-add-profile (a branch that Sangita created and pushed to the remote), then added a commit on that branch.

At the same time, Player Two (Sangita) fetched the addison-add-faqs branch (created by Addison) and made a commit.

Here's what your individual clones look like:

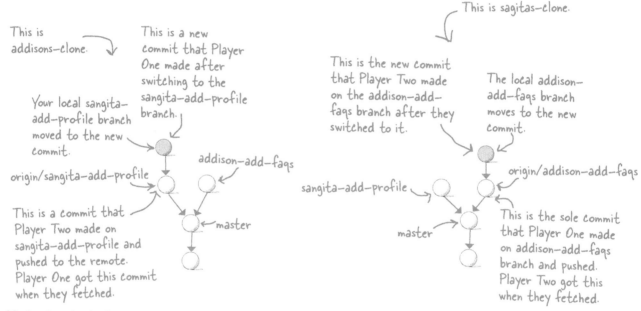

Notice that the fetch got you the other player's branch, but it was a remote tracking branch (for example, in addisons-clone, there is origin/sangita-add-profile). Switching to it gives you a local branch with the same name (sangita-add-profile) as the remote tracking branch. And now it's just another branch in your repository. You can commit on it, but that means that your local branch has now added to the commit history of that branch. In other words, your branch is now *ahead* of its remote tracking branch. So is there a way to know where things stand? That's what we are going to find out next.

Relax

There's a lot going on here.

This is a long chapter, with pretty involved commit histories and a lot of new concepts. Take breaks, get some sleep, and give your brain time to absorb all the new material.

Reason 3 for remote tracking branches: knowing you need to push

Sit back and let it wash over you.

In Chapter 5 we warned you that one of the most common mistakes people can make in Git is to forget to push, and this is where remote tracking branches really come in handy. Remember that fetching updates the remote tracking branches to the latest commit that Git sees in the remote. In other words, remote tracking branches are your local mirror to the remote—they inform you (and Git) what the commit graph looked like when you last fetched. So if you make any new commits, Git can use the remote tracking branches to tell you what's changed. Imagine that your remote and your clone have only one branch—`master`. If you haven't made any changes, this is what Git status will look like:

```
File  Edit  Window  Help
$ git status
On branch master
Your branch is up to date with 'origin/master'.

nothing to commit, working tree clean
```
← This means you haven't made any new commits.

Here, Git is telling you that since your last fetch (which updated the remote tracking branch `origin/master`) you've made no commits to the `master` branch. Now suppose you make a commit on the `master` branch—what does `git status` have to say?

```
File  Edit  Window  Help
$ git status
On branch master
Your branch is ahead of 'origin/master' by 1 commit.
   (use "git push" to publish your local commits)

nothing to commit, working tree clean
```
After committing, you are 1 ahead.

Git even advises you on what to do!

This is what your clone would look like:

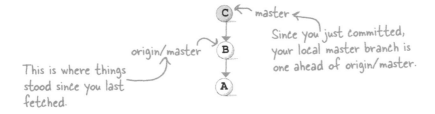

This is where things stood since you last fetched.

Since you just committed, your local master branch is one ahead of origin/master.

This is another good reason to keep checking your Git status. For any branch that has a remote tracking branch, Git can compare your local branch with the remote tracking branch and inform you that you might want to consider pushing your commits.

Exercise

Take a few minutes to see how `git status` can help you know where your branch is in relation to your remote tracking branch.

We've combined the instructions for both players here. If you are playing solo, then be sure to read all the way through and play both parts.

✳ **Player One:** Navigate to the location where you have `addisons-clone`. From your last exercise you should still be on the `sangita-add-profile` branch. (If you are not, switch to it.) Use the `git status` command and read its output. Can you explain what you are seeing?

✳ **Player Two:** You are going to head over to the location where you have `sangitas-clone`. Make sure you are on the `addison-add-faqs` branch, and then use `git status` to see what Git has to say about your current branch. Care to elaborate on what you are seeing here?

Both players: take notes here. ⟶

If you are playing solo, read this instruction carefully.

✳ **Both players** should now push. (If you are playing solo, be sure to do a push from both `addisons-clone` and `sangitas-clone`.) Then use `git status` again. You should see "Your branch is up to date with..." Explain what just happened:

More space for your notes. ⟶

⟶ Answers on page 344.

Reason 4 for remote tracking branches: getting ready to push

Remote tracking branches can tell you where your branch is in relation to the remote tracking branch. However, remember, remote tracking branches don't update themselves. They wait for you to run the `git fetch` command. What does that mean? Let's go back to a hypothetical repository where you have a `master` branch in the remote and in your clone, and you are merrily working away. There is a chance that, in the meantime, your fellow collaborator pushed a new commit on the `master` branch to the remote! Let's take a look.

Your clone is unaware of the new commit, since you haven't fetched yet!
This presents a conundrum.

My head hurts. The master branch in the remote has changed, **and** so has my local master branch. So, how will this work?

Precisely! As you can see, your `master` branch and its counterpart in the remote have *diverged*. Commit B's child in the remote is commit D, while in your clone, commit B's child is C.

Reason 4 (continued)

It's not uncommon to see the remote counterpart of a branch diverge away from your local branch—especially when two or more collaborators are working together on the same branch and pushing to the remote. Suppose your local branch (say it's master) has indeed diverged from its counterpart in the remote. What happens when you push?

We'll show you some best practices in a few.

Be sure to read this carefully before you proceed.

```
File Edit Window Help
$ git push
To github.com:looselytyped/hawtdawg-all-ears.git
 ! [rejected]        master -> master (fetch first)
error: failed to push some refs to 'github.com:looselytyped/hawtdawg-all-ears.git'
hint: Updates were rejected because the tip of your current branch is behind
hint: its remote counterpart. Integrate the remote changes (e.g.
hint: 'git pull ...') before pushing again.
hint: See the 'Note about fast-forwards' in 'git push --help' for details.
```

Oof! That's gonna leave a mark.

Notice that Git tells you to pull. We realize this isn't something we do often, but we are going to ignore Git's advice for now.

Git rejected your attempt to push. The reason is simple: Git sees new commits on the master branch in the remote *and* the master branch in your clone and cannot reconcile them automatically. So what do you do now? Well, this is where remote tracking branches really shine. The name—remote tracking branches—has two distinct parts:

| remote tracking | | branches |

You don't get to create or delete or rename (or, for that mattter, do anything) with remote tracking branches. They are for Git's bookkeeping. However, you can update them using the git fetch command. Every time you fetch, the remote tracking branches are updated to look like their remote counterparts. In other words, remote tracking branches "track" the remote.

And because they are branches, you can merge them into other branches!

You'll see why this is such a big deal in a minute.

So how does any of this help with our current conundrum? Look to the next page.

Reason 4 (still going)

So far, you've discovered that remote tracking branches inform you that you might want to push commits (Reason 3), but they don't seem to be of much help in *letting you push*— particularly if your local branch has diverged from its remote counterpart. Or are they? What happens if you invoke the `git fetch` command in that scenario? Let's take a look:

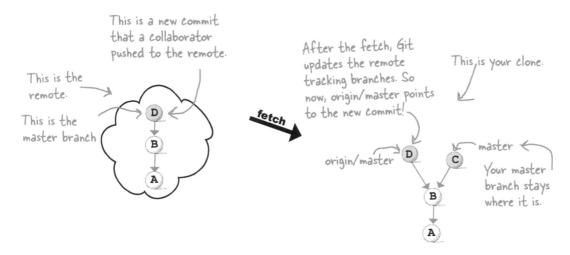

Remember, the `git fetch` command updates all remote tracking branches to look like their remote counterparts. In this scenario, the remote tracking branch `origin/master` now points to commit D (since that's what the remote `master` branch is pointing to).

If you want to push your changes (and you know Git won't let you), you'll need to help Git reconcile the difference between `origin/master` (which is what the remote `master` branch has, since you *just* fetched) and your local `master` branch.

Let's see how to do that next!

Brain Power

Take a long, hard look at the commit history for the clone shown above. If you were to merge `origin/master` into the `master` branch, would that be a fast-forward merge, or would it create a merge commit?

Hint: Have the two branches diverged?

Reason 4 (Yep! Almost there!)

You now know that remote tracking branches *are*, in fact, branches. Which means you can merge `origin/master` into your local `master` branch. Here's what that would look like:

We're still in the discussion phase. Just relax.

```
File Edit Window Help
$ git status
On branch master          Yep. We are on master.
                                         Git sees new commits
                                         on origin/master and
                                         your local master.
Your branch and 'origin/master' have diverged,
and have 2 and 1 different commits each, respectively.
  (use "git pull" to merge the remote branch into yours)

nothing to commit, working tree clean
                                         We are going to ignore
                                         Git's advice for now.
                          Merge origin/
                          master into master.
$ git merge origin/master
Merge made by the 'recursive' strategy.    This may bring up your
  FAQ.md | 11 ++++++++++                   default editor so you can
  1 file changed, 11 insertions(+)         type in a commit message.
```

Merging `origin/master` into your local `master` is just the same as any other merge. Recall from Chapter 2 that *if* the two branches have diverged, then Git will attempt to create a child commit and present you with your configured editor to type in a commit message. If the branches haven't diverged, then it'll be a fast-forward merge.

After merging `origin/master` into your local `master`, your local `master` branch has both—the changes introduced in the remote master and your changes—which means you've reconciled the differences between the two branches. You can now attempt to push!

State of the clone after the merge.

This is the child commit after the merge.

origin/master

E
D   C
B   master
A

You can't merge into the remote tracking branch because you can't switch to it.

You can get merge conflicts!

When you merge changes that appear on the remote tracking branches into your local branches, there is a possibility that you will get one or more merge conflicts.

Just remember—merging remote tracking branches into local branches is no different than any other merge. Use all the skills you acquired in Chapter 2. You've got this!

there are no
Dumb Questions

Q: Whoa, not so fast! You said I can "attempt to push"—what are you not telling me?

A: You got us—we were trying to be sneaky there. There is a chance that while you were busy merging the remote tracking branch into your local (which may lead to a conflict that you'll have to resolve), a fellow collaborator pushed again to the remote master. Which means that if you try to push, Git will reject your push once again, because it'll see new commits on the remote that aren't in your local. If so, you'll have to repeat the cycle all over again—perform a `git fetch`, followed by a merge of the remote tracking branch into your local branch, and try again.

Remember, Git defers to you for anything it can't automatically resolve.

Q: That seems arduous. This could go on forever, and I might never get a chance to push. How does that make any sense?

A: It's not as bad as it seems. Sure, if you have many developers all pushing directly to a shared branch, you might run into contentious pushes. But worry not! We'll be describing a reasonable workflow for you and your fellow collaborators here soon.

Q: If remote tracking branches are indeed branches, what's to stop me from merging, say, `origin/master` into a random feature branch? Will Git prevent me from doing that?

A: Nope! You are absolutely on point. Remote tracking branches are just branches, and while they help a local branch track a remote branch, there is nothing stopping you from merging, for example, `origin/master` into your `feat-a` branch. This is why you should check your status first (which, among other things, tells you which branch you're on).

As to whether you should be merging remote tracking branches into other branches, that's part of the workflow we'll talk about soon.

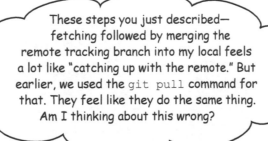

These steps you just described—fetching followed by merging the remote tracking branch into my local feels a lot like "catching up with the remote." But earlier, we used the `git pull` command for that. They feel like they do the same thing. Am I thinking about this wrong?

You aren't wrong! That's exactly right, in fact. Fetching gets you anything new in the remote, and merging the remote tracking branch into the local branch means your local is now "caught up" with its remote tracking branch. Which is exactly what `git pull`'s job is.

And that is the secret we are going to share with you on the next page. But if you are looking for the teaser trailer, here it is—`git pull` is the same as doing a `git fetch` followed by a `git merge`!

Cue the evil twin reveal sound effect.

We feel this is going to do really well in "Git: The Musical."

git pull is git fetch + git merge!

There! We said it. The `git pull` command essentially does what we just described—it first performs a `git fetch` (updating the remote tracking branches), then merges the remote tracking branch of the branch *you are on* into its local counterpart.

Why is this important? Because sometimes when you pull, Git's behavior might not align with your expectations. Consider this scenario once again:

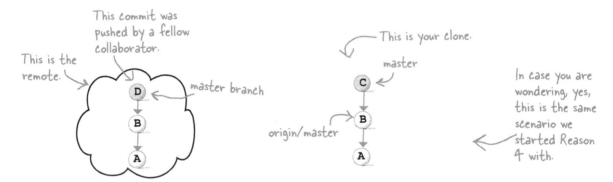

Your local `master` has diverged away from the `master` in the remote. What happens if you do a `git pull`? (Remember, Git is going to perform a `git fetch` followed by a `git merge` for you.)

```
File Edit Window Help
$ git pull
hint: Pulling without specifying how to reconcile divergent branches is
hint: discouraged. You can squelch this message by running one of the following
hint: commands sometime before your next pull:
hint:
hint:    git config pull.rebase false  # merge (the default strategy)
hint:    git config pull.rebase true   # rebase
hint:    git config pull.ff only       # fast-forward only
hint:
hint: You can replace "git config" with "git config --global" to set a default
hint: preference for all repositories. You can also pass --rebase, --no-rebase,
hint: or --ff-only on the command line to override the configured default per
hint: invocation.
hint: Waiting for your editor to close the file...   AND Git pops up your default editor
                                                      to type in a commit message.
```

Cool your jets, Git! You see, Git performed the fetch and initiated the merge in the blink of an eye—and if you had not realized that the remote's `master` branch had diverged from your local, then its behavior would be startling.

Now you know that git pull is `git fetch` + `git merge`. So which is the better option?

Use git fetch + git merge. Avoid git pull.

We don't like surprises (we don't even do well even at our own birthday parties). Our take on this: `git pull`, though convenient, is too magical. Personally, we prefer to use `git fetch` followed by `git merge` to "catch up with the remote." And we have good reasons for this!

If you are wondering why we brought up git pull, well, you'll see it being referenced in many a tutorial and blog post. We just want you to know what it does.

1 **Doing a `git fetch` does not affect your local branches.**

Remember, `git fetch` has no effect on your local branches, which means you can perform `git fetch` anytime. Earlier, we told you to get in the habit of fetching often—this way you can then use `git status` to see if your local branch has diverged, and know that you have to merge the remote tracking branch into your local branch. On the other hand, `git pull` *does* update your local branches to look like the remote. That means you can only pull when you are ready to update your local branch.

2 **Doing a `git fetch` gives you an opportunity to think about what to do.**

After you perform a `git fetch`, you can always check your `git status` to know where your local branch stands in relation to its remote tracking branch, then decide what you want to do. You can even `diff` the two (like we showed you in Chapter 3) because they are both branches. Using `git pull` gives you no such opportunity.

Does this mean that using `git pull` is completely off the table? No, not really. Our recommendation—continue using our suggested workflow: `git fetch` followed by `git merge`. As you get more experience with Git, you can always decide what works best for you.

Brain Power

Consider this scenario: you haven't added any commits to your local branch, but when you perform a `git fetch`, your remote tracking branch receives new commits from the remote (because a fellow collaborator pushed some commits to that branch). What would happen if you then merged the remote tracking branch into your local branch?

Alternatively, what if you *had added* commits to your local branch, but when you fetched, you received no new commits? What would be the result of merging the remote tracking branch into your local branch?

Hint: In both scenarios, ask yourself—
have the two branches diverged?

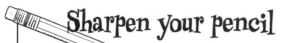

Sharpen your pencil

This is for Player One (Addison).

And if you are by yourself, then you're up!

In this exercise you are going to see how you can use `git fetch` followed by a merge to "catch up with the remote." Here's what you've done so far: you have a local branch called `addison-add-faqs` to which you've made some commits. Since you were stuck, you asked Player Two (Sangita) to help out. After Sangita was done, she pushed her commits to the remote. You just don't know that yet, because you haven't fetched!

➤ Start by fetching, then `switch` to the `addison-add-faqs` branch. Here's a place to jot down the commands you are going to use:

Remember, the order here does not matter. You can fetch no matter what branch you are on.

➤ Next, use the `git status` command to see where things stand. Explain what you are seeing here.

➤ Merge the `origin/addison-add-faqs` branch into your local `addison-add-faqs` branch. Was that a fast-forward merge? Why or why not?

➤ Check your status again. Can you push? Go ahead, try it. Did it do anything? Why is that?

Answers on page 345.

Sharpen your pencil

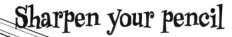

This is for Player Two.

And if you are by yourself, then yeah, you should do this exercise.

Let's use `git fetch` followed by a merge to "catch up with the remote." Recall you created the `sangita-add-profile` branch and pushed it upstream. You then asked Addison to help you add some content to the profile, which she did in a new commit. Addison pushed her changes upstream. You are going to use the workflow we described to get Addison's commit into your local `sangita-add-profile` branch.

➤ You are going to `fetch` first, then switch to the `sangita-add-profile` branch. List the commands you are going to use here:

You can always switch before fetching. Remember, fetch only affects the remote tracking branches.

➤ Next up, see what `git status` has to say. Explain what it tells you.

➤ Merge the `origin/sangita-add-profile` branch into your local `sangita-add-profile` branch. That should be a fast-forward merge. Why is that?

➤ Check your status again. Can you push? Go ahead, try it. Did it do anything? Why or why not?

→ Answers on page 346.

The ideal scenario

You know that when two branches diverge, merging them will create a child commit. But what if they haven't diverged? Well, that would result in a fast-forward merge, right? Take a look at the following two scenarios, which depict the state of affairs *in your clone after you fetched*:

Scenario 1

You've added new commits to master.

origin/master

We are showing you what your clone looks like right after you fetch.

Scenario 2

You've made no new commits on the master branch.

The origin/master branch moved after you fetched.

In Scenario 1, you've added one or more commits to the `master` branch. But when you fetched, the remote had no new commits, so `origin/master` did not move.

In Scenario 2, you've made no changes to your local `master` branch. However, when you fetched, you got some new commits on your remote tracking branch.

In both cases, you can see that the remote tracking branch and its local counterpart have *not* diverged. Which means when you merge the remote tracking branch into the local branch, you *will* get a fast-forward merge. This is exactly what happened when we showed you the `git pull` command at the beginning of the chapter. Here is the console output from early on in this chapter:

```
File  Edit  Window  Help
$ git pull
remote: Enumerating objects: 4, done.
remote: Counting objects: 100% (4/4), done.
remote: Compressing objects: 100% (3/3), done.
remote: Total 3 (delta 0), reused 0 (delta 0), pack-reused 0
Unpacking objects: 100% (3/3), 518 bytes | 259.00 KiB/s, done.
From github.com:looselytyped/hawtdawg-all-ears
   32b1d92..1975528  master      -> origin/master
Updating 32b1d92..1975528
Fast-forward
 FAQ.md | 7 ++++++
 1 file changed, 7 insertions(+)
 create mode 100644 FAQ.md
```

There it is!

This is because `git pull` performs a merge under the covers. Even if you had fetched and merged `origin/master` into `master`, you would have gotten the same result. And a fast-forward merge is exactly what you want! So how do you get there? How can you make it so that when you do catch up with the remote, it's always a fast-forward merge?

We mentioned this in Chapter 2 as well—when merging, fast-forward is the best-case scenario.

A typical workflow: getting started

Here's a summary of what you've learned so far. Things get complicated when your local branch diverges from its counterpart in the remote. Why? Because when you do attempt to catch up, it will result in a merge, and potentially merge conflicts. So can you avoid the merge?

What if you try to make it so that the remote only sees commits that *you* push to it? In other words, no one else should be pushing to that branch. And how do you do that? Well, ideally, every contributor should work on their own feature branches. This way, no one execpt you pushes to your remote branch. Problem solved!

Let's see what this looks like. You are assigned a new task, so you start by making sure that the integration branch (say, `master`) in your clone is "caught up" with the remote.

You then follow the same workflow we described in Chapter 2. Create a new branch based on the integration branch, make your commits, and when you think you are in a good place, push. The important takeaway here is that *this feature branch is yours and yours alone.* No one else is pushing to this branch, which means you'll never see a merge (and potentially a corresponding merge conflict) between your local branch and the remote tracking branch.

And now you are ready to merge.

> If you were thinking this is Scenario 1 from the previous page, you are absolutely correct. Only your local branch introduces new commits.

> This is important! You always want to try and create new feature branches from the latest commits on integration branches.

> Remember, catching up involves fetching, then merging origin/master into master.

> It's a good habit to keep pushing your work to the remote, even if you aren't done yet. This way there is a copy of your work on the remote in case something happens to your workstation.

there are no Dumb Questions

Q: What if I need to work on the same branch as a fellow teammate? Say it's a big task and can't be done solely by one individual. What then?

A: There's nothing wrong with that approach. Some tasks are pretty involved and involve multiple contributors working together on the same branch to get things done. Just remember—there is always the possibility that a colleague might have pushed commits to the common branch while you were busy working. When you are ready to push, be sure to fetch first, then merge the remote tracking branch into your local branch, *then* push.

Q: If I am the only one pushing new commits on a branch, is there even a need to fetch? Why bother?

A: You are absolutely correct—if you are the only one adding commits to a branch, then the remote only has commits that you've pushed so far. Which means when you fetch, Git won't see anything new in the remote, so there will be nothing to update on your local tracking branch.

Remember, fetching updates *all* remotes in your clone, including the integration branches like `master`. While there is no immediate benefit to the branch you are working on, it's still good practice to make sure your remote tracking branches are up to date with the remote. So keep fetching!

A typical workflow:
getting ready to merge

The majority of your workflow will consist of working on your local feature branch (and occasionally pushing). But eventually, you'll want to get your code into an integration branch (for the sake of this example, we'll call it `master`). So what does that look like?

You've seen that you need to be sure that when you create a feature branch, you are always basing it on the latest commits on the `master` branch at that time.

However, the role of the integration branch is to incorporate everyone's work! Which means that while you were busy chugging away, your collaborators might have merged their work into `master`. Before you merge, it's a good idea to know if your work will play well with theirs. How do you do that? Just before you merge your work, merge the work on `master` into your feature branch. Effectively, your feature branch is now caught up with the integration branch.

In case you are wondering, this is the first time in this book that we've merged the integration branch into a feature branch. Always a first time for everything, huh?

There are two ways to go about doing this:

① **Do a `git fetch` and merge `origin/master` into `master`. Then merge `master` into your feature branch.**

② **Do a `git fetch`, then merge `origin/master` into your feature branch.**

We alluded to this in the last "No dumb questions" segment.

This is your clone after updating the integration branch.

This is a commit you made on your feature branch.

This is a commit on the integration branch.

The integration branch does not move after your merge into your feature branch.

Your feature branch moves to the merge commit.

Whichever option you pick, the end result will be the same. Your feature branch now contains all your new work *and* the work your contributors put into the integration branch. You can now do some spot checks or run tests to make sure it all works well together.

Now you are ready to merge!

Our lawyers made us put this here.

⚠ Watch it!

Obligatory merge conflict warning

This workflow involves a merge, which can always lead to a merge conflict. Be advised!

A typical workflow:
merge locally, or issue pull requests?

You know that you have two options to merge your work into the integration branch: you either merge locally into the integration branch, or push your branch upstream and issue a pull request. We spoke of the differences between the two at the end of Chapter 5: merging locally means that you are adding commits to the integration branch locally (which you'll have to push upstream after the merge). The second option means that you will merge using your Git repository manager (like GitHub)—that is, the merge happens in the remote.

We prefer using pull requests to merge our code into the integration branch for one simple reason: we want to avoid adding commits to integration branches in our clone. Remember, it's not just you working on a shared repository. Your colleagues are working on it as well. Suppose you do merge into the integration branch locally—another contributor could be doing the same thing at the same time in their clone. If they beat you to the punch and push the integration branch to the remote, what happens when you attempt to push? Git will reject your push, because the remote branch has now diverged from your local copy. This is exactly the problem we've been trying to avoid!

With pull requests, you are merging in the remote, of which there is only one. This means you are not updating the integration branch locally anymore.

there are no
Dumb Questions

Q: What if there are no new commits on the integration branch? Do I still need to merge the integration branch into my feature branch before I push?

A: There is no downside to following the workflow. If there are no new commits on the integration branch, then Git will simply report "Already up to date".

The key thing is to develop a consistent workflow so it becomes automagic.

Q: Wait. We merge the integration branch into my feature branch, and then merge the feature branch back into the integration branch? Seems like a lot of merging is going on. Why not just merge my feature branch into the integration branch directly?

A: The objective here is to get your work into the integration branch. However, it's a good idea to check that everything will be well *after* the merge.

When you merge the integration branch into your feature branch, you are essentially "catching up" with the integration branch. You can resolve any conflicts and check to make sure all is well. If something does not seem right, you can still create additional commits in your feature branch to fix those issues.

The second merge, which involves merging your feature branch into the integration branch, gets you where you want to be—your work is now integrated.

A typical workflow visualized

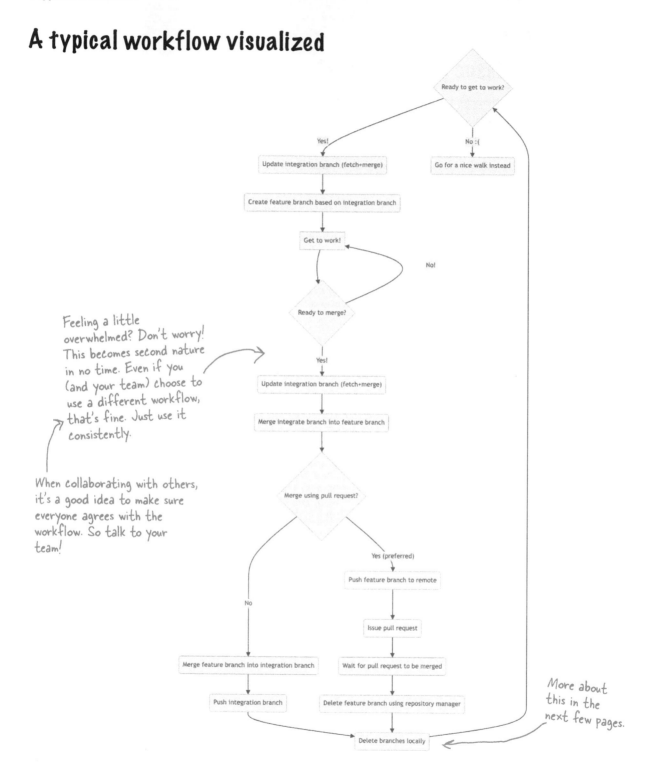

Feeling a little overwhelmed? Don't worry! This becomes second nature in no time. Even if you (and your team) choose to use a different workflow, that's fine. Just use it consistently.

When collaborating with others, it's a good idea to make sure everyone agrees with the workflow. So talk to your team!

More about this in the next few pages.

Test Drive

You are in the final stretch! All your commits have been pushed to the remote and it's time to merge.

We've combined the instructions for both players here.

➤ Both players are going to use the GitHub interface to create a pull request to merge their code into the `master` branch. Player One will create a pull request for the `addison-add-faq` branch to be merged into `master`, while Player Two does the same for the `sangita-add-profile` branch.

Feel free to check Chapter 5 if you need a reminder on how to create a pull request, but here is the short version. You'll start by clicking on the "Pull requests" tab at the top, then pull down the "compare" menu and pick your branch. Then select "Create pull request."

This has to be the username of whoever forked our repository.

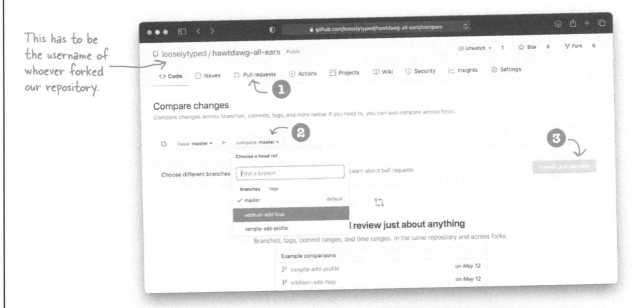

➤ Ask your collaborator to merge your pull request in. **Be sure** to click the "Delete branch" button after your pull request is merged in.

⟶ This is one of the exercises with no solution shown.

Cleaning up remote branches

Remember the scouting rule, "Always leave the campground cleaner than you found it"? Well, that applies to working with remotes as well. Your workflow depends on creating branches, making commits on them, and pushing and pulling. But eventually you are going to be done with the task at hand, and you'll need to delete that branch after merging into an integration branch. But what about the remote tracking branch and the corresponding branch in the remote?

Remember, git fetch fetches anything new from the remote and tracks those changes using remote tracking branches.

Let's start by looking at branches you manage (that is, branches that you might have created, pushed, and are now done with) and wish to delete in your clone *and* in the remote. You learned how to delete a local branch back in Chapter 2—you can use the branch command with the -d (or --delete) flag to delete the local branch. But that still leaves the remote tracking branch and the counterpart branch in the remote. The answer is counterintuitive—you *push a branch deletion* to the remote. Let's say you want to delete a branch called feat-a in the remote.

You use the push command.

Or you can use the --delete flag.

The name of the remote, which by default is origin

Name of the branch you want to delete in the remote

git push   -d   origin   feat-a

Recall that when you push a branch for the first time, you have to set the upstream (using either the --set-upstream or -u flags). When you do, Git creates the branch in the remote, then creates the remote tracking branch in your clone.

Similarly, when you push a deletion, Git will first delete the branch in the remote, and then clean up the remote tracking branch in your clone. Doesn't seem that counterintuitive anymore, does it?

If you follow our recommended approach of using pull requests, delete the branch using the "Delete branch" button in GitHub after your pull request is merged in. This takes care of the branch in the remote. But it still leaves the remote tracking branch and the local branch.

Solution? Next page.

Watch it!

Git errors out when you push a deletion

If Git reports an error like error: failed to push some refs, *that means that a branch with that name does not exist in the remote.*

- *Check the name of the origin and the branch you supplied to* git push -d.

- *You can always check GitHub and see if you see that branch in the branch drop-down menu. It might have already been deleted.*

Cleaning up remote branches (continued)

Remote tracking branches are managed by Git, so it's best to have Git delete them when they no longer have a remote counterpart. Remote tracking branches show up in the clone for two different reasons: you created a local branch and pushed it upstream, or a fellow collaborator created a branch, pushed upstream, and you did a fetch.

The easiest way to clean up all remote tracking branches that no longer have a remote counterpart is use the -p (or --prune) flag that the fetch command supports. With this option, you get all the new branches and commits that show up in the remote but also clean up any remote tracking branches that no longer have a remote counterpart! A twofer? Yes, ma'am!

Suppose you are Addison and you list all the branches in your repository:

```
File  Edit  Window  Help
$ git branch -vv
                      ⟵ List all the branches in very verbose mode.

* addison-add-faqs     d7a1f12 [origin/addison-add-faqs] add third FAQ
  master               1975528 [origin/master] add first FAQ
  sangita-add-profile b584453 [origin/sangita-add-profile] update profile
```

You have a local `addison-add-faqs` branch and the associated remote tracking branch, `origin/addison-add-faqs`. Now, let's say that the `addison-add-faqs` was deleted—perhaps you deleted the branch using GitHub's interface after your pull request was merged in. If you did a `git fetch`, with the -p (shorthand for --prune) flag, this is what you would see:

```
File  Edit  Window  Help
$ git fetch -p ⟵ You can use the --prune flag here.        Git tells you that the
                                                           remote branch was deleted.
From github.com:looselytyped/hawtdawg-all-ears
- [deleted]         (none)        -> origin/addison-add-faqs
                              Listing the branches tells you
                              the remote is gone as well.
$ git branch -vv
* addison-add-faqs     d7a1f12 [origin/addison-add-faqs: gone] add third FAQ
  master               1975528 [origin/master] add first FAQ
  sangita-add-profile b584453 [origin/sangita-add-profile] update profile
```

When you fetched, asking Git to prune along the way, Git compared the list of branches in the remote with the list of remote tracking branches in your clone. It noticed that the `addison-add-faqs` branch was deleted in the remote, so it deleted your remote tracking branch for you. All that's left is to delete the local branch (which we covered in Chapter 2).

Exercise

This is for both players.

If you are playing solo, do this exercise in both clones.

Let's do some cleanup. In the last exercise, each player merged the other's pull request into the shared `hawtdawg-all-ears` repository. But you still have your local branches and the corresponding remote tracking branches—not to mention, your `master` branch does not contain the latest commits after the merge!

✱ Using your terminal, navigate to your clone. Invoke the `git branch` command with `-vv` and write down what you see:

File Edit Window Help

✱ Next, invoke the `git fetch` command with the prune (`-p`) flag. Pay close attention to what Git reports in the output. Then use `git branch -vv` and write down what you see:

File Edit Window Help

✱ Your feature branch has been deleted in the remote, and Git pruned away the remote tracking branch. All that remains is your local feature branch. Delete it. Here's some space for you to type out the commands you will use:

✱ One final task—you need to update your local `master` branch. Remember, you've already fetched, so your `origin/master` has all the commits in the remote. Merge `origin/master` into the `master` branch.

✱ Use the `git log` command with the `--graph --oneline --all` flags to see the beautiful collaborative history you've built throughout this chapter.

Answers on page 347.

We know we've been telling you to get in the habit of fetching often. The real advice here is to get in the habit of using git fetch -p (or --prune) often. This ensures that your list of remote tracking branches always reflects what's available in the remote. This way you know which local branches you should delete locally.

What a trip it's been. We certainly hope you had fun collaborating in this chapter as you learned how to use remotes to work with others. You saw how to use remote tracking branches and how to pair the `git fetch` command with the `git merge` command to catch up with the remote.

You are ready! Go forth and collaborate.

Thanks so much for your help, Addison! I think the FAQ page and the sample profile are really going to help our customers.

Thank you, Sangita! Think you can show me some tips for working with Git next?

Bullet Points

- Git shines at collaboration. It allows multiple contributors to work on a shared repository. Every contributor can clone the same repository and work independent of others.

- Your clone is unaware of any changes that occur in the remote, including branches and commits that collaborators push to the remote.

- The `git pull` command updates a specific branch. It fetches all new commits on the remote and updates the local branch's commit history to look like the remote's.

- Git uses remote tracking branches as liaisons between local branches in a clone and their counterparts in the remote.

- Remote tracking branches are branches that are fully managed by Git. Git creates, updates, and deletes them.

- Git uses remote tracking branches to know which branch in the remote should be updated when you push a local branch to the remote.

- When you push a new branch to the remote, you have to set the upstream. Git records the upstream as a remote tracking branch.

- Git offers another command, `git fetch`, that retrieves all new branches and commits in the remote, then updates the remote tracking branches in the clone. The `git fetch` command does **not** affect the local branches in the clone.

- You can use the `-a` (shorthand for `--all`) flag with the `git branch` command to see all the branches in your clone, including local and remote tracking branches.

- You can also use the very verbose (`-vv`) flag with the the `git branch` command to list all your branches alongside their remote tracking branches (if any).

- To work on a branch that somebody else created and pushed to the remote, you can use the `git switch` command (like you would any other branch). Git will create a new local branch with the same name as the remote tracking branch. This allows multiple people to share their work.

- If you add commits to a local branch that has an associated remote tracking branch, Git can compare the commits and inform you that you need to push.

- Prior to pushing, it's good practice to first `fetch`. Since `fetch` only updates the remote tracking branches, Git can tell you if the local branch has diverged away from the remote branch.

- To update the local branch with any commits on the remote tracking branch, you can merge the remote tracking branch into the local branch.

- These two steps—`git fetch` followed by `git merge`—are what `git pull` does.

- It's best to avoid using the command `git pull`. Instead, use `git fetch` followed by `git merge`. This gives you the opportunity to think about what you want to do if your local branch has diverged away from the remote.

- The `git fetch` command supports a prune (`-p` or `--prune`) flag. This updates the remote tracking branches in your clone with all new branches and commits. It also deletes any remote tracking branches that no longer exist in the remote.

- Listing all your branches with the `-vv` flag will mark any remote branch that has been deleted as "gone," indicating that the local branch no longer has a remote counterpart.

Collaborative Crossword

Why not solve this crossword with a partner? After all,
two HEADs are better than one.

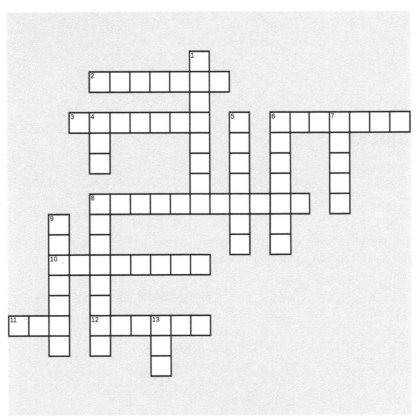

Across

2 The flag -vv, used with the git branch command, stands for "very ___"

3 GitHub is a repository ___

6 You created a branch called addison-___-___ (2 words)

8 Sounds like git pull, but it's different (2 words)

10 Remote ___ branches are a different kind of branch created automatically

11 The argument you'll supply to the git clone command is a ___

12 You can use an ___ to type commit messages

Answers on page 348.

Down

1 When you fork, check the URL to make sure it includes your GitHub ___

4 The -a flag (used with the git branch command) stands for ___

5 This command sends changes from your local branch to the remote (2 words)

6 The HawtDawg employee working on the FAQ page

7 The git ___ command downloads new commits and branches from the remote

8 Git allows multiple people to work in ___

9 This command lets your local branch catch up with the remote (2 words)

13 In the exercises, Sangita is Player ___

Exercise Solution

From page 280.

This exercise is for both players.

You are going to spend a little time looking around the repository you cloned. Each player should navigate to the location where they have their respective clones. **For those playing solo**, navigate to `addisons-clone` for this exercise.

✱ Start by using `git log --graph --oneline --all` to inspect your repository's history. Use the space provided below to sketch it out:

There is only one branch, called master.

The master branch has only one commit, identified by 32bld92, authored by Marge.

Sharpen your pencil
Solution

From page 281.

This exercise is for the player playing Addison. If you are by yourself, do this exercise.

➤ Player One, it's time for you to make some edits to the repository. Using your terminal, navigate to the location that contains `addisons-clone`. First, create a new branch based on the `master` branch. Call the new branch `addison-first-faq`. Use the following space to list the commands you will use. (**Hint:** Always be sure to check the status and verify what branch you are on before creating new branches.)

```
git switch master
git branch addison-first-faq
git switch addison-first-faq
```

➤ Using your text editor, create a new text file called `FAQ.md` with the following contents:

This is what the FAQ.md file should look like.

You can find this file in the code you downloaded for this book under chapter06 in a file called FAQ-1.md. Be sure to rename it to FAQ.md!

```
# FAQ

## How many photos can I post?

We know you want to show off your fabulous furry face, so we've given you
space to upload up to 15 photos!

For those who are camera-shy, we recommend posting at least one to bring
your profile some attention.

Showcase your best self—whether that means a fresh-from-the-groomer glamour
shot or an action shot from your last game of fetch.
```

`FAQ.md`

➤ Save the file, add `FAQ.md` to the index, and then commit it with the message "addison's first commit".

➤ Using `git log --graph --oneline --all`, sketch out your commit history here:

Your ID will be different.

This is Addison's first commit on the addison-first-faq branch. Our ID is 1975528.

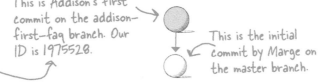

This is the initial commit by Marge on the master branch.

➤ If you were to merge the `addison-first-faq` branch into `master`, would that create a child commit, or would it be a fast-forward merge? Explain your answer here:

This will be a fast-forward merge because addison-first-faq and master have not diverged.

Exercise
Solution

This exercise is for Player One
(Addison) and for solo players. →

From page 282.

Your task this time around is to make the work that Addison did on the `addison-first-faq` branch available on the remote. As we showed you in Chapter 5, you can do this in one of two ways: merge locally and then push the integration branch, or push the `addison-first-faq` branch to the remote and then issue a pull request on GitHub. We're going to keep it simple and do the merge locally for this exercise. (In general, though, if you're working with a team, be sure to conform to the established conventions.)

✱ Start by merging the `addison-first-faq` branch into the `master` branch. It might help to list the commands you are going to use before you do the merge. (**Hint:** Always check your status. Remember, you **will** need to switch to the `master` branch because you are merging `addison-first-faq` *into* the `master` branch.)

```
git switch master
git merge addison-first-faq
```

Note that this was a fast-forward merge.

✱ Next, push the `master` branch to the remote using the `git push` command.

```
git status
git push
```

Always use the status prior to pushing to verify branch information.

Alternatively, you could use the git branch command.

✱ Since your work in the feature branch has been merged into master, you can safely delete the `addison-first-faq` branch.

```
git branch -d addison-first-faq
```

Sharpen your pencil
Solution

From page 285.

Put yourself in Sangita's (Player Two's) shoes (if you aren't already there). Why does it matter whether or not your clone has the latest commit on the master branch?

> An integration branch like master is where everyone's work comes together. I always want to work off the latest commit on the integration branch—this means that I'll have everyone else's work already integrated before I start my work.

Exercise
Solution

From page 286.

This exercise is for Player Two (Sangita) and for solo players.

✳ Let's make sure Sangita's clone has all the commits Addison pushed up to the remote's master branch. Navigate to sangitas-clone in your terminal. Write down the commands you will use to update your local master branch with the commits on the remote.

> git switch master
>
> git pull

Always be sure to be on the right branch prior to pulling!

✳ Next, run the commands you listed to update your local master branch.

Exercise Solution

From page 293.

This exercise is for Player One;
if you're playing solo, then it
applies to you, too.

✱ It's time for you to spend a little time investigating how remote tracking branches work in your respective clones. Using your terminal, navigate to `addisons-clone`. List all your branches and their respective remote tracking branches (if any) using the `git branch` command with the `-vv` (double-v) flag:

```
File Edit Window Help
$ git branch -vv
* master 1975528 [origin/master] add first FAQ
```

✱ Create a new branch called `addison-add-faqs` based on `master` and switch to it. We've provided this space so you can list out the commands you are going to use:

git switch master
git branch addison-add-faqs
git switch addison-add-faqs

✱ Edit the `FAQ.md` file in the repository and **add** a second FAQ, like so:

Add this
entry to the
FAQ.md file.

Or you can use the FAQ-2.md
file we provided in the source
code for Chapter 6. Be sure to
overwrite the existing FAQ.md.

```
## Where do I list my favorite treats?


Open the Hawt Dawg app and click on "Edit Profile."

Scroll down to the section called "Passions" and tell
potential mates and friends all about the treats and toys
that make your tail wag.

When you're done, click "Save Changes" to show the world.
```

FAQ.md

✱ Add the `FAQ.md` file to the index, and commit it with the commit message "add second FAQ".

continued on the next page...

Exercise Solution

From page 294.

Still Player One!
Solo players, too. →

✱ Use the `git branch` command with the `-vv` flag and write out what you see. (Note: you will not see the remote tracking branch for the newly created `addison-add-faqs` branch just yet.)

```
File Edit Window Help
$ git branch -vv
* addison-add-faqs c08f7f7 add second FAQ
  master           1975528 [origin/master] add first FAQ
```
↖ You'll get a different ID.

✱ Next, push the `addison-add-faqs` branch to the remote. List the command you are going to use here:

git push –u origin addison-add-faqs ← Alternatively, use the
‑‑set-upstream flag.

✱ Use the `git branch` command again, with the "very verbose" flag. Do you see the remote tracking branch?

```
File Edit Window Help
$ git branch -vv
* addison-add-faqs c08f7f7 [origin/addison-add-faqs] add second FAQ
  master           1975528 [origin/master] add first FAQ
```

Lightning Round!

✱ How many branches (including remote tracking branches) are in your repository?

Four. The master and addison-add-faqs branches and their corresponding remote tracking branches.

✱ How many branches are there in the remote?

Two. The master and addison-add-faqs branches.

✱ True or false? Your local `addison-faq-branch`, `origin/addison-faq-branch`, and the remote's `addison-faq-branch` all point to the same commit.

True, because we just pushed and we have made no additional commits in our local since.

✱ Does Sangita's clone know of the newly created `addison-add-faqs` branch?

No. Only the remote is aware of the push.

Exercise Solution

This exercise is for Player Two, or if you are playing solo.

If you are playing solo, these steps might seem repetitious, but don't skip them. This is setting you up for the discussion to follow.

From page 295.

✱ Just like Player One, you, too, are going to spend a few minutes investigating how remote tracking branches work. Since you are playing Sangita, using your terminal, navigate to `sangitas-clone`. Using the `git branch` command with the `-vv` (double-v) flag, list your branches and their respective remote tracking branches, if any:

```
File Edit  Window Help
$ git branch -vv
* master 1975528 [origin/master] add first FAQ
```

✱ Create a new branch based on `master`, call it `sangita-add-profile`, and switch to it. List the commands you are going to need here:

git switch master
git branch sangita–add–profile
git switch sangita–add–profile

✱ Using your text editor, create a new file in `sangitas-clone` called `Profile.md`. Add the following contents:

We've provided this in a file called Profile–1.md in the source code for chapter06. Be sure to rename it Profile.md!

```
# Profile


Name:  **Roland H. Hermon**


Age:  **3**


Breed:  **Beagle**


Location:  **Philadelphia**
```

Profile.md

✱ Add the `Profile.md` file to the index and commit it with the message "add sample profile".

continued on the next page...

Exercise Solution

From page 296.

Yep! Still Player Two and solo players!

✱ Use the `git branch` command along with the "very verbose" (`-vv`) flag to inspect all your branches and their remote tracking branches (if any) again. (Pay attention to the newly created `sangita-add-profile` branch.)

```
File Edit Window Help
$ git branch -vv
  master                   1975528 [origin/master] add first FAQ
* sangita-add-profile 2657e9f add sample profile
```
⤷ You'll get a different ID. That's OK.

✱ Push the `sangita-add-profile` branch to the remote. Start by listing the command you are going to use to do that:

git push –u origin sangita-add-profile ⟵ Alternatively, use the `--set-upstream` flag.

✱ Finally, use the `git branch` with the `-vv` flag again. Does your newly created `sangita-add-profile` branch now have a remote tracking branch?

```
File Edit Window Help
$ git branch -vv
  master                   1975528 [origin/master] add first FAQ
* sangita-add-profile 2657e9f [origin/sangita-add-profile] add sample profile
```

Lightning Round!

✱ How many branches (including remote tracking branches) are in your repository?

Four. The master and sangita-add-profile branches and their corresponding remote tracking branches.

✱ How many branches are there in the remote?

Two. The master and sangita-add-profile branches.

✱ True or false? Your local `sangita-add-profile`, `origin/sangita-add-profile`, and the remote's `sangita-add-profile` all point to the same commit.

True, because we just pushed and we have made no additional commits in our local since.

✱ Does Addison's clone know of the newly created `sangita-add-profile` branch?

No. Only the remote is aware of the push.

Who Does What?
Solution

From page 297.

You've built quite the repertoire of Git commands so far! Let's see if you can match each command to its description:

clone — Displays details about the remote

remote — Shows a list of all your branches

branch — Lists all branches along with their remote tracking branches (if any)

push — Is another way to initialize a Git repository

branch -vv — Updates the remote branch with any new commits you made locally

Sharpen your pencil
Solution

From page 301.

Each player will do this exercise in their respective clone. You're ready! We know it!

If you are playing solo, you will do this exercise twice— once in each clone.

Let's practice the `git fetch` command and see its effects on the remote tracking branches in your repository. To recap, the remote has *both* the `addison-add-faqs` and the `sangita-add-profile` branches.

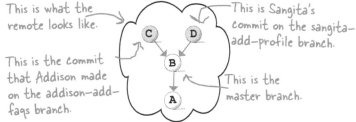

This is what the remote looks like.

This is Sangita's commit on the sangita-add-profile branch.

This is the commit that Addison made on the addison-add-faqs branch.

This is the master branch.

➤ Using your terminal, navigate to your clone—if you are Player One, that would be `addisons-clone`; if you are Player Two, that would be `sangitas-clone`. If you're playing solo, start with `addisons-clone` followed by `sangitas-clone`. List all the branches in your repository using `git branch --all` (or `git branch -a`) and write them here:

```
File Edit Window Help
$ git branch --all
* addison-add-faqs
  master
  remotes/origin/HEAD -> origin/master
  remotes/origin/addison-add-faqs
  remotes/origin/master
```

This is the output from Player One (Addison's) clone.

➤ Use the `git fetch` command to fetch anything new in the remote.

➤ Ask your Git repository to list all of its branches again. Write them here and note what has changed.

```
File Edit Window Help
$ git branch --all
* addison-add-faqs
  master
  remotes/origin/HEAD -> origin/master
  remotes/origin/addison-add-faqs
  remotes/origin/master
  remotes/origin/sangita-add-profile
```

There it is!

Sharpen your pencil Solution

From page 306.

This is for Player One (Addison).

And if you are by yourself, then you're up!

Player One, you are going to lend Sangita a hand with her sample profile. In your last exercise, you invoked the `git fetch` command in your clone, so you are caught up with the remote. You are going to add some helpful content to the sample profile in her `sangita-add-profile` branch.

➤ You are going to switch to the `sangita-add-profile` branch (the one that Sangita pushed to the remote). Start by listing the command you are going to use.

> *git switch sangita-add-profile*

➤ Next, use the `--vv` flag with the `git branch` command, and jot down what you see here:

```
File Edit Window Help
  addison-add-faqs     c08f7f7 [origin/addison-add-faqs] add second FAQ
  master               1975528 [origin/master] add first FAQ
* sangita-add-profile  2657e9f [origin/sangita-add-profile] add sample profile
```

➤ Update the `Profile.md` file you see in your clone, and **add** the following line to the bottom of the file:

Add this line to the bottom of the Profile.md file.

We've provided this in a file called Profile-2.md in the source code for chapter06. Be sure to rename it Profile.md!

```
Skills: Following scent trails, digging holes, treeing
squirrels, looking after small children, guarding the pack,
stealing chimkin when the little humans isn't looking
```

`Profile.md`

➤ Add the `Profile.md` file to the index, and then commit it using the commit message "update profile".
➤ Can you describe what you just accomplished? Take your notes here:

> Since I fetched, I got the branch that Sangita pushed to the remote.
> Switching to it creates a local branch with the remote automatically set.
> Then I created a new commit on that branch, adding to the commit history
> that already has Sangita's commits.

Sharpen your pencil
Solution

From page 307.

This is for Player Two.  And if you are by yourself, then yeah, you should do this exercise.

Just like Player One, you are going to extend yourself and help Addison out by adding a new question to the FAQ.md file that she's been working on. You've already fetched all the remotes in your last exercise, so you are going to switch to the addison-add-faqs branch first and then make some edits to the FAQ.md file.

➤ To get started, switch to the addison-add-faqs branch. (Yep, the one that Addison pushed to the remote.) Start by listing the command you are going to use.

> *git switch addison-add-faqs*

➤ Next, use the --vv flag with the git branch command, and jot down what you see here:

```
File Edit Window Help
* addison-add-faqs      c08f7f7 [origin/addison-add-faqs] add second FAQ
  master                1975528 [origin/master] add first FAQ
  sangita-add-profile   2657e9f [origin/sangita-add-profile] add sample profile
```

➤ You are now going to add a new question in the FAQ.md file that you see in your clone:

Add this line to the bottom of the FAQ.md file.

Feel free to use the FAQ-3.md file that we've put in the source code for this chapter. Just be sure to rename it to FAQ.md.

```
## Photos are nice and all, but I don't see very well. How can
I smell the other dogs?


We regret that we are unable to offer our customers smell-o-
vision at this time.

As soon as human technology catches up to dog noses, we'll be
sure to add a scent feature to the app.

In the meantime, why not meet up at the dog park to get a whiff
of your new friend?
```

FAQ.md

➤ Add the FAQ.md file to the index, and commit it with the message "add third FAQ".

➤ Take a moment to think about what just happened here. Take your notes here:

> *Since fetching, I have all the branches in the remote, including the one Addison pushed, except it's a remote tracking branch in my clone. Switching to it gives me a local branch, and I can commit on it, adding to the history that Addison started on that branch.*

Exercise Solution

From page 310.

Take a few minutes to see how `git status` can help you know where your branch is in relation to your remote tracking branch.

We've combined the instructions for both players here. If you are playing solo, then be sure to read all the way through and play both parts.

✱ Player One: Navigate to the location where you have `addisons-clone`. From your last exercise you should still be on the `sangita-add-profile` branch. (If you are not, switch to it.) Use the `git status` command and read its output. Can you explain what you are seeing?

✱ Player Two: You are going to head over to the location where you have `sangitas-clone`. Make sure you are on the `addison-add-faqs` branch, and then use `git status` to see what Git has to say about your current branch. Care to elaborate on what you are seeing here?

> Git is telling me that my branch is "ahead" by one commit. This makes sense because since I fetched, I made one commit in my local branch that isn't there on the remote tracking branch.

✱ Both players should now push. (If you are playing solo, be sure to do a push from both `addisons-clone` and `sangitas-clone`.) Then use `git status` again. You should see "Your branch is up to date with..." Explain what just happened:

> Since I pushed, Git is telling me that my branch is up-to-date with the remote. Since I pushed, Git updated the remote with my latest commit, and the remote tracking branch. In other words, after the push, the remote, the remote tracking branch, and my local branch all point to the same remote.

Sharpen your pencil
Solution

From page 318.

This is for Player One (Addison).

And if you are by yourself, then you're up!

In this exercise you are going to see how you can use `git fetch` followed by a merge to "catch up with the remote." Here's what you've done so far: you have a local branch called `addison-add-faqs` to which you've made some commits. Since you were stuck, you asked Player Two (Sangita) to help out. After Sangita was done, she pushed her commits to the remote. You just don't know that yet, because you haven't fetched!

➤ Start by fetching, then `switch` to the `addison-add-faqs` branch. Here's a place to jot down the commands you are going to use:

> git fetch
> git switch addison-add-faqs

The order does not matter here since fetching only affects remote tracking branches.

➤ Next, use the `git status` command to see where things stand. Explain what you are seeing here.

> git status tells me that my local addison-add-faqs branch is one behind the remote tracking branch. That's because when I fetched, Git retrieved the commit that Sangita made on the addison-add-faqs branch and pushed that to the remote. Since my local branch does not have that, Git is telling me I need to "catch up."

➤ Merge the `origin/addison-add-faqs` branch into your local `addison-add-faqs` branch. Was that a fast-forward merge? Why or why not?

> Yes, it was. Since I last pushed, I have not changed the addison-add-faqs branch. Which means my branch is just behind the remote, and has not diverged away from the remote.

➤ Check your status again. Can you push? Go ahead, try it. Did it do anything? Why is that?

> Git told me "Everything is up-to-date." This is because I haven't added anything new to the addison-add-faqs branch so there is nothing to push.

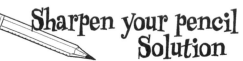

Sharpen your pencil
Solution

From page 319.

This is for
Player Two. →

And if you are by
yourself, then yeah,
you should do this
exercise.

Let's use `git fetch` followed by a merge to "catch up with the remote." Recall you created the `sangita-add-profile` branch and pushed it upstream. You then asked Addison to help you add some content to the profile, which she did in a new commit. Addison pushed her changes upstream. You are going to use the workflow we described to get Addison's commit into your local `sangita-add-profile` branch.

➤ You are going to `fetch` first, then switch to the `sangita-add-profile` branch. List the commands you are going to use here:

> git fetch
> git switch sangita-add-profile

← I can do this in any order
since fetching does not
affect my local branches.

➤ Next up, see what `git status` has to say. Explain what it tells you.

> git status tells me that my local sangita-add-profile branch is one
> behind the remote tracking branch. That's because when I fetched, Git
> retrieved the commit that Addison made on the sangita-add-profile
> branch and pushed that to the remote. Since my local branch does not
> have that, Git is telling me I need to "catch up."

➤ Merge the `origin/sangita-add-profile` branch into your local `sangita-add-profile` branch. That should be a fast-forward merge. Why is that?

> Yes, it was. Since I last pushed, I have not changed the sangita-add-profile branch.
> Which means my branch is just behind the remote, and has not diverged away from
> the remote.

➤ Check your status again. Can you push? Go ahead, try it. Did it do anything? Why or why not?

> Git told me "Everything is up-to-date." This is because I haven't added anything new
> to the sangita-add-profile branch, so there is nothing to push.

Exercise Solution

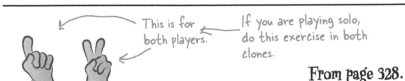

This is for both players.

If you are playing solo, do this exercise in both clones.

From page 328.

Let's do some cleanup. In the last exercise, each player merged the other's pull request into the shared `hawtdawg-all-ears` repository. But you still have your local branches and the corresponding remote tracking branches—not to mention, your `master` branch does not contain the latest commits after the merge!

✱ Using your terminal, navigate to your clone. Invoke the `git branch` command with `-vv` and write down what you see:

```
File Edit Window Help
$ git branch -vv
  addison-add-faqs    d7a1f12 [origin/addison-add-faqs] add third FAQ
  master                1975528 [origin/master] add first FAQ
* sangita-add-profile b584453 [origin/sangita-add-profile] update profile
```

✱ Next, invoke the `git fetch` command with the prune (`-p`) flag. Pay close attention to what Git reports in the output. Then use `git branch -vv` and write down what you see:

```
File Edit Window Help
$ git branch -vv
  addison-add-faqs    d7a1f12 [origin/addison-add-faqs: gone] add third FAQ
  master                1975528 [origin/master: behind 6] add first FAQ
* sangita-add-profile b584453 [origin/sangita-add-profile: gone] update profile
```

Git deleted the remotes.

✱ Your feature branch has been deleted in the remote, and Git pruned away the remote tracking branch. All that remains is your local feature branch. Delete it. Here's some space for you to type out the commands you will use:

You can't be on the branch you are deleting! Switch first!

git switch master
git branch -d addison-add-faqs

We are showing you what we did in Addison's clone.

✱ One final task—you need to update your local `master` branch. Remember, you've already fetched, so your `origin/master` has all the commits in the remote. Merge `origin/master` into the `master` branch.

Always verify which branch you're on first.

git branch
git merge origin/master

✱ Use the `git log` command with the `--graph --oneline --all` flags to see the beautiful collaborative history you've built throughout this chapter.

Collaborative Crossword Solution

Why not solve this crossword with a partner? After all, two HEADs are better than one.

From page 331.

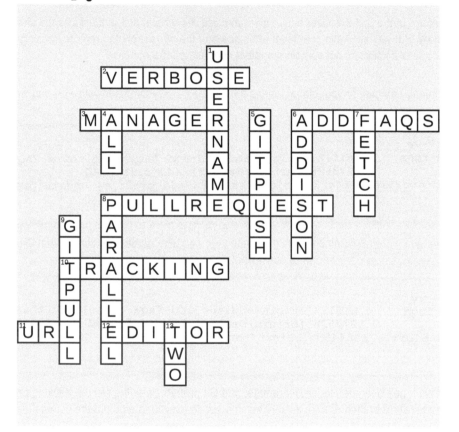

7 searching Git repositories
Git a Grep

The truth is, your project and its commit history are going to grow over time. Every so often, you will need to search your files for a particular piece of text. Or perhaps you'll want to see who changed a file, when it was changed, and the commit that changed it. Git can help you with all of that.

And then there is your commit history. Each commit represents a change. Git allows you to search not only for every instance of a piece of text in your project, but also for when it was added (or removed). It can help you search your commit messages. To top it off, sometimes you want to find the commit that introduced a bug or a typo. Git offers a special facility that allows you to quickly zero in on that commit.

What are we waiting for? Let's go search some Git repositories, shall we?

Taking things to the next level

Business is booming! Trinity's event-planning business has really blossomed, thanks to repeat customers. Speaking of which, Gitanjali and Aref have hired Trinity again—this time to plan their wedding.

Exercise

You'll find Trinity and Armstrong's repository for Gitanjali and Aref's wedding plans here: *https://github.com/looselytyped/gitanjali-aref-wedding-plans*

✱ Clone this repository locally. Start by listing the command you are going to use here:

✱ Take a look around the repository and answer the following questions:

How many branches are there in the repository? _____

How many commits are there on the master branch? _____

✱ Finally, use the `git log --graph --oneline --all` command to take a look at the history. Read the commit messages carefully.

⟶ Answers on page 387.

there are no Dumb Questions

Q: In the last chapter, you made me fork before cloning. Now we're back to just cloning. What's up with that?

A: In the last chapter, our exercises involved pushing commits to the remote. In order to do that, you need permissions to write to the repository, which you automatically get when you fork the repository, because GitHub will copy over the original repository to your account.

This chapter revolves around searching Git repositories, so as long as you have a clone, you will be able to do everything that we ask of you. In other words, you'll be working only in your clone—no pushing or pulling required. However, if you wish, you can always fork and then clone. Just be sure you use the right clone URL. After forking, the clone URL will have your username in it, instead of ours.

A walk through the commit history

Let's take a quick tour of the commit history for the `gitanjali-aref-wedding-plans` repository so we are all on the same page.

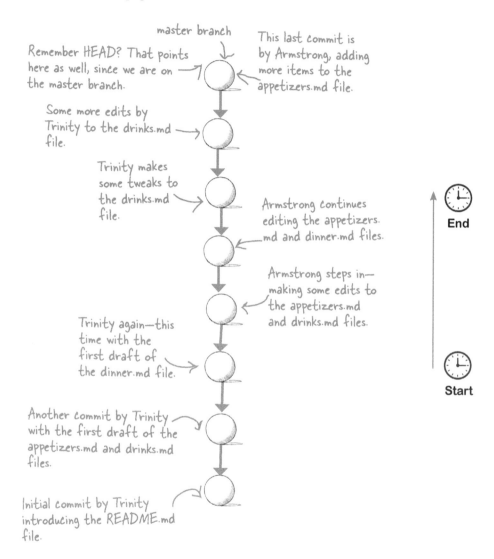

master branch

Remember HEAD? That points here as well, since we are on the master branch.

This last commit is by Armstrong, adding more items to the appetizers.md file.

Some more edits by Trinity to the drinks.md file.

Trinity makes some tweaks to the drinks.md file.

Armstrong continues editing the appetizers.md and dinner.md files.

Armstrong steps in— making some edits to the appetizers.md and drinks.md files.

Trinity again—this time with the first draft of the dinner.md file.

Another commit by Trinity with the first draft of the appetizers.md and drinks.md files.

Initial commit by Trinity introducing the README.md file.

End

Start

As you can see, there's been a lot of activity in this repository, with both Trinity and Armstrong committing several times. We only have one branch—`master`—and we are on it: HEAD is pointing to the same commit ID as `master` is.

We talked about HEAD in Chapter 4, so if you need a refresher, "head" back there. (See what we did there?) We'll be right here waiting.

Cubicle conversation

Armstrong: Hey, Trinity! I just got off the phone with Gitanjali. We had discussed offering nonalcoholic options to the guests, and I see the change in the `drinks.md` file, but I don't remember making it. Did you?

Trinity: I guess one of us has. Why does it matter?

Armstrong: Well, the sample menus we sent Gitanjali and Aref don't have nonalcoholic options listed, so I was wondering if we sent the samples before we made the change or if something slipped through the cracks at the printer's.

Trinity: Well, that's why we use Git! We can easily tell when a particular line or set of lines was changed in a file.

Armstrong: Really? Show me—that's a good thing to know.

Trinity: The magic incantation is a command called `git blame`. For each line in a file, it will show you the commit ID, author info, timestamp, and commit message that last affected that line.

Armstrong: I'm going to try that right now. Cheers!

Seeing who changed what and when with git blame

Every commit you make introduces "diffs"—files that were added or removed or edits to existing files, like adding or removing content—from the previous change. And Git is absolutely brilliant at tracking those changes: it can tell you exactly when a line was changed, who changed it, and the ID of the commit that introduced that change. To see this, use the `git blame` command:

Invoke the blame command.

The name and path of the file you want to inspect

```
git blame          README.md
```

Next, let's dissect the output.

Using git blame

Let's spend a few minutes looking at what `git blame` has to offer. To see the revisions made to the `drinks.md` file over its lifetime, you'd run:

Relax. It's not your turn yet.

git blame drinks.md

And you would see this:

git blame shows you each line in the file, with details about the commit that last revised that line.

Let's zoom in on this line.

```
File Edit Window Help
99fd56e6 (Trinity 2021-07-05 14:01:36 -0400   1) # Gitanjali and Aref Reception:
Signature Drinks                                   This is the
99fd56e6 (Trinity 2021-07-05 14:01:36 -0400   2)  line number.
c3668177 (Trinity 2021-07-20 05:20:02 -0400   3) * Autumn in Manhattan:
c3668177 (Trinity 2021-07-20 05:20:02 -0400   4)    Pumpkin-spice bitters give a fall
feeling to this classic bourbon-vermouth cocktail
c3668177 (Trinity 2021-07-20 05:20:02 -0400   5) * Orchard Mimosa:
c3668177 (Trinity 2021-07-20 05:20:02 -0400   6)    Champagne meets apple cider,
garnished with a cinnamon-sugar rim
c3668177 (Trinity 2021-07-20 05:20:02 -0400   7) * The Log Cabin:
c3668177 (Trinity 2021-07-20 05:20:02 -0400   8)    Apple brandy and maple syrup will
take you on an autumn trip through our favorite couple's history
0b90575d (Trinity 2021-07-25 08:30:44 -0400   9)
0b90575d (Trinity 2021-07-25 08:30:44 -0400  10) **Nonalcoholic substitutes for all
spirits are available upon request.**
```

Looking more closely, here's how to explain each portion of this line of `git blame`'s output:

The commit ID that last changed this line

Name of the author of the commit

The time and date the commit was made

The line number

The content of the line

c3668177 (Trinity 2021-07-20 05:20:02 -0400 7) * The Log Cabin:

Navigate the log with the up and down arrow keys.

The `git blame` command, much like `git log` and `git diff`, uses the pager to display its output. So you can use the up/down arrow keys if the output exceeds the length of your terminal window, and you'll need to type "q" (for quit) to get back to the prompt.

The "q" is for "quit pager."

As you can see, `git blame` can tell you who last changed a line and details about the commit that recorded that change. This is a super handy and quick way to figure out who last edited or added a line.

`git blame` *cannot* tell you whether a line was added or how it changed—it only gives details about the last revision to that line. Furthermore, since `git blame` only looks at the lines in the file at the time you run it, it cannot tell you about deleted lines.

git blame using Git repository managers

The `git blame` command is so useful that most Git repository manager web interfaces give you an easy way to look at its output. If you navigate to the repository on GitHub and look at the contents of any file, this is what you'll see:

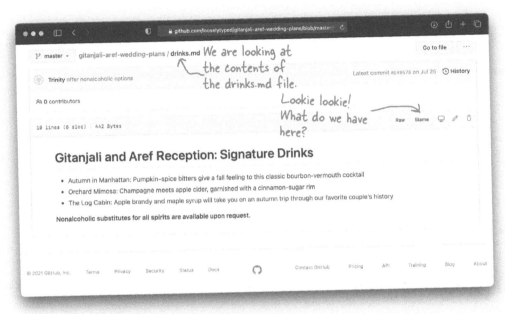

If you were to click on the "Blame" button, this is what you'd see:

If multiple lines were edited in the same commit, GitHub helpfully collates them and displays the date in a slightly more "human" format. Otherwise, it's the same output!

A few more details about git blame

When you run the `git blame` command, pay attention to which commit HEAD is pointing to. By default, Git will show you revisions made to change the file as it existed at the time of that commit.

These two commands are functionally identical.

git blame HEAD drinks.md   **git blame drinks.md**

This means that we can ask `git blame` to show us the revision history of a file at any commit, simply by giving it the commit ID and the filename! Suppose one of the commits you see in the `git blame` output happens to be c3668177. You can supply that ID to `git blame`, and it will show you the revision history of the file as it looked at the moment the commit was made.

git blame c3668177 drinks.md

Supply the commit ID to git blame.

Followed by the name of the file.

Note: order matters. Always put the commit ID first, followed by the filename.

Sharpen your pencil

Let's get you some hands-on experience with `git blame`.

➢ You are going to use the `git blame` command to look over the revisions that have been made to the `appetizers.md` file in the `gitanjali-aref-wedding-plans` repository that you cloned at the beginning of this chapter. Start by listing out the command you are going to use:

➢ Next, answer the following questions:

How many authors have contributed to this file? _____

When was the last edit to this file made? _____

Who last edited line number 5? _____

When you are done, be sure to hit the "q" key to return back to the prompt.

➢ Next, use the GitHub web interface to see if you can see the `git blame` output there as well.

⟶ Answers on page 388.

Serious Coding

All throughout this book we've explored tons of commands. Many, like `log` and `branch`, support a slew of flags that can tweak their behavior. And so does the `git blame` command! Don't want to see the author and timestamp info? Supply the `-s` (for suppress) command and Git will only display the commit ID and line numbers. You can even tweak how the `git blame` output formats dates.

As you've seen, you can supply the `git blame` command a commit ID to see the revisions for a particular file at a particular point in your commit history. You can even supply the name of a branch instead—in case you want to see how a file was modified in another branch. (Recall that every branch points to a commit ID—so when you supply the `git blame` command with a branch name, you are asking Git to use the commit ID that branch points to.)

Searching Git repositories

Armstrong: You think sometimes we get carried away?

Trinity: What do you mean?

Armstrong: We work on so many different projects and sometimes I feel that we overuse certain words and phrases. I feel like we may have used both *autumn* and *fall* in the menus for Gitanjali and Aref's wedding reception.

Trinity: Well, we can always search the project, right?

Armstrong: Yeah, but I just switched workspaces to work on the Zimmermans' annual company outing plans, and it seems like a pain to switch back. Maybe I'll do it later when I get a minute.

Trinity: I'll give you a hint—look up the `grep` command. I have a feeling it's going to make your life a lot easier.

Armstrong: You always have the answer, don't you?

Searching Git repositories with grep

Sit back and let it wash over you.

Every so often you might have to search your Git repository for a particular word or phrase. You probably know that most editors can perform a global search across all the files in a project. But guess what? Git can help here too! The command you are looking for is `git grep`, and you can supply it any string, like so:

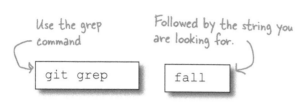

Use the grep command

Followed by the string you are looking for.

```
git grep
```

```
fall
```

If you are looking for a phrase, wrap it in double quotes:

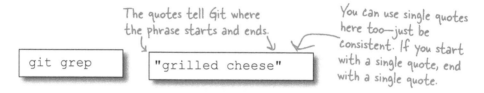

The quotes tell Git where the phrase starts and ends.

You can use single quotes here too—just be consistent. If you start with a single quote, end with a single quote.

```
git grep
```

```
"grilled cheese"
```

Let's say you want to find all the places where you used Aref's name. You can grep for it (using `git grep Aref`), and this is what Git will present you:

git grep lists the files and individual lines that contain your search term.

```
File Edit Window Help
README.md:# Gitanjali/Aref wedding plans
README.md:This repository will help us manage Gitanjali and Aref's wedding night menus.
appetizers.md:# Gitanjali and Aref Reception: Appetizers
dinner.md:# Gitanjali and Aref Reception: Dinner Menu
drinks.md:# Gitanjali and Aref Reception: Signature Drinks
```

There are a couple of things to note about `git grep`'s output. First, Git will list out every instance that contains the string you are searching for, which means you might see the same filename listed multiple times (if the word you are looking for happens to be in a file more than once). Git also lists files in alphabetical order, making it easier to scan if you are looking for a particular file.

Uppercase letters appear before lowercase letters.

As with `git blame`, Git grep displays the search results in a pager, so you'll use the up/down arrow keys to move around and the "q" key to quit the pager.

Next, let's look at some useful options that the `git grep` command supports.

git grep options

It shouldn't surprise you that the grep command also supports plenty of flags. Here are some of the more useful ones:

Case-insensitive search

The git grep command, by default, respects the case of the string you supply it. If you search for "cheese", Git grep will not list any instances that have "Cheese" (uppercase "C") or "CHEESE" (all uppercase) or anything that does not match "cheese" exactly. But often you don't know (or remember) whether you *politely* asked for cheese or screamed it at the top of your lungs. You can use the -i (or its longhand version --ignore-case) to make your search case-insensitive:

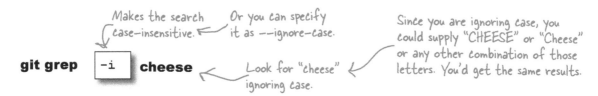

Makes the search case-insensitive.

Or you can specify it as --ignore-case.

Look for "cheese" ignoring case.

Since you are ignoring case, you could supply "CHEESE" or "Cheese" or any other combination of those letters. You'd get the same results.

git grep `-i` **cheese**

Displaying line numbers

You might have noticed that git grep's output only lists the names of files and the corresponding content that contains the search term. That's fine for some searches, but if you ever want grep to list line numbers, then you'll need to supply it the -n (shorthand for --line-number) flag. This option is useful if the files contained in your repository tend to be long.

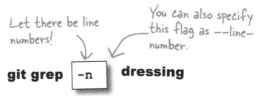

Let there be line numbers!

You can also specify this flag as --line-number.

git grep `-n` **dressing**

List only filenames

Sometimes you don't care to know what lines match, only which files contain certain terms. The -l (lowercase "L," which is shorthand for --name-only) only lists the names of the files that matched. This list, too, is alphabetized. However, a file will be only listed once, even if there are multiple lines that match within that file.

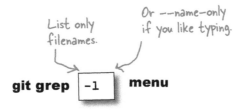

List only filenames.

Or --name-only if you like typing.

git grep `-l` **menu**

The git grep flags combo

With a side of fries—yes, please!

Naturally, it often makes sense to combine these flags. Our favorite combination when using the `git grep` command is to search in case-insensitive mode while displaying line numbers. This is how you would go about doing that:

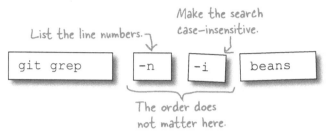

List the line numbers.

Make the search case-insensitive.

```
git grep    -n    -i    beans
```

The order does not matter here.

Watch it!

Git grep only searches files that Git knows about!

The `git grep` command's functionality is very specific—**by default**, it only searches files that Git knows about. That is, `git grep` only searches files that Git is tracking.

This means that if you have files in your repository that you haven't added to the index yet, `git grep` will not search those!

Also, there is a way to tell Git to ignore some files in a directory (more about this in the next chapter). Git's `grep` command will also ignore these files. This is both a boon and a curse: it's great if you don't want to search these files because they aren't technically part of your repository, but it works against you if you do want to search them for a particular use case.

For the latter scenario, you might be better off using your editor's search facilities or tools like Bash's `grep` command.

Serious Coding

There is a mechanism called "regular expressions" that lets you specify patterns to look for—for example, if you wanted to look for any word that is exactly 10 characters long, you can specify it as a regular expression pattern that looks like `\w{10}`. The `git grep` command supports both basic and extended regular expression syntax!

We can almost hear a few knuckles being cracked right now!

there are no Dumb Questions

Q: Why would I use the `git grep` command over my editor's search facilities?

A: Some kinds of projects have files that aren't technically part of the repository. For example, if you are working with source code, you might have a dependencies folder. Your editor might not know to ignore those files when searching, so you might find a lot more matches than you care about. But Git knows to ignore those files since it isn't tracking them. We realize we haven't told you how to tell Git to ignore these files, but it's one thing we are going to talk about in the next chapter.

Q: I am familiar with Bash's grep command. Why would I prefer one over the other?

A: Git's grep, by default, does not search your files. Rather, it searches its index and database, so it can make good use of Git's efficient internal storage.

This means that Git's grep can be a lot faster than Bash grep. On the other hand, if you wish to search all files in a project, including tracked *and* untracked files, Bash's grep is your friend.

However, it's not an either/or—depending on the use case, we've found that we reach for one or the other.

Exercise

Time to exercise your new Git grep sleuthing skills. Navigate to the `gitanjali-aref-wedding-plans` repository in your terminal.

✽ How can you search for all files that contain the word "menu"? Jot that down here:

✽ How many files did you find?

✽ Next, make the search case-insensitive. List the command here:

✽ How many matches did you get this time around?

✽ Finally, if you also want to see the line numbers, what would the `git grep` command look like?

→ Answers on page 389.

Where git blame falls short

The `git blame` command is pretty rad. It gives lots of information about a certain file, and you can easily see who changed any line of the file, including details about the commit that affected that line.

However, Git blame works at a line level! Git blame can tell you *when* a particular line was last changed, but it can't tell you *what* changed in that line when that commit was made. And finally, `git blame` only looks at one file at a time.

That's quite a mouthful, so be sure to read it again.

Consider a **single-line file** in a repository that has seen three changes in three commits, like so:

1 **The brown fox jumps over the tired dog**

Note: commit 2 came after commit 1, and commit 3 came after commit 2.

Commit 2 changed the word "tired" to "lazy."

2 **The brown fox jumps over the [-tired-]{+lazy+} dog**

This is the output of git diff with the --word-diff flag.

3 **The {+quick+} brown fox jumps over the lazy dog**

You can find this history in the source code for this chapter. Look for a folder called why-pickaxe.

Commit 3 added the word "quick."

If only there was a way to search my commit history for a piece of text.

If you were to run the `git blame` command giving this file as its argument, it would tell you that commit number 3 changed the line. (Recall that there is only one line in this file.) Except you don't know what changed.

So what if you want to know when the word "lazy" showed up in that line? Or when the word "tired" disappeared?

You might have guessed one option—use the `git diff` command. Start by comparing the third commit with the second, and if you don't find what you are looking for, then `diff` the second commit with the first. Which would work, except it isn't really efficient and can get rather tiresome if you have more than a handful of commits.

The solution? Well, Git knows the commits you've made, and you know that a commit records the state of the files as they were in the index at that time. Which means Git should be able to compare every commit with its predecessor and see if a particular piece of text was added or deleted.

git log's "pickaxe" capability (-S)

It's not as scary as it sounds. We pinky promise.

We are in the discussion phase.

If you ever wanted to know when a particular piece of text was added or removed, you need look no further than our good friend and ally, the `git log` command. It offers several options to search the "diff" that each commit introduces—that is, `git log` can help you search the *changes* introduced by each commit. Consider the first two commits we showed you on the previous page:

The word "tired" showed up in this commit.

(1) The brown fox jumps over the tired dog

The word "tired" was deleted in this commit.

(2) The brown fox jumps over the [-tired-]{+lazy+} dog

If you are interested in when the word "tired" *first* appeared or disappeared, you can use the `git log` command with the -S (uppercase "S") flag. This lets you search the diffs of each commit like so:

The search capabilities offered by git log are referred to as the "pickaxe" options. -S is one way to do this. We'll show you another search option soon.

Invoke the log command.

Use the -S flag, supplying it the text you are searching for.

```
git log        -S tired
```

The text you are searching for must be an argument to the -S flag.

This, too, uses the pager, so you'll use the arrow keys to navigate, and "q" to quit.

And this is what Git will show you:

```
File Edit Window Help
commit 8c05de2eaf10764d0337a799a2ca7b423f8904ba
Author: Raju Gandhi <raju.gandhi@gmail.com>
Date:   Thu Jul 29 13:43:53 2021 -0400

    qualify dog

commit b76b2b04b317cc6951fd6ff1c64ca7eea2345bb2
Author: Raju Gandhi <raju.gandhi@gmail.com>
Date:   Thu Jul 29 09:03:27 2021 -0400

    introduce pangram
```

Git lists the two commits that either add or remove the word "tired."

git log -S versus blame

There are a couple of differences between the `git log`'s search results and those of `git blame`. First, the pickaxe option (-S) is not restricted to a single file. In our example, using the pickaxe option to search for "tired" searches your entire repository—it's not limited to a single file. You *can* restrict `git log` to only display the log for a single file by supplying the filename at the end.

git log -S tired ` pickaxe-demo.md `  *Supply the name of the file at the end.*

Think about it this way—`git blame` is a way to attribute changes in a single file, while `git log`'s pickaxe option is a search mechanism for your entire repository.

Exercise

Let's put your searching skills to work. Start by navigating to the `gitanjali-aref-wedding-plans` repository.

✱ How can you go about finding every commit that adds or removes the word "classic" in your repository? Start by listing the command you would use here:

✱ Execute! How many commits did your search reveal? _____

⟶ Answers on page 389.

Brain Power

Here's a puzzler for you—in the previous exercise, can you tell whether the word was added or removed? If so, which commit added it and which one removed it? What else could the `git log` command provide that would help here? **Hint:** Remember, each commit introduces a set of changes, or "diffs."

Watch it!

Make sure you get the order flags and arguments right!

If you get a `fatal: ambiguous argument` *error from Git when using the* `-S` *flag, it's most likely because you misplaced the flag and argument order. The string you are searching for* **must follow** *the* `-S` *flag, or else you'll confuse Git.*

Using the "patch" flag with git log

If you ever wanted to see the actual diff that each commit introduced, you can use yet another flag with `git log`, which is `-p` (shorthand for `--patch`). This is true for every instance of `git log` that we've shown you in this book. For example, you could combine the `-p` flag with our favorite combo of `git log` flags like so:

Still discussing. There's an exercise soon.

Supply the -p flag. ↙ ← Or you could use --patch.

git log --oneline --all --graph `-p`

With the "patch" flag, Git will display your commit graph just as you are used to seeing it, along with the differences introduced in each commit:

Here's the commit ID abbreviated.

Followed by the diff.

```
File Edit Window Help
* 5555624 (HEAD -> master) qualify fox
| diff --git a/pickaxe.md b/pickaxe.md
| index 832d941..84102df 100644
| --- a/pickaxe.md
| +++ b/pickaxe.md
| @@ -1 +1 @@
| -The brown fox jumps over the lazy dog
| +The quick brown fox jumps over the lazy dog
```

We've truncated the log just to highlight the juicy details.

Back to searching—combine the pickaxe flag (`-S`) with the `-p` (`--patch`) flag, and `git log` will show you every commit that has the search string in its diff, as well as the diff itself!

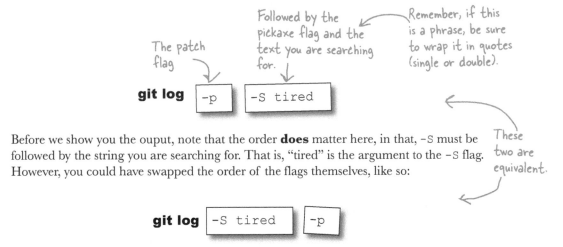

The patch flag

Followed by the pickaxe flag and the text you are searching for.

Remember, if this is a phrase, be sure to wrap it in quotes (single or double).

git log `-p` `-S tired`

Before we show you the ouput, note that the order **does** matter here, in that, `-S` must be followed by the string you are searching for. That is, "tired" is the argument to the `-S` flag. However, you could have swapped the order of the flags themselves, like so:

These two are equivalent.

git log `-S tired` `-p`

So does this get us closer to knowing when the word "tired" appeared or was deleted? Let's find out.

Using the "patch" flag with git log (continued)

If you provide the patch (-p) flag along with the search term (-S), here is what Git has to offer:

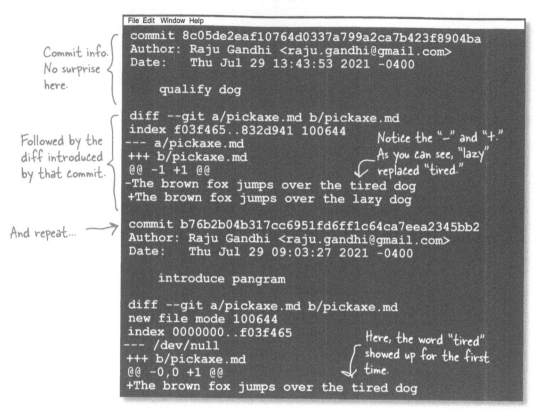

Commit info. No surprise here.

```
File Edit Window Help
commit 8c05de2eaf10764d0337a799a2ca7b423f8904ba
Author: Raju Gandhi <raju.gandhi@gmail.com>
Date:    Thu Jul 29 13:43:53 2021 -0400

        qualify dog
```

Followed by the diff introduced by that commit.

```
diff --git a/pickaxe.md b/pickaxe.md
index f03f465..832d941 100644
--- a/pickaxe.md
+++ b/pickaxe.md
@@ -1 +1 @@
-The brown fox jumps over the tired dog
+The brown fox jumps over the lazy dog
```

Notice the "−" and "+." As you can see, "lazy" replaced "tired."

And repeat...

```
commit b76b2b04b317cc6951fd6ff1c64ca7eea2345bb2
Author: Raju Gandhi <raju.gandhi@gmail.com>
Date:    Thu Jul 29 09:03:27 2021 -0400

        introduce pangram

diff --git a/pickaxe.md b/pickaxe.md
new file mode 100644
index 0000000..f03f465
--- /dev/null
+++ b/pickaxe.md
@@ -0,0 +1 @@
+The brown fox jumps over the tired dog
```

Here, the word "tired" showed up for the first time.

Recall that the `git log` command displays commits in reverse chronological order, so the commit that introduced the word "tired" is at the bottom of the output, preceded by the commit that changed "tired" to "lazy."

And one last piece that'll make your life easier—like the `diff` command, the `log` command also supports the `--word-diff` flag when displaying patches! So if the above is too verbose for you and you like your output to be as succinct as you can make it, here is the final incantation that does the trick:

The `--word-diff` flag shows how individual words differ rather than whole lines. We spoke of this in Chapter 3.

git log -p --oneline -S tired `--word-diff`

Here again, as long as the search text follows the `-S` flag, you can supply these arguments in any order.

Using the "patch" flag with git log (almost there)

All together now! We are going to use the pickaxe flag and the patch flag alongside all our other
`git log` flags, like so:

git log -p --oneline -S tired --word-diff ← You can add the --graph and --all flags here as well.

And you see this:

Abbreviated commit ID followed by commit message.

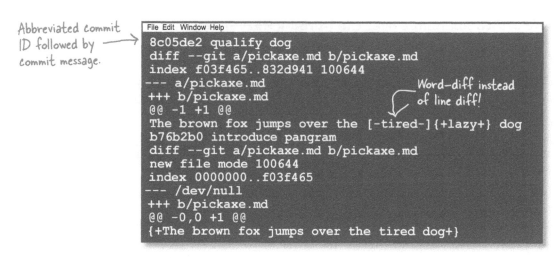

```
File Edit Window Help
8c05de2 qualify dog
diff --git a/pickaxe.md b/pickaxe.md
index f03f465..832d941 100644
--- a/pickaxe.md
+++ b/pickaxe.md
@@ -1 +1 @@
The brown fox jumps over the [-tired-]{+lazy+} dog
b76b2b0 introduce pangram
diff --git a/pickaxe.md b/pickaxe.md
new file mode 100644
index 0000000..f03f465
--- /dev/null
+++ b/pickaxe.md
@@ -0,0 +1 @@
{+The brown fox jumps over the tired dog+}
```

Word-diff instead of line diff!

Now, not only can you see every commit that added or removed the word "tired," you can see
the diff itself!

Exercise

✱ Search the `gitanjali-aref-wedding-plans` repository for all commits that add or delete the word "walnut",
using the patch and word-diff flags. Which commit added the word, and which one removed it?

→ **Answers on page 390.**

git log's other "pickaxe" flag (-G)

Git log's -S flag can help you find every commit where the text you are looking for was either added or deleted, which is super handy. But what if you want to find every time a particular piece of text showed up in the diff of a commit? Let's go back to our single-line-file example and take a look at the diffs of the last two commits—keep an eye out for the word "lazy":

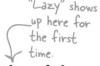

"Lazy" shows up here for the first time.

2 **The brown fox jumps over the [-tired-]{+lazy+} dog**

3 **The {+quick+} brown fox jumps over the lazy dog** ◄—

This diff does not affect the word "lazy," but the line that contains it did change in this commit. In this case, the word "quick" was added.

The -S flag in this case will only list commit 2 because it only lists commits where the text you are searching for ("lazy" in this case) was either added or deleted. The -S flag will **not** list commit 3 because it does not affect the *number of times* lazy appears—rather, commit 3 affects the line that contains the word "lazy."

Why would you ever perform a search like this? Maybe someone introduced a typo somewhere on the line that contains the word "lazy"—searching for "lazy" will highlight anytime that line was changed in some way. Or if you want to see how the arguments of a function have changed over time—you could just search for the name of the function.

As we discussed, git log's -S flag will not do the trick for this. Rather, you want to use the -G option. You use it just like the -S option, and it will highlight every commit whose diff includes the word you are looking for.

Everything that we've talked about with the -S flag applies to the -G flag—you can display the individual patches for each commit listed with the -p (or --patch) flag, and you can use --word-diff and --oneline flags as well.

 Serious Coding ——————————————————

We've even more good news for all those regular expression aficionados—the -G option accepts regular expressions as arguments (unlike -S, which by default only accepts strings). So let your regular expressions flag fly high!

Exercise

* Search for the word "classic" in the commit history of the `gitanjali-aref-wedding-plans` repository, except this time you are going to use the `-G` flag. Be sure to display abbreviated commit IDs, and use the `--word-diff` option. Start by listing the command here:

* How many commits reported the word "classic" in your commit history?

* Compare this with the output of the `-S` flag—why do you see more commits with the `-G` flag than you did with the `-S` flag?

→ Answers on page 390.

Sharpen your pencil

> Some of these commands are not like the others. Some don't work!

Let's say you were searching for the word "classic" in the `gitanjali-aref-wedding-plans` repository. Listed below are several combinations of `git log`'s pickaxe options, except a few of them won't work. Can you identify them? **Hint:** Look carefully at the order of flags and arguments.

```
git log -p --oneline -S classic
```

```
git log -G -p classic
```

```
git log -p -G classic --oneline --all
```

```
git log -p classic -S
```

```
git log -S classic --all
```

→ Answers on page 391.

Searching commit messages

We've seen how we can use the `git log` command to search the diffs of individual commits. But the `git log` command has yet another trick up its sleeve—it can help you search the commit messages as well. You might be wondering—how could this be useful? You can always list all the commits using the `git log` command and scan them, right? Sure. That works if you have a handful of commits—but as projects grow, you might end up with hundreds or thousands of commits. Searching those commit messages certainly sounds like a good job for the computer.

Not your turn just yet!

Suppose you wanted to find every commit that uses the phrase "first draft" in its commit message:

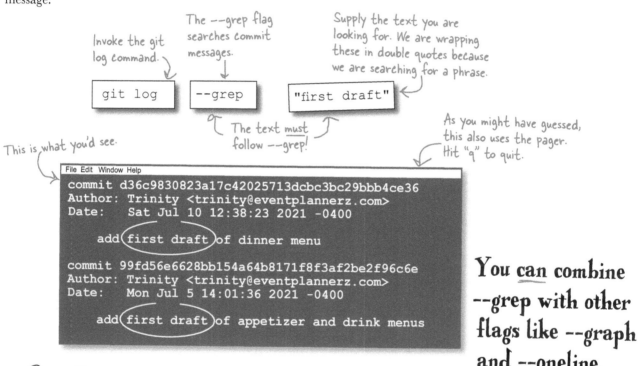

Invoke the git log command.

The --grep flag searches commit messages.

Supply the text you are looking for. We are wrapping these in double quotes because we are searching for a phrase.

```
git log        --grep        "first draft"
```

The text _must_ follow --grep!

This is what you'd see.

As you might have guessed, this also uses the pager. Hit "q" to quit.

```
File Edit Window Help
commit d36c9830823a17c42025713dcbc3bc29bbb4ce36
Author: Trinity <trinity@eventplannerz.com>
Date:    Sat Jul 10 12:38:23 2021 -0400

    add first draft of dinner menu

commit 99fd56e6628bb154a64b8171f8f3af2be2f96c6e
Author: Trinity <trinity@eventplannerz.com>
Date:    Mon Jul 5 14:01:36 2021 -0400

    add first draft of appetizer and drink menus
```

You can combine --grep with other flags like --graph and --oneline.

 Exercise

✱ What command would you use to find every commit that has the word "menu" in the `gitanjali-aref-wedding-plans` repository?

✱ How many commits did you find? List their IDs here:

Answers on page 391.

Git log flag soup

The `git log` command sure is a flexible fella, isn't it? The sheer number of options it offers is mind-blowing, and we haven't even covered the entire list! Just to bring it all together, here is our latest `git log` edition of flag soup:

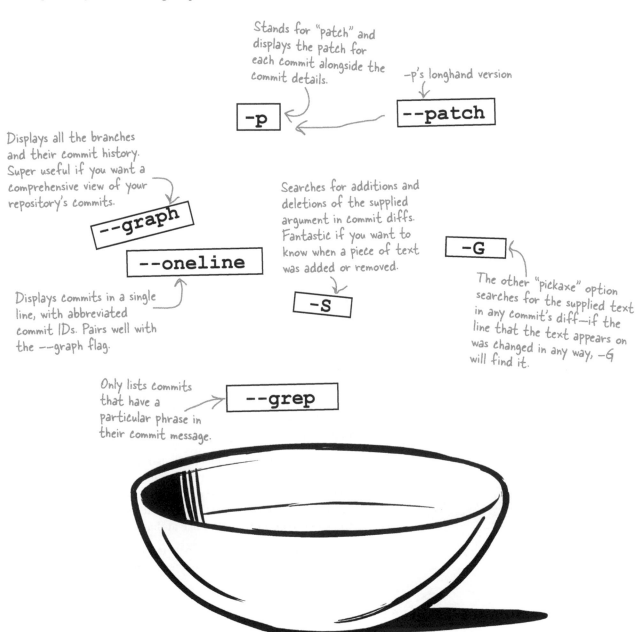

Stands for "patch" and displays the patch for each commit alongside the commit details.

`-p`

-p's longhand version

`--patch`

Displays all the branches and their commit history. Super useful if you want a comprehensive view of your repository's commits.

`--graph`

`--oneline`

Displays commits in a single line, with abbreviated commit IDs. Pairs well with the --graph flag.

Searches for additions and deletions of the supplied argument in commit diffs. Fantastic if you want to know when a piece of text was added or removed.

`-S`

`-G`

The other "pickaxe" option searches for the supplied text in any commit's diff—if the line that the text appears on was changed in any way, -G will find it.

Only lists commits that have a particular phrase in their commit message.

`--grep`

*I've held my tongue long enough! It's nice that the git log command can show me all the commits that somehow affected a piece of text, but sometimes seeing the diff isn't enough. What if I want to see exactly what **all** the files in my repository looked like when I made that commit? A commit is a snapshot, right? I assume I can "flip back" to that commit if I want to. Isn't that the point of making commits?*

Yes, yes, and...YES! A commit is a snapshot of the state of the index at the time you made the commit—it captures what every file looked like at the time you made the commit.

While we're talking about it, you've already "flipped" between commits! Remember what happens every time you switch branches? Git rewrites your working directory to look like the commit that the branch points to. In other words, you "flipped" to the commit the branch points to.

But each branch only points to the latest commit. To your point, suppose you identified a commit where a particular piece of text was added or modified using the pickaxe option. While the patch flag can tell you what changed, it can't show you exactly what your repository looked like at that time.

But Git can. And going back to your analogy, Git gives you a mechanism to "flip back" to that commit. Shall we take a look?

What does it mean to check out a commit?

A commit in Git is a snapshot. It's a mechanism to freeze-dry the contents of your index and keep them in storage (that is, Git's object database). So how do you get them out when you want to see what you tucked in there? Git offers a command called `checkout` that, when supplied a commit ID, rewrites your working directory to look exactly like it did when you made the commit. Consider the `gitanjali-aref-wedding-plans` repository. If you list the files as they stand in the `master` branch, you'll see this:

Hold on! Just soak it in for now.

All the files in the master branch

```
File Edit  Window Help
$ ls
README.md        appetizers.md  dinner.md        drinks.md
```

If you were to go back to the beginning of this chapter where we listed the commit history for the `gitanjali-aref-wedding-plans` repository, you'd notice that in the very first commit, Trinity only added one file, namely `README.md`. If you were to check out the very first commit, Git would rewrite your working directory to look like it did *at that point in time*:

Pretend we checked out commit ID 6b11ec8.

```
File Edit  Window Help
$ ls
README.md
```

As you might imagine, this isn't that different from switching branches. When you switch branches, Git looks at the commit ID recorded in the branch's sticky note and "rehydrates" all the files that were freeze-dried in that commit—and it replaces all the files in your working directory with those files.

master branch

HEAD points here as well.

This is the very first commit, with ID 6b11ec where Trinity added the README.md file.

 Sharpen your pencil

> ➤ Using your `git log` sleuthing skills, find the commit with the message "add first draft of appetizer and drink menus". Jot down the commit ID here, because you are going to need it for a future exercise.

> ➤ Who made this commit, and what changes did they introduce in this commit? **Hint:** Use the patch option to view the diffs.

——————➤ Answers on page 392.

Checking out commits

↞ *Ooh! Looking good!*

We know what it means to check out a commit. So how do we go about checking out a particular commit?

Invoke checkout.

Supply it a commit ID.

```
git checkout
```

```
6b11ec8
```

And this is what you'll see:

```
File Edit Window Help
$ git checkout 6b11ec8 ←──── Invoke the checkout command, passing it
                                the commit ID.
Note: switching to 'b6c8c82'.

You are in 'detached HEAD' state. You can look around, make experimental
changes and commit them, and you can discard any commits you make in this
state without impacting any branches by switching back to a branch.

If you want to create a new branch to retain commits you create, you may
do so (now or later) by using -c with the switch command. Example:

  git switch -c <new-branch-name>

Or undo this operation with:

  git switch -

Turn off this advice by setting config variable advice.detachedHead to
false
                      ┌─ Git reports all went well and displays the
                      └─ commit message for commit ID 6b11ec8.
HEAD is now at 6b11ec8 add README
```

We don't see any errors, so it seems to have worked. However, Git certainly seems a tad worried about *something*. Let's spend a few minutes dissecting its message.

Remember HEAD? If you recall, we spoke at length about HEAD (even interviewed it) in Chapter 4. To refresh your memory, HEAD serves multiple purposes in Git. The most important, and the one most pertinent to the conversation at hand, is that whichever commit HEAD points to will be the parent of the next commit! And *that*, right there, is the reason why Git emits this scary wall of text when you check out a commit.

Before you proceed to the next page, go back and read the output of the `git checkout` command carefully.

Sit back and, let it wash over you. We'll get you busy here soon enough.

The master branch is still here.

But HEAD now points here.

Detached HEAD state

When you check out a commit using its ID, Git says You are in 'detached HEAD' state. What this means is that you are no longer on a branch. And why does that matter? There are two things to keep in mind:

❶ **The commit that HEAD points to will be the parent of the next commit.**

❷ **There is nothing stopping you from making edits to your repository and making a commit at this point!**

What would your history look like if you did make a commit? Here's what your commit history would look like:

The master branch is still here.

HEAD points to the commit that master points to.

The master branch

You started with HEAD here.

This is the new commit. HEAD now points here.

Before

Since HEAD points here, this will be the parent of the next commit.

After

No one cares about me. :-(

As you can see, you've now created a new timeline, except there is no branch reference. While that might seem innocuous, what would happen if you then decided to switch back to the master branch? HEAD would move to the commit that the master branch points to—leaving your new commit behind. Whoops!

You switch to master after creating a new commit.

The moral of the detached HEAD ~~story~~ state

Git gives you a tremendous amount of flexibility and power. As you can see, you can check out any arbitrary commit and start making new commits. The risk you run is if you switch away to another commit or branch—you'd leave all your commits behind, and unless you remember the commit IDs, there is no easy way to get back to them! ⟵

Git will warn you when you are leaving unreferenced commits behind. But the point still stands—if you miss the warning, you'll have to figure out how to get those commits back!

The lesson here? If you ever want to see what your repository looked like at a particular point in time, use Git's checkout facilities to do just that. However, be sure to create a branch first and switch to it before making any edits when you are in detached HEAD state! Remember, branches are cheap. If you decide later on that you don't care to keep those changes around, simply delete the branch. This way, your work resides safely on a branch, and you can always switch back to it if you like, without running the risk of losing your changes. Win-win!

Exercise

Why don't you try checking out a commit?

✱ Using your terminal, navigate to the `gitanjali-aref-wedding-plans` repository. Start by listing the files in your working directory:

File Edit Window Help

✱ In the last exercise, you recorded a commit ID. This commit, created by Trinity, introduces two new files—`appetizers.md` and `drinks.md`. Jot down the command you would use to check out this commit:

✱ Next, list the files in your working directory again.

File Edit Window Help

✱ What file is missing, and why is that? Explain your answer:

⟶ Answers on page 393.

---

there are no
Dumb Questions

Q: This discussion has left me a little unsettled. If there is a chance I might lose my work, why does Git even permit us to check out commits?

A: Git's power lies in individual commits and in the directed acyclic graph that is the commit history. By capturing the state of the index in its entirety every single time you commit, Git allows you to relive that moment any time you like. Furthermore, you might have a good reason to want to go back—maybe you've thought of a better way to solve the problem at hand. That's pretty flexible, right?

And Git isn't leaving you out in the cold—it not only warns you about the state of your repository, it also provides hints on what you ought to do so you don't risk losing any work.

Checking out commits is definitely swimming at the deep end of the pool, but Git's right there, watching over you.

Who Does What?

This chapter has been a whirlwind of Git's search capabilities. Why don't you see if you can match each command with its description?

log --grep	Moves HEAD to the specified commit.
grep	Searches the diffs of all commits.
blame	Searches commit messages only.
log -S	Displays all the commits where the line that includes that text was changed in some way.
checkout	Searches all the tracked files for a piece of text.
log -G	Shows the commit and author information for each line in a file.

➞ **Answers on page 394.**

Cubicle conversation

Trinity: Are you seeing this? Seems we have a typo in our `appetizers.md` file.

Armstrong: Uh oh! What do you mean?

Trinity: It's spelled B-L-I-N-I-S, not B-L-I-N-N-I-S! I know I had this right in the first draft because I used the spell checker then.

Armstrong: Wonder when that happened? I guess you could use the pickaxe option to find when "blinnis" first appeared in the diff of a commit, right?

Trinity: You really are a quick learner, aren't you? I absolutely could. But let me show you another way to find out which commit introduced a particular change. It's called `git bisect`. It helps you search all your commits using an efficient search algorithm called binary search.

Armstrong: Do tell.

Trinity: Let's say you have five commits in your repository. You know you have a typo in the latest commit, but it wasn't there in the first commit.

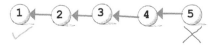

Now suppose I show you the state of the repository as it looked in commit 3, and after looking around you conclude the typo isn't there. That is, commit 3 is "good." What would that tell you?

Armstrong: That means the typo appeared in commit 4 or 5!

Trinity: Right! And what if commit 3 is "bad," as in, the typo was there?

Armstrong: We know it wasn't in commit 1, so it has to be in 2 or 3 itself.

Trinity: Yep. You just did a binary search of commits—you pick two commits and find one somewhere in between—say, commit 3. If the typo isn't there, that means it's either in commit 4 or 5. Otherwise you go further back, eventually zeroing in on the right commit.

Armstrong: And Git can help you with this? That's awesome!

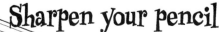

Sharpen your pencil

Before we get into our next discussion, why don't you work through an example or two that can get you acquainted with how the binary search algorithm (which, as we are sure you've figured out, is going to become important soon enough) works. Your mission, should you choose to accept it, is to find the number we call out in a list of numbers. Here are the rules:

1. You'll always start at the middle of the list. If there isn't an exact middle because the list has an even number of items, choose an item as close to the middle as possible (for instance, in a list of four items, pick the second or third).

2. If the number we ask you to find is greater than the number in the middle, you will move to the right. If the number we ask of you is less than the number in the middle, you move to the left. If you've found the number, stop.

3. When you move (left or right), you'll move to the middle of the remaining numbers. Once again, if there is no true middle, pick one close to the middle.

4. Go back to step 2.

Here's an example of us working through it so you get an idea of how to proceed. Given this list, let's find 61.

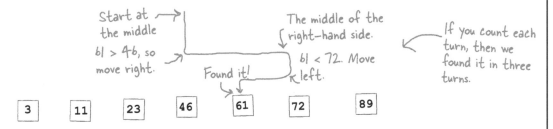

Your turn! Find the number 9 using the binary search algorithm:

How many turns did it take you?

→ Answers on page 395.

Searching for commits using git bisect

Git log's pickaxe options (-S and -G) are incredibly powerful. However, they fall short when you don't know exactly what to search for. Consider a scenario where you've found a bug in the master branch. You don't know what's causing it, so you don't know what to search for—which means the pickaxe options are no help.

But perhaps you *do* know of a way to verify the functionality of your application—either by visually inspecting the files or by running the application. Maybe you have some automated tests you can run. So how do you go about identifying the commit that introduced the bug? Well, you now know of the git checkout command. You could find the parent commit of the commit you are on and check that out. Git will diligently replace all the files in your working directory with the files as they were in that commit. You can take a look around, run your application, maybe do some tests, and if you find the bug, you're done! But if you don't, well, back to the drawing board—go back one more commit. Wash, rinse, repeat.

Or you could do a binary search of the commits in your commit history! (Where is the mind-blown emoji when you need it?)

You might have noticed in the last exercise that binary searching *can be* significantly faster than searching a list of numbers linearly. And Git can help you search your commits using the same algorithm.

The command to start a binary search of commits in Git is the bisect command. But before we show you how to use it, take a glance at the workflow.

Start here.

Start the bisect process

Tell Git a "bad" commit

Tell Git a "good" commit

Git finds and checks out out a middle commit

Is the bug there?

Yes → Tell Git it's a "bad" commit

No → Tell Git it's a "good" commit

Is this the commit that introduced the bug?

No

This workflow is a lot easier than meets the eye.

Yes → Stop the bisect process

End here.

Git's bisect command automates the process of finding a commit for you to inspect so you can decide if the bug you are looking for exists or not, over time narrowing down the list of commits that could be where the bug first showed up.

Let's see how this plays out on the command line.

Using git bisect

Let's walk through a `git bisect` session together. We'll use a hypothetical repository that has five commits. We just noticed that the latest commit has a bug in it. Let's go ahead and assume that the first commit is good.

> Sit back and read. We'll get to the exercise.

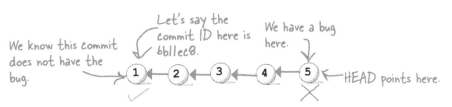

We know this commit does not have the bug.

Let's say the commit ID here is 6b11ec8.

We have a bug here.

HEAD points here.

To start bisecting commits, we have to first tell Git to kick off a bisecting session.

```
File  Edit  Window  Help
$ git bisect start                 ←——— Start bisecting. Git does not report
                                          anything. But you can use git status.
$ git status
On branch master
Your branch is up to date with 'origin/master'.

You are currently bisecting, started from branch 'master'.
  (use "git bisect reset" to get back to the original branch)

nothing to commit, working tree clean
```

> Here we go! This is gonna be fun!

Next you have to tell Git the "bad" commit ID—in this scenario, HEAD has the bug, so let's tell Git that.

```
File  Edit  Window  Help
$ git bisect bad        Again, Git does not
                        report anything.
```

This is equivalent to saying git bisect bad HEAD.

Then you tell Git the "good" commit ID, which in this case is commit ID 6b11ec8.

```
File  Edit  Window  Help
$ git bisect good 6b11ec8
Bisecting: 3 revisions left to test after this (roughly 2 steps)
[b6c8c826ed98583a175ea4616ba9aad48ec0b1ad] replace meat dishes with vegetarian items
```

By telling Git where the "bad" and "good" commits are, you are giving Git a range of commits to search. Git immediately gets to work—starting a binary search. It finds a commit somewhere halfway between the "bad" and "good" commits, and uses the `git checkout` command to check out that commit.

You are in business! Now go find that pesky commit, will ya?

Using git bisect (continued)

The `git bisect` session is all set up, and Git has already checked out a commit for you. Git status confirms this:

```
File Edit Window Help
$ git status                          Yep! You are in detached
                                      HEAD state.
HEAD detached at b6c8c82
You are currently bisecting, started from branch 'master'.
  (use "git bisect reset" to get back to the original branch)

nothing to commit, working tree clean
```

Where do things stand? Recall that checking out a commit means Git has replaced all the files in your working directory to look like they did when you made that commit:

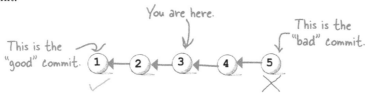

At this point, you can look at the files in your project in your editor and see if you spot the bug. Or you could run the application, run your tests, what have you. You'll probably draw one of two conclusions—the bug is in this commit, or the bug is *not* in this commit. If you **do see** the bug in this commit, then you tell Git just that:

```
File Edit Window Help
$ git bisect bad    You still see the bug.    Along the way, Git informs you how many
                                              more commits it thinks it will have to check.
Bisecting: 0 revisions left to test after this (roughly 1 step)
[d36c9830823a17c42025713dcbc3bc29bbb4ce36] add first draft of dinner menu
```

On the other hand, you might not see the bug. Then you use `git bisect good`.

Telling Git whether a commit is bad or good tells Git which direction to keep searching in. If you say "bad", Git knows to search in commits that came before the commit you are on. Otherwise, it will search commits that came after that one.

Regardless, Git will simply repeat what it did when you started—check out another commit and give you a chance to keep inspecting commits till you finally home in on the commit that started the trouble.

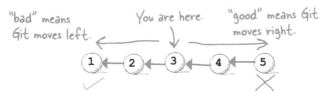

Finishing git bisect

After a few iterations with `git bisect` (depending on how many commits it has to search), Git will show you the commit that you've identified as the one that introduced the bug:

```
File Edit Window Help
$ b6c8c826ed98583a175ea4616ba9aad48ec0b1ad is the first bad commit
commit b6c8c826ed98583a175ea4616ba9aad48ec0b1ad
Author: Armstrong <armstrong@eventplannerz.com>
Date:   Tue Jul 13 04:25:01 2021 -0400          There it is!

    replace meat dishes with vegetarian items

 appetizers.md | 4 ++--
 dinner.md     | 4 ++--
 2 files changed, 4 insertions(+), 4 deletions(-)
```

So now you know which commit introduced the bug. You can inspect the files to see how the bug managed to creep in, or perhaps even decide to revert the commit (see Chapter 4)!

But before you proceed with making any changes, remember that you are still in the `git bisect` session. You'll need to signal to Git that you are done:

```
File Edit Window Help
$ git bisect reset    reset ends the              Git returns you
                      bisect session.             to where you were
Previous HEAD position was d36c983 add first draft of dinner menu  when you started
Switched to branch 'master'                       git bisect.
Your branch is up to date with 'origin/master'.
```

Be sure to reload the files in your editor!

As you proceed through the `git bisect` session, Git is checking out one commit after another. Each time it is rewriting your working directory to look like it did when you made that commit. If you have the files of your project open, there is a possibility that your editor will not realize those files have changed on disk and will continue to present you a version of the file that isn't what is in your working directory.

Many editors, like VS Code, will auto-update, so that you are always seeing the correct version of the file—but this isn't true of all editors. Many editors provide a "refresh" button to force reloading the contents of your files, so be sure to use it. Alternatively, just close and reopen your editor every time Git checks out a new commit. This way you can be sure you are looking at the right revision of the files.

Exercise

Can you spend a few minutes helping Trinity figure out which commit introduced the "blinnis" typo? Here are a few details you will need:

- HEAD has the bug. In other words, HEAD is "bad."

- We looked over the Git log for you—we know that the commit with ID 6b11ec8 is "good."

✱ Navigate to the `gitanjali-aref-wedding-plans` repository using your terminal. Start a `git bisect` session.

✱ Be sure to tell Git about the "bad" and "good" commits.

✱ Every time Git checks out a commit, be sure to reload the files in your editor. **Keep an eye on the `appetizers.md` file.**

✱ See if you can identify the commit that introduced the typo. Write down the commit ID here:

✱ Be sure to finish your Git bisect session using `git bisect reset`.

⟶ Answers on page 396.

Gitanjali and Aref's wedding was a hit! We are getting swamped with emails requesting our services.

We're going to need to do even more hiring, then!

And I get to teach them all Git! Woot!

Bullet Points

- Git provides a variety of useful tools to search the contents of repositories, the commit log, and commits.

- You can annotate any tracked file in a Git repository using `git blame`. This will show you, on a per-line basis, details about the latest commit that changed that line, including the commit ID, the author info, and the date the change was made.

- Most Git repository managers like GitHub make it easy to annotate files using `git blame` in your browser.

- You can supply `git blame` a specific commit ID to see the revision history of a file at the time that commit was made.

- You can search the contents of all tracked files in your repository using the `git grep` command.

- The `git grep` command by default is case-sensitive when searching. You can use the `-i` (shorthand for `--ignore-case`) flag to make your search case-insensitive.

- The `git grep` command also supports the `-n` (shorthand for `--line-number`) flag that will display the line number for a match.

- The `git grep` command lists every match it finds. You can restrict the output to list just the names of the files using the `-l` (shorthand for `--name-only`) flag.

- To find which commit added or removed a piece of text, you can use the `-S` flag that the `git log` command supports. The `-S` flag is one of two "pickaxe" options that Git supports, and it accepts as its argument the text you want to search for.

- The pickaxe options search the entire commit history but can be limited to inspect the history of a single file by supplying the name of the file to the `git log` command.

- The `git log` command can also display the patch introduced in every commit using the `-p` (shorthand for `--patch`) flag. This can be combined with the `-S` flag to see if the search text was added or removed in a particular commit.

- Searching for text in a Git repository using the `-S` flag only reveals commits that added or removed that piece of text. To find all commits where the line that contains a piece of text changed, there is the `-G` flag that `git log` supports.

- The `--grep` flag with the `git log` command searches commit messages.

- You can "flip back" to any commit in your commit history using the `git checkout` command.

- When you check out a commit, Git will rewrite your working directory to look like it did when you made that commit.

- Checking out a commit puts you in "detached HEAD" state. This means that you are no longer working on a branch.

- You can continue to make edits and commits, but switching away from that commit history means you will abandon your commits (since they are not referenced by a branch).

- It's best not to make any commits when you are in detached HEAD state. Always work on branches.

- You can search for commits that introduced a typo or a bug using the `git bisect` command, which uses the binary search algorithm to navigate your commit history, and quickly zero in on the commit you are looking for.

- At each step in a `git bisect` session, Git checks out a commit, leaving you in detached HEAD state. Since Git will rewrite your working directory, you can look around to see if you spot the unwelcome behavior.

- Depending on whether you see the issue, you can tell Git if the current commit is "good" or "bad," which informs Git which direction in the commit history to search. This repeats till you've isolated the commit with the reported issue.

Searching for Clues

You're not done searching just yet—time to dig up the answers to this chapter's crossword.

Across

4 -S and -G are sometimes called Git's ___ search options

5 Using this flag with the git log command lets you search commit messages

9 The git __ command tells you who did what and when for a particular file

11 When capital letters don't matter to your search, use this flag with the git grep command (2 words)

13 Using the -n flag with the git grep command will show __ numbers in the output

14 Trinity's business partner

17 To find the commit where a bug was introduced, search commits with the git ___ command

Down

1 A very efficient type of search algorithm

2 One of our favorite flags to use with the git log command for concise output

3 Trinity and Armstrong's initial files track appetizers, dinner, and _____

6 To get a snapshot of your file at the time of a commit, ___ ___ that commit (2 words)

7 The output of the git log --grep command is displayed using this

8 Like flags, you can supply these to lots of Git commands

10 The ____ brown fox jumps over the lazy dog

12 You are in _____ HEAD state when you check out a commit

15 Git offers a few different ways to ___ for a piece of text in a repository

16 Using this flag with the git log command will combine your commit history with diffs

———————▶ Answers on page 397.

Exercise
Solution

From page 351.

You'll find Trinity and Armstrong's repository for Gitanjali and Aref's wedding plans here: *https://github.com/looselytyped/gitanjali-aref-wedding-plans*

✱ Clone this repository locally. Start by listing the command you are going to use here:

git clone https://github.com/looselytyped/gitanjali-aref-wedding-plans.git

✱ Take a look around the repository, and answer the following questions:

How many branches are there in the repository? |

How many commits are there on the master branch?   8

✱ Finally, use the `git log --graph --oneline --all` command to take a look at the history. Read the commit messages carefully.

Sharpen your pencil
Solution

From page 356.

Let's get you some hands-on experience with `git blame`.

➤ You are going to use the `git blame` command to look over the revisions that have been made to the `appetizers.md` file in the `gitanjali-aref-wedding-plans` repository that you cloned at the beginning of this chapter. Start by listing out the command you are going to use:

> git blame appetizers.md

➤ Next, answer the following questions:

How many authors have contributed to this file? __2__

When was the last edit to this file made? __July 26, 2021__

Who last edited line number 5? __Armstrong__

➤ Next, use the GitHub web interface to see if you can see the `git blame` output there as well.

Exercise Solution

From page 361.

Time to exercise your new Git grep sleuthing skills. Navigate to the `gitanjali-aref-wedding-plans` repository in your terminal.

✱ How can you search for all files that contain the word "menu"? Jot that down here:

> git grep menu

✱ How many files did you find?   1

✱ Next, make the search case-insensitive. List the command here:

> git grep —i menu

✱ How many matches did you get this time around?   2

✱ Finally, if you also want to see the line numbers, what would the `git grep` command look like?

> git grep —i —n menu

Exercise Solution

From page 364.

Let's put your searching skills to work. Start by navigating to the `gitanjali-aref-wedding-plans` repository.

✱ How can you go about finding every commit that adds or removes the word "classic" in your repository? Start by listing the command you would use here:

> git log —S classic

✱ Execute! How many commits did your search reveal? _____1_____

Exercise Solution

From page 367.

✳ Search the `gitanjali-aref-wedding-plans` repository for all commits that add or delete the word "walnut", using the patch and word-diff flags. Which commit added the word, and which one removed it?

b6c8c82 added it

e9beff3 removed it

Exercise Solution

From page 369.

✳ Search for the word "classic" in the commit history of the `gitanjali-aref-wedding-plans` repository, except this time you are going to use the `-G` flag. Be sure to display abbreviated commit IDs, and use the `--word-diff` option. Start by listing the command here:

git log -p --oneline -G classic --word-diff

✳ How many commits reported the word "classic" in your commit history?

2

✳ Compare this with the output of the `-s` flag—why do you see more commits with the `-G` flag than you did with the `-s` flag?

Searching with the -S flag only shows one commit. This is because -S only looks for when "classic" was added (or removed). The -G flag looks for commits that affect the line that contains "classic," which changed in the commit with ID c366817.

Sharpen your pencil
Solution

From page 369.

> Some of these commands are not like the others. Some don't work!

Let's say you were searching for the word "classic" in the `gitanjali-aref-wedding-plans` repository. Listed below are several combinations of `git log`'s pickaxe options, except a few of them won't work. Can you identify them? **Hint:** Look carefully at the order of flags and arguments.

The search string ("classic" in this case) must follow the −G flag.

```
git log -p --oneline -S classic
```

```
git log -G̶-p classic
```

```
git log -p -G classic --oneline --all
```

```
git log -p c̶l̶a̶s̶s̶i̶c̶ -S
```

```
git log -S classic --all
```

Similarly, "classic" must be an argument to the −S flag.

Exercise
Solution

From page 370.

✱ What command would you use to find every commit that has the word "menu" in the `gitanjali-aref-wedding-plans` repository?

> git log --grep menu

✱ How many commits did you find? List their IDs here:

> Two. d36c983 and 99fd56e

Sharpen your pencil
Solution

From page 373.

➤ Using your `git log` sleuthing skills, find the commit with the message "add first draft of appetizer and drink menus". Jot down the commit ID here, because you are going to need it for a future exercise.

99fd5be

➤ Who made this commit, and what changes did they introduce in this commit? **Hint:** Use the patch option to view the diffs.

This commit was authored by Trinity. This commit introduces two new files—appetizers.md and drinks.md. I know they are new files because I see "new file mode" for both files in the diff output.

Exercise
Solution

From page 376.

Why don't you try checking out a commit?

✲ Using your terminal, navigate to the `gitanjali-aref-wedding-plans` repository. Start by listing the files in your working directory:

```
File Edit Window Help
README.md    appetizers.md
dinner.md    drinks.md
```

✲ In the last exercise, you recorded a commit ID. This commit, created by Trinity, introduces two new files—`appetizers.md` and `drinks.md`. Jot down the command you would use to check out this commit:

> git checkout 99fd5be

✲ Next, list the files in your working directory again.

```
File Edit Window Help
README.md    appetizers.md    drinks.md
```

✲ What file is missing, and why is that? Explain your answer:

> Checking out commit ID 99fd5be flipped me back to a point in time before
> dinner.md was added. Since Git rewrote my working directory to look like it
> did when that commit was made, the dinner.md file is no longer available to me.

Who Does What?
Solution

From page 377.

This chapter has been a whirlwind of Git's search capabilities. Why don't you see if you can match each command with its description?

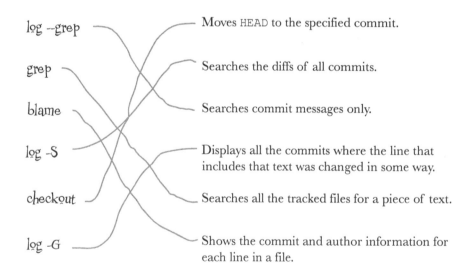

log --grep

grep

blame

log -S

checkout

log -G

Moves HEAD to the specified commit.

Searches the diffs of all commits.

Searches commit messages only.

Displays all the commits where the line that includes that text was changed in some way.

Searches all the tracked files for a piece of text.

Shows the commit and author information for each line in a file.

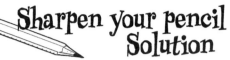

Sharpen your pencil
Solution

From page 379.

Before we get into our next discussion, why don't you work through an example or two that can get you acquainted with how the binary search algorithm (which, as we are sure you've figured out, is going to become important soon enough) works. Your mission, should you choose to accept it, is to find the number we call out in a list of numbers. Here are the rules:

1.   You'll always start at the middle of the list. If there isn't an exact middle because the list has an even number of items, choose an item as close to the middle as possible (for instance, in a list of four items, pick the second or third).

2.   If the number we ask you to find is greater than the number in the middle, you will move to the right. If the number we ask of you is less than the number in the middle, you move to the left. If you've found the number, stop.

3.   When you move (left or right), you'll move to the middle of the remaining numbers. Once again, if there is no true middle, pick one close to the middle.

4.   Go back to step 2.

Here's an example of us working through it so you get an idea of how to proceed. Given this list, let's find 61.

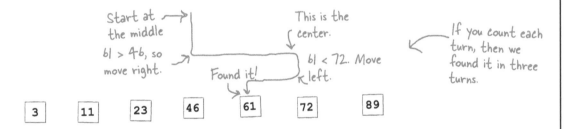

Your turn! Find the number 9 using the binary search algorithm:

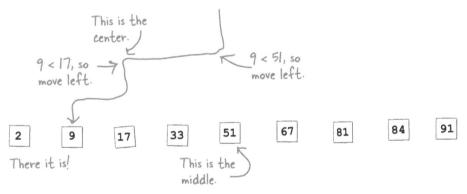

How many turns did it take you?

Three

Exercise Solution

From page 384.

Can you spend a few minutes helping Trinity figure out which commit introduced the "blinnis" typo? Here are a few details you will need:

- HEAD has the bug. In other words, HEAD is "bad."

- We looked over the Git log for you—we know that the commit with ID 6b11ec8 is "good."

✱ Navigate to the `gitanjali-aref-wedding-plans` repository using your terminal. Start a `git bisect` session.

✱ Be sure to tell Git about the "bad" and "good" commits.

✱ Every time Git checks out a commit, be sure to reload the files in your editor. **Keep an eye on the `appetizers.md` file.**

✱ See if you can identify the commit that introduced the typo. Write down the commit ID here:

b6c8c82 is the bad commit. ← Is this what you got?

✱ Be sure to finish your Git bisect session using `git bisect reset`.

Searching for Clues Solution

You're not done searching just yet—time to dig up the answers to this chapter's crossword.

From page 386.

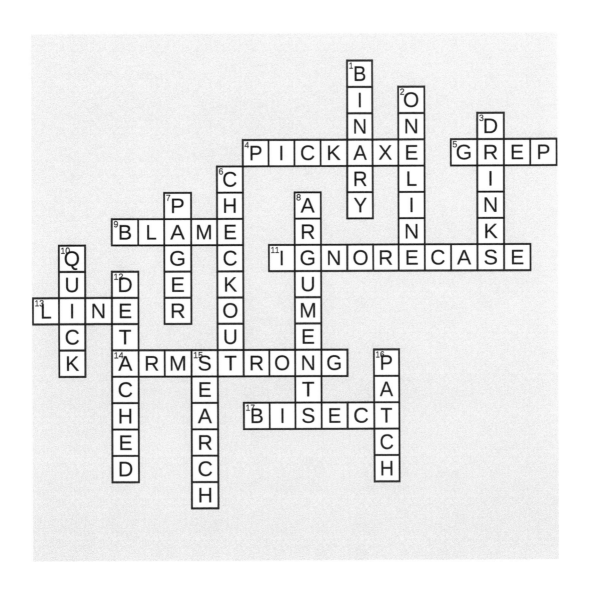

8
making your life easier with Git
#ProTips

On behalf of everyone here at the Head First family, we'd like to welcome you aboard.

We'll do everything we can to ensure a pleasant experience with us today. Thank you for choosing us.

So far in this book, you've learned how to use Git. But you can also bend Git to your will. That's where the ability to configure Git plays a vital role. You've already seen how to configure Git in previous chapters—in this chapter we'll be exploring a lot more of what you can configure to make your life easier. The configuration can also help you define shortcuts: long-winded Git commands begone!

There's a lot more you can do to make your interaction with Git easier. We'll show how you can tell Git to ignore certain types of files so that you don't accidentally commit them. We'll give you our recommended ways of writing commit messages and tell you how we like to name our branches. And to top it off, we'll even explore how a graphical user interface to Git can play an important role in your workflow. #letsgo #cantwait

Configuring Git

Git ships with a certain set of defaults. So far in this book, you've used the `git config` command to set or override some of these settings to better suit your needs. However, it doesn't stop here—you can tweak Git's behavior to do all kinds of things to make your life easier. Understanding where Git stores this configuration, and all that it is capable of, can really improve your overall experience.

Here's a quick reminder of how we told Git our name, so it knows to give us credit every time we commit:

You will probably recall also using this to set our email (Chapter 1), our default editor (Chapter 2), and Git's behavior when it comes to pushing branches (Chapter 5).

The `git config` command can accept a flag (`--global`, in this case), an option (`user.name`), and finally the value to which we set the option ("Raju Gandhi"). The `--global` flag is of particular interest because it tells Git how to treat this configuration change.

You've worked with a few different repositories in this book, and you've probably noticed that no matter what repository you were in, your name and email address were always the same. That's because of the `--global` flag. This flag tells Git that you want this setting applied to any and all Git repositories that you work with on that particular workstation. This is also why you didn't have to be in any particular directory when you ran this command! Next, we'll look at where your configuration resides and what else you can do with it.

there are no Dumb Questions

Q: I recall setting `user.name` **and** `user.email`**, but these look like very specific things we are setting. Is there a place I can find a list of everything that Git allows me to configure?**

A: You are right that `user.name` and `user.email` are "special." Unfortunately, there isn't one single comprehensive location in Git's documentation that lists the entire set of things you can configure. If you view the documentation for the `git config` command (using `git help config` or `git config --help`), you'll see a list of more than 600 settable items. But that isn't the entire list! You'll often find additional configurable items for individual commands if you read the help page for that particular command.

Don't let this overwhelm you, though. We'll get you to a good place, and as you gain more experience with Git and start to spot default settings that you wish to change, you can always use your favorite search engine.

The global .gitconfig file

What happens when you invoke the `git config` command with the `--global` flag? Git realizes you want a particular setting available across all of the repositories you work with, so it installs that setting in a file called `.gitconfig` in your home directory. For Linux and macOS users, your home directory will be `~/` and for Windows users, this defaults to the directory with your username under `C:\Users`. You can use your terminal to locate this file:

Change directories to "~" (home) directory.

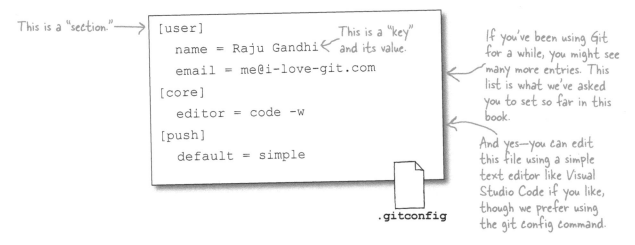

```
File Edit Window Help
$ cd ~
$ ls -A                    There it is!
.bashrc    .gitconfig   .profile
Desktop    Documents    Library
```

We truncated this list— you'll probably see lots of files and folders here.

If you were to open this file using a text editor, this is what you'd see:

This is a "section." ───→

```
[user]                        This is a "key"
    name = Raju Gandhi        and its value.
    email = me@i-love-git.com
[core]
    editor = code -w
[push]
    default = simple
```

.gitconfig

If you've been using Git for a while, you might see many more entries. This list is what we've asked you to set so far in this book.

And yes—you can edit this file using a simple text editor like Visual Studio Code if you like, though we prefer using the git config command.

As you can see, this file has a bunch of *sections* (wrapped in square brackets), each followed by one or more *keys* and their values. A `setting.key` combination is referred to as an *option*—for example, `user.name` is an option. Perhaps you can see how the Git command works: supplying the `--global` flag edits the `.gitconfig` file in your home directory. And supplying, say, `user.name` means we are attempting to configure the `name` key under the `user` section.

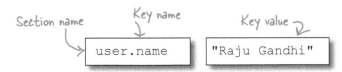

Section name   Key name   Key value

```
user.name       "Raju Gandhi"
```

The .gitconfig file isn't always visible

The `.gitconfig` *file (like the* `.git` *directory in a repository) is referred to as a "hidden" file. If you were to use the Finder or File Explorer to navigate to your home directory, you might not see it. That's because most operating systems, by default, do not list hidden files. You'll need to turn on the ability to see hidden files.*

For Mac users, open a new Finder window, navigate to your home directory, and if you don't see the `.gitconfig` *files, use* `Command + Shift + .` *(yep, that's a period at the end) to turn on displaying hidden files. For Windows users, open a new File Explorer window, navigate to your home directory, and click on the "View" tab, then check the "Hidden files" checkbox.*

Exercise

Why don't you spend a few minutes working with your global Git configuration?

✳ Using the terminal, navigate to your home directory, then list all the files, including hidden ones. See if you can spot the `.gitconfig` file. Use this space to write out the commands you are going to use:

You might recall that the command to *check* the value of a key is nearly identical to setting it. For example:

> **git config --global user.email "me@i-love-git.com"**   Sets your email address globally.

> **versus**

> **git config --global user.email**   Not supplying a value means you are asking Git to show you the value of a particular option.

✳ Using the terminal, see if you can check the value of the `core.editor` key. List the command you are going to use here first:

✳ Using your text editor, open the global Git configuration file. Spend a few minutes looking around—do the sections and key-value pairs listed seem familiar to you?

⟶ Answers on page 435.

If there is a "global" configuration, does that mean there is a "local" configuration? If so, what does that even mean?

Brilliant question! Git is all about flexibility. It knows that different situations have different requirements, and it aims to do everything it can to help you out. Let's say that most of your Git use involves projects at work—it makes sense for you to set your work email address in the global configuration. This way, no matter which repository you work on, the email address recorded in every commit across all repositories on that workstation would be your work email address.

But then you decide to work on a personal project or contribute to an open source project in your free time. Just for that project, you would rather record your personal email address for every commit. Git allows you to install a specific configuration for a particular repository, overriding the global one. Let's see how to do that next.

Project-specific Git configuration

The global Git configuration is a great place to store options that you want Git to use most of the time (like your name, which probably doesn't change often). But every so often, you might prefer a different setting for a particular project. Git to the rescue—we can override global options for a particular project. The `git config` command supports another flag, `--local`, that writes a configuration file for a specific repository:

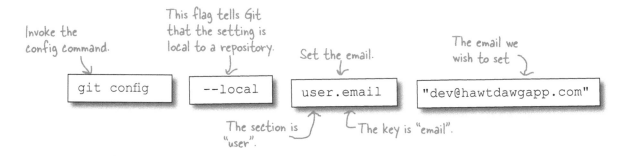

Invoke the config command.

This flag tells Git that the setting is local to a repository.

Set the email.

The email we wish to set

```
git config          --local          user.email          "dev@hawtdawgapp.com"
```

The section is "user".

The key is "email".

Two points of note: the **default behavior** of the `git config` command is to install options locally. In other words, you can skip the `--local` flag and get the exact same behavior. You'd have to use the `--global` flag for it to **not** be a local install. Secondly, **you have to be in a Git repository** when you issue the `git config` command without the `--global` flag! Otherwise, Git will report a `fatal: not in a git directory` error. That makes sense—you are telling Git you want to set a *specific* option for a *particular* repository, the one you are in right now.

Git stores the local configuration in a file called "config" inside the hidden .git folder.

What happens when you install a option locally? Git stores it in, you guessed it, a special location inside the hidden `.git` directory of the repository you are in. As long as you are working in that repository, Git will use the option as dictated by the local configuration. If you change directories and start working with another repository that does not have a local configuration, Git falls back to using the global setting.

Watch it!

Be careful of typos

The `git config` command does not check if the section and key name you supply are valid! Let's say you accidentally supply the option as `user.nme`—Git will record it in a new key-value pair, leaving you wondering why Git isn't acknowledging your change. Always check for typos before you issue the `git config` command.

there are no Dumb Questions

Q: Let's say that I set my work email address in the global `.gitconfig` file, but set my personal email address locally for one particular repository. The commits in that particular repository will use my personal email address, right?

A: Exactly! Git first reads the global configuration file (in your home directory), followed by the one local to your repository—in that order—and then merges them into one. Sections and keys that are unique to each file will remain untouched—however, if you have the `user.email` key set to a different value in your local configuration than what's in the global one, the local one wins.

Just think of the "distance" between each configuration and your repository—the closer it is, the higher its priority.

Q: I can't see myself using the local configuration. Can you give me some examples of where this might be useful?

A: You are right—it is rather unusual. You usually want Git to behave consistently, and having different configurations for different repositories can be unsettling.

However, one scenario where this plays in our favor is the exact scenario we described earlier, where we want to use a personal email instead of a work one for one specific repository.

Or suppose you want your "name" to show differently for a particular project. For example, you are proofreading a manuscript, and you want any commits that you make to show up under the pseudonym "Proofreader." This would be a good use case to install a different name for a specific repository.

Regardless, knowing how to dictate Git's behavior is a valuable skill. We'll be using Git's configuration for another topic in this chapter, and we certainly hope you find good use for it in the future.

Q: Once I set an option, how do I change it later?

A: Simply rerun the command to set the option with a new value, and Git will update the configuration file you are targeting with the new value. Easy peasy.

Q: How do I delete an entry?

A: The `git config` command offers an `--unset` flag that will remove an entry. Suppose you want to remove the value for `user.email` from the configuration of a specific repository—that is, you want to remove a "local" configuration. This is how you'd go about doing it:

```
git config --local --unset user.email
```

If this was a global configuration, you'd have to pass the `--global` flag alongside the `--unset` flag to affect the `.gitconfig` in your home directory.

Also, recall that Git stores your configuration as a plain-text file. You can always choose to open the file using a text editor like Visual Studio Code and edit it. Be sure to make a backup first, though. (Better safe than sorry, right?)

Q: What happens if I run the --local flag with the git config command, but I am not in a Git repository?

A: When you run the `git config` command with the `--local` flag, Git attempts to find a place to store your configuration. Git will look for a `.git` directory in the current folder—if it finds one, it installs the option there. Otherwise, it navigates to the parent of the current folder and looks again. It continues to navigate up the directory tree till it finds a `.git` folder.

If the search fails, Git will error out with `fatal: --local can only be used inside a git repository`.

Our advice: if you want to configure a repository with a local option, be sure to invoke the `git config` command with the `--local` flag when you are in the root directory of the repository you want to configure (that is, the directory containing the hidden `.git` folder). This way you know exactly which repository you are affecting.

Listing your Git configuration

Installing options and configuring Git to your whims is all fine and dandy, but sometimes you might just want to list everything you have configured. The `git config` command offers a `--list` flag that lists all the options you've set, global or local. Imagine you've set a bunch of options in the global configuration, and you've introduced a different email address using the `git config` with the `--local` flag. Here is what we see when we use the `--list` option on our own machine (yours will be different):

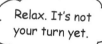

Relax. It's not your turn yet.

```
File Edit Window Help
$ git config --list
user.name=Raju Gandhi
user.email=me@i-love-git.com
core.editor=code -w
push.default=simple
core.repositoryformatversion=0
core.filemode=true
core.bare=false
core.logallrefupdates=true
core.ignorecase=true
user.email=me@hawtdawgapp.com
```

Note that user.email is listed twice.

The --list config lists your entire configuration—global and local.

You will see entries you might not recognize. That's OK—those are some defaults that Git sets up.

As you can see, the `--list` flag lists **all** the options that Git sees, including some that Git sets up automatically. Recall that Git reads the global configuration first, followed by the local configuration. The `--list` flag lists the options in the order Git encounters them—entries at the top are global, followed by any local entries. You'll notice that the previous listing displays `user.email` twice—the first is the value Git sees in the global configuration file; the second is the one that we installed locally in that repository.

Naturally, you might be curious whether a particular option was set globally or locally. To answer that question the `git config` command supports another flag, `--show-origin`, which, alongside the `--list` option, will show you where Git picked up a particular setting.

Supply the --show-origin flag to the git config command.

These entries come from the global .gitconfig file in your home directory.

These are local to the repository.

```
File Edit Window Help
$ git config --list --show-origin
file:/root/.gitconfig      user.name=Raju Gandhi
file:/root/.gitconfig      user.email=me@i-love-git.com
file:/root/.gitconfig      core.editor=code -w
file:/root/.gitconfig      push.default=simple
file:.git/config      core.repositoryformatversion=0
file:.git/config      core.filemode=true
file:.git/config      core.bare=false
file:.git/config      core.logallrefupdates=true
file:.git/config      core.ignorecase=true
file:.git/config      user.email=me@hawtdawgapp.com
```

We aren't done yet. We'll soon show you another little trick that uses Git's configuration capabilities. Stay tuned!

Sharpen your pencil

Flex those Git configuration muscles for a bit, will ya?

➤ What command will you use to list your global Git configuration as well as the name of the file where you set this configuration?

Note that you don't have to be in any specific directory to run this version of the `git config` command!

➤ Next, create a new folder called `a-head-above`. We chose to create this folder inside another folder called `chapter08` next to the exercises we did for other chapters just to keep things nice and tidy (but you do you!).

➤ Using your terminal, change directories to the `a-head-above` directory, and initialize a new Git repository.

➤ Using the `--local` flag with the `git config` command, change your name for this repository alone. If you've been using your full name so far in this book, use only your first name, or just your initials. Or, use the name of your favorite fictional character! What command will you use? (Hint: The option you are to set is `user.name`.)

➤ List your entire Git configuration again, along with the origin of the configuration. What has changed? Explain your answer here:

➤ Create a file called `README.md` with the following contents, add it to the index, and commit it with the commit message "docs: add a README file":

You might notice that this is a slightly different commit-message format. We'll be talking more about this soon.

We've included this file under the chapter08 folder in the source code for this book.

```
# Making your life easier with Git

1. You can override the global configuration on a
per-repository basis
```

README.md

➤ Finally, use `git log` (with no flags), and inspect the author name.

⟶ Answers on page 436.

Git aliases, aka your personal Git shortcuts

You've certainly been busy in this book—you've typed a variety of Git commands so many times that they are second nature by now. However, some commands, especially those that use a variety of flags (we are looking at you, `git log`!) can be annoying to type out every single time—not to mention that you can introduce errors when you do.

We have good news! Git allows you to define an *alias*, which allows you to wrap any Git command, including all the necessary flags, into a shortcut. When you invoke the shortcut, Git will automagically expand into whatever that shortcut is assigned to. Perhaps this is best explained with an example. Let's say you create an alias called `loga` that expands to `git log --online --graph --all`:

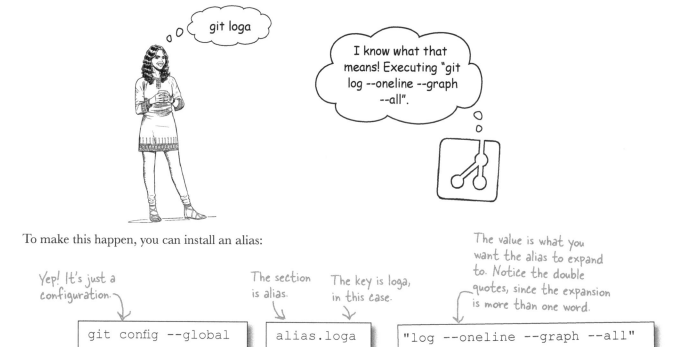

git loga

I know what that means! Executing "git log --oneline --graph --all".

To make this happen, you can install an alias:

Yep! It's just a configuration.

The section is alias.

The key is loga, in this case.

The value is what you want the alias to expand to. Notice the double quotes, since the expansion is more than one word.

```
git config --global        alias.loga        "log --oneline --graph --all"
```

This is just another piece of configuration, and as you might've guessed, it gets stuffed in the `.gitconfig` file in your home directory. Everything you've learned so far about adding/editing/viewing the Git configuration also applies to aliases.

Now, instead of having to type `git log --oneline --graph --all`, you simply invoke `git loga` and you get the exact same output! How awesome is that?!

When you "set" an alias, the section in the `.gitconfig` file is called "alias" (which you must get right) and the key can be anything you want it to be. Just be sure to make the key relevant and somewhat memorable—in our case we picked **loga** because we are invoking the **l**og command with the **o**neline, **g**raph, and **a**ll flags, not to mention it's pretty similar to log (with the "a" at the end).

Tweaking the behavior of Git aliases

Git aliases allow you to move quickly and accurately, while at the same time allowing the flexibility that all Git commands offer. Just remember, Git aliases are unforgiving when it comes to what they *expand into*. For example, if you had an alias called `loga` that expanded into `git log --oneline --graph --all`, but for some reason you did not want to see "all" branches, you'd be forced to type out `git log --oneline --graph` (or use another alias if you had it). In other words, once you define an alias, you can't tell it *not* to do what it's designed to do.

However, Git aliases are extremely flexible when it comes to supplying additional arguments or flags. For example, let's say you define an alias, c (yep, lowercase C), to expand into `git commit`. But you know that when you commit, you use the `-m` flag to supply a commit message. This is what that would look like:

For commands that we use often, we like terse aliases. c for commit is an alias we use daily!

Invoke the alias.

You can supply any arguments and flags like you normally would.

```
git c -m "my first commit"
```

Git will execute this.

```
git commit -m "my first commit"
```

As you can see, Git takes any additional flags and arguments that you supply to an alias, expands them, and diligently passes them to the command.

Pay close attention to the commands you use often, including any flags that you always seem to need. Those are ideal candidates for aliases. But don't get too specific! Remember, the alias will always expand into what you define it to be. You can always add more (like we just demonstrated) when the need arises.

Also, it's not unusual to have multiple aliases that invoke the same command, with different variations. For example, you might define "b" to expand into `branch`, and "ba" to expand into `branch -a` (or `--all`).

Finally, **always make your aliases lowercase**. This fits with how Git commands work—and they are easier to type.

> ⚠️ **Watch it!**
>
> ### Never define an alias name to match a Git command name!
>
> *Let's say you decide to define an alias, "log", that expands into "log --oneline --graph". Git will always look to see if there is a command called `log` **before** it looks to see if there is an alias called `log`. So, when you invoke `git log`, Git will find the `log` command and invoke that. In other words, you have no way of invoking the alias. Kinda defeats the purpose of having the alias to begin with, right?*

Sharpen your pencil

Can you think of any Git commands that could really use an alias? Think of how many times you've used Git's `status`, `add`, `branch`, `switch`, and `diff` commands in this book!

Here's some space for you to jot down some ideas. (We've got you started with one of our favorites.)

Alias	Expands to
git a	git add

Also, be sure to look ahead at the solution to see what we've listed, in case you see some aliases you might adapt in your day-to-day workflow. (We've listed most of our favorites.)

⟶ Ideas on page 437.

there are no Dumb Questions

Q: Can I make a local alias for a specific repository?

A: Absolutely. But the question is—should you? You see, aliases are all about making your life easier, and having different aliases do different things in different repositories almost seems like the antithesis of making your life easier. We feel that aliases only make sense in the global configuration.

Q: Let's say I make an alias but forget it later. Is there a way to ask Git what it expands to?

A: Let's say you have an alias s that expands to "status". Invoke `git help s` and Git will respond with `'s' is aliased to 'status'`.

Watch it!

Don't get too used to your shortcuts

The more you use your aliases, the more they become muscle memory in every interaction you have with Git. Git aliases, just like any other shortcut, are not always available. Suppose you are working on a remote server or a colleague's workstation—you will most likely have to revert back to using Git's defaults for both commands and flags. So don't lose touch with how things really work in Git. You never know when you'll have to fall back to the basics.

Exercise

You are going to spend a little time creating a few aliases of your own.

✳ Fire up your terminal. You're going to be installing these aliases globally, so it doesn't matter which directory you do this exercise from.

✳ The first alias you are to install is **loga**, which you'll set to expand to `log --oneline --graph --all`. List the command to use here first:

Execute this command.

✳ Use the `git config` command to check if the alias was correctly installed. Here's some space for you to jot down the command to use:

✳ Let's go meta! You are going to create an alias that lists your entire configuration. Define an alias called **aliases** that expands into `git config --list --show-origin`. Be sure to write out the command you are going to use.

✳ Navigate to the location where you created the `a-head-above` repository. Invoke the `loga` alias. Did you get what you expect to see? Next, invoke the `aliases` config—is the `aliases` alias listed as well?

Just now we had you modify your global configuration. Feel free to "unset" these aliases if they are not to your liking—we won't be offended, we promise!

———————————▶ Answers on page 438.

Telling Git to ignore certain files and folders

At times, you'll want to tell Git to ignore certain files in a repository. Case in point—when you navigate to a directory using the Finder, macOS tends to create a file called `.DS_Store` that it uses to store internal settings. Windows users, on occasion, might have noticed the pesky `Thumbs.db` or `Desktop.ini` files.

Many editors tend to create specific files and/or folders to store their own project-specific settings. Visual Studio Code, based on how you use it, often creates a `.vscode` folder. IntelliJ (from JetBrains) creates an `.idea` folder.

Often, software projects have files that you will never track in your Git repository. For example, most JavaScript projects tend to have a `node_modules` folder that houses dependencies. Java projects often have a `build` directory that stores all the compiled source code. Since both the `node_modules` folder and the `build` directory contain "generated" artifacts, you can always recreate them using the appropriate tooling. There's no reason to stuff them into your Git repository.

Finally, you might have project files that contain sensitive information you do not wish to commit, even accidentally.

Consider one of the operating-system-specific files; if Git sees one of these files in your working directory, it will report it in the output of the `git status` command:

> Sit back, and let it wash over you.

Different teams have different policies when it comes to editor-specific files and folders. We usually prefer to keep these files out of our Git repositories, but be sure to talk to your team first.

```
File Edit Window Help
$ git status
On branch master
Untracked files:
  (use "git add <file>..." to include in what will be committed)
    .DS_Store
nothing added to commit but untracked files present (use "git add" to track)
```

There it is! Gah! (shakes fist at the infuriating file)

One option is to pretend they don't exist. However, for many projects, this list of unneeded files can get long. After a while, it gets hard to discern which files you care about and which you don't! Git, once more, has an answer, in the form of a special file called `.gitignore` that can help eliminate this annoyance once and for all.

The effects of a .gitignore file

You learned in Chapter 1 that when you intialize a Git repository, Git creates a hidden `.git` folder where it houses a bunch of things, including the object database and any repository-specific configurations, like a work or personal email that is different from your global configuration as we just discussed.

Nothing for you to do here.

This directory containing the `.git` folder is called the "root" of your project. In this root directory, you can create a `.gitignore` file. This file allows you to tell Git which files it should, well, ignore. Essentially, the `.gitignore` file keeps **untracked files** out of your Git repository. Consider a hypothetical repository:

Read that again—the .gitignore file is for untracked files only!

List all the files and folders, including hidden ones.

```
File Edit Window Help
$ ls -A
.DS_Store   .git   README.md

$ git status
On branch master
Untracked files:
  (use "git add <file>..." to include in what will be committed)
        .DS_Store

nothing added to commit but untracked files present (use "git add"
to track)
```

There it is!

Nooooool!!

Now suppose we add a `.gitignore` file at the root of the project. Since we want to ignore the `.DS_Store`, we can simply list the name of that file in the `.gitignore` file. How does that help us? Let's take a look:

We include a .gitignore file.

`.DS_Store`

`.gitignore`

```
File Edit Window Help
$ ls -A
.DS_Store   .git   README.md

$ git status
On branch master
Untracked files:
  (use "git add <file>..." to include in what will be committed)
        .gitignore
nothing added to commit but untracked files present (use "git add" to track)
```

Still there

Git ignores the .DS_Store file now.

Anticlimactic? Maybe. But notice that Git ignores the `.DS_Store` file. Why? Because the `.gitignore` file instructs it to. Now that Git is ignoring the file, you can't even add it to the index, which means you can't accidentally commit it. Pretty sweet, right?

However, now Git sees the `.gitignore` file as "untracked." How do you go about managing this file? Let's talk about that next.

Managing the .gitignore file

The `.gitignore` file plays a very important role in any Git repository. In fact, we would go as far as to say that any repository that you will work with **will** have a `.gitignore` file.

Don't believe us? Navigate to github.com and browse through some of the public repositories. Go on! We dare ya!

After creating the `.gitignore` file, you should add it to the index and then commit it. This makes it consistent across all collaborators working on the repository, and any changes to it will be part of your commit history.

As to the contents of the file, a good starting point is to think about how you'll use your repository. If it's just you working on it, then at a minimum, you will want to ignore all those files that your operating system introduces for its internal bookkeeping, like the `.DS_Store` file on macOS. Use your favorite search engine to search for a sample `.gitignore` file and copy-paste its contents into your `.gitignore` file.

Insert the name of your operating system here.

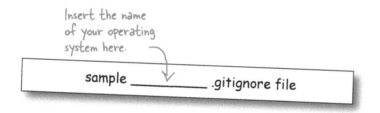

sample _____ .gitignore file

If you are working with a bunch of collaborators and you all happen to use different operating systems, then you'll need to list out all the files that you'll need to ignore across all those operating systems.

The .gitignore files for many projects can get pretty long. However, once you get the initial version committed, they don't tend to change that often.

And then get to work. As you do, you'll see files and folders that you know you'll never add to the repository but that clutter the output of commands like `git status`. Add those file and folder names to the `.gitignore` file. You can always search for a sample `.gitignore` file for a particular kind of project (Java, JavaScript, Xcode, what have you) to get to a good starting point.

Just be aware! Before you use a sample `.gitignore` file, look it over carefully. Be sure to pull in your team (if you have one) to take a look too—share it with them, or issue a pull request so they can review your changes before you merge it in. Once you ignore a file or a folder, Git will continue to ignore it unless you remove that entry from the `.gitignore` file.

See? All that hard work creating pull requests is about to finally pay off!

It's not easy to create a .gitignore file

Many, if not all, operating systems make it astonishingly hard to create a hidden file like the .gitignore *file. (Any file or folder prefixed with a period is considered hidden.) You have a couple of options:*

Use your terminal

The easiest option is to use your terminal. The command to use is touch, *which creates files, much like* mkdir *(discussed in Chapter 1) creates directories. The* touch *command takes the name of the file you wish to create as an argument. Suppose you want to create a* .gitignore *file in the* a-head-above *directory. This is what that would look like:*

```
File Edit Window Help
$ pwd
/tmp/a-head-above       Navigate to the directory
                        where you want to create
                        the file.

$ ls -A
.git   README.md  ← There is no .gitignore file.

                       Invoke the touch command, supplying it the
$ touch .gitignore     name of the file you want to create.
$ ls -A
.git   .gitignore   README.md
     There it is!
```

Once you have the file, you can edit it using your text editor and add as many entries as you like.

Use a text editor

The other option available to you is using a text editor like Visual Studio Code. You can create a new file using the File menu. When you attempt to save it, Visual Studio Code will give you the option to name the file and pick a location—provide it the name .gitignore *and pick the directory where you want to save it. Visual Studio Code will give you a warning that you are about to create a hidden file. Just confirm and you are good to go.*

Visual Studio Code's warning dialog when creating a hidden file.

Names that begin with a dot "." are reserved for the system.

If you decide to go ahead and use a name which begins with a dot the file will be hidden.

Cancel   Use "."

Click the Use "." button to continue.

A sample .gitignore file

Let's spend a few minutes looking over a sample .gitignore file and examining some of its capabilities. The file we are about to show you is from one of our projects. It accomodates ignoring both macOS and Windows-specific files. Since we like to use extensions with Visual Studio Code, we exclude some folders that one of the extensions generates.

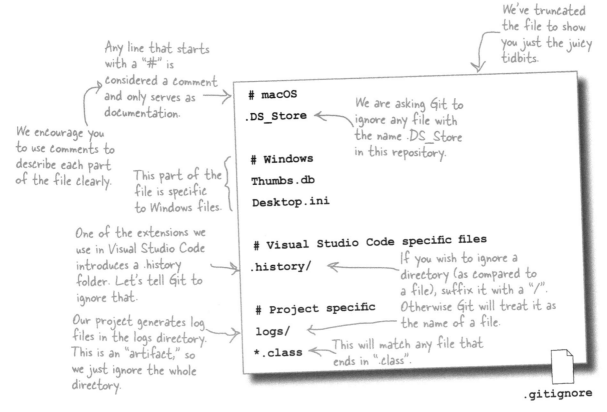

We've truncated the file to show you just the juicy tidbits.

Any line that starts with a "#" is considered a comment and only serves as documentation.

We encourage you to use comments to describe each part of the file clearly.

This part of the file is specific to Windows files.

We are asking Git to ignore any file with the name .DS_Store in this repository.

One of the extensions we use in Visual Studio Code introduces a .history folder. Let's tell Git to ignore that.

Our project generates log files in the logs directory. This is an "artifact," so we just ignore the whole directory.

If you wish to ignore a directory (as compared to a file), suffix it with a "/". Otherwise Git will treat it as the name of a file.

This will match any file that ends in ".class".

```
# macOS
.DS_Store

# Windows
Thumbs.db
Desktop.ini

# Visual Studio Code specific files
.history/

# Project specific
logs/
*.class
```

.gitignore

As you can see, the .gitignore file allows you to ignore both files and folders. Since our project is a Java project that produces .class files and writes its logs in the logs directory, we ignore both of those. Not only that, you can specify "patterns" to match—for example, *.class will match any files that have the class extension.

An important thing to note is that if you want to ignore a folder, you need to append it with a forward slash (/). Without the trailing slash, Git will treat it as a filename.

Finally, the .gitignore file can be as short or long as it needs to be—individual entries in the file are listed one per line. We are huge proponents of documenting our work, so we are liberal with comments. These are prefixed with a hash mark (#), which tells Git to simply discard them.

This pattern format is very comprehensive and allows for all kinds of special use cases. Be sure to look into Git's documentation if you'd like to know more.

Sharpen your pencil

Let's introduce a `.gitignore` file in the `a-head-above` Git repository you created for this chapter.

➤ Fire up your terminal and navigate to the location where you created the repository.

➤ Using the terminal and the `touch` command, create a `.gitignore` file at the root of the project. Use this space to list the command you will use:

➤ Using your favorite search engine, search for a sample `.gitignore` file for your particular operating system.

➤ Open your own `.gitignore` file in your text editor and update it to match the sample you found. Be sure to comment to document why you made some entries.

➤ Look over the `.gitignore` file to make sure you understand exactly what you are choosing to exclude from your repository.

➤ Finally, add the `.gitignore` file to the index and commit it with the message "chore: add .gitignore file".

Yet another departure from our usual commit-message format. We'll explain soon, we promise!

Answers on page 439.

---

there are no Dumb Questions

Q: I get that the `.gitignore` file allows me to keep untracked files from being added to the index, which means I can't commit them. But what if I want to ignore a file that I've already committed?

A: Let's say you accidentally commit a file which you should have been ignoring to begin with. You'll start by deleting the file (using the `git rm` command). Remember that this means you'll have to make a commit to record that you are deleting the file.

Then be sure to add the name of the file to your `.gitignore` file, which you'll have to add and commit again.

Going forward, even if that file shows up in your working directory, `git status` will not report it and you can no longer add it to the index, which means you can't commit it.

Serious Coding

As you might have guessed, ignoring operating-system-specific files can get repetitive, especially if you have many Git repositories. Each one will essentially list the same set of files again and again. Git allows you to define a global `.gitignore` file to avoid the repetition. For any project, Git will combine the global `.gitignore` file with any project-specific `.gitignore` file you provide to generate a complete list of files to ignore.

Thie setup, as you might have guessed, involves tweaking the `.gitconfig` file in your home directory. Once you have some more experience with Git, we encourage you to explore this some more. Search online for the phrase "global gitignore" to get started.

Commit early, commit often

Commits are the bread and butter of your interaction with Git. Each commit represents a snapshot of the index at the time you made the commit, allowing you to capture the state of your work at a particular point in time. You've explored, at length, how you can build a commit history for a branch and use branches to have multiple, parallel efforts in flight at the same time. You also know that you can push a branch to the remote.

Once you make a commit, you are entrusting your work to Git's memory (the object database). When Git begins to act like your "second brain," you've reached Git enlightenment. Your journey begins with this mantra: *commit early, commit often*. This means don't make large swaths of changes before you decide to commit. Find yourself in a good place when working on a task? Commit. Small or big changes? Don't wait to commit—just commit!

You might be drumming up some counterarguments to our stance here, so we've anticipated a few. If nothing else, think of it as us heckling ourselves.

Argument	**Counterargument**
Ugh! This is so annoying. Now I have to remember to make a commit every time I make any change. I'll end up with a repetitive stress injury from all that typing!	First of all, you know how to create aliases now. That's why we love "c" as an alias for "commit"—sure saves a bunch of typing.
	Second, you might be in the habit of constantly saving your work in Microsoft Word or Apple Pages because you've been burned one too many times. Think of committing as hitting the "Save" key.
My thoughts are messy! I might try a bunch of different approaches to solve a problem—I don't want the world to know how I arrived at a solution. That's like washing my dirty laundry in public.	We love you and that brain of yours, and (we are pretty sure) so do your colleagues. As you start out with Git, we'd rather you adopt good habits at the expense of doing things strictly right. Don't let the perfect be the enemy of the good.
	Git does offer you some facilities to clean up and reorder commits, but that's a pretty advanced subject.
Nope. I'm still undecided.	Think of everything that commits represent and what you can do with them—they capture your work, you can diff them, you can revert them, you can use them as the basis for new branches. Use this to your advantage.

As far as mantras go, "commit early, commit often" sounds great. But what does that really mean in practice? How big or small should my commit be? How often is "often"?

Think scope, not size! Suppose you are editing a friend's manuscript and you catch some inconsistent verb tenses. Fix those throughout the chapter, and make a commit. If you also notice a bunch of typos along the way, fixing those would be a different commit. You shouldn't need to make a separate commit for every typo you fix—group them into one commit, or go chapter by chapter.

Pretend you are tasked with adding a new feature to a project. As a first step, you realize you need to rename a bunch of files. Rename, commit. Then make the changes you need to. Commit. Update the documentation to reflect the new functionality. Then commit.

See a pattern? Think about *what* you are putting into the commit. The size of the commit is of secondary concern to what you are packing into it.

As for when should you commit? If you feel you are done with a particular change, go ahead and add those files to the index, then make a commit. Remember, you can choose which files you add to the index—so if you somehow make different kinds of changes across many files, add only those that belong together to the index. The index is a useful ally—take advantage of it!

We have a lot more advice on writing good commit messages. The great thing about commit messages is that they force you to think about what you are putting in them, so why don't we look at that next?

Write meaningful commit messages

Since we are on the subject of committing early, committing often, another piece of advice we'll give you is to *always write meaningful commit messages*. This helps you if you ever need to go back and look over your commit history, and makes it easy for your collaborators to understand why you did what you did.

Think about all the places where a good commit message can be your ally. The output of the `git log` command is certainly an obvious one. But we did introduce you in Chapter 7 to the `--grep` flag for the `git log` command, which lets you search commit messages. How much more useful would that be if the commit messages you were searching were more descriptive? How about finding a bad commit using the `git bisect` command (which we also discussed in Chapter 7)?

As you are working, it's easy to fall into the trap of making quick and dirty commit messages like "temporary" or "still doesn't work." While that satisfies our "commit early, commit often" mantra, it does not add much value to your commit history. Good luck trying to remember what that commit was all about a few hours or days later! Here are some guidelines for writing a good commit message:

You might be wondering why we didn't use this protocol from the beginning of this book. Our approach to teaching is to tease things apart so we can tackle them one piece at a time. At this point in the book, you are comfortable enough with Git's workflow that you can start to think about how to do things better.

1 **Always use the imperative mood**

Avoid messages like "updated documentation" or "fixes login bug." Write a commit message as if you were giving the computer a command, for example, "update documentation" and "fix intermittent bug when logging in."

We give credit where it's due. This piece of advice comes from the prolific Tim Pope, published in a brilliant blog post that you can find here: https://tbaggery.com/2008/04/19/a-note-about-git-commit-messages.html

2 **Avoid using the -m (or --message) flag with the `git commit` command**

Throughout this book, we've asked you supply commit messages to the `git commit` command using the -m flag. But you're ready to level up. Our advice going forward is to simply invoke the `git commit` command with no flags. This will prompt Git to bring up Visual Studio Code or your default configured editor so you can type a message.

You can use all of your text editor's capabilities to craft a good commit message. You can even introduce double and single quotes, new lines, ampersands, and other characters that are notoriously hard to enter at the command line. In other words, with a text editor at your disposal you no longer have to wrestle with the limitations of the command line.

Here's an example of a commit message that is best written out using a text editor. Writing this at the command line would be cumbersome.

```
remove the "is required" label for city from address form

This is no longer needed; we can deduce the city name from the zip
code supplied.
```

The anatomy of a good commit message

Let's dive deeper into what a good commit message should look like. Our approach is to write a commit message the same way we'd write an email—with a header, and optionally, a body.

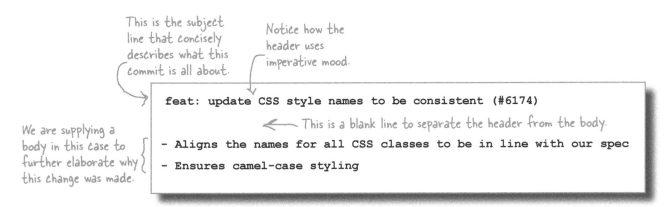

This is the subject line that concisely describes what this commit is all about.

Notice how the header uses imperative mood.

```
feat: update CSS style names to be consistent (#6174)

- Aligns the names for all CSS classes to be in line with our spec
- Ensures camel-case styling
```

← This is a blank line to separate the header from the body.

We are supplying a body in this case to further elaborate why this change was made.

The most important thing to remember about a commit message is that it should focus on the *why* of a change, not the *how* or the *what*. Of course, this may not always be possible, but it's a good ideal to keep in mind.

Before we go further, it's important to realize what this particular format buys you. You see, using the `git log` command with the `--oneline` flag will display the first line (header) for every commit. Here's the log of the `a-head-above` repository you've been working with so far in this chapter:

You probably recall that GitHub shows you the commits for any repository. GitHub and other repository managers, like the `--oneline` option, display only the first line of every commit message.

```
File  Edit  Window  Help
$ git log --oneline
b892542 (HEAD -> master) chore: add .gitignore file
03638ff docs: add a README file
```

This is why we jam-pack so much information into so little space. The terse output of the `--oneline` flag with the `git log` command is often enough to give a sense of what the commit history looks like and just enough detail about each commit. To see the full commit messages, including the bodies, you can always use the `git log` command (with no flags).

The anatomy of a good commit message: headers

Let's spend a few minutes dissecting our header, displayed here in its full glory:

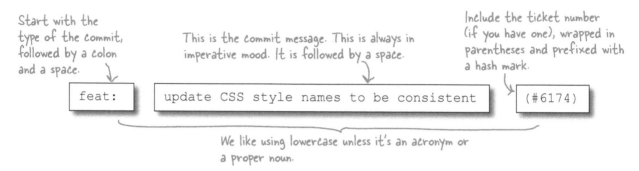

Start with the type of the commit, followed by a colon and a space.

This is the commit message. This is always in imperative mood. It is followed by a space.

Include the ticket number (if you have one), wrapped in parentheses and prefixed with a hash mark.

`feat:`

`update CSS style names to be consistent`

`(#6174)`

We like using lowercase unless it's an acronym or a proper noun.

We'll start with the type. We like to prefix our commit messages with the kind of change introduced in that commit. Here's an abbreviated list of "types" we find useful:

`feat:` use this when introducing a new feature or enhancement

`fix:` use this when fixing a bug

`docs:` use this to describe any documentation change

`chore:` use this when you make changes that affect tooling, like Git

An example would be adding or modifying the .gitignore file.

`test:` use this when you introduce or modify tests

The commit type is usually obvious from the kind of task you've been assigned. You should work with your team to document a list of "types" so that everyone uses them consistently.

The type is followed by a colon and a space, then the commit message describing the change (again, in imperative mood—that is, as if you are commanding the computer to take action on your part). Notice that our preference is to use all lowercase, unless we are spelling out acronyms (like CSS) or proper nouns (like Git).

We usually end this by spelling out the ticket number (if there is one) wrapped in parentheses and prefixed with a hash mark.

Brain Power

Cast your mind back to past projects. Can you think of a few types that could describe the commits you might make in those projects? Jot down some ideas here from your own mind or your favorite search engine.

Code Magnets

Oh my! We applied the types to our commit messages correctly, but somehow they got jumbled up. Can you help us out and reassign the correct types to the commit messages we so diligently typed out? (You might have to use the same magnet more than once.)

| feat |
| chore |
| docs |
| fix |

`correct question count in quiz counter`

`redo label alignment after logging out`

`update .gitignore file to exclude Windows DAT files`

`allow users to add multiple email addresses to profiles`

`introduce a chat feature`

⟶ Answers on page 439.

The anatomy of a good commit message: bodies

Getting the header right is a very good first step, and a descriptive header is often sufficient to describe why a particular commit was made.

But for many commits, a single-line header isn't enough. Perhaps you wish to provide more information about the change or explain why you chose a particular approach. This is where the body of the commit message comes into play. Here's the commit message we laid out for you a few pages ago:

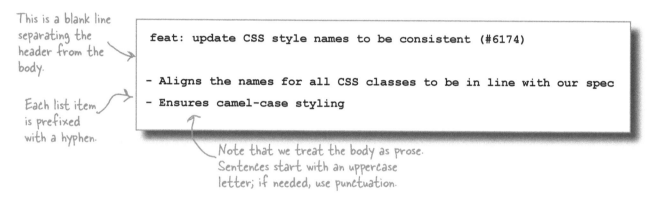

This is a blank line separating the header from the body.

Each list item is prefixed with a hyphen.

```
feat: update CSS style names to be consistent (#6174)

- Aligns the names for all CSS classes to be in line with our spec
- Ensures camel-case styling
```

Note that we treat the body as prose. Sentences start with an uppercase letter; if needed, use punctuation.

There is only one rule—**you must separate the body from the header using a blank line**. Outside of that, the guidelines for writing the body are pretty relaxed—it's free-form text and can be as short or long as you need it to be. If you decide to write more than one paragraph, then be sure to insert a blank line between paragraphs. That's it!

What should you say? We have found ourselves writing blocks of text to further elaborate on a change or add links to online documentation or blog posts. Sometimes we link to past issues that were solved using a similar technique to establish precedent. We've even included what we did to test out our work, particularly if the testing setup was elaborate. Anything you think will help someone reading the commit log make sense of a change is fair game.

We prefer using hyphens in place of asterisks when creating lists, and we encourage you to do the same. This aligns well with the Markdown format, which you've used throughout this book.

There you have it! Go forth and write perfect commit messages.

And if you make a mistake or a typo when you commit? Don't forget about the --amend option, which you learned about in Chapter 4. Amend away!

Fussy much?

We've described our preferred way to write commit messages—feel free to tweak this method so that it works best for you and your team. The most important thing is **always be consistent**—having a messy commit history will do you no good in the long run.

One nuance that often goes unnoticed is that choosing the type forces you to think hard about what you are going to put in a commit. By separating your work into different types of commits, you are being intentional about the changes you are making. This is where Git's index comes in: it gives you a place to organize your work before you commit. You can see how this would work—even if you've made different kinds of changes to several files, you add only the files that logically represent one type of change to the index. Commit them with an appropriate commit message. Then repeat.

Perhaps you can see why we encourage you to use a text editor to compose your commit messages as opposed to the command line option—it allows you to really think through your message, while giving you the flexibility to write it out in the best manner possible.

A shoutout

Once again, we give credit where credit is due. We've taken a lot of inspiration from the hugely influential Google Angular project. The Angular team laid out a rigorous commit message protocol that has persuaded lots of other people (yours truly included) to be just as thorough when drafting commit messages. Navigate to *https://github.com/angular/angular* and take at a look at how they organize their commit history.

Another online resource we routinely point to is Conventional Commits (*https://www.conventionalcommits.org*). This takes what the Angular project did a step further—by formalizing it into a specification and explaining why you should adopt a structured approach to commit messages.

Serious Coding

Conventional Commits, along with many other teams and organizations, encourages using footers to reference related ticket numbers or additional information that might be pertinent to the change you are introducing in a commit. While we've occasionally found this useful, it depends on the kind of work you are doing. If you are curious whether this would fit your workflow, the Conventional Commits website has some details on what footers should include.

Sharpen your pencil

Review the following commit messages and see if they fit the format that we've recommended in the last few pages. Examine each message and if it does not look right, explain why. For the sake of this exercise, assume we always had a ticket to work with, and remember, not all commit messages need a body.

Jot down your observations here.

```
allow ESC key to be used to dismiss dialog box (#1729)


This commit allows the application to capture the ESC
key and dismiss any alert dialog box being displayed.
```

```
fix: remove duplicate error-trapping code
```

```
docs: fix link in documentation (#3141)


Point the "Help" link to https://hawtdawgapp.com/docs
```

```
Updates chapter 8
```

Answers on page 440.

Create helpful branch names

If you think of a repository as a story, then commits represent its plot points—and branches are the narrative arc. So be just as diligent when naming your branches as when drafting your commits.

We bet you're wondering if we have any thoughts on the subject. Funny you should ask! Here's how we suggest you name your branches:

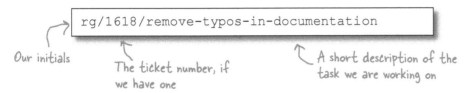

Our initials

The ticket number, if we have one

A short description of the task we are working on

We mentioned in Chapter 2 that Git allows forward slashes in branch names. We recommend using them to separate the different parts of the branch name. Let's take a look at each segment of the branch name:

rg

Prefix the name of the branch with your initials. This makes it easy to discern who created which branches when you list them (using the `git branch` command with the `-a` or `--all` flag).

1618

We have always recommended that you check your Git status before adding files to the index or making commits. Since Git always displays the branch name in the output of the `git status` command, which will now include the ticket number, you'll always have it when you're about to commit. No need to dig up your notes or fire up the task tracking tool—it's right there!

remove-typos-in-documentation

Finally, we arrive at a brief description of the task at hand. We usually just grab the title of the ticket, lowercase it, convert the spaces to hyphens, and remove any superfluous words. Done! By incorporating a clear (but short) description of the task, we leave ourselves a mental bookmark. If we have to switch tasks, this will make it easier for us to remember what we were working on when we come back.

Naming is hard. Having a strategy can make it easier, and being consistent about it can make your life and your collaborators' lives easier.

If you are feeling inspired to rename any branches, recall from Chapter 4 that you can use the —m (or ——move) option with the git branch command to rename branches. Just putting it out there! ;-)

there are no
Dumb Questions

Q: **The workflow you've prescribed in this book recommends using each branch to do one thing and one thing only. Once I merge our branch into the integration branch, I'm just going to delete it. This seems like a lot of trouble for something so short-lived, doesn't it?**

A: Sure. But remember, the point of branches is to allow you to work on multiple things at the same time. Having a consistent naming strategy can help you switch between branches quickly, and a good branch name can get you in the right frame of mind, especially if it's been a while since you worked on that task.

Q: **You say to put a short description of the task in the branch name. But we also do that in the header of the commit message. Wouldn't those be always the same?**

A: Sometimes—particularly if the task is small and well defined and resolving it involves only one commit. However, many times completing a task is a process that generates a lot of commits. Each commit header should tell us exactly what changes we introduced in that commit.

Exercise

Your mission, should you choose to accept it, is to craft some appropriate branch names. We'll give you a ticket number and a description: you come up with a good branch name. There are no wrong answers here!

* 6283: Allow user to export report in HTML format

* 70: Reformat tables in online documentation

* 2718: Allow multiple photos in profile

Answers on page 441.

Integrate a graphical user interface into your workflow

Throughout this book, you've used the command line prompt to interact with Git. While the command line is truly the most powerful interface to using Git, sometimes it can be cumbersome. Consider a situation where you quickly want to peruse a set of commits to see which files each commit affected. Could you do this using the `git log` command and the right combination of flags? Absolutely. But it might take some digging through the documentation to figure out the right flags to supply.

In case we piqued your curiosity, the flag you are looking for is --stat, which you can supply to the git log command.

Or you could use a graphical user interface (GUI) that does this for you. *GUI is pronounced "gooey."*

The first thing to know about GUI tools is that, for any operation, they invoke Git commands. In other words, they can't do anything that the Git command line can't do. But they can make things easier and more convenient. Here are a few options we like:

 Sourcetree

We showed you a screenshot of Sourcetree in Chapter 2.

Features: Free. Available for macOS and Windows

We've used Sourcetree, a brilliantly designed Git GUI, for years, and highly recommend it. We'll discuss it more on the next page.

URL: *https://www.sourcetreeapp.com*

GitHub Desktop

Features: Free. Available for macOS and Windows

GitHub's official desktop app makes working with Git *and* GitHub easier. It allows you to fork repositories, create and view pull requests, and do plenty of things that are specific to GitHub. If you use GitHub as your repository manager, GitHub Desktop might just be the GUI tool you are looking for.

URL: *https://desktop.github.com*

GitLens

Features: Free. Available anywhere Visual Studio Code is available

GitLens, while not truly a GUI, is an absolutely fantastic extension for Visual Studio Code. It presents Git-specific information in real time, without you having to leave your editor. Want to see the `git blame` for a particular file? Right there in your editor! Want to see a `diff`? Push a button to get a split-screen view comparing the current version of the file with a previous committed version. GitLens is certainly worth a look if you are a Visual Studio Code user.

Any editor worth its salt will have a plug-in or extension for Git.

URL: *https://marketplace.visualstudio.com/items?itemName=eamodio.gitlens*

Start with one, and if you find yourself pushing up against its limitations, look for another one. You can always fall back to the command line—this is why we keep insisting on teaching you Git on the command line first!

One huge benefit of GUI-based tools is the sheer amount of information they can show you at a glance, not to mention that many operations are a click away. Here is a whirlwind tour of the "History" view in Sourcetree, which shows you your commit graph and the additions recorded in that commit:

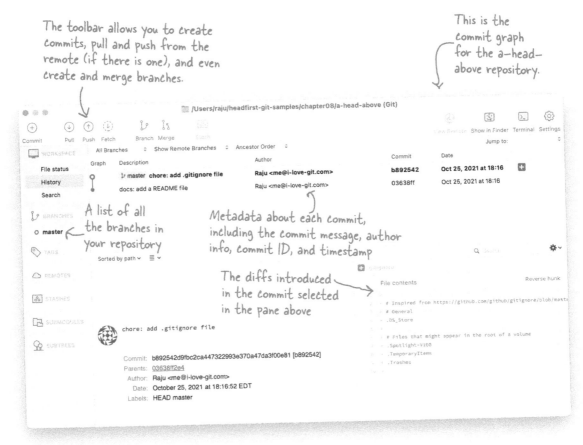

The toolbar allows you to create commits, pull and push from the remote (if there is one), and even create and merge branches.

This is the commit graph for the a-head-above repository.

A list of all the branches in your repository

Metadata about each commit, including the commit message, author info, commit ID, and timestamp

The diffs introduced in the commit selected in the pane above

It takes a little while to get used to the GUI and to know where to go looking for a specific piece of information, but the windowed environment can certainly make some things easier.

We believe that to really understand Git and use it to maximum benefit, the command line is the way to go. We are also strong advocates for using the right tool for the right job. That's why we use tools like Sourcetree side by side with the terminal, reaching for whichever we feel best accomplishes the task at hand. We do not encourage a this-versus-that mentality—both the command line and a GUI-based tool should, and we hope will, find a place in your workflow.

The command line versus a GUI

Tonight's talk: **"Who's more useful?"**

The command line:

I am the definitive interface to Git. I know all the commands and all the flags. I absolutely own this space.

Information overload much? I let our readers stay focused—one thing at a time is actually great. Slow and steady wins the race.

That's fine—until our readers need to do something that you don't support. Then what? Huh?

You just don't appreciate the beauty of simple things, do you?

Maybe we both have a place in our readers' workflow. Use the best tool for the job, right?

The GUI:

No argument there! But you are also very single-minded—you can only display one thing at a time. It's the status *or* the log *or* the list of branches. I, on the other hand, can provide *so* much information at a glance. I'm pretty amazing.

My focus in life is convenience. I make sure our readers don't have to remember every single flag and combination. Ugh!

I'll be the first to admit I can't do everything, but I can get our readers 80% of the way there, and what they want is usually to click a button or select a menu item. I also give them easy-to-understand icons and tooltips. You are a barren landscape of text.

Not to mention, I can integrate with text editors to give our readers real-time information about how they are affecting the repository, without making them switch to the terminal to interact with Git.

This could be the beginning of a beautiful friendship.

Read that license!

We absolutely adore open source projects. In fact, we like to think of ourselves as advocates for open source. After all, Git is open source, and we wrote a whole book on it!

But we need to tell you something: just about every open source project picks a license that describes how you can use it. Be sure to peruse the license of any project you use so you'll know what you are allowed to do with it: some licenses prohibit using the project in certain circumstances (for example, a license might allow educational but not commercial applications). Yes, we know it's boring. Do it anyway.

Bullet Points

- Git is extremely customizable. You can set and override many settings using the `git config` command.

  - The `git config` command, used with the `--global` flag, allows you to create settings that affect every repository you work in on that particular workstation.

  - Using the `git config` command, you can set the value for a particular setting.

- All global settings are stored in a file called `.gitconfig`, which is stored in the home directory under your account. It consists of sections, and keys under a section, each associated with a value.

- You'll have to configure some settings, like `user.name` and `user.email`, to be able to use Git. Others, like `core.editor`, override Git's defaults and are optional.

- You can store certain settings at the repository level (that is, local to a specific repository) using the `--local` flag with the `git config` command.

- To list all settings, use the `git config` command with the `--list` option.

- Git allows you to create aliases, which act like shortcuts to invoke certain Git commands. Aliases can also include flags and arguments.

- Aliases are configurations, under the "alias" section. The key can be any word, and its value is what the alias will expand to. You can invoke an alias like you would any Git command (e.g., `git loga`).

- Most, if not all, projects require that some files never be committed. You can tell Git to ignore an untracked file. Once ignored, it will remain forever untracked.

- To tell Git to ignore a file, create a `.gitignore` file at the root of your repository that lists all the files you wish to ignore.

- "Commit early, commit often" is the mantra when it comes to working with Git. Recording snapshots of your work regularly is a good habit to develop.

- Think of each commit in terms of its scope, not its size. Try to group changes together logically.

- Use consistent and informative commit messages. This can be helpful when reading the output of the `git log` command or searching for a commit using `git bisect` (see Chapter 7), to name a few examples.

- Create contexual and meaningful branch names that help discern which branches are yours and what their purposes are.

- Consider using a graphical user interface (GUI) tool to aid in your work with Git. Remember, it's not one or the other—you can and should use a GUI side by side with the command line.

Wouldn't it be nice if this were the end of the book? No more terminals or commands or anything else? Sigh...

Congratulations!

You've made it to the end.

Though there is still the appendix.

And the index.

And there's a website...

You aren't getting away that easily!

(Go ahead, you can admit it—you just can't get enough of Git, can you?)

Configuration Crossword

Just one more puzzle to go! Can you configure your answers to these crossword clues?

Across

2 Some commit messages include this after the header

4 Use this flag with the git config command to remove an entry from your .gitconfig file

8 You can tell Git to ___ files you don't want to track

9 Your configuration includes (key, ____) pairs

11 Google project that inspired many people to use structured commit messages

14 You can rename branches by using this flag with the git branch command

16 It's best to set your aliases to be the same for every repository, using this flag with the git config command

17 Write your commit message headers in this commanding grammatical mood

20 When deciding how and when to commit, consider ___, not size

21 If you have a ___ number, include it at the end of your commit message header

Down

1 We recommend prefixing your commit messages with a commit ___

3 Commit early, commit ____

5 The alias we gave "log --oneline --graph --all"

6 This part of the commit message operates like the subject line in an email

7 In alias.loga, "alias" is the section and "loga" is the ___

10 Use this flag with the git config command to store certain settings in one specific repository

12 ___ user interface tools

13 The git ___ command lets you personalize Git

15 When using open source software, be sure to read this

18 Git's nickname for a shortcut that lets you type complex commands quickly

19 Command to create a new file from the command line

→ **Answers on page 442.**

Exercise Solution

From page 402.

Why don't you spend a few minutes working with your global Git configuration?

✱ Using the terminal, navigate to your home directory, then list all the files, including hidden ones. See if you can spot the `.gitconfig` file. Use this space to write out the commands you are going to use:

ls –A

You might recall that the command to *check* the value of a key is nearly identical to setting it. For example:

git config --global user.email "me@i-love-git.com"

versus

git config --global user.email

✱ Using the terminal, see if you can check the value of the `core.editor` key. List the command you are going to use here first:

git config ––global core.editor

✱ Using your text editor, open the global Git configuration file. Spend a few minutes looking around—do the sections and key-value pairs listed seem familiar to you?

Sharpen your pencil
Solution

From page 407.

Flex those Git configuration muscles for a bit, will ya?

➤ What command will you use to list your global Git configuration as well as the name of the file where you set this configuration?

git config --list --show-origin

Note that you don't have to be in any specific directory to run this version of the `git config` **command!**

➤ Next, create a new folder called `a-head-above`. We chose to create this folder inside another folder called `chapter08` next to the exercises we did for other chapters just to keep things nice and tidy (but you do you!).

➤ Using your terminal, change directories to the `a-head-above` directory, and initialize a new Git repository.

➤ Using the `--local` flag with the `git config` command, change your name for this repository alone. If you've been using your full name so far in this book, use only your first name, or just your initials. Or, use the name of your favorite fictional character! What command will you use? (Hint: The option you are to set is `user.name`.)

git config --local user.name "Raju" ← *We decided to use our first name.*

➤ List your entire Git configuration again, along with the origin of the configuration. What has changed? Explain your answer here:

I see several new entries in the local .git/config file. I also see two entries for user.name, one in my global .gitconfig file and one in the local .git/config file with the value "Raju".

➤ Create a file called `README.md` with the following contents, add it to the index, and commit it with the commit message "docs: add a README file":

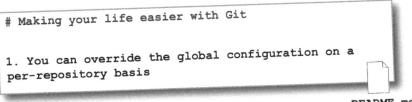

```
# Making your life easier with Git

1. You can override the global configuration on a
per-repository basis
```

README.md

➤ Finally, use `git log` (with no flags), and inspect the author name.

Sharpen your pencil
Solution

From page 410.

Can you think of any Git commands that could really use an alias? Think of how many times you've used Git's `status`, `add`, `branch`, `switch`, and `diff` commands in this book!

Here's some space for you to jot down some ideas. (We've got you started with one of our favorites.)

Alias	Expands to
git a	git add
git s	git status
git c	git commit
git b	git branch
git sw	git switch

Also, be sure to look ahead at the solution to see what we've listed, in case you see some aliases you might adapt in your day-to-day workflow. (We've listed most of our favorites.)

Exercise Solution

From page 411.

You are going to spend a little time creating a few aliases of your own.

✱ Fire up your terminal. You're going to be installing these aliases globally, so it doesn't matter which directory you do this exercise from.

✱ The first alias you are to install is **loga**, which you'll set to expand to log --oneline --graph --all. List the command to use here first:

> git config --global alias.loga "log --oneline --graph --all"

Execute this command.

✱ Use the `git config` command to check if the alias was correctly installed. Here's some space for you to jot down the command to use:

> git config --global alias.loga

✱ Let's go meta! You are going to create an alias that lists your entire configuration. Define an alias called **aliases** that expands into git config --list --show-origin. Be sure to write out the command you are going to use.

> git config --global alias.aliases "config --list --show-origin"

✱ Navigate to the location where you created the a-head-above repository. Invoke the loga alias. Did you get what you expect to see? Next, invoke the aliases config—is the aliases alias listed as well?

> Invoking git loga showed me one commit just like it would have been displayed using git log --online --graph --all.
>
> Listing my aliases using git aliases shows me the global and local aliases, including the aliases alias.

Just now we had you modify your global configuration. Feel free to "unset" these aliases if they are not to your liking—we won't be offended, we promise!

Sharpen your pencil Solution

From page 417.

Let's introduce a `.gitignore` file in the `a-head-above` Git repository you created for this chapter.

➤ Fire up your terminal and navigate to the location where you created the repository.

➤ Using the terminal and the `touch` command, create a `.gitignore` file at the root of the project. Use this space to list the command you will use:

touch .gitignore

➤ Using your favorite search engine, search for a sample `.gitignore` file for your operating system.

➤ Open your own `.gitignore` file in your text editor and update it to match the sample you found. Be sure to comment to document why you made some entries.

➤ Look over the `.gitignore` file to make sure you understand exactly what you are choosing to exclude from your repository.

➤ Finally, add the `.gitignore` file to the index and commit it with the message "chore: add .gitignore file".

Code Magnet Solution

From page 423.

Oh my! We applied the types to our commit messages correctly, but somehow they got jumbled up. Can you help us out and reassign the correct types to the commit messages we so diligently typed out? (You might have to use the same magnet more than once.)

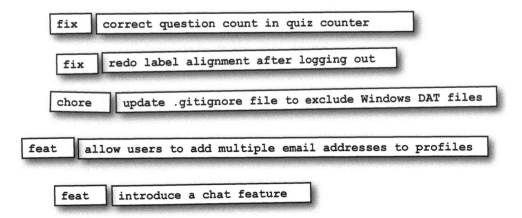

fix	correct question count in quiz counter
fix	redo label alignment after logging out
chore	update .gitignore file to exclude Windows DAT files
feat	allow users to add multiple email addresses to profiles
feat	introduce a chat feature

Sharpen your pencil Solution

From page 426.

Review the following commit messages and see if they fit the format that we've recommended in the last few pages. Examine each message and if it does not look right, explain why. For the sake of this exercise, assume we always had a ticket to work with, and remember, not all commit messages need a body.

```
allow ESC key to be used to dismiss dialog box (#1729)


This commit allows the application to capture the ESC
key and dismiss any alert dialog box being displayed.
```

This commit message does not specify a type. Other than that, it does everything else right. The header is in imperative mood, lists the ticket number, and has a blank line between header and body.

This commit message does not list the ticket number at the end. Otherwise, it gets everything else right. It starts with a type, followed by a colon and a space, and is written like we are giving the computer a command.

```
fix: remove duplicate error-trapping code
```

```
docs: fix link in documentation (#3141)


Point the "Help" link to https://hawtdawgapp.com/docs
```

This commit gets everything right. It has a type and lists the ticket number at the end.

This commit message has a few issues. There is no type, the first letter is uppercase, and it is not in imperative mood. It also does not list the ticket number.

```
Updates chapter 8
```

Exercise Solution

From page 428.

Your mission, should you choose to accept it, is to craft some appropriate branch names. We'll give you a ticket number and a description: you come up with a good branch name. There are no wrong answers here!

✱ 6283: Allow user to export report in HTML format

      rg/6283/allow-user-to-export-report

In all three cases, we used our initials. Note how we put just enough in the branch name to remind us of what we are working on.

✱ 70: Reformat tables in online documentation

      rg/70/reformat-tables-in-documentation

✱ 2718: Allow multiple photos in profile

      rg/2718/allow-multiple-photos-in-profile

Configuration Crossword Solution

Just one more puzzle to go! Can you configure your answers to these crossword clues?

From page 434.

appendix: *leftovers*

The Top Five Topics We Didn't Cover

Ooh! Cake!

We've covered a lot of ground, and you're almost finished with this book. We'll miss you, but before we let you go, we wouldn't feel right about sending you out into the world without a *little* more preparation. Git offers a *lot* of functionality, and we couldn't possibly fit all of it in one book. We saved some really juicy bits for this appendix.

this is a new chapter   **443**

#1 Tags (remember me forever)

You know that Git branches are sticky notes—a branch is simply a named reference to a commit. You also know that if you make a new commit on a branch, Git moves the branch to point to the new commit ID on that branch. Tags, like branches, are also named references to commits, except that once they are created, they **never** move. Tags are very useful if you want to name a commit so you can find and get it to easily. We use tags to record "landmarks" in a project history. For example, we could tag the commit that marks a specific version of our software, like v1.0.0. Or the commit that fixed a particularly nasty bug. To create a tag, Git offers the `git tag` command:

Invoke the tag command. → `git tag` `v1.0.0` ← Supply the name of the tag.

By default, the `tag` command will record the current ID (that is, where HEAD points to) in the tag. However, you can supply a specific commit ID after the tag name.

`git tag` `v2.0.0` `049896f` ← Supply a specific commit ID to tag.

Tag names follow the same rules as branch names. They don't allow spaces (we like using hyphens instead), but they can have forward slashes and periods.

To list all the tags in your repository, you can simply supply the `-l` (lowercase "L," which is shorthand for `--list`) flag to the `git tag` command.

Tags, like branches, are part of your commit history, and you can fetch (and push) tags from the remote to share them with the rest of your team. Both the `fetch` and `push` command support the `--tags` flag. Supplying this flag ensures that the commit history for everyone working on a shared repository accurately reflects all tags that are part of your commit history.

← The git pull command also supports the --tags flag.

One thing to watch out for—try to avoid naming a tag the same name as a branch. Much like we encourage putting your initials in branch names, we encourage finding appropriate prefixes for tag names. We like using the letter "v" (for "version") to label version numbers.

Serious Coding

A *tag*, like a branch, is a named reference to a commit. As long as you have a tag pointing to a commit, it will always be reachable, even if it has no branch or child commit pointing to it.

#2 Cherry-pick (copying commits)

Imagine you're working on a new feature and notice a bug in the code. You fix the bug and make a commit (preferably prefixed with the "type" "fix"). Then you learn that your teammates are getting affected by the same bug. Your branch includes the fix, but you aren't ready to merge your branch in just yet. So what's to be done? The commit that contains the bug fix is on your feature branch—how can you apply *just* that fix to the integration branch?

In case you were wondering where you heard the term cherry-pick before, we mentioned it in Chapter 3.

You have two options. First, you could create a new branch based on the integration branch, manually reapply your bug fix, commit, and issue a pull request.

Second, you could use another Git command, called `cherry-pick`, which allows you to copy a commit to another branch. Since you want the fix to be on the `master` branch, you'd first switch to the `master` branch. Let's see how this would play out:

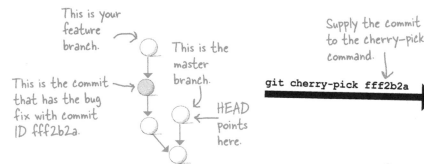

This is your feature branch.

This is the master branch.

This is the commit that has the bug fix with commit ID fff2b2a.

HEAD points here.

Supply the commit ID to the cherry-pick command.

`git cherry-pick fff2b2a`

We cherry-picked this commit.

Git creates a copy of the commit on the master branch.

Having the ability to cherry-pick commits does not mean you shouldn't create a feature branch to apply your work, nor does it mean avoiding your team's conventions around how that change is applied to the integration branch (issue a pull request or merge locally and push). It does, however, avoid you having to redo a change manually—you can rely on Git's memory to confidently apply the changes introduced in a commit by simply asking it to copy them to a new location in your commit history.

Note that you can get a merge conflict since Git will replay your changes on the `master` branch.

Recall that when calculating the commit ID, Git uses the commit's parent commit ID. This means that the cherry-picked commit *will* have a different commit ID than the original.

This is yet another reason why separating your work into different types of commits is a good idea. You never know when you might have to reach and copy a commit over to another branch.

⚠ Watch it! Don't overuse cherry-picking!

The best way to integrate your work is to merge your feature branch into the integration branch. Cherry-picking commits should be only used as a last-ditch effort, in situations where you absolutely can't merge the branch where the work was done. Remember, when you are cherry-picking commits, you are making copies of those commits, which contain the same set of changes as the original. Doing this too often can make it hard to decipher your commit history.

#3 Stashes (pseudo-commits)

You are knee deep in work. You've edited a bunch of files, maybe even added a few files to the index. You check your status and realize you are on the wrong branch! Oops. You should have been on your feature branch, but instead you're on the `master` branch.

```
File Edit  Window Help
$ git status
On branch master
Changes to be committed:
   (use "git restore --staged <file>..." to unstage)
      modified:    README.md  ← You have some
                              changes staged.
Changes not staged for commit:
   (use "git add <file>..." to update what will be committed)
   (use "git restore <file>..." to discard changes in working directory)
      modified:    README.md
      modified:    stashes.md  ← And you have a bunch of tracked
                              files that have been modified in
                              your working directory.
```

Recall that when you switch branches, Git will rewrite your working directory to look like it did when you made the most recent commit on that branch. This means that if you've modified a file that looks different in the two branches, Git won't let you switch because it would have to overwrite your changes.

How can you switch branches now that you have a few changes in flight? Git allows you to stash away your changes using the `git stash` command.

```
File Edit  Window Help
$ git stash
Saved working directory and index state WIP on master: 52beb88
docs: talk about stashes

$ On branch master
nothing to commit, working tree clean
```

Invoke the git stash command.

Now your status is clean.

When you ask Git to stash your changes, Git stuffs them away in a special location. This leaves your working directory clean. You can now switch branches.

Recall all those times when someone asked you to clean your room? You take everything in sight, shove it all in a drawer, and ta-da! Clean room. See, you're already an expert in stashing.

You can think of a stash as a sort of pseudo-commit. The difference is that stashing records the changes in both your working directory and the index, as opposed to a commit, which only records what is in your index. The other difference is that a commit adds to your commit history, while a stash does not. If you push, your stashes don't go along for the ride—they remain in your local Git repository.

This is important. Stashes are local to your repository and are not designed to be shared.

So now that you've stashed your changes—how do you get them back?

#3 Stashes (pseudo-commits, continued)

You switch branches, and now you'd like you all that work you stashed away back (pretty please with sugar on top). When you stash something, Git puts your work in a stack. This allows you to create multiple stashes, and much like a stack of pancakes, your latest stash created will be at the top. Git allows you to "pop" a stash. This means asking Git to take the topmost (latest) stash, recover all the changes recorded in it, and bring them back, just as they were recorded in the stash.

Mmm...pancakes.

This is often referred to as a "last in, first out" (LIFO) structure.

```
File Edit Window Help
$ git stash pop --index          Gets all the changes in the latest
                                 stash and brings them back.

Changes to be committed:
  (use "git restore --staged <file>..." to unstage)
        modified:   README.md

Changes not staged for commit:
  (use "git add <file>..." to update what will be committed)
  (use "git restore <file>..." to discard changes in working directory)
        modified:   README.md
        modified:   stashes.md

Dropped refs/stash@{0} (ee4e422f6d0f4b126ed94b7fdd3e963134a7cc2a)
```

Git brings back the changes you staged.

Information about the stash you just applied

Git diligently remembers which changes were in the index and which were in the working directory, and it puts them back. Now that you are on the right branch and those changes you made are in the right place, you can get back to work!

There's a lot more to stashes—you can supply them with a commit message (just like a standard commit message), list them, view the changes you've put in them and even apply specific stashes (rather than just popping the last one you created). And while stashing, by default, only stows away any changes to tracked files, Git allows you to pick whether you want all files (tracked and untracked), only files in the index, or even individual files.

Watch it!

Don't overuse stashes

It's tempting to use stashes to store "work in progress" items. Sometimes stashes may seem like a good way to stuff away some work while you try an alternative approach to solving a problem. But you already have a solution for this exact problem: branches!

We'll admit—we don't use stashes very often. (That's why they are in the appendix of this book!) One of the times we reach for them is when we are faced with the exact scenario we just described, where we've made some edits, haven't committed just yet, and find ourselves on the wrong branch.

#4 reflog (reference log)

You know that every time you switch branches or check out a specific Git commit using the git checkout command, HEAD moves. You also know that when you make a commit on a branch, both the branch and HEAD move to the new commit on that branch. What happens when you do a reset? HEAD moves to the commit you reset to. Turns out, a lot of operations involve HEAD, like moving around in Git repositories, or adding to (or removing from) your commit history.

Git maintains a log called the reflog (short for *reference log*), which is updated every time HEAD moves. You can see the reflog for any repository using the git reflog command:

```
File Edit Window Help
30589cb (HEAD -> master) HEAD@{0}: checkout: moving from rg/docs-describe-reflog to master
18de9d8 (rg/docs-describe-reflog) HEAD@{1}: commit: docs: describe reflog
30589cb (HEAD -> master) HEAD@{2}: checkout: moving from master to rg/docs-describe-reflog
30589cb (HEAD -> master) HEAD@{3}: commit: docs: update README and stashes docs
640227f HEAD@{4}: reset: moving to HEAD
640227f HEAD@{5}: reset: moving to HEAD
640227f HEAD@{6}: commit: docs: talk about stashes
4cdf9f2 HEAD@{7}: commit (initial): docs: add a README file
```

Looking closely at one entry in the reflog, we can discern a lot about what happened:

This is the commit ID that HEAD moved to.

This describes the operation—in this case, we moved from a feature branch to the master branch.

```
30589cb (HEAD -> master) HEAD@{0}: checkout: moving from rg/docs-describe-reflog to master
```

Reading the reflog and getting used to all the information Git records in it can take a little. However, it's important because the reflog is your safety net. Suppose you reset a commit (which might make a commit unreachable) and then change your mind. Well, since the git reset command moves both HEAD and the branch pointer, the reflog can tell you where you were before you reset.

Here's another example: say you are in detached HEAD state. You switch away to another branch or commit, but now you can't recall which commit you had checked out previously. Reflog to the rescue!

Stashes and the reflog have a lot in common. Like the stashes list, the reflog is maintained last-in, first-out (LIFO): the latest movement of HEAD is listed at the top. If you were to make another commit or switch branches, that would be inserted at the top of the list, and the current topmost item would move down one.

Another thing stashes and the reflog share is that the reflog, like your stashes, is local to your repository—it is not shared.

While the reflog isn't something you'll use a lot in your day-to-day work with Git, it is certainly a powerful ally if you ever find yourself in a pickle. So stay calm and use reflog.

#5 rebase (another way to merge)

Merging branches is an integral part of working with Git. A merge unites work from separate branches. You know that when you merge two branches, you can either get a fast-forward merge (where the proposing branch jumps forward) or a merge commit. Git offers another way to merge your work: rebase.

Before we dive into the details of what rebase offers us and how it is different than doing a merge, let's consider a hypothetical scenario: suppose you are working on a feature branch (rg/feat-a in this case) and are ready to merge. However, your feature branch and the integration branch (master) have diverged. You already know what will happen if you merge your feature branch *into* the integration branch—you'll get a merge commit:

Here, the merge commit (E), which Git created, represents the union of the work that happened in the two branches.

What if, instead of creating a branch off commit A, you had created the rg/feat-a branch branch after commit B (on the master branch) had already been created? In other words, you do the same work (same diff) in commits C and D, but instead of building off commit A, you build your work on top of commit B?

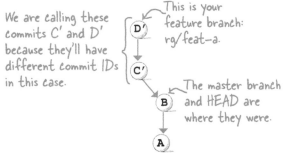

If you think about it, commit D' (D prime) is effectively the union of the work in the master and the rg/feat-a branch, because it started with everything the master branch had to offer! That is, D' *is* the merge of the master and feat-a branches.

And this is exactly what Git's rebase capability allows you to do—it allows you to merge two branches by moving one branch on top of another, effectively merging the two without actually merging.

If you were to merge rg/feat-a into the master branch, it would be a fast-forward merge, which further solidifies our argument.

#5 rebase (another way to merge, continued)

When you rebase one branch onto another, you are asking Git to replay all the commits on the current branch on top of the latest commit on the other branch. Perhaps this is best explained by an example—let's revisit the one example from the previous page:

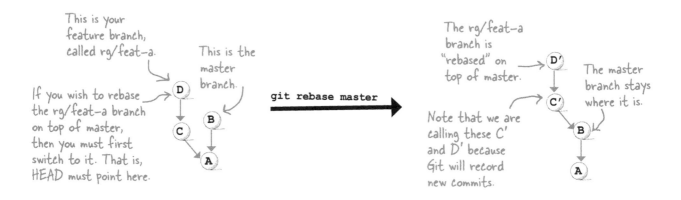

Performing a rebase involves another Git command, called `git rebase`. You start by switching to the branch you want to rebase—rg/feat-a branch in this case. If you rebase this branch on `master`, Git iterates over all the commits in the feature branch, starting with the first commit (C). It records a new commit (C′) that has the same changes contained in commit C, except the new commit's parent will be B (as opposed to A). It then proceeds to the next commit on the feature branch, D in this case, and records a new commit (D′) with the same changes as D—except its parent will be the C′. It does this till all the commits have been re-recorded, then it moves the feature branch to point to the latest commit (D′).

Note that the branch being rebased moves to the newly recorded commit (D′), as opposed to merging, where the proposing branch moves to the merge point.

As you can see, there are a few differences between merging and rebasing. Your history is very different. Rebasing "flattens" the history—you end up with a straight line, with C′ being the parent of D′, B being the parent of C′, and so forth. Rebasing is also more involved than merging, since Git rewrites your commits, which changes their IDs, as opposed to merging, which leaves commit IDs the same. This means that you should not rebase public commits.

If merging and rebasing have the same results, which one should you reach for when aiming to integrate your work? Merging is much more straightforward and does not involve Git having to rewrite your commit history. This means you can safely merge branches, even those with public commits. Since you are just learning the ropes, use merges. As you get more familiar with Git, and the different kinds of workflows that teams use, you can decide whether you should merge or rebase.

This isn't goodbye!

**Bring your brain over to
https://i-love-git.com**

Don't know about the website? We've got updates, interesting links and posts, and so much more!

Index

C

S

O'REILLY®

Learn from experts.
Become one yourself.

Books | Live online courses
Instant Answers | Virtual events
Videos | Interactive learning

Get started at oreilly.com.

Milton Keynes UK
Ingram Content Group UK Ltd.
UKHW051823120924
448259UK00007B/111